Applerouth
PO Box 14161
Atlanta GA 30324
Email: info@applerouth.com

Director: Richard Vigneault
Writers: Jed Applerouth, Sarah Fletcher, Matthew Kiesner, Zdenka Sturm, Emma Vigneault, Richard Vigneault, Joshua White
Contributing Writers: Desirina Boskovich, Debora Crichton, Eric Garbe, Jennifer Gaulding, Ian Harkins, Katie Rose, Forrest Tuttle
Editors: Alyssa Aiello, Jenna Berk, Kalianna Cawthon-Freels, Debora Crichton, Marsha Fletcher, Sarah Fletcher, Eric Garbe, Ian Harkins, Matthew Kiesner, Tal Kitron, Tina Motway, Zdenka Sturm, Emma Vigneault, Richard Vigneault, Joshua White

Layout Design: Azekeal McNees, Richard Vigneault
Interior Illustrations: Azekeal McNees, Tina Motway

October 2023

Version 5.0

Manufactured in the United States of America.

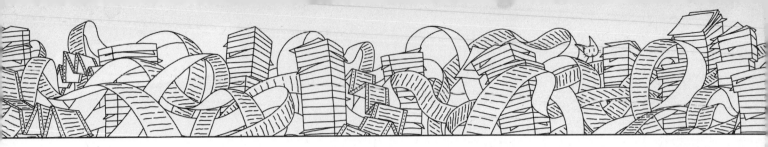

Special Thanks

A shout-out to the people who made this book possible.

Thanks to our Curriculum team:

- **Sarah Fletcher**, for her her scientific rigor and brilliance in all things math.
- **Matthew Kiesner**, for being a multi-talented, passage-producing prodigy.
- **Azekeal McNees**, for his unbridled enthusiasm and organizational genius.
- **Zdenka Sturm,** for her mathematical mind and attention to every detail.
- **Richard Vigneault**, for choosing to work with such fine people.
- **Joshua White,** for his indispensible mind and inspiring spirit.

Thanks to our support team:

- **To our editing champions:** Alyssa Aiello, Jenna Berk, Kalianna Cawthon-Freels, Marsha Fletcher, Sarah Fletcher, Matthew Kiesner, Tal Kitron, Azekeal McNees, Zdenka Sturm, Richard Vigneault, Joshua White
- **To the tutors who lent their time and expertise:** John Cadenhead, Debora Crichton, Shara-Sue Crump, Marshall Findlay, Eric Garbe, Natalie Gallagher, Philip Silverman

Thanks to the Applerouth family:

- **The Applerouth employees,** for every ounce of support and patience.
- **The tutors**, for their dedication to their students and their craft.
- **The tutors again**, for testing, editing, and refining Applerouth's strategies.
- **The tutors one last time**, for making us all proud of what we do.
- **To Jed Applerouth,** for starting this crazy thing, for creating such a fun, effective, and empathetic style, and for always believing that a no-good clown impersonator from Gdansk could amount to more than a hill of beans in this cruel world.

Contents

Letter from Jed

Every year over a million students partake in the time-honored ritual of taking the SAT. If you are reading this book, then your time has come to join the ranks and see just how high you can raise your score.

The SAT, like any other test, can be studied and mastered. Succeeding on the SAT does not require the waving of a magic wand. It requires a combination of effort and the proper tools. We've worked hard to create the ultimate SAT preparation tool. And now it's in your hands.

We kept several principles in mind when we designed this book:

- Keep things simple and clear.

- Break things into smaller steps and build on them.

- Keep things visually interesting.

- Use humor whenever possible: it's okay to laugh while learning!

This book is comprehensive. We've analyzed every aspect of the new SAT to bring you the strategies included in this book. Use it well, and hit the scores you need to get into the schools of your dreams. If you are looking for additional information or resources to help you along the way, please check us out online at www.applerouth.com.

Thanks and good luck!

SAT FAQs

You probably have a lot of questions about the SAT. We've answered some Frequently Asked Questions below, but you can always go to applerouth.com for more information.

What is the Digital SAT?

The Digital SAT, administered by the College Board, is a test that allows you to show your college readiness. It test your knowledge in reading comprehension, grammar, and math.

Why did the SAT go digital?

The new testing format provides some clear advantages: (1) a shorter testing experience for students due to its adaptive nature, (2) faster scoring, (3) more reliable test dates that do not rely on the secure storage of hundreds of thousands of paper test forms, and (4) a test that students can easily take on their personal or school-issued devices.

Can I take the digital SAT wherever and whenever I want?

No, there is no "at-home" testing option. You will still test during the school day or at nationwide test dates on the weekend.

What do I need to be able to take the digital SAT?

You will need a device that can run College Board's testing app, Bluebook. You can use your own laptop if it's Mac or PC, or you could use a tablet. Unfortunately, Bluebook does not run on personal Chromebooks, but it can be added to school Chromebooks by an administrator.

Should I go ahead and download Bluebook before the actual test?

Yes! Bluebook also provides free practice tests, so you download it as you begin studying for the digital SAT. https://bluebook.app.collegeboard.org/

Is Bluebook easy to use?

Yes! It also provides helpful tools, including an answer-eliminator, a Desmos calculator, and a way to mark questions for further review. Getting to know Bluebook before testing is a great place to start.

Can I have scratch paper and a calculator when testing?

Yes, you will receive three sheets of scratch paper to use during your test. You can bring any calculator as long as it's on their list of approved calculators. Additionally, you can use the Desmos calculator built into Bluebook on every math question.

How is the digital SAT scored?

The digital SAT has a scaled score range from 400 to 1600. The Reading & Writing section and math section are weighted equally, each worth 800 points. Unlike previous versions of the SAT, the digital SAT does not provide any subscores.

What is adaptive testing?

Unlike a linear test, where every question has been predetermined, an adaptive test analyzes how you are doing and then provides different questions to match your ability. There are two types of adaptive testing: item adaptive, which uses your answer from the previous question to determine the following question, and section adaptive, which waits until you've finished each section before adjusting the difficulty. The digital SAT is section adaptive, which allows you to move around and review questions in each module.

What is the difference between the digital SAT and PSAT/NMSQT?

The PSAT is quite similar to the digital SAT, having the same structure, number of questions, and timing. The only difference is that the PSAT leaves off some of the most advanced math and the scale is 160 to 760 per section, making a maximum score 1520.

For high school juniors, the PSAT is also the National Merit Scholarship Qualifying Test. If you score in the top one percent of your state, you will be invited to enter the process to become a National Merit Scholar, which upon completion grants you a college scholarship. National Merit uses its own qualifying score scale (the sum of twice your Reading & Writing section score and your Math section score, divided by 10), which converts your PSAT score to a scale with a maximum score of 228.

How important is my SAT score?

This depends on the schools you are applying to. Some schools will expect your score to be at a certain minimum and admission will be difficult, if not outright impossible, without reaching that score. Other schools consider the SAT alongside GPA and other aspects, such as recommendations, essays, and extracurricular activities. And some colleges don't use the SAT for consideration for admission. It's important to check with the admission office of every school you'll be applying to make sure you know their expectations.

If I'm applying to test optional schools, should I still take the SAT?

Yes, test optional means that the colleges still consider the SAT, but won't disqualify a student for not submitting the scores. At many test optional schools, applicants who submit SAT scores are more likely to be accepted than those who do not. Additionally, SAT scores can qualify you for merit based scholarships and aid that can dramatically reduce the cost of attending college.

If my school offers the SAT during the school day, should I take it?

Absolutely! Your school is paying for the test, so you should take advantage of that opportunity. Digital SAT test administered during school days are considered the same as those offered on national test dates.

How often should I take the SAT?

You should always check with the specific colleges you're applying to for their requirements, but here are our recommendations. Generally, three times should be adequate to achieve your optimal score, but there is usually no penalty for taking the SAT as many times as you need to achieve the score you seek. An increasing number of schools will "superscore" your tests and create a composite SAT score, combining the highest section scores from different administrations to create your "Super" score. Because SATs vary in difficulty from one administration to the next, it's in your best interest to take this test multiple times until you reach your target score. Just as there are easier and harder tests, students have good and bad days. The more you take this test, the more comfortable and confident you become. You eventually move into a zone where you know what to expect and achieve a level of mastery of the testing process. As students move from their first to their second SAT, they tend to achieve their biggest score increases. Students generally see smaller gains through their third SAT.

Should I set goals for each test I take?

Absolutely! Always keep your ultimate goal in mind, and view each test as a stepping stone towards this goal. Set distinct section goals for each test you plan to take. Say, for example, your introductory score is a 540 reading & writing and 520 math, giving you a total score of 1060, and you want to hit a total of 1200. Set short term goals for each test you plan to take, and write them down. "In October my goal is 560 reading & writing and 550 math. In December my goal is 580 reading & writing and 570 math. My goal for June is 610 reading & writing and 590 math." As you write your goals, enumerate the steps you will take to achieve them, such as practicing with this guide and taking mock tests. Setting and attaining short term goals has a positive impact on your sense of confidence and your level of motivation. Use these short term goals to help you attain your ultimate goal.

When should I take the SAT?

Fall and winter of junior year are ideal times to take the first SAT. The December SAT is a natural first test. For students who are enrolled in Algebra II as juniors, we generally recommend March as the first official SAT; this gives them a semester to hone their Algebra II skills. The majority of our students, having finished Algebra II as sophomores, are ready to jump in at the beginning of junior year.

Keep your schedule in mind! If you have a major time commitment in the fall, wait until the winter to start your prep. It is quite common to prep intensely and take two SATs back to back. Once you've knocked out a test or two, it's fine to take breaks and come back for one later in the year. Many of our students see their greatest gains on the June SAT. This has to do with our students' growing familiarity and comfort with the test as well as their freedom from academic and extracurricular obligations. Once school is out, students can really focus on the June SAT. Ideally students will take the SAT two to three times their junior year.

Many schools will offer an in-school version of the SAT during the Spring semester. Keep an eye out for this, as this is an efficient way to get another attempt at the test. And you won't have to get up early on a weekend!

SATs administered during the fall of their senior year are available as back-ups. The August, October, November, and December tests of senior year will all count for regular admissions. The October test is generally the last SAT that will count for Early Decision / Early action.

How do I register for the SAT?

Log in to www.collegeboard.org. Click "Sign up/Log in" and create an account. Follow the instructions. Make sure to sign up early to secure a spot at a preferred location. The good locations can fill up quickly.

What do I need to take the digital SAT?

You will need to have downloaded Bluebook on your device. A few days before the test, you will be reminded to download an update. That update will contain your test, so you'll have no issue with school wifi when you're testing.

Make sure that your device is fully charged before you leave.

On test day, you should bring:

- Your fully-charged device
- Power cord for your device
- Your printed admission ticket
- Your driver's license or other form of photo ID
- A few pencils to write down your work (paper will be provided)
- A calculator if you prefer your handheld one over Desmos
- Snacks and water
- Layers of clothing, in the event you are in a cold or hot room

When will I receive my scores?

The Bluebook app will not immediately grade your test. The College Board provides scores back between two to three weeks.

How do I report my SAT scores to schools?

When you sign up for an SAT administration, you can select up to four schools to receive your SAT scores free of charge. You can send your scores to additional schools for a fee. After the test, you can log onto your College Board My SAT account to send your scores to schools.

Do I have to send all of my SAT scores?

College Board allows you to send particular scores and withhold others. If a college superscores the SAT, it is in your best interest to send all tests which contain a personal best on any section. Keep in mind, a few colleges require that you send all of your scores. That will be made clear during the application process.

What is extended time? Do I need it? Can I get it?

Some students with diagnosed learning differences are allowed to take the SAT with accommodations such as extended time. Only a licensed psychologist can make the diagnosis of whether a student needs extended time to compensate for a learning disability. In most cases, before the College Board will consider granting extended time or any other accommodation, your high school must acknowledge and provide you appropriate accommodations. Once approved for accommodations, they will be applied to your Bluebook testing app.

Will colleges know if I took the SAT with accommodations?

No, it's unlawful for the College Board to disclose if a student took the test with extended time or any other accommodations, as that violates medical privacy.

SAT Structure and Scoring

Let's review the test's structure and address the complexity in the scoring.

Timing and Structure

The digital SAT is divided into two sections, Reading & Writing and Math, each with two modules.

Reading & Writing Module 1 27 questions, 32 minutes	Reading & Writing Module 2 27 Questions 32 minutes
Math Module 1 22 questions 35 minutes	Math Module 2 22 questions 35 minutes

Two questions in each module are "pretest" questions, which is the College Board's term for experimental questions that are not graded. There is no way to determine which two questions in the module are pretest.

Modules and Adaptive Testing

Each section of the digital SAT starts with a module that will have a mix of easy, medium, and hard questions. After you complete the first module, the app will assess your answers and either assign you an higher module with more difficult questions, or a lower module with more easier questions. The test will not notify you of which module you receive and it's important to recognize that the higher module will still have easy questions.

NEW ADAPTIVE SAT STRUCTURE

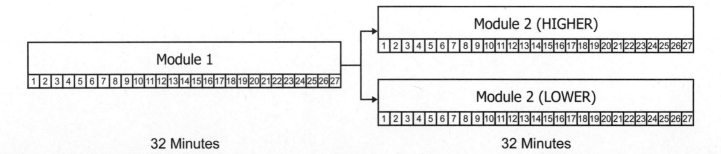

The official score reports don't give much info

When you receive your official score report, you'll find that there is not a lot of information provided. The score report only provides 7 bars that don't directly relate to how many questions you missed.

SAT Scores

Total Score   1240 400-1600   80th*

Section Scores

Reading and Writing   **630** 200-800   81st*

Math   **610** 200-800   77th*

*Percentiles represent the percent of graduating SAT test takers from the past 3 years who scored equal to or lower than you.

Knowledge and Skills

View your performance across the 8 content domains measured on the SAT.

Reading and Writing

Information and Ideas (26% of section, 12-14 questions)

Craft and Structure (28% of section, 13-15 questions)

Expression of Ideas (20% of section, 8-12 questions)

Standard English Conventions (26% of section, 11-15 questions)

Math

Algebra (35% of section, 13-15 questions)

Advanced Math (35% of section, 13-15 questions)

Problem-Solving and Data Analysis (15% of section, 5-7 questions)

Geometry and Trigonometry (15% of section, 5-7 questions)

Also, notice that the score report gives no indication whether you made it to the higher or lower second module. Let's explore why they do this.

A peek behind the curtain...

On the digital SAT, each question is given a unique point value, or "weight," which is scored via an algorithm. Weighting is based on the difficulty of the question, the skills required to find a solution, and the "guessability" of the answer. More challenging questions are not necessarily more valuable, because an easier question that involves important skills may be assigned a higher point value.

This is why the score reports are so vague, because, with the algorithmic scoring, they can't say "if you miss one question, you get a 790, and if you miss two questions you get a 780." It keeps the College Board from having to say "it's complicated" when students ask about the scores.

What should you do?

There's a lot going on behind the scenes of the digital SAT. This may lead to some you to wonder:

- Should I try to answer a certain number of questions in module 1 to get the lower module?

- Should I try to figure out which questions are pretest?

- Should I try to analyze the relative weight of each question?

The short answer to all of these questions is **no**. Trying to decode the algorithm is not the best way to succeed on the digital SAT. Let's head to the next chapter to learn the best way to approach the test.

Don't be this poor fellow – there is no need to worry about all this complicated background info!

Main Strategy

For all questions on the SAT, there is one overarching strategy.

....

Don't stress the numbers

There's a lot to think about on the digital SAT, and it can be stressful knowing that an algorithm is assessing your performance as you're taking the test. It's similar to being at bat in a baseball game; there's a lot you *could* think about, but only one thing you <u>should</u> focus on: the ball.

Baseball fanatics love statistics, as every batter has their stats–runs batted in (RBI), on-base percentage–and so does every pitcher–earned runs average (ERA) and total strikeouts.

But when you're at bat, should you be thinking about these statistics? Does keeping these stats in the front of your mind make it more likely that you'll hit the ball? No, because it's <u>each individual pitch</u> that matters.

Keep your eye on the ball

Yes, there is a lot of stuff going on behind the scenes, but your job is to keep your eye on the ball. With the SAT, you should **focus on the question in front of you**. Don't ponder whether this question is one of the two pretest questions. Don't worry about how much weight the question has in the algorithm. Focus on answering the question. You'll do much better with this approach rather than trying to game the algorithm.

How To Use This Book

This book is divided into to the key sections of the SAT: Reading, Writing, and Math. Each chapter contains strategies, illustrated explanations, and practice sections.

Active Learning

Practice is the key to raising your SAT score. Many books are designed like lectures, spewing a list of all the rules and formulas you need to memorize and calling it a day. That kind of passive learning is not very fun (and frankly does very little to raise your score). This book is instead designed to empower and guide you, much as a private tutor would, in the kind of smart practice that will prepare you for test day.

TIP

Cover up solutions with an index card or a piece of paper while you work the example: no peeking!

EXAMPLES and SOLUTIONS

A large portion of this book is dedicated to working through example problems to show you the best way to approach the material. Give every example a shot before you read the solution. Then, check your work and answer against the solution, reading for tips that will help you solve future problems.

Exercises

Many chapters have **exercises**: interactive practice sections designed to bridge the gap between learning a concept and putting it into practice on a sample test problem. When you see this pencil icon, it means stop reading and start exercising your new skills. Answers can be found either below the exercise or at the **bottom of the next page**.

> 1. Good testing habits can be built through _____.

Answers: | 1. practice

Portals

In every section of the book, you'll find **portals** in the margins leading you to other pages in the book that can provide more information or context for the current topic. These portals are designed to help you **make connections** between different concepts, boosting your understanding of multiple topics at once!

Practice Problems

This book includes hundreds of different practice problems that are modeled after real SAT questions. Even the passages mimic the length, tone, and appearance of those that you'll see on test day. After completing each chapter, complete the practice problems attached and be sure to check your answers in the back of the book!

Peppers

Math problems can vary in difficulty. The last few questions of the multiple choice and grid-ins on the Math test are particularly tricky and often combine a number of concepts into a single question. Unless you're going for a near-perfect score, it's often not worth the time investment to chip away at these tough problems for 1 or 2 lousy points. Like very spicy peppers, they're not for everyone!

We have marked the most difficult practice problems with a **pepper icon**. Give these problems a shot, but don't feel like you haven't fully mastered a section simply because the pepper problem is giving you trouble.

Study Schedules

There is no single "right" way to study for the SAT. But there IS a right book.

Two approaches to prepping for the SAT

You should consider your own unique strengths and weaknesses when deciding on the study plan that will work best for you. Let's look at two approaches to SAT prep:

(1) *The Comprehensive Review*

Each week complete a series of lessons and practice problems from each section: Reading, Writing, and Math. In Week 1, you may tackle Words in Context in Reading, Punctuation in Writing, and Basic Algebra in Math. This balanced approach will keep you moving forward on all fronts.

(2) *Isolate and Focus*

Take a practice test. Celebrate your strengths and identify the areas that need improvement, then use the table of contents to target those areas where you lost the most points. If your Reading score is lower than the other sections, put your energy there. If you are grappling with Math, go there first. You can use the practice sections and additional tests to gauge your progress and guide your preparation.

Spread out your SAT review over time

Memory researchers have found that packing all of your review into long sessions is not nearly as effective as spacing your study over multiple, shorter sessions. Each time you review a concept, you strengthen and reinforce it, etching the material deeper into your brain, where it will remain until you need it on test day!

Sample Study Schedules

Let's admit it: this is a big book! You likely don't have the time or need to work through every single page. Based on the amount of time you have before your test, it might make sense to focus on the chapters that cover only the most commonly tested concepts. Below, we've provided recommended syllabi based on the amount of time you have to study.

One Day Syllabus

If you only have one day to prepare, you should read the **overviews** of each section. These chapters will let you know what's on each section and give you a brief outline of recommended strategies.

One Week Syllabus

If you only have one week to prepare, you should read the **overviews** listed above as well as chapters that cover **core strategies** and **frequently tested concepts**. The chapters below will give you the most bang for your buck.

One Month Syllabus

If you have one month to prepare, you have enough time to move beyond core strategies but not quite enough time to work your way through the full book. Below, we've broken down your month into four structured weeks of content.

Week One

Reading
Reading Overview & Strategy 28
Reading Introduction..............................33

Writing
Writing Introduction 130
Boundaries... 135

Math
Math Overview & Strategy 238
Math Toolkit.. 245
Foundations 269
Functions 319

Week Two

Reading
Words in Context 48
Central Ideas and Details 86

Writing
Form, Structure, and Sense 161

Math
Polynomials 359
Advanced Functions............................. 405
Systems of Equations........................... 447

Week Three

Reading
Text Structure and Purpose....................65
Command of Evidence............................97

Writing
Transitions 216

Math
Modeling 481
Problem Solving & Data Analysis Part 1.. 545

Week Four

Reading
Cross text Connections 75
Inference 116

Writing
Rhetorical Synthesis............................. 224

Math
Problem Solving & Data Analysis Part 2.. 583
Geometry 635

Not sure where to start? We've got your back.

Not all chapters are worth the same amount of "points" on the test. Some content in the book covers core topics or strategies that will help on just about every problem you come across; others cover less common or more difficult content meant for students seeking a very high score.

The **Reading & Writing** chapters are in the order that the questions appear in each module. You can work linearly through these chapters, building your skills in the order you will see on the test. Alternatively, you can review the question types you missed on a practice test and put your focus there.

It's worth noting that the Standard English Conventions domain is the only section that requires you to remember grammatical rules. Not every module will test every type of grammar, so reviewing this unit regardless of how you did on your mock test score will prepare you for the range of ideas you could see on the official test.

Customize a study plan for Math

There are a lot of topics that can come up on the Math section, and so many pages of comprehensive Math instruction in this book. Based on your score goals, you might want to skip or focus on different topics. Here are tips for strategically approaching the Math section of this book.

- **Practice Tests** - All students should start out by taking a practice test to find their strengths and weaknesses.

- **Challenge Problems -** The trickiest problems throughout the book are marked with chili pepper icons. If you are aiming for a 650 or higher on Math, seek out and tackle these questions. Also be sure to try the Challenge Problem Sets on page 697. If you are aiming for below a 650, consider skipping these.

- **Desmos Calculator Tips -** Throughout the math section we provide tips and tricks for getting the most out of the Desmos calculator that is provided in the Bluebook app. The table of contents on page 249 will point you to all of these tips, and we recommend all students check out each of the listed pages, even if you are otherwise skipping a chapter.

- **Geometry and Data Analysis -** The SAT casts a wide net when it comes to these domains - you can expect just 5-7 problems from each of these two domains, which means any given topic may or may not show up on your specific test. If these topics are new to you, you can pick up points by covering the most basic questions from each of these units. If you are aiming for over 700, you want to make sure you are ready regardless of what they decide to throw at you. Check your practice test results before plowing through these larger units.

TIP

The math modules on the SAT organize the problems by difficulty rather than concept, and almost every concept can be tested in low, medium, or high difficulty problems.

Most of the units build on each other, so if you have several topics to work on, start with the ones that come earlier in the book.

Reading & Writing

Tags: Reading Strategy • Writing Strategy

Structure and Timing

The Reading & Writing modules each contain 27 questions with an accompanying text, typically a short paragraph.

2 modules

32 minutes

27 questions

Passage Types

TIP

Every literature and poem text comes from a published work, often by a famous author. The others texts are written by the test writers but always reference real people and events.

On each module you will find a mix of six different passage types:

Literature: Expect these text to be at least a hundred year old and may go back to the 1700s. You'll always be given the author's name and publication date for context.

Poetry: Poems can go all the way back to Shakespeare.

Social Science: texts about economics, psychology urban planning, behavior, or sociology.

History: texts about archeology, historical figures, and important events.

Humanities: texts about artists and the art they make.

Natural Science: texts about biology, chemistry, physics, or Earth science.

Content Domain and Skills

There are four content Domain areas in the Reading & Writing section. The first two domains contain the reading comprehension questions, and the second two domains contain the grammar and revision questions.

TIP

This is the order of questions used on each module. Only the Standard English Conventions domain will mix up the order of questions.

Content Domain	Skill/Knowledge Testing Points	Operational Question Distribution
Craft and Structure (Reading)	• Words in Context • Text Structure and Purpose • Cross-Text Connections	13-15 Questions ~28%
Information and Ideas (Reading)	• Central Ideas and Details • Command of Evidence (Textual, Quantitative) • Inferences	12-14 Questions ~26%
Standard English Conventions (Writing)	• Boundaries • Form, Structure, and Sense	11-15 Questions ~26%
Expression of Ideas (Writing)	• Transitions • Rhetorical Synthesis	8-12 Questions ~20%

The key to a higher score is building better habits

The reading and writing is consistent in its structure, so the best thing you can do is to familiarize yourself with the question types and the strategies and/or content tested within those. We'll building better reading, answering, and pacing habits, including:

1. **Identifying** question types and **recalling** any specific strategies

2. Coming up with **your own answer** to questions

3. Eliminating wrong answers with **throwaways**

4. Proving the right answer with **evidence**

Build habits through regular practice

Like all habits, these won't simply appear overnight; your Reading & Writing score will increase with practice, practice, practice! These strategies might slow you down or feel awkward at first. When you're tired, you might forget and slip into old habits. But over time, text-by-text, these strategies will become second nature.

As a result, you'll become a **better reader** and a **better test-taker**!

Learning Bluebook

Tags: Reading Strategy • Writing Strategy

Practice and Prepare

The SAT is taken through the College Board's official *Bluebook* app. Becoming familiar with this app is the first step towards a great SAT score. Once you download Bluebook for your laptop or tablet, you can preview test features or take full-length practice tests.

Click here to try out test features without a timer.

Test Preview

Full-Length Practice

Click here to launch a timed practice test that will be scored on your College Board account.

Digital Tools

The Bluebook app offers several basic tools to help you mark questions for review, eliminate answers, add notes, and more.

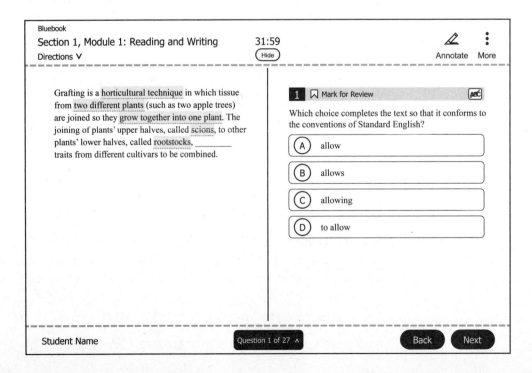

Digital Tools of the Bluebook App

Become familiar with the layout and functionality of the Bluebook app before testing day. Practicing with the app now will allow you to be more confident and save time on the official test.

Annotate - Near the top right of the Bluebook app is an annotation button that will allow you to **highlight text** and make notes. Before you use this tool, you must select some text. With this done, click the annotation button to highlight the text and open a new text box that will let you enter a note.

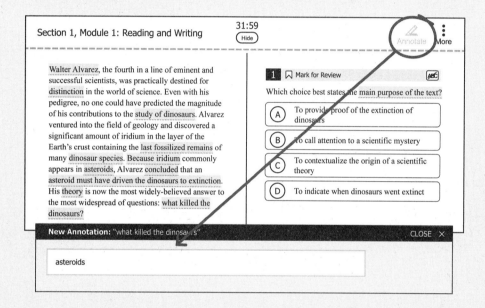

 Answer Eliminator - Clicking this button allows you to cross out any answer choices that you believe are incorrect.

Mark for Review - Clicking the flag button labels the question as one you want to return to after finishing the section. Pull up the list of items at the bottom, you'll see all of your marked items.

More – Clicking this button lets you take an emergency break and access a Help tool that explains test features and functionality.

Directions ∧ **Directions -** Clicking here brings up the standard directions for the Digital SAT reading section.

The questions in this section address a number of important reading and writing skills. Each question includes one or more passages, which may include a table or graph. Read each passage and question carefully, and then choose the best answer to the question based on the passage(s).

All questions in this section are multiple-choice with four answer choices. Each question has a single best answer.

UNIT | Reading Introduction

Chapters

Overview

In this unit, you'll learn some overarching strategies for the reading portions of the Reading & Writing modules. You'll learn how to use **throwaways** to eliminate wrong answers and logic words to focus on the **central claims or arguments** in a text.

Reading Strategy

Tags: Reading Strategy

Neutral talk

Try to catch yourself thinking in judgy language; when you do, rephrase with **goal-oriented, neutral language** instead. Replace the unhelpful thought

"Be faster!"

with the helpful thought

"Spend less time rereading and more time underlining."

or

"After 45 seconds on a question, make my best guess and move on."

First, get rid of judgy language

It's easy to think that reading comprehension is something that just kind of *happens* inside your brain: that you are either SMART, SLOW, GOOD AT READING, or NOT GOOD AT READING, and that's all there is to it. This is what we might call **judgy language**: it's full of judgments and conclusions that would be rude if said to someone else. So why say them to yourself?

Aside from being upsetting, this language does nothing to point us toward solutions. How are you supposed to respond to a goal of DO BETTER, BE SMARTER, or REMEMBER MORE? Say "Okay"? Instead, we're going to **focus on concrete, behavioral goals** that will naturally drive up your Reading score.

Reading is about behavior, not IQ

The truth is that **reading is a skill anyone can improve**. The future version of you who consistently gets a higher score on the Reading section is physically DOING things (like, with your *muscles*) that are leading to a higher score.

Reading is an <u>activity</u> you can practice!

Step-by-step strategy for answering questions

The right strategy will keep you focused on the task at hand, earning points one-by-one. You'll tackle questions using a **three-step process** that will help you quickly identify the correct answer.

Read the Question   *Read Text with the Question in Mind*   *Eliminate Wrong Answers*

READ THE QUESTION FIRST

Rather than read the text without any context, start with the question on the right and determine the **question type** and the **goal**. Learning the question types may seem like a lot at first, but there are only eleven different categories and this book has chapters about all of them.

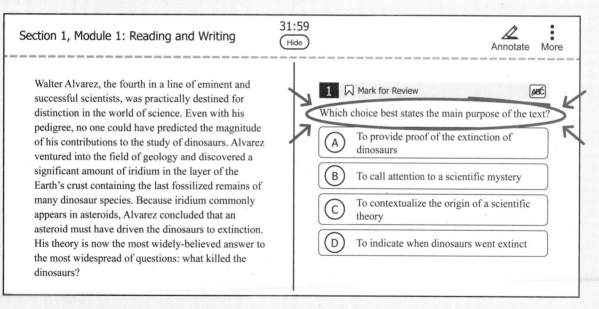

Section 1, Module 1: Reading and Writing   31:59 (Hide)   Annotate   More

Walter Alvarez, the fourth in a line of eminent and successful scientists, was practically destined for distinction in the world of science. Even with his pedigree, no one could have predicted the magnitude of his contributions to the study of dinosaurs. Alvarez ventured into the field of geology and discovered a significant amount of iridium in the layer of the Earth's crust containing the last fossilized remains of many dinosaur species. Because iridium commonly appears in asteroids, Alvarez concluded that an asteroid must have driven the dinosaurs to extinction. His theory is now the most widely-believed answer to the most widespread of questions: what killed the dinosaurs?

1 ⬚ Mark for Review   ABC

Which choice best states the main purpose of the text?

(A) To provide proof of the extinction of dinosaurs

(B) To call attention to a scientific mystery

(C) To contextualize the origin of a scientific theory

(D) To indicate when dinosaurs went extinct

Why read the question first?

It may seem counterintuitive to skip the passage, but it all comes down to **giving your brain a break**. If you read the text without knowing what the question is asking, your brain will try to hold as much information as possible in case it ends up being important. Why bother? Read the question to **prime your brain** to focus only on what *really* matters!

READ THE TEXT WITH THE QUESTION IN MIND

Now that you know the question, you can focus on the task at hand. Read the passage and focus on what is important to that question. Use the highlighter and annotation tools to mark any key ideas.

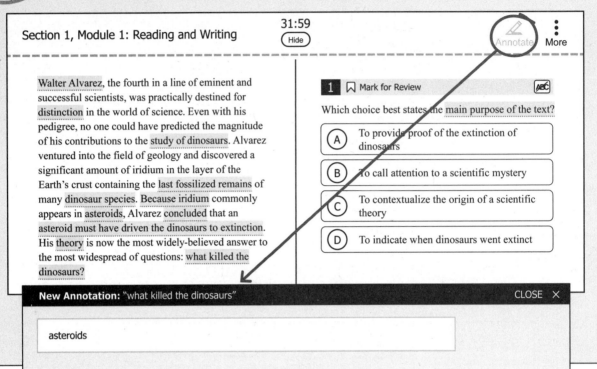

ELIMINATE WRONG ANSWERS

Finally, eliminate wrong answers one-by-one. If a choice has a single word that contradicts the passage (what we call a "throwaway" word), that choice is wrong! Find your right answer through the magical **process of elimination**. Once you've narrowed down your choices, pick the option with no throwaways and the most supporting evidence in the passage.

Section 1, Module 1: Reading and Writing

31:59 Hide

Annotate More

Walter Alvarez, the fourth in a line of eminent and successful scientists, was practically destined for distinction in the world of science. Even with his pedigree, no one could have predicted the magnitude of his contributions to the study of dinosaurs. Alvarez ventured into the field of geology and discovered a significant amount of iridium in the layer of the Earth's crust containing the last fossilized remains of many dinosaur species. Because iridium commonly appears in asteroids, Alvarez concluded that an asteroid must have driven the dinosaurs to extinction. His theory is now the most widely-believed answer to the most widespread of questions: what killed the dinosaurs?

1 Mark for Review

Which choice best states the main purpose of the text?

A To provide proof of the extinction of dinosaurs

B To call attention to a scientific mystery

C To contextualize the origin of a scientific theory

D To indicate when dinosaurs went extinct

Throwaways

Tags: Reading Strategy

....

A single word can make an answer choice wrong

In order for an answer choice to be correct, every single word must be supported by the text. An answer choice that matches perfectly with text except for one little word is a wrong answer.

Save time!

Many students get stuck debating between two answers that both sound pretty great. They waste time trying to "feel out" which one is more correct.

Instead, by focusing on throwaways, you make the Reading section feel more concrete and move from question to question MUCH faster.

Find the best answer, not just a good one

Wrong answers range from **clearly wrong** to **almost right**. Reading and Writing questions, especially difficult ones, will usually contain at least one or two choices that are "almost right." Focusing on throwaways will help you to weed out the contenders and focus on the real deal.

Common Throwaway offenders

Watch out for any of these stock bad answers:

* aren't **relevant** or **true**
* might be true but **don't answer the question asked**
* might be true but are **too broad**
* might be true but are **too narrow**
* address the **wrong part of the text**
* reference the text, but **do not answer the question accurately**
* are **too extreme**

Paraphrase

Remember to put each question into your **own words**, then read that paraphrase before each choice. For example:

"David Kahn's quote..."

BOX 'EM

Throughout this chapter, whenever you spot a throwaway, draw a box around it.

Alternate Strategy:
After putting it into a box, put that box inside of another box, then mail that box to yourself, and, when it arrives, *SMASH IT WITH A HAMMER.*

EXAMPLE 1

It is highly doubtful that the Allied forces would have won World War II without the help of Polish mathematician Marian Rejewski. At age fourteen, Rejewski enrolled in a secret cryptology course for German speakers. Soon his full-time occupation was decoding the German Enigma machine. Combining his usage of pure mathematics with information provided by French intelligence, Rejewski succeeded in decoding the Enigma, and consequently, the Allied forces were able to intercept German intelligence transmissions for six years. Historian David Kahn says that Rejewski's stunning achievement "elevates him to the pantheon of the greatest cryptanalysts of all time." On the 100th anniversary of his birthday, a sculpted memorial was presented to his hometown of Bydgoszcz, Poland.

1. Which choice best describes the function of the quotation in the text as a whole?

   A) It reveals the origins of Rejewski's success.
   B) It offers evidence to support a prior claim.
   C) It suggests the value perceived in a historical event.
   D) It argues that Rejewski has been underappreciated.

1. Which choice best describes the function of the quotation in the text as a whole?

   A) It reveals the origins of Rejewski's success.

   The second sentence offers some information about the origins, but that has nothing to do with the Kahn quote.

   B) It offers evidence to support a prior claim.

   This answer is really close, but what Kahn offers is an opinion about Rejewski, not evidence.

   C) It suggests the value perceived in a historical event.

   No throwaways here! The historical event is "Rejewski's stunning achievement" and that achievement makes him one of the best.

   D) It argues that Rejewski has been underappreciated.

   Khan's quote does nothing to suggest that Rejewski is underappreciated.

EXAMPLE 2

Coleman Hawkins, one of the first great saxophonists of the Harlem Renaissance, was a consistently modern improviser who possessed an encyclopedic knowledge of music. Hawkins was a giant of the jazz scene for more than forty years. His musical odyssey began in front of the keys of a piano at the age of five; he moved on to the cello before settling on the tenor saxophone. In the 1920s and 30s, the saxophone was primarily considered a novelty instrument used in marching bands. However, Hawkins saw a greater potential for this instrument. His lyrical tones and innovative style helped usher in a new age of avant-garde jazz known as Bebop and placed the saxophone at the center of the new jazz aesthetic. Succeeding generations of saxophonists, whose members included Sonny Rollins, Lester Young, and John Coltrane, acknowledged the profound influence that "Hawk" had on their musical styles.

2. The text supports which of the following statements about Hawkins?

   A) He broke new ground for jazz saxophonists.
   B) His innovative lyrics helped usher in a new musical era.
   C) His music earned international acclaim for many decades.
   D) His modernist style alienated more traditional musicians.

SOLUTION

Paraphrase

"The passage says that…"

2. The text supports which of the following statements about Hawkins?

(A) He broke new ground for jazz saxophonists.

   No throwaway here: each word has support in the passage.

B) His innovative  lyrics helped usher in a new musical era.

   The passage says he has a "lyrical tone," but we never read about Hawkins writing actual lyrics. He was a sax player!

C) His music earned international acclaim for many decades.

   He was definitely acclaimed. But there's no mention of international acclaim. Don't assume anything you can't find evidence for in the passage!

D) His modernist style alienated more traditional musicians.

   This COULD be true, but nowhere in the passage do we read about a negative reaction to Hawkins.

Claims and Logic

Tags: Reading Strategy

NOTE

Question types that often focus on claims:

• Text Structure & Purpose
• Cross Text Connections
• Central ideas & Details
• Command of Evidence
• Inference
• Rhetorical Synthesis

TIP

Remember to **skip to the question before reading the text!** Even though we know we're focusing on claims, it's important to practice the main strategy on every question!

What is the main claim, argument, or theory?

The SAT Reading & Writing section places significant emphasis on your ability to recognize and interpret a claim, argument, or theory being made in a given text. You can expect to come across **12 to 18 questions** that specifically test your comprehension of a presented claim. That's a lot of points up for grabs! So before we focus on specific question types, let's get some practice identifying claims.

Sometimes an author will share multiple points of view before stating their main idea; sometimes the author will come right out with multiple supporting details before concluding with a central claim. The key is to tell the difference between background details and main ideas. Let's get some practice!

EXAMPLE 1

An agrivoltaic system occurs when agriculture and solar panels coexist on the same parcel of land. Henry Williams and Max Zhang have studied how the placement of solar panels can affect both the efficiency of the panel and the surrounding crops. By using a computational fluid dynamics–based microclimate model and solar panel temperature data, Williams and Zhang claim to have found a "sweet spot" for the mounting height of the panels that will allow cooling for both the panel and the ground below, and therefore allow more types of crops to grow in dry, arid environments.

1. Which choice best states the main purpose of the text?

   A) To introduce the invention of agrivoltaic systems
   B) To determine the proper mounting height for solar panels
   C) To call attention to a promising discovery
   D) To indicate a necessary change in the growing of crops

SOLUTION

After reading the question, let's read the text and focus on the **main claim** it is highlighting:

> ...**Williams and Zhang claim** to have found a **"sweet spot"** for the **mounting height** of the panels that will **allow cooling** for both the **panel** and the **ground below**, and **therefore** allow **more types of crops** to grow in dry, arid environments.

The claim is about how Williams and Zhang have figured out how to place crops and solar panels on the same piece of land in a way that benefits both.

Now we're ready to **eliminate wrong answers** using throwaways:

A) To introduce the invention of agrivoltaic systems

The text never states that Williams and Zhang invented the idea of agrivoltaic systems.

B) To determine the proper mounting height for solar panels

The text states that they claimed to have found a correct height, but we don't know the specifics of how they did it.

C) To call attention to a promising discovery

Their claim is the promising discovery, so this matches.

D) To indicate a necessary change in the growing of crops

Necessary is a strong word and the text only says that it works in a specific climate, so this is not the best answer.

Choice C is best.

TIP

Always be on the lookout for main ideas and claims! Use your scratch paper or annotation tools as needed to keep your mind focused on what's *really* important in each text.

NOTE

Expect to see logic words featured in 10 to 15 texts per test, including transitions questions that directly test you on effective use of logic words.

Question types that often focus on logic words:

- Words in Context
- Centra Ideas and Details
- Text Structure and Purpose
- Command of Evidence
- Inference
- Transitions

Logic words are key to identifying claims

Many authors signal that a main point is coming by using a "transition word" like **but, however, therefore,** and **although**. Typically, whatever comes after one of these words is pretty important, so take note of transition words whenever you see them! This will help you spot shifts in the author's argument and identify the logical flow of the text as a whole.

TRANSITION WORDS	
Conclusion	Logical Shift
Thus	But
Consequently	However
Therefore	Although
Because	Nevertheless
Hence	Nonetheless

EXAMPLE 2

Most of the carbon emitted by human activity is absorbed by the ocean, yet modeling this process has been difficult to refine. A team of researchers, led by Dr Laura Cimoli, have been studying how deep sea underwater waves, created on boundaries between water of differing temperatures and salinity, can affect carbon absorption. Combining multiple types of oceanic observations, the team concluded that turbulence between deep sea waves can dramatically affect how much carbon gets absorbed by the ocean.

2. What choice best states the main idea of the text?

A) Researchers have obtained evidence that provides the best way to reduce carbon emissions.
B) Researchers have identified an underlying factor that impacts carbon absorption.
C) Deep sea underwater waves are created by differences in water temperature and salinity.
D) Deep sea underwater waves are easily understood by direct observations.

Most of the carbon emitted by human activity is absorbed by the ocean(yet)modeling this process has been difficult to refine. A team of researchers, led by Dr Laura Cimoli, have been studying how deep sea underwater waves, created on boundaries between water of differing temperatures and salinity, can affect carbon absorption. Combining multiple types of oceanic observations, the team(concluded)that turbulence between deep sea waves can dramatically affect how much carbon gets absorbed by the ocean.

So there was a problem and this team came up with a solution! Let's eliminate answers with that in mind:

A) Researchers have obtained evidence that provides the best way to reduce carbon emissions.

Strong language, like saying it's the "best" is usually there to make an answer choice wrong. Furthermore, the text is about carbon absorption, not emission.

B) Researchers have identified an underlying factor that impacts carbon absorption.

There was an unknown and this team figured it out.

C) Deep sea underwater waves are created by differences in water temperature and salinity.

This is mentioned, but it's just a detail—not the main idea.

D) Deep sea underwater waves are easily understood by direct observations.

Again, we have a detail and the passage never said anything about it being easy.

Choice B is best.

PORTAL

We'll get more into specifics about different types of transitions when we get to the *Transitions* chapter on page 216.

TIP

If you're not focused on the main ideas, you're more likely to be fooled by wrong answer choices that reference a distracting detail from the text.

Logic words keep you focused on the main idea

When you're reading the text, it's important to recognize that not every word is important. Part of your job is to focus on the words and phrases that matter for the question asked. Let's look at a question type that asks us to identify claims using logic words.

EXAMPLE 3

In January 2023, Boston unveiled a new monument by Hank Willis Thomas to commemorate the lives and relationship of Corretta and Martin Luther King Jr., as the two met and fell in love in the city. The sculpture, consisting of a pair of 20-foot-tall bronze arms intertwined in embrace, allows visitors to walk between the arms in hope of feeling the connection between the two subjects. The initial response, however, has been mostly negative, with some members of the King family disapproving. In contrast, American Culture professor Kristin Ann Hass claims that this initial controversy should be expected, as many famous modern public art pieces, from Paris's Eiffel Tower to the Washington DC's Vietnam War Memorial, were originally met with scorn. Hass predicts that the critical consensus on the monument will likely _____

3. Which choice most logically completes the text?

A) remain negative as few will disagree with the King family's assessment.
B) become overwhelmingly positive in a short period of time.
C) focus on creating a more traditional replacement in its place.
D) gradually become more positive as the monument gains familiarity.

TIP

Logic words are used by authors to guide your understanding of their main idea.

SOLUTION

This is an **inference** question, and these texts often rely on claims and logic. We'll explain this question type in its own chapter later, but for now all you need to know is that <u>the answer choices finish the text</u>. Read the passage, underline the claim, and circle any logic words. Check your notes against ours on the next page.

Now let's check and see how similar your notes are.

In January 2023, Boston unveiled a new monument by Hank Willis Thomas to commemorate the lives and relationship of Corretta and Martin Luther King Jr., as the two met and fell in love in the city. The sculpture, consisting of a pair of 20-foot-tall bronze arms intertwined in embrace, allows visitors to walk between the arms in hope of feeling the connection between the two subjects. The initial response (however) has been mostly negative, with some members of the King family disapproving. (In contrast) American Culture professor <u>Kristin Ann Hass claims that this initial controversy should be expected, as many famous, and widely beloved, modern public art pieces, from Paris's Eiffel Tower to the Washington DC's Vietnam War Memorial, were originally met with scorn.</u> Hass predicts that the critical consensus on the monument will likely _____

Now that we know the claim, we can use it to best conclude the essay. Focus on eliminating choices using throwaway words:

A) remain negative as few will disagree with the King family's assessment.

The examples of the Eiffel Tower and the War Memorial show how public art can go from negative to positive.

B) become overwhelmingly positive in a short period of time.

The word overwhelmingly is too optimistic.

C) focus on creating a more traditional replacement in its place.

The expert makes no claim about a replacement.

D) gradually become more positive as the monument gains familiarity.

This matches the claim and is the most logical conclusion.

Choice D is best.

TIP

Watch out for choices, like choice B here, which sound similar to the claim but promise too much with superlative words.

UNIT

Craft and Structure

Chapters

Overview

In this unit, you'll explore how the building blocks of writing (words, sentences, and paragraphs) create **meaning**. You'll get in the mind of the author(s) of the texts and compare and contrast ideas between two different authors.

Many years ago, the SAT Reading section tested the depth of a student's vocabulary and regularly trotted out dusty old words that haven't been regularly used since the Victorian era.

The College Board took a more high-tech approach for the digital SAT: they used an algorithm to analyze the **most common words in college textbooks**, removed all the prepositions, articles, and conjunctions, as well as any technical words that apply only to a specific discipline.

The result is a collection of words that are actually useful, **many of which you're likely familiar with already**.

Words in Context

Tags: Craft and Structure • Words in Context

Which word best fills the blank given the context?

Every SAT begins with a handful of Words in Context questions. Typically, the question will present a sentence or two with **one word missing**. Your job is to find the best fit for the sentence out of the four words provided. We'll look at a few different types of Words in Context questions, including:

- **Definition –** when we need to pick a word that matches a definition provided in the text

- **Antonym/Contrast –** when we need to pick a word that contrasts with an idea or definition in the text

- **Cause and Effect –** when we need to pick a word that provides a logical outcome for what's described in the text

- **Words in Literature –** when we need to pick a word that matches the meaning of an underlined word in a piece of prose

Main Strategy

We'll get familiar with the nuances (details) of each question type, but first let's practice the main strategy we'll use for Words in Context questions:

1. *Read the text & look for logic clues*

2. *Plug in answer choices*

3. *Pick the best fit*

TIP

This strategy will keep us on the right track, even if we don't perfectly know the meaning of vocab when we start reading the question and text.

Strategy Practice

Before worrying about building vocabulary or tackling specific question types, focus on practicing the three-step strategy with the example below.

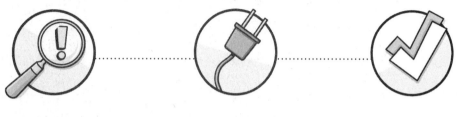

*Read the text &
look for logic clues*

Plug in Choices

Pick the Best Fit!

EXAMPLE 1

While studying the movement of sand dunes, Karol Bacik and Nathalie Vriend realized that they needed to further _____ how two sand dunes interact: by creating a model that tracked the motion of a large and small sand dune, they discovered that over time their size and their velocity would eventually reach an equilibrium.

1. Which choice completes the text with the most logical and precise word or phrase?

   A) separate
   B) diminish
   C) relocate
   D) investigate

SOLUTION

Step one: Read the text and look for any logic clues.

While studying the movement of sand dunes, Karol Bacik and Nathalie Vriend **realized** that they needed to **further** _____ how two sand dunes interact: by creating a model that tracked the motion of a large and small sand dune, they **discovered** that over time their size and their velocity would eventually reach an equilibrium.

Continued on next page →

There are several clues you can use to determine which word fits best. The scientists *realized* they needed to go *further*. The colon tells you that the next clause will give more details and you learn that they *discovered* something. All these logic clues point to picking an answer that emphasizes the need to discover more information.

Step two: Plug in the answer choices.

A) ... realized that they needed to further <u>separate</u> how two sand dunes interact

> *Nothing in the second part says that the sand dunes are separated*

B) ... realized that they needed to further <u>diminish</u> how two sand dunes interact

> *Diminish would make it smaller or less important. That doesn't make sense here.*

C) ... realized that they needed to further <u>relocate</u> how two sand dunes interact

> *They could relocate the dunes, but not how the dunes interact, so this isn't logical.*

D) ... realized that they needed to further <u>investigate</u> how two sand dunes interact

> *This looks good. They **investigate** and then make a **discovery**. This relationship seems logical.*

Step three: Pick the best fit.

1. Which choice completes the text with the most logical and precise word or phrase?

    A) separate
    B) diminish
    C) relocate
    D) **investigate**

D

PORTAL

Learn more about the introductory role of colons in the *All About Clauses* chapter of the Writing section on page 146.

Question Types

Words in Context questions follow **four general types**. Let's spend some time familiarizing ourselves with each, so that we can better spot the underlying logic.

Definition

Definition type questions are the most common Word-in-Context questions. The text given either provides the definition or a clear example of the word needed.

Here are some common logic clues to look out for:

(1) *Colon*

The colon is one of the most common clues that let you know that you're dealing with a definition question. The rule for using colons is that <u>the clause after the colon needs to explain the clause before the colon</u>. So if the word blank is before the colon, look for clues after the colon to help determine which specific word is the best fit.

(2) *For example/to illustrate/such as*

These words and phrases often set up an example that support the definition of the missing word. Pick the answer choices that best matches the given example.

EXAMPLE 2

In 1972, Cornell University hosted an exhibition titled "The Civilization of Llhuros," which featured 150 objects from an "ancient" Iron Age civilization. The entire exhibit turned out to be _____: Cornell professor of art Norman Daly had crafted the objects and invented the story of Llhuros.

2. Which choice completes the text with the most logical and precise word or phrase?

   A) revolutionary
   B) impactful
   C) fabricated
   D) uninspired

Step one: Read the text and look for any logic clues.

> In 1972, Cornell University hosted an exhibition titled "The Civilization of Llhuros," which featured 150 objects from an "ancient" iron age civilization. The entire exhibit turned out to be _____: Cornell professor of art Norman Daly had crafted the objects and **invented** the story of Llhuros.

Looking over the text, we have a colon right after the blank. This means that the clause after the colon has to define the word we need. The best clue after the colon is "invented," so we need to pick an answer that matches.

Step two: Plug in the answer choices.

A) The entire exhibit turned out to be <u>revolutionary</u>:

Maybe, but "invented" doesn't necessarily mean something is revolutionary.

B) The entire exhibit turned out to be <u>impactful</u>:

Again, maybe, but impactful does not have a strong connection with "invented."

C) The entire exhibit turned out to be <u>fabricated</u>:

Fabricated is a strong match with "invented."

D) The entire exhibit turned out to be <u>uninspired</u>:

Sounds like Norman Daly created an entire fictional culture. That doesn't sound uninspired.

Step three: Pick the best choice.

2. Which choice completes the text with the most logical and precise word or phrase?

A) revolutionary
B) impactful
C) **fabricated**
D) uninspired

C

Antonym and Contrast

Antonym and contrast questions typically give you the opposite definition and then a transition to show you that you're looking for the antonym.

Here are some common logic clues to look out for:

(1) *Transitions and conjunctions*

The best signal that you're dealing with an antonym or contrast question are words like *but*, *yet*, *however*, or *although*.

(2) *Words that show disappointment*

Sometimes the plan or experiment does not go as planned. Keep an eye out for words like *unfortunately*, *regrettably*, *ironically*, or *discouragingly*.

(3) *Words that show surprise*

While less negative than disappointment, the results of a study or experiment could surprise researchers. Words like *peculiarly*, *unexpectedly*, *inadvertently*, and *unusually* show that things didn't go as planned.

EXAMPLE 3

Hurricanes are one of the most destructive forces in nature, yet for all their damage, they may also provide benefits for coastal ecosystems. Lee Smee and Joseph Reustle studied how hurricanes in the Gulf of Mexico affected bays popular for fishing. Their conclusion was that the hiatus of fishing, caused by the hurricanes, _____ the local ecology.

3. Which choice completes the text with the most logical and precise word or phrase?

A) rebuilt
B) destroyed
C) marginalized
D) reorganized

Step one: Read the text and look for any logic clues.

> Hurricanes are one of the most **destructive** forces in nature, **yet** for all their damage, they may also provide **benefits** for coastal ecosystems. Lee Smee and Joseph Reustle studied how hurricanes in the Gulf of Mexico affected bays popular for fishing. Their **conclusion** was that the hiatus of fishing, caused by the hurricanes, _____ the local ecology.

Yes, hurricanes are destructive, yet they also provide benefits. This means the answer must emphasize a benefit of hurricanes.

Step two: Plug in the answer choices.

(A) Their conclusion was that the hiatus of fishing, caused by the hurricanes, <u>rebuilt</u> the local ecology.

That sounds like a benefit!

B) Their conclusion was that the hiatus of fishing, caused by the hurricanes, <u>destroyed</u> the local ecology.

This is definitely not a benefit!

C) Their conclusion was that the hiatus of fishing, caused by the hurricanes, <u>marginalized</u> the local ecology.

Being marginalized is typically negative, so that wouldn't be a benefit.

D) Their conclusion was that the hiatus of fishing, caused by the hurricanes, <u>reorganized</u> the local ecology.

Being reorganized is pretty neutral and logic clues tell us that we need to show a benefit.

Step three: Pick the best choice.

3. Which choice completes the text with the most logical and precise word or phrase?

   (A) rebuilt
   B) destroyed
   C) marginalized
   D) reorganized

A

54

Cause and Effect

Cause and effect questions ask you to follow the logic of events and pick a word that helps support the outcome presented.

Here are some common logic clues to look out for:

① *Words that explain why something happened*
Usage of words like *because*, *therefore*, *since*, and *accordingly* show events are related.

② *Words that show conclusion*
Words and phrases like *resulted in*, *proved*, *confirmed*, and *ascertained* show that a conclusion has been reached.

EXAMPLE 4

Although found in a variety of foods including fruits, nuts, and tea, tannins are considered an antinutrient. Tannins bind with proteins in a way that renders them _____, and therefore nutritionally inert.

4. Which choice completes the text with the most logical and precise word or phrase?

A) indigestible
B) delectable
C) irresistible
D) potent

SOLUTION

Step one: Read the text and look for any logic clues.

Although found in a variety of foods including fruits, nuts, and tea, tannins are **considered** an **antinutrient**. Tannins bind with proteins in a way that **renders** them _____, and **therefore** nutritionally **inert**.

In this text, you need to pick a word that would lead to tannins making nutrition inert (non-active).

Step two: Plug in the answer choices.

A) Tannins bind with proteins in a way that renders them <u>indigestible</u>, and therefore nutritionally inert.

Making something indigestible sounds like it could make some nutritionally inert.

B) Tannins bind with proteins in a way that renders them <u>delectable</u>, and therefore nutritionally inert.

Delectable means tasty, which is different from nutritionally inert.

C) Tannins bind with proteins in a way that renders them <u>irresistible</u>, and therefore nutritionally inert.

Irresistible doesn't have anything to do with making something nutritionally inert.

D) Tannins bind with proteins in a way that renders them <u>potent</u>, and therefore nutritionally inert.

Potent would make them more packed with nutrients, not inert.

Step three: Pick the best choice.

4. Which choice completes the text with the most logical and precise word or phrase?

A) indigestible
B) delectable
C) irresistible
D) potent

A

Words in Literature

Occasionally, a word in context question will use something from literature. These are easy to spot, as the test will tell you the author, title, and year of the text. Additionally, there will not be a blank in lieu of a word. Instead, you will have to determine a synonym for a word selected from the text. Even if the text is a 100+ years old, the SAT won't pick a super obscure word. The word selected will be easy, although it may be used in a less common or figurative way. The key here, just like the other types, is to use context clues.

EXAMPLE 5

The following text is from Jane Austen's 1818 novel *Persuasion*.

> A few years before, Anne Elliot had been a very pretty girl, but her bloom had vanished early; and as even in its height, her father had found little to admire in her, (so totally different were her delicate features and mild dark eyes from his own), there could be nothing in them, now that she was <u>faded</u> and thin, to excite his esteem.

5. As used in the text, what does the word "faded" most nearly mean?

    A) Detached
    B) Distant
    C) Pale
    D) Evaporated

SOLUTION

Step one: Read the text and look for any logic clues.

> A few years before, Anne Elliot had been a very **pretty** girl, **but** her **bloom** had **vanished early**; and as even in its height, her father had found little to admire in her, (so totally different were her delicate features and mild dark eyes from his own), there could be nothing in them, now that she was <u>faded</u> and **thin**, to excite his esteem.

We need a word that contrasts with *pretty* and connects to *thin*.

Step two: Plug in the answer choices.

~~A)~~ ... there could be nothing in them, now that she was <u>detached</u> and thin, to excite his esteem.

> *Detached describes personality and the description of Anne is only physical in this text, so we should probably find a physical description.*

~~B)~~ ... there could be nothing in them, now that she was <u>distant</u> and thin, to excite his esteem.

> *Distant doesn't describe someone's appearance.*

(C) ... there could be nothing in them, now that she was <u>pale</u> and thin, to excite his esteem.

> *She could be pale and thin and those could be seen as negatives by her father.*

~~D)~~ ... there could be nothing in them, now that she was <u>evaporated</u> and thin, to excite his esteem.

> *Evaporated seems like an awfully odd way to describe someone's appearance.*

Step three: Pick the best choice.

5. As used in the text, what does the word "faded" most nearly mean?

    A) Detached
    B) Distant
    (C) **Pale**
    D) Evaporated

C

58

Troubleshooting

What if you've done step one and two of the strategy and you are still not certain of the answer? Here are some additional approaches to try.

(1) Determine what type of word you need

Look over the text and the answer choices to determine if you need to pick a noun, verb, or adjective. This will help you to better grasp the logic of the text.

(2) Determine if the word needed is positive, negative, or neutral

Use context clues in the text to figure out if you need a positive, negative, or neutral word.

(3) Come up with your own word.

Imagine that this was an open-ended question where you could enter in your own word for the blank. What word would you choose to best match the tone of the text? Is there a synonym for that word among the answer choices?

(4) Use word roots to determine the meaning of words

Many English words use common Latin and Greek roots, prefixes, and suffixes. Paying attention to word roots and relating them to words with the root that you do know can help you infer the meaning of unfamiliar words.

(5) Use process of elimination

If you're able to eliminate even one word, that still increases your chances of getting the question correct. Some questions will create difficulty by using an uncommon word as the answer. For those questions, if you're able to eliminate three answers, it's perfectly fine to pick the answer with the unfamiliar word.

Recapping Words in Context

Words in Context questions ask you to pick a vocab word that best fills in a blank or replaces an underlined word. Whether you're matching or contrasting a given definition, completing a logical thought, or matching a word in a piece of literature, follow the three-step strategy:

(1) Read the text & look for logic clues

(2) Plug in answer choices

(3) Pick the best fit

Practice Set

1

The Acosta Bridge in Jacksonville, Florida, is the unlikely home to a mural by artist David Nackashi. Depicting three cows in shallow water, the Acosta mural is a _____ the history of this section of the St. James River: settlers referred to the area as "the Cowford" as this shallow part of the river gave herds a place to cross.

Which choice completes the text with the most logical and precise word or phrase?

A) tribute to
B) revision of
C) satire of
D) provision for

2

Created by artisan, engineer, and alchemist Bi Sheng, the Chinese system of movable type, the first of its kind in 1040 CE, _____ Guttenberg's European version by over 400 years.

Which choice completes the text with the most logical and precise word or phrase?

A) influenced
B) predated
C) conceived
D) disputed

3

Sculptor Paul Richards' 1985 installation *Wave Organ*, which uses pipes to acoustically amplify the sound of waves as they crash along the San Francisco coast, was _____ Bill Fontana's 1976 innovative underwater recordings of Kirribilli Wharf in Australia.

Which choice completes the text with the most logical and precise word or phrase?

A) inspired by
B) critical of
C) a byproduct of
D) derisive towards

4

Frustrated with the _____ of existing terms, author Nnedi Okorafor coined the term Africanfuturism to describe the genre of science fiction that is rooted in African experiences and perspectives and that focuses on "what is and can/will be" rather than "what could have been."

Which choice completes the text with the most logical and precise word or phrase?

A) arrangement
B) limitations
C) precision
D) obscurity

5

Campbell's Soup, beloved by many for its ease of preparation and homey appeal, was _____ to the status of an American classic when its distinctive can was featured in Andy Warhol's famous artworks.

Which choice completes the text with the most logical and precise word or phrase?

A) demoted
B) elevated
C) archived
D) reinstated

6

In 1972, Dougal Robertson, his wife Lyn, and their two children were traveling from Panama to the Galapagos via sailboat. Along the way, they met with serious misfortune when their boat, The Lucette, was sunk by a pod of orcas. The tightly-knit family demonstrated remarkable ____ and trust with one another, surviving on a small dinghy for 38 days before being rescued.

Which choice completes the text with the most logical and precise word or phrase?

A) aggression
B) resilience
C) ineptitude
D) forethought

7

Bananas are picked while still green and refrigerated to a chilly 56 degrees Fahrenheit: cool enough to delay ripening without thwarting it all together. Conversely, when they reach their destination, the bananas are stored in airtight rooms and exposed to ethylene gas, which is a naturally produced plant hormone that ____ ripening.

Which choice completes the text with the most logical and precise word or phrase?

A) hastens
B) stymies
C) hinders
D) reverses

8

Modern composting, which can generate tons of material, is so effective because it uses aerobic decomposition: oxygen, bacteria, and moisture to ____ a rapid breaking down of organic matter into beneficial compost.

Which choice completes the text with the most logical and precise word or phrase?

A) facilitate
B) disallow
C) complicate
D) reconcile

9

Despite the widely accepted narrative that workers are busier than ever before, the average number of work hours per week has not actually gone up significantly since the 1980s. According to the 2014 American Time Use Survey numbers, employed people logged an average of 7.8 hours per workday—a manageable 39 hours per work week, nothing like the excessive fifty-, sixty-, or eighty-hour work weeks so often ____

Which choice completes the text with the most logical and precise word or phrase?

A) claimed.
B) avoided.
C) circumvented.
D) proscribed.

10

For over a century, Arctic explorers have discovered small patches of land, only to find that these "ghost islands" have vanished. The answer to why these islands disappear has _____ scientists until recently. Swiss and Danish surveyors have concluded that these are not actual islands, but recently splintered icebergs that have patches of dirt and rubble left over from landslides.

Which choice completes the text with the most logical and precise word or phrase?

A) frustrated
B) eluded
C) confronted
D) avoided

11

While hiking the mountains of central Switzerland, geologist Heinz Infanger not only discovered a rich vein of rock crystals, but also primitive tools dating back to the Alpine Mesolithic period. Although these tools were certainly used to extract the rock crystal, the application and significance of the rock crystals themselves has been _____ by time.

Which choice completes the text with the most logical and precise word or phrase?

A) verified
B) obscured
C) disengaged
D) devalued

12

The 1960s American folk duo Richard and Mimi Fariña used the mountain dulcimer, a stringed-instrument from Appalacha, in _____ way: typically used for accompaniment, as its frets are set to play a specific scale rather than chromatically, Richard Fariña was adept at using it to play creative lead melodies, which are featured on the duo's many instrumental songs.

Which choice completes the text with the most logical and precise word or phrase?

A) an unknowable
B) a disruptive
C) an innovative
D) an orthodox

13

In New York, every street tells its own part of the city's rich history. Take for example Great Jones Street, built in 1789. This nearly 225-year-old street is named after a lawyer named Samuel Jones. Unperturbed by the fact that the city already had a Jones Street (named for his brother-in-law), Mr. Jones simply _____ the Great – creating his street's memorable name. In 1973, American author Don DeLillo chose this spot as the setting for his acclaimed novel, *Great Jones Street*.

Which choice completes the text with the most logical and precise word or phrase?

A) appended
B) tallied
C) reinstated
D) argued

14

Against the backdrop of abject poverty and worker exploitation in the newly industrialized America, Emma Goldman emerged as the voice of the disenfranchised lower classes, speaking and writing against the status quo. An immigrant herself, having fled from ethnic and political violence in Russia, she led strikes and political rallies in her fight for economic and political freedom at home and abroad. In time, she became a symbol of social and political activism. Her ideology is immortalized by the _____ words of her epitaph: "Liberty will not descend to a people; a people must raise themselves to Liberty."

Which choice completes the text with the most logical and precise word or phrase?

A) enduring
B) vibrant
C) uncertain
D) turbulent

15

Bronze has traditionally been the medium for grandiose sculpture documenting history's greatest figures. However, contemporary artist Simone Leigh and her sculpture *Last Garment* uses bronze to capture a simple, everyday moment. The sculpture represents a woman in a simple dress bending over a pile of laundry. The statue sits inside a reflecting pond, allowing the shine of the still water to reflect upon the bronze. The result _____ the polish of the brass, makes the form-clinging dress appear soaked, and gives life to a statue designed to give dignity to the most back-breaking of work.

Which choice completes the text with the most logical and precise word or phrase?

A) accentuates
B) obscures
C) distracts from
D) engenders

16

PFAS (per- and poly-fluoroalkyl substances) are found in many products including non-stick cookware. Dr. Sung Kyun Park is concerned about PFAS pollution because the bonds between fluorine and carbon within them create what are considered "forever chemicals" and do not _____ naturally over time.

Which choice completes the text with the most logical and precise word or phrase?

A) maintain
B) decompose
C) persist
D) expand

17

Award winning author Rebecca Roanhorse writes speculative fiction that centers around indigenous histories, mythologies, and experiences, but she says that this theme is _____ to her main goal of telling stories about interesting characters and their relationships with each other and the world they inhabit.

Which choice completes the text with the most logical and precise word or phrase?

A) secondary
B) crucial
C) involuntary
D) superfluous

Biologist Li-Li Li conducted a study with Asian elephants from the Myaing Hay Wun Elephant Camp in Yaikkyi, Myanmar, in order to better understand how elephants balance competition and cooperation when attempting to access food. While elephant societies tend to be hierarchical and competitive, Li's research discovered that elephants are also likely to engage in cooperative behaviors that _____ selfish impulses.

Which choice completes the text with the most logical and precise word or phrase?

A) reinforce
B) mitigate
C) exacerbate
D) exhibit

The following text is from Henry David Thoreau's 1851 speech that was later titled "Walking."

Nowadays almost all man's improvements, so called, as the building of houses, and the cutting down of the forest and of all large trees, simply deform the landscape, and make it more and more tame and cheap. A people who would begin by burning the fences and let the forest stand!

As used in the text, what does the word "cheap" most nearly mean?

A) Frugal
B) Penniless
C) Ruined
D) Paltry

The following passage is adapted from Charles W. Chesnutt's 1899 book *The Conjure Woman*.

One day my wife requested me to build her a new kitchen. The house erected by us, when we first came to live upon the vineyard, contained a very conveniently arranged kitchen; but for some peculiar reason my wife wanted a kitchen in the backyard, apart from the dwelling-house, after the usual Southern fashion. Of course I had to build it.

As used in the text, what does the word "arranged" most nearly mean?

A) Controlled
B) Designed
C) Predetermined
D) Restrained

Text Structure and Purpose

Tags: Craft and Structure • Structure • Purpose

Everything in a text serves a purpose

Each Reading & Writing module will have between 0 and 4 Text Structure and Purpose (TSP) questions. The content of TSP texts can be either a **historical work of literature** or a **contemporary academic passage**. The question will ask about the job or function that a part of the text (word, phrase, or sentence) is doing. Generally, you'll be asking:

> *Why did the author include this part of the text?*

We want to **shift our mindset** to imagine being the author of the text, purposefully choosing our words in order to communicate something.

TIP

TSP questions can be tricky because they are about the form and rhetoric of the texts. As with many of the other reading question types, we need to focus on the claim of the text.

Main Strategy

We want to think practically about the structure or purpose of the text, not get wrapped up in distracting details. So we'll follow a 3-step strategy:

1. *Focus on the question as you read the text*
2. *Answer in your own words*
3. *Eliminate wrong answers and pick the best fit*

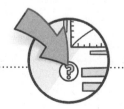

Focus on the question as you read the text.

Answer in your own words

Eliminate wrong answers and pick the best fit

Part of a Test

Some TSP questions will ask you to explain the purpose of a single phrase or sentence in the context of the text as a whole. We want to focus on what specifically those words **add** to the text as a whole.

EXAMPLE 1

The following text is from Mark Twain's 1902 short story "The Californian's Tale."

> Thirty-five years ago I was out prospecting on the Stanislaus, tramping all day long with pick and pan and horn, and washing a hatful of dirt here and there, always expecting to make a rich strike, and never doing it. It was a lovely region, woodsy, balmy, delicious, and had once been populous, long years before, but now the people had vanished and <u>the charming paradise was a solitude.</u> They went away when the surface diggings gave out. In one place, where a busy little city with banks and newspapers and fire companies and a mayor and aldermen had been, was nothing but a wide expanse of emerald turf, with not even the faintest sign that human life had ever been present there.

1. Which choice best describes the function of the underlined phrase in the text as a whole?

    A) It establishes the location has changed very little in the thirty-five years that have passed.
    B) It indicates that the speaker may prefer the area's lack of people.
    C) It reinforces the damage people had done to once pristine wilderness.
    D) It establishes the speaker's preference to avoid contact with other people.

Step one: Read the text and pay attention to focus of the question

Thirty-five years ago I was out prospecting on the <u>Stanislaus</u>, tramping all day long with pick and pan and horn, and washing a hatful of dirt here and there, always expecting to make a rich strike, and never doing it. It was a <u>lovely region</u>, woodsy, balmy, delicious, and <u>had once been populous</u>, long years before, <u>but</u> now the people had vanished and <u>the charming paradise was a solitude</u>. They went away when the surface diggings gave out. In one place, where a busy little city with banks and newspapers and fire companies and a mayor and aldermen had been, was nothing but a wide <u>expanse of emerald turf</u>, with not even the faintest sign that human life had ever been present there.

The text describes a place that was once populated but now is empty. The speaker describes this as not necessarily a bad thing, as he appreciates being alone.

Step two: Answer in your own words

"Charming paradise" is pretty positive and "solitude" is neutral, so we can assume that he feels pretty ok about being there alone.

Step three: Eliminate wrong answers and pick the best fit

A) It establishes the location has changed very little in the thirty-five years that have passed.

It sounds like it has changed quite a bit.

(B) It indicates that the speaker may prefer the area's lack of people.

This seems to match the positive description of the place

C) It reinforces the damage people had done to once pristine wilderness.

There is no damage, as the last sentence says that there is no evidence of humans ever being there.

D) It establishes the speaker's preference to avoid contact with other people.

Just because the speaker appreciates an empty place does not mean he avoids contact with people.!

B

Whole Text

Other TSP questions will ask you analyze the overall structure of the text. To ace these questions, you wanto have a strong understanding of the main idea and supporting details in the text. To do that, focus on **claims** and **logic words**.

EXAMPLE 2

Although she was widely recognized as artist Pablo Picasso's muse, as she would often model for the famous Spanish modern artist, Dora Maar was an accomplished artist in her own right. Maar excelled at Surrealist photography, where real-world things are transformed into something ethereal and unknown. Maar's most famous photograph, 1936's *Père Ubu*, exemplifies this approach: a close-up of a baby armadillo becomes nearly unrecognizable due to the image's high contrast lighting and upright angle.

2. Which choice best describes the overall structure of the text?

   A) It discusses Pablo Picasso's influence over Dora Maar and then provides an example of her work.
   B) It argues that the photographs of Dora Maar should be seen as an influence on the paintings of Pablo Picasso.
   C) It uses an example of Dora Maar's photography to diminish the importance of Pablo Picasso on her work.
   D) It introduces a lesser known aspect of Dora Maar's output and provides a noteworthy example of her photography.

Step one: Read the text and pay attention to focus of the question

Although she was widely recognized as artist Pablo Picasso's muse, as she would often model for the famous Spanish modern artist, Dora Maar was an accomplished artist in her own right. Maar excelled at Surrealist photography, where real-world things are transformed into something ethereal and unknown. Maar's most famous photograph, 1936's *Père Ubu*, exemplifies this approach: a close-up of a baby armadillo becomes nearly unrecognizable due to the image's high contrast lighting and upright angle.

Continued on next page →

Step two: Answer in your own words

This passage is about Dora Maar's art and why she's significant.

Step three: Eliminate wrong answers and pick the best fit

A) It discusses Pablo Picasso's influence over Dora Maar and then provides an example of her work.

This is close but the text never describes Picasso's influence over Maar. Did he influence Père Ubu? Maybe, but that's not in the text.

B) It argues that the photographs of Dora Maar should be seen as an influence on the paintings of Pablo Picasso.

Yes, she was a model for Picasso, but that doesn't mean that Maar's photographs influenced his paintings.

C) It uses an example of Dora Maar's photography to diminish the importance of Pablo Picasso on her work.

The text is not against Picasso; it's just focused on Maar.

D) It introduces a lesser known aspect of Dora Maar's output and provides a noteworthy example of her photography.

Perfect! It talks about her and mentions a famous photograph she created.

D

Practice Set

The following text is from W. E. B. Du Bois' 1911 novel *The Quest of the Silver Fleece*.

The boy wearily dropped his heavy bundle and stood still, listening as the voice of crickets split the shadows and made the silence audible. A tear wandered down his brown cheek. They were at supper now, he whispered—the father and old mother, away back yonder beyond the night. They were far away; they would never be as near as once they had been, for he had stepped into the world. And the cat and Old Billy—ah, but the world was a lonely thing, so wide and tall and empty! And so bare, so bitter bare! Somehow he had never dreamed of the world as lonely before; he had fared forth to beckoning hands and luring, and to the eager hum of human voices, as of some great, swelling music.

Which choice best states the function of the underlined phrase in the text as a whole?

A) It foreshadows that the boy will not be successful in his journey.

B) It justifies the boy's negative feelings expressed later in the text.

C) It establishes context for why the boy feels as he does at that moment.

D) It implies that the boy's actions were not of his own choosing.

The following text is from Sir Rabindranth Tagore's 1895 memoir *Glimpses of Bengal*. In the text, the word *beel* refers to a lake-like wetland.

Where the waters cover cultivated tracts the rice grows through, often from considerable depths, giving to the boats sailing over them the curious appearance of gliding over a cornfield, so clear is the water. The water loses its beauty when it ceases to be defined by banks and spreads out into a monotonous vagueness. In the case of language, meter serves for banks and gives form and beauty and character. Just as the banks give each river a distinct personality, so does rhythm make each poem an individual creation; prose is like the featureless, impersonal beel. Again, the waters of the river have movement and progress; those of the beel engulf the country by expanse alone. So, in order to give language power, the narrow bondage of meter becomes necessary; otherwise it spreads and spreads, but cannot advance.

Which choice best states the main purpose of the text?

A) It provides farming advice by relating water management to choices made in literature.

B) It criticizes regional environmental practices and suggests officials use a holistic approach.

C) It uses a description of a location as a metaphor to explain the author's preferences in writing.

D) It discusses the beauty found in the environment before revealing that this beauty comes at a cost.

3

The field of organic electronics has benefited from the discovery of new semiconducting polymers with molecular backbones that are resilient to twists and bends, meaning they can transport charge even if they are flexed into different shapes. It had been assumed that these materials resemble a plate of spaghetti at the molecular scale, without any long-range order. However, an international team of researchers found that for at least one such material, there are tiny pockets of order within. These ordered pockets, just a few ten-billionths of a meter across, are stiffer than the rest of the material, giving it a 'fruitcake' structure with harder and softer regions.

Which choice best states the main purpose of the text?

A) It presents a commonly understood theory and then offers a potential contradiction.

B) It explains the necessity of using organic electronics by analyzing differences in their molecular structures.

C) It argues for greater research into a subject by presenting a recent discovery that needs to be addressed.

D) It uses an analogy involving common items to explain a discovery that otherwise may be difficult to comprehend.

4

The following text is from Walt Whitman's ca. 1817 poem "A Noiseless Patient Spider."

A noiseless patient spider,
I mark'd where on a little promontory it stood isolated,
Mark'd how to explore the vacant vast surrounding,
It launch'd forth filament, filament,
        filament, out of itself,
Ever unreeling them, ever tirelessly speeding them.

And you O my soul where you stand,
Surrounded, detached, in measureless oceans of space,
Ceaselessly musing, venturing, throwing,
        seeking the spheres to connect them,
Till the bridge you will need be form'd,
        till the ductile anchor hold,
Till the gossamer thread you fling
        catch somewhere, O my soul.

Which choice best describes the function of the underlined portion in the text as a whole?

A) It contrasts the behavior of the spider with the intentions of the speaker.

B) It criticizes what the spider can accomplish due to its small size.

C) It contextualizes the scale of the space in which the spider casts its webs.

D) It justifies why the spider is perceived as being noiseless.

5

One of the most fascinating natural phenomena is the schooling of fish. Each one moves independently, yet the configuration of the whole persists. How do they manage to move in perfect concert with each other, maintaining formation while moving forward? For mackerel, the answer may lie in the prominent vertical stripes on their back. Fish are particularly aware of moving stripes – <u>the same way humans are alert to blinking lights.</u> The light bouncing off a mackerel's stripe could signal changes in position to other fish, helping them rapidly adjust their position and speed.

Which choice best describes the function of the underlined phrase in the text as a whole?

A) It provides evidence for the theory stated in the text.

B) It emphasizes a key difference between human traffic and mackerel schools.

C) It offers an analogy to better understand how the vertical stripes function.

D) It foregrounds the structural similarities between humans and mackerel.

6

The following text is from Louisa May Alcott's 1873 novel *Work: A Story of Experience.*

Christie was one of that large class of women who, moderately endowed with talents, earnest and true-hearted, are driven by necessity, temperament, or principle out into the world to find support, happiness, and homes for themselves. Many turn back discouraged; <u>more accept shadow for substance</u>, and discover their mistake too late; the weakest lose their purpose and themselves; but the strongest struggle on, and, after danger and defeat, earn at last the best success this world can give us, the possession of a brave and cheerful spirit, rich in self-knowledge, self-control, self-help.

Which choice best states the function of the underlined phrase in the text as a whole?

A) It sets up that Christie will have a difficult journey.

B) It acknowledges a hurdle that Christie should avoid.

C) It elaborates on the desire expressed in the previous sentence.

D) It introduces a conflict that arises later in the text.

7

It might seem counterintuitive to learn that the Sun is surrounded by an atmosphere. The heliosphere surrounds the entire solar system with a "bubble" of hot plasma radiating outward from the sun. Although solar plasma is not very similar to the composition of the Earth's atmosphere, astrophysicists borrow terms commonly used by terrestrial meteorologists—including wind, weather, and climate—to describe what happens in the heliosphere. On the other hand, the Sun's atmosphere is similar to the Earth's in that it impedes high-energy radiation.

Which choice best describes the overall structure of the text?

A) It presents a controversial theory, then explains the origins of that theory.

B) It discusses similarities between the Sun and Earth, then considers how other objects in space might also be similar.

C) It describes an environment, then further explains that environment by making a comparison.

D) It describes a situation, then explains various reasons why this situation may pose a threat.

8

In 1859, naturalist Alfred Russel Wallace, while exploring the wildlife on the Malay Archipelago, noticed a difference between the types of animals living on the island of Bali and the island of Lombok, despite only 35 kilometers of water separating them. He used this observation to draw what is now known as the Wallace line, which separates Southeast Asian fauna from its Australian counterpart. Wallace struggled to explain why the line exists and assumed sea level changes may have separated the two regions. A better justification for the Wallace line emerged from the theory of plate tectonics: the Australian plate, which contains islands now part of the eastern half of the Malay Archipelago, had spent eons isolated from Asia and therefore nurtured its own unique fauna.

Which choice best states the main purpose of the text?

A) To present a scientific observation that was later determined to be false

B) To criticize a theory that oversimplifies a complex relationship

C) To chronicle a discovery and its eventual explanation

D) To contrast two opposing theories regarding the distribution of fauna

9

The following text is from William Shakespeare's 1609 poem "Sonnet 8."

Music to hear, why hear'st thou music sadly?
Sweets with sweets war not, joy delights in joy:
Why lov'st thou that which thou receiv'st not gladly,
Or else receiv'st with pleasure thine annoy?
If the true concord of well-tuned sounds,
By unions married, do offend thine ear,
They do but sweetly chide thee, who confounds
In singleness the parts that thou shouldst bear.
Mark how one string, sweet husband to another,
Strikes each in each by mutual ordering;
Resembling sire and child and happy mother,
Who, all in one, one pleasing note do sing:
Whose speechless song being many, seeming one,
Sings this to thee: 'Thou single wilt prove none.'

Which choice best describes the overall structure of the text?

A) The speaker questions a preference, then accepts its validity.

B) The speaker analyzes the effect of music, then uses it to create a comparison.

C) The speaker criticizes a person, then directs that critique to a family.

D) The speaker condemns an harmonic theory, then offers an alternative.

The following text is adapted from August Strindberg's 1871 play "The Outlaws."

> VALGERD. Close the window.
> [Gunlöd is silent.]
> VALGERD. Gunlöd!
> GUNLÖD. Did you speak, mother?
> VALGERD. What are you doing?
> GUNLÖD. I am watching the sea.
> VALGERD. When will you learn to forget?
> GUNLÖD. Take everything away
> from me but memories!
> VALGERD. Look forward—not back. You have
> had three winters to make your farewell.
> GUNLÖD. You speak truly—three winters!
> For here never came a summer!
> VALGERD. When the floating ice
> melts, then shall spring be here.
> GUNLÖD. The Northern Lights melt no ice.
> VALGERD. Nor your tears.

Which choice best describes the function of the underlined sentence to the overall structure of the text?

A) It presents an optimistic view in contrast to Gunlöd's mood.

B) It reveals that Valgerd has been trying to dismiss Gunlöd's feelings.

C) It causes a reversal of how Valgerd and Gunlöd see each other.

D) It concedes that a change in season with not affect Gunlöd's personality.

Cross-Text Connections

Tags: Craft and Structure • Cross-Text Connections

Comparing and contrasting two authors' claims

Every SAT Reading & Writing section will have one Cross-Text Connection question, which could appear in either module. It's one of the easiest question types to spot, as it has two paragraphs labeled **Text 1** and **Text 2**. Furthermore, the question almost always looks like this:

> Based on the texts, what would the author of Text 2 most likely say about *thing/idea/claim* from Text 1?

Main Strategy

Your job is to understand **two claims** and how they compare and contrast. To do that, we'll follow a familiar three-step strategy:

(1) *Read the question to see what's being compared between the two texts.*

(2) *Read Text 1 and 2 with the comparison in mind.*

(3) *Use throwaways to eliminate wrong answers.*

Determine what you'll be comparing between the two texts   *Read Text 1 and 2 with the comparison in mind*   *Use throwaways to eliminate wrong answers*

TIP

The Cross-Text Connections question always marks the end of the Craft and Structure questions.

TIP

By now you can see how important a skill it is to understand the main claims made in a passage! This one has TWO claims! Crazy!

EXAMPLE 1

Text 1

American folk rock band The Byrds had established an iconic sound of rich vocal harmonies and electric 12-string guitar hooks, but in 1968 the band's sixth album represented a departure. The band was in flux, having lost several original members, and the remaining members decided to record an album of country music called *Sweetheart of the Rodeo.* This choice was not successful, as it was not well received by fans of either traditional country or rock music, and sold fewer copies than any of their previous albums.

Text 2

Sweetheart of the Rodeo was not well received by most, but ended up becoming a pivotal album for the beginning of alternative country music. By including guitarist Gram Parsons on the album, The Byrds would launch the career of one of the most influential musicians in 1970s roots music. The album's mixing of traditional country music with counterculture sensibilities would become a template for many subsequent bands.

1. Based on the texts, how would the author of Text 2 most likely respond to the description of *Sweetheart of the Rodeo* in Text 1?

   A) As definitive, because it offers ample background information that led to the creation of the album.
   B) As incomplete, because it does not mention who left The Byrds and who replaced them.
   C) As shortsighted, because it focuses on the initial reception of the album and leaves out its later significance.
   D) As untruthful, because it states the album did not sell well, when in fact it has become a classic.

Step one: Read the question to determine what you'll be comparing between the two texts.

> Based on the texts, how would the author of Text 2 most likely respond to the description of *Sweetheart of the Rodeo* in Text 1?

We need to focus on how Text 1 describes the album, and then how Text 2 would respond.

Step two: Read text 1 and 2 with the comparison in mind.

Text 1

American folk rock band The Byrds had established an iconic sound of rich vocal harmonies and electric 12-string guitar hooks, but in 1968 the band's <u>sixth album</u> represented a <u>departure</u>. The band was in <u>flux</u>, having lost several original members, and the remaining members decided to record an album of country music called *Sweetheart of the Rodeo*. This choice was <u>not successful</u>, as it was <u>not well received</u> by fans of either traditional country or rock music, and <u>sold fewer copies</u> than any of their previous albums.

Text 1 focuses on how the album was not successful.

Text 2

Sweetheart of the Rodeo was not well received by most, but ended up becoming a <u>pivotal album</u> for the beginning of alternative country music. By including guitarist Gram Parsons on the album, The Byrds would <u>launch the career</u> of one of the most <u>influential musicians</u> in 1970s roots music. The album's mixing of traditional country music with counterculture sensibilities would become a <u>template for many subsequent bands</u>.

Text 2 focuses on how the album ended up being influential later on.

Continued on next page →

Step three: Use throwaways to eliminate wrong answers.

A) As definitive, because it offers ample background information that led to the creation of the album.

Definitive would include all information and Text 2 adds a lot of details missing from Text 1.

B) As incomplete, because it does not mention who left The Byrds and who replaced them.

Text 2 is interested in Gram Parsons, a new member, and how the album influenced other musicians. There is no suggestion that the author of Text 2 wants more details about The Byrds before recording the album.

C) As shortsighted, because it focuses on the initial reception of the album and leaves out its later significance.

Shortsighted means to not see the bigger picture. This works well here because Text 2 talks about the greater impact of the album, while Text 1 focuses only on the initial reception.

D) As untruthful, because it states the album did not sell well, when in fact it has become a classic.

Nothing in Text 1 is not true. The issue is that Text 1 only focuses on what happened right after the album was released.

C

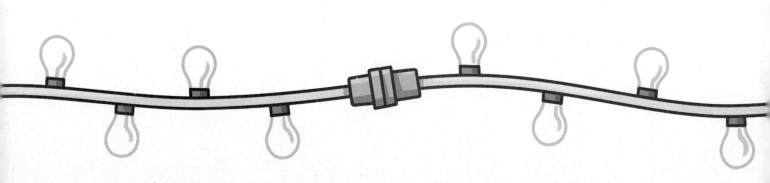

Practice Set

1

Text 1

High-occupancy vehicle lanes, better known as HOV lanes, are a common feature in many urban area freeways. These lanes restrict access to only vehicles containing at least two, and in some cases three, people and promise a faster commute. Communities install these lanes to reduce congestion and decrease air-pollution by affecting commuters' behavior and rewarding carpooling.

Text 2

HOV lanes are a byproduct of a time when urban planners saw traffic as a negative result of the need to commute. The rationale is that HOV lanes reward commuters for making better choices, but never address why they needed to commute by car in the first place. Rather than devote more resources to enable commuters, a healthier urban plan would focus on building public transportation options and encourage neighborhood planning where residents can work, shop, and live without resorting to becoming a commuters.

Based on the texts, how would the author of Text 2 most likely respond to the commuters referenced in Text 1?

A) By suggesting that city planning focus on the needs of residents rather than the needs of commuters.
B) By acknowledging that HOV lanes do relieve compliant commuters of long travel times.
C) By lamenting that commute length continues to increase despite the implementation of HOV lanes.
D) By criticizing the use of HOV lanes because too few commuters are able to use them.

Text 1

"Blitzscaling" has become a popular term in business circles thanks to the book written by Reid Hoffman and Chris Yeh. In *Blitzscaling*, Hoffman and Yeh advocate that start-up companies should try to grow their market share as quickly as possible in order to increase their value to investors. This philosophy "prioritizes speed over efficiency in an environment of uncertainty," and promises early investors sizable returns.

Text 2

While the initial appeal of "blitzscaling" has investors excited to get in before the company gets too big, there still are lots of questions about the long term viability of this strategy. Many advocates equate growth in users or subscribers or clients as profit, but having a large user base does not mean robust, sustained profits. Some early adopters of "blitzscaling" practices are now struggling to find new customers and keep their current customers happy.

Based on the texts, how would the author of Text 2 most likely respond to the quote in Text 1?

A) It shows that by focusing on speed, "blitzscaling" can produce growth in various marketplaces.

B) It does not address how "blitzscaling" works in more certain environments.

C) It focuses on short-term gains which may not lead to long-term success.

D) It does not acknowledge how companies could better balance speed and efficiency.

Text 1

Cattle require vast swaths of land to graze, with each cow utilizing a minimum of 10 acres of pasture. A cow eats an average of 24 pounds of food a day, significantly more than other meat producing animals such as chickens. Whether cattle eat grass in a pasture or grain from a feedbag, many acres are needed to grow their food.

Text 2

The cattle that roam our Western states have been fighting a silent war against desertification, where once thriving grasslands become barren. Cattle are part of the ruminant family of mammals, cloven hoof grazers that travel in large herds across many acres. The grazing itself does the region a surprising amount of good, as cow manure acts as a fertilizer and also helps distribute seeds. Cattle's cloven hooves help to till the grasslands, aerating the soil and allowing for better water retention. Ruminants shepherd the land, ensuring an ample supply of food for the herd.

Based on the texts, how would the author of Text 2 respond to the description of cattle in Text 1?

A) By agreeing that eliminating cattle herds from the Western states would improve environmental conditions

B) By replying that grazing cattle herds can have some positive impact against desertification

C) By arguing that Western states should raise more grazing cattle rather than raising chickens

D) By encouraging cattle ranchers to increase the number of cattle per acre in order to better improve pastures

4

Text 1

The night before Hollywood's shining stars are honored at the Oscars, there is another, less prestigious award show. The Golden Raspberry Awards, first held in 1981, highlights the worst performances of the previous year in film. No one is safe from being nominated for a Razzie, not even entertainment's biggest names. Sylvester Stallone holds the record for most Razzies, and ironically Neil Diamond won the inaugural Worst Actor Razzie the same year he was nominated for a Golden Globe for the same role. The award show encourages the industry's best to own up to their regrettable performances, a humbling lesson that has value for all of us.

Text 2

The 2023 Golden Raspberry nominations sparked controversy with their inclusion of Ryan Kiera Armstrong for Worst Actress for her performance in *Firestarter*. The issue was that Armstrong was only twelve years old at the time. Many other actors took umbrage with nominating a child for a mocking award. The Razzies responded by apologizing, removing Armstrong's nomination, and making a rule stipulating that every nominee must be at least 18 years of age.

Based on the texts, how would the author of Text 2 most likely respond to the characterization of the Golden Raspberry Awards as presented in Text 1?

A) It focuses on the history of the award and does not reference any of its recent successes.

B) It presents a positive representation of an award that has generated controversy with its nominations.

C) It implies that Neil Diamond enjoyed being nominated for both a Razzie and a Golden Globe, when he only won one of them.

D) It states that actors need a humbling lesson, but many nominees continue to have successful careers.

Text 1

By the 1920s, most homes in the United States were connected to electrical power. Though invented decades earlier, electric light bulbs were suddenly demanded by household consumers. The shift to electric lighting strained the supply of electricity. In 1924, the largest light bulb manufacturers responded to the energy crisis. These companies shifted their focus to producing more energy-efficient bulbs, although this effort also had the consequence of creating bulbs with a shorter lifespan.

Text 2

On Christmas Eve in 1924, a group of lightbulb manufacturers met on the shore of Lake Geneva to end their rivalry. At the time, recent innovations allowed lightbulbs to be produced cheaply and to last for over 2,500 hours. This was great for consumers, but it reduced profits for manufacturers. The group, known as the Phoebus Cartel, dedicated their resources toward an advantageous solution: creating lightbulbs that would reliably break before only 1,000 hours of use. Integrity and progress were sacrificed for great profits, but the self-sabotage did have the unintended benefit of creating more energy-efficient bulbs.

Based on the texts, how would the author of Text 2 most likely characterize the conclusion presented in Text 1?

A) As cynical, given how electric lighting has improved in energy efficiency since its invention

B) As optimistic, given that light bulb manufacturers have struggled to remain profitable

C) As questionable, given the increase in energy efficiency was not a direct aim of the lightbulb manufacturers

D) As outdated, given the modern shift toward light-emitting diode (LED) and other highly efficient lighting technologies

6

Text 1

Grown for centuries by farmers in Totontepec, Mexico, a rare, giant species of maize could offer a solution to a global agricultural problem. Mass produced maize typically requires massive amounts of nitrogen fertilizers, a potent polluter, in order to produce profitable yields. In contrast, the giant maize grown in Totontepec is able to self-fertilize thanks to exposed roots that drip a viscous fluid into the ground which provide nitrogen fixation. Its secret is that the mucus hosts a type of bacteria able to convert nitrogen from the atmosphere into a form that the plant can use. Unlocking this symbiotic relationship could be the secret to globally increasing food yields while decreasing the reliance on nitrogen fertilizers.

Text 2

Scientific journalism loves to report on a new discovery–perhaps a medicine or food–found in a remote part of the globe. Oftentimes these breakthroughs were invented, nurtured, and finetuned by that region's indigenous people. Sadly, when mainstream science learns of these advancements, they are quickly gobbled up with little-or-no compensation for their stewards, an insidious practice known as biopiracy. It is important to recognize the value of under-the-radar inventions and ethically compensate those whose traditional practices advance scientific discoveries.

Based on the texts, how would the author of Text 2 respond to the discovery presented in Text 1?

A) With skepticism since maize is already a common global crop
B) With measured optimism as long as it does not result in biopiracy
C) With relief since nitrogen fixation can impact a variety of crop yields
D) With regret as the farmers from Totontepec will not be paid for their innovation

UNIT | Information and Ideas

Chapters

Overview

In this unit, you'll learn strategies for answering reading questions about the main ideas of text and the details that support them. Then you learn how analyze evidence and synthesize it into the text.

Central Ideas & Details

Tags: Information and Ideas • Central Idea • Details

Introduction

A Reading & Writing module will have between 0 and 3 Central Ideas and Details questions. In many ways, these feel like good old-fashioned reading comprehension questions. No advanced analysis of claims or vocabulary to sort out.

Most Central Ideas and Details questions fit into one of three categories: main ideas, specific details, and character studies. The strategies are a bit different for each of these subcategories, but each begins with **reading the question first** to tune our focus when reading the text.

Main Idea Strategy

When you see that the question is asking for the main idea of the text, zoom your focus out to the bigger arguments and points. Don't worry too much about challenging words of phrases, as long as you can determine the central idea or main takeaway of the text.

(1) *Read the question first, then the text with the question in mind.*

(2) *Summarize the* **main idea** *in your own words.*

(3) *Eliminate answers by looking for throwaways.*

Read the question first, then the text with the question in mind | Summarize the main idea in your own words | Eliminate answers by looking for throwaways

TIP

Take a moment after reading to **summarize the main idea in your own words**. This will make sure you are zoomed out to the right level before looking at those distracting answer choices.

EXAMPLE 1

When George Smith discovered and translated *The Epic of Gilgamesh* into English in 1872, the Western world knew little about the ancient civilization of Mesopotamia. Sparked by Smith's translation, interest and funding for Assyriology surged, and Smith would go on to chronicle the history of the ancient Middle Eastern empire for future generations of archaeologists to study. His translation of Gilgamesh also revealed the story of a great flood that paralleled other ancient deluge stories. Seeing these similarities would lay the groundwork for the study of comparative mythology, where scholars attempt to make connections between stories created by cultures otherwise isolated from each other.

1. Which choice best states the main idea of the text?

   A) It justifies Smith's choice to translate *The Epic of Gilgamesh* into English by detailing the translation's success.
   B) It provides historical context to challenge the renewed popularity of *The Epic of Gilgamesh*.
   C) It offers an overview of George Smith's academic career and how he helped to fund the study of the ancient Middle East.
   D) It chronicles the reemergence of *The Epic of Gilgamesh* and how that influenced academic studies.

TIP

Focus on the text as a whole. Incorrect answers often seem correct when you consider only a portion of the text.

The main change we see occur in this paragraph is a "surge" in interest of certain types of stories related to the *Epic of Gilgamesh*.

SOLUTION

(1) *Read the question first, then the text with the question in mind.*

What is the main idea of the text?

When George Smith discovered and translated *The Epic of Gilgamesh* into English in 1872, the Western world knew little about the ancient civilization of Mesopotamia. Sparked by Smith's translation, interest and funding for Assyriology surged, and Smith would go on to chronicle the history of the ancient Middle Eastern empire for future generations of archaeologists to study. His translation of Gilgamesh also revealed the story of a great flood that paralleled other ancient stories of catastrophic deluges. Seeing these similarities would lay the groundwork for the study of comparative mythology, where scholars attempt to make connections between stories created by cultures otherwise isolated from each other.

Continued on next page ➡

② *Summarize the main idea in your own words.*

This passage is about why the translation of The Epic of Gilgamesh is important.

③ *Eliminate answers by looking for throwaways.*

Which choice best states the main idea of the text?

A̶) It justifies Smith's choice to translate The Epic of Gilgamesh into English by detailing the translation's success.

In order to justify, the text would need to provide more evidence for why Smith translated it.

B̶) It provides historical context to challenge the renewed popularity of *The Epic of Gilgamesh*.

Challenge is a clear throwaway in this answer choice.

C̶) It offers an overview of George Smith's academic career and how he helped to fund the study of the ancient Middle East.

The text is not mostly about George's career, and this doesn't reference any info from the last two sentences.

D)) It chronicles the reemergence of *The Epic of Gilgamesh* and how that influenced academic studies.

Nothing looks wrong here.   **D**

TIP

Key Detail Strategy

Key detail questions ask about information that is directly presented in the text. We want to **sharpen our focus** to avoid answer choices that get a detail incorrect or make assumptions beyond what is stated in the text.

① *Read the question first and identify what detail to focus on.*

② *Read the passage with that detail in mind.*

③ *Eliminate answers by looking at throwaways.*

Read the question first and identify the detail   *Read the passage with the detail in mind*   *Eliminate answers by looking for throwaways*

EXAMPLE 2

Since the Renaissance, European painters focused on realism, striving to grasp the subtleties of anatomy, perspective, and light. For hundreds of years, the ability to paint realistically was a key skill. With photography gradually taking over the role of documentarian in the 1860s, painters started working in a more expressive mode. They began to paint in ways that emphasized the brushstrokes and color palette. Progressively, some painters began to include unrealistic color and distortion to create a more expressive interpretation of the subject matter. Eventually a few painters abandoned painting real subjects altogether and invented abstract painting where the brushstrokes no longer represent anything from the real world. This period, roughly from 1860 to 1970, is known as the era of Modern Art and contains some of the most challenging and provocative paintings ever seen.

2. According to the text, how did photography affect the art of painting?

A) It took jobs away from painters because photography was more realistic.
B) It led to painting evolving into a different visual style.
C) It justified the decision of painters to abandon realism.
D) It allowed painters to imagine unrealistic color and distortion.

ART

It's subjective.

SOLUTION

TIP

We find the best information about the detail of how photography affected the art of painting in the third and fourth sentences of the text.

(1) *Read the question first and determine what detail to focus on.*

How did photography affect the art of painting?

(2) *Read the passage with that detail in mind.*

Since the Renaissance, European painters focused on realism, striving to grasp the subtleties of anatomy, perspective, and light. For hundreds of years, the ability to paint realistically was a key skill. <u>With photography gradually taking over the role of documentarian in the 1860s, painters started working in a more expressive mode. They began to paint in ways that emphasized the brushstrokes and color palette.</u> Progressively, some painters began to include unrealistic color and distortion to create a more expressive interpretation of the subject matter. Eventually a few painters abandoned painting real subjects altogether and invented abstract painting where the brushstrokes no longer represent anything from the real world. This period, roughly from 1860 to 1970, is known as the era of Modern Art and contains some of the most challenging and provocative paintings ever seen.

"painters started painting in a more expressive mode"

(3) *Eliminate answers by looking at throwaways.*

How did photography affect the art of painting?

A) It took jobs away from painters because photography was more realistic.

This might be true, but it's not stated in the text.

(B) It led to painting evolving into a different visual style.

This matches "painting in a more expressive mode."

C) It justified the decision of painters to abandon realism.

Justified is very strong language and not a safe inference to make. Also this answer says painters, which implies all painters, rather than some painters.

D) It allowed painters to imagine unrealistic color and distortion.

This could be right if the answer swapped "use" for "imagine," but this won't work as is.

B

Character Study Strategy

Character study questions always come from literature. The text will be a quick description of a character, and then the question will ask you what is **true** about the character according to the text.

(1) *Read the question to determine which character to focus on.*

(2) *Read the passage and focus on **words that describe** the character.*

(3) *Eliminate answers by looking at throwaways.*

Read the question first and identify the character to focus on

Read the passage and focus on words that describe the character

Eliminate answers by looking for throwaways

EXAMPLE 3

The following text is from H. C. McNeile's 1921 short story, "A Question of Personality."

> For years now, personally conducted tours had come round Frenton's factory. Old Frenton was always delighted when his friends asked him if they might take their house-parties round: he regarded it as a compliment to himself. For he had made the works, watched them grow and expand till now they were known throughout the civilized world. They were just part of him, the fruit of his brain—born of labour and hard work and nurtured on the hard-headed business capacity of the rugged old Yorkshireman.

3. According to the text, what is true about Frenton?

   A) Frenton expects his house-party guests to say nice things about his factory.
   B) Frenton takes pride in his business and enjoys showing his works to others.
   C) Frenton did not always make good financial decisions when managing his works.
   D) Frenton worked hard to build his fruit canning business.

SOLUTION

(1) *Read the question to determine which character to focus on.*

According to the text, what is true about Frenton?

(2) *Read the passage and focus on words that describe the character.*

For years now, personally conducted tours had come round Frenton's factory. Old Frenton was always delighted when his friends asked him if they might take their house-parties round: he regarded it as a compliment to himself. For he had made the works, watched them grow and expand till now they were known throughout the civilized world. They were just part of him, the fruit of his brain—born of labour and hard work and nurtured on the hard-headed business capacity of the rugged old Yorkshireman.

Frenton owns a factory and he takes pride in it.

(3) *Eliminate answers by looking at throwaways.*

According to the text, what is true about Frenton?

A) Frenton expects his house-party guests to say nice things about his factory.

There is not a lot of evidence that Frenton expects compliments.

(B) Frenton takes pride in his business and enjoys showing his works to others.

This seems to be supported throughout the text.

C) Frenton did not always make good financial decisions when managing his works.

The passage says that he nurtured his factory, but there is nothing to suggest that did not make good financial decisions.

D) Frenton worked hard to build his fruit canning business.

In the passage, fruit refers to output, not literal fruit. There is no information regarding what kind of factory Frenton owns.

B

Practice Set

1

The following text is from John Muir's 1901 book *Our National Parks*.

The tendency nowadays to wander in wildernesses is delightful to see. Thousands of tired, nerve-shaken, over-civilized people are beginning to find out that going to the mountains is going home; that wildness is a necessity; and that mountain parks and reservations are useful not only as fountains of timber and irrigating rivers, but as fountains of life. Awakening from the stupefying effects of the vice of over-industry and the deadly apathy of luxury, they are trying as best they can to mix and enrich their own little ongoings with those of Nature, and to get rid of rust and disease.

Which choice states the main idea of the text?

A) Until recently, people had preferred to avoid nature rather than use it therapeutically.

B) People are beginning to realize the positive effects of visiting nature.

C) Many people who visit nature are unequipped to endure such an experience.

D) Using nature to harvest resources is a byproduct of an over-civilized life.

2

Plastics are extremely durable synthetic polymers, yet more than 30% are made into disposable items such as packaging, which are typically discarded within a year of manufacture. The associated throw-away culture has led to an escalating plastic waste management problem, and widespread accumulation of plastic debris in the natural environment. Debris is now present on shorelines and at the sea surface from pole to pole. It has major environmental impacts and is recognized as one of the key challenges of our century.

According to the text, what is true about plastic debris?

A) It has become a problem primarily around the polar regions.

B) It has become a global pollution problem thanks to disposable items.

C) It accounts for 30% of all debris found in natural environments.

D) It is a common ingredient in single-use synthetic polymers.

3

Many world religions use choral singing or group chanting to enhance group togetherness. Colleges commonly have "fight songs" sung at sporting events, and many fraternal organizations have songs known only to their members that are used in the initiation process. Summer camps and scouting organizations use sing-a-longs to help nurture a sense of community. Even the workplace has a long history of group singing, from the sea shanties on sailing ships to the field hollers of agricultural workers.

Which choice best states the main idea of the text?

A) Singing can be found in a variety of international music types.

B) College fight songs are structurally similar to sea shanties.

C) Initiation processes can often include learning secret songs.

D) Singing has often been used to create social bonding.

Being invisible to the naked eye, microbes managed to escape scientific scrutiny until the mid-17th century, when Dutch scientist Antonie van Leeuwenhoek invented the microscope. These cryptic organisms continued to thwart scientists' efforts to probe, describe, and classify them until about 40 years ago, owing largely to similar body structures that are hard to visually differentiate and obscure body functions that make them notoriously difficult to grow in a lab.

Which choice states the main idea of the text?

A) Scientific understanding of microbial life was a slow progression.

B) Microbes continue to be misunderstood by today's scientists.

C) Antonie van Leeuwenhoek was the first scientist to grow microbes in a laboratory.

D) Confirmation of microbial life occurred relatively recently.

When it comes to four-legged animals such as cats, horses and deer, or even humans, the concept of a gait is familiar, but what about unicellular green algae with multiple limb-like flagella? Long before there were fish swimming in the oceans, tiny microorganisms were using long slender appendages called cilia and flagella to navigate their watery habitats. Now, new research reveals that species of single-celled algae coordinate their flagella to achieve a remarkable diversity of swimming gaits. The latest discovery, published in the journal *Proceedings of the National Academy of Sciences*, shows that despite their simplicity, microalgae can coordinate their flagella into leaping, trotting or galloping gaits just as well.

Which choice best states the main idea of the text?

A) Movement among four-legged animals is different from movement among organisms with flagella.

B) Gaits similar to those found in larger animals have been observed in microorganisms.

C) Scientists have recently discovered that microalgae are capable of movement.

D) Research into microalgae has only recently begun.

A recent example of nanotech innovation is graphene: a material made from a single layer of carbon atoms assembled hexagonally. At one atom wide, it's so thin it's essentially two-dimensional. Graphene is flexible, transparent, and light, but thanks to the unbreakable bonds between carbon atoms, it's also very strong—207 times stronger than steel. A "magic" material like this can revolutionize technological devices from cellphones to solar cells. And it's already under development in next-generation water filtration systems, which will turn salty ocean water into potable fresh water, or remove toxins to make contaminated water safe to drink.

According to the text, what is true about graphene?

A) It is the first manmade material created that is only one atom thick.

B) It derives its strength from carbon atom bonds.

C) It uses carbon to filter salt from seawater.

D) It will replace steel in a variety of applications.

7

One of only two venomous lizards found in North America, the Gila monster (*Heloderma suspectum*) may have an ominous name, but it's rarely a threat to people. In fact, Gila monster venom contains a hormone called extendin-4, which is similar to a human hormone, glucagon-like peptide-1 analog (GLP1), found in the human digestive tract. GLP-1 assists in the production of insulin to combat peaks in a human's blood sugar level. Extendin-4 has shown to work better than GLP-1, as its effects last longer. Scientists have been able to recreate extendin-4, calling the synthetic hormone "exenatide."

Which choice best states the main idea of the text?

A) It introduces an unique reptile to an audience unfamiliar with venomous lizards.

B) It presents a scientific discovery from an unexpected source.

C) It details how scientists are able to recreate exenatide.

D) It advocates for the conservation of Gila monsters and their habitat.

8

The following text is from Getrude Atherton's 1896 short story *The Striding Place*.

Weigall, continental and detached, tired early of grouse shooting. To stand propped against a sod fence while his host's workmen routed up the birds with long poles and drove them towards the waiting guns, made him feel himself a parody on the ancestors who had roamed the moors and forests of this West Riding of Yorkshire in hot pursuit of game worth the killing. But when in England in August he always accepted whatever proffered for the season, and invited his host to shoot pheasants on his estates in the South. The amusements of life, he argued, should be accepted with the same philosophy as its ills.

According to the text, what is true about Weigall?

A) Weigall prefers to visit England in August, but otherwise spends his time on the European mainland.

B) Weigall accepts that grouse hunting is an ironic charade compared to his ancestors' hunting practices.

C) Weigall is not physically capable of hunting grouse by himself and needs his servants' assistance.

D) Weigall has become too tolerant of less than satisfactory experiences.

Twenty-three years ago, a man musing about work while driving down a California highway revolutionized molecular biology when he envisioned a technique to make large numbers of copies of a piece of DNA rapidly and accurately. Known as the polymerase chain reaction, or PCR, Kary Mullis' technique involves separating the double strands of a DNA fragment into single-strand templates by heating it, attaching primers that initiate the copying process, using DNA polymerase to make a copy of each strand from free nucleotides floating around in the reaction mixture, detaching the primers, then repeating the cycle using the new and old strands as templates. Since its discovery in 1983, PCR has made possible a number of procedures we now take for granted, such as DNA fingerprinting of crime scenes, paternity testing, and DNA-based diagnosis of hereditary and infectious diseases.

Which choice best states the main idea of the text?

A) Ideas can appear in the strangest of places.
B) DNA technology has been stable for over twenty years.
C) Mullis' innovation has multiple applications.
D) PCR usage is widespread and underappreciated.

The following text is adapted from Edith Wharton's 1912 novel *The Reef*.

"Unexpected obstacle. Please don't come till thirtieth. Anna." All the way from Charing Cross to Dover the train had hammered the words of the telegram into George Darrow's ears, ringing every change of irony on its commonplace syllables: rattling them out like a discharge of musketry, letting them, one by one, drip slowly and coldly into his brain, or shaking, tossing, transposing them like the dice in some game of the gods of malice; and now, as he emerged from his compartment at the pier, and stood facing the wind-swept platform and the angry sea beyond, they leapt out at him as if from the crest of the waves, stung and blinded him with a fresh fury of derision.

According to the text, what is true about George Darrow?

A) He is very upset that he needs to visit Anna.
B) He is bothered by the tone of the telegram he received from Anna.
C) He gets nervous and annoyed on train rides.
D) He remained calm until arriving at the sea.

Command of Evidence

Tags: Information and Ideas • Command of Evidence

True statements are supported by evidence

Command of Evidence questions ask you to understand a logical connection between an argument, claim, or statement and a supporting piece of evidence. There are two ways the test goes about doing this:

- **Textual** questions, which ask you to consider how some new information strengthens or weakens a claim from the text.

- **Quantitative** questions, where you need to combine information from the text and a table or graph to support or finish a statement.

Main Strategy

The strategy for both types of Command of Evidence questions is the same. As usual, we will **read the question first** to help us focus on what we need to answer the question.

1 *Read the question to determine the goal*

2 *Read the text to find the author's claim*

3 *Pick the answer that provides the best supporting evidence or conclusion*

Read the question to determine the goal

Read the text to find the author's claim

Pick the answer with supporting evidence or conclusion

Textual Command of Evidence Questions

Textual evidence questions come in two general flavors. The most common of the two involves selecting an answer that contains a **quote** from a piece of literature that supports the claim made in the text.

EXAMPLE 1

In the introduction to their 1881 book *The History of Women's Suffrage Vol 1*, authors Elizabeth Cady Stanton, Susan B. Anthony, and Matilda Joslyn Gage argue that women's status as a second class citizen arose from a time when violence justified political power.

1. Which quote from the text best illustrates this claim?

   A) "The prolonged slavery of woman is the darkest page in human history."

   B) "A survey of the condition of women through those barbarous periods, when physical force governed the world, when the motto, "might makes right," was the law, enables one to account for the origin of woman's subjection to man."

   C) "The slavish instinct of an oppressed class has led her to toil patiently through the ages."

   D) "Woman's steady march onward, and her growing desire for a broader outlook, prove that she has not reached her normal condition."

TIP

In order to evaluate how the evidence relates to the text, you will first have to determine the **main point or argument** of the text.

SOLUTION

(1) *Read the question to determine the goal*

Which quote from the text best illustrates this <u>claim</u>?

(2) *Read the text to find the author's claim*

In the introduction to their 1881 book, *The History of Women's Suffrage Vol 1*, authors Elizabeth Cady Stanton, Susan B. Anthony, and Matilda Joslyn Gage argue that <u>women's status as a second class citizen arose from a time</u> when <u>violence justified</u> political power

We need to find an answer that focuses on an earlier time and on a link between physical violence and political power.

(3) *Pick the answer that provides the best supporting evidence*

A) "The prolonged slavery of woman is the darkest page in human history."

   This is an opinion about that time, but not the justification for it.

B) "A survey of the condition of women through those barbarous periods, when physical force governed the world, when the motto, 'might makes right,' was the law, enables one to account for the origin of woman's subjection to man."

   Yes, this discusses a point in history when being physically stronger meant a lot.

C) "The slavish instinct of an oppressed class has led her to toil patiently through the ages."

   This choice explains why women accepted their position, but doesn't say why that position occurred in first place.

D) "Woman's steady march onward, and her growing desire for a broader outlook, prove that she has not reached her normal condition."

   This choice is more about now than the origins of women's oppression.

B

Complete the sentence with supporting evidence

The second type of textual command of evidence questions asks you to pick a choice that provides the best **evidence to support the claim** in the text. The difference is that these are not necessarily quotes from pre-existing sources.

EXAMPLE 2

Ada King, Countess of Lovelace, is well celebrated for her mathematical innovations and is widely considered a trailblazer in computer science. As the daughter of Lord Byron, she had access to the best education available in the 19th century, which allowed her to grow her passion for math and programming. History professor Corinna Schlombs has noticed that King's other interests, specifically embroidery, also had a strong influence on the programming language she created: _____

2. Which finding, if true, would most directly support Corrina Schlombs' claim?

   A) during her education, she learned French and Italian, as was common for English aristocrats at the time.

   B) she borrowed the loop notation used in embroidery to create notation shortcuts for her work with the Analytical Engine.

   C) she programmed how to calculate Bernoulli numbers, which are important to number theory.

   D) her interests extended beyond math, as she also conducted biological experiments to better understand the mechanics of bird wings.

SOLUTION

(1) *Read the question to determine the goal*

Which finding, if true, would most directly support Corrina Schlombs' claim?

(2) *Read the text to find the author's claim*

Ada King, Countess of Lovelace, is well celebrated for her mathematical innovations and is widely considered a trailblazer in computer science. As the daughter of Lord Byron, she had access to the best education available in the 19th century, which allowed her to grow her passion for math and programming. History professor Corinna Schlombs has noticed that King's other interests, specifically embroidery, also had a strong influence on the programing language she created: _____

Schlombs specifically mentions embroidery, so we should look for answers that mention it.

(3) *Pick the answer that provides the best conclusion*

A) during her education, she learned French and Italian, as was common for English aristocrats at the time.

This isn't what Schlombs is discussing.

B) she borrowed the loop notation used in embroidery to create notation shortcuts for her work with the Analytical Engine.

This choice mentions embroidery and how it influenced her math work.

C) she programmed how to calculate Bernoulli numbers, which are important to number theory.

Schlombs makes no mention of Bernoulli numbers, only embroidery.

D) her interests extended beyond math, as she also conducted biological experiments to better understand the mechanics of bird wings.

Neat, but no relationship to embroidery.

B

Undermine a claim with new information

Occasionally you'll see a textual evidence question that flips the script. Here, you need to be the skeptic and try to **disprove the claim** in the passage. When you see words like *discredit*, *undermine*, or *oppose*, then you've found one of these questions. The strategy will still work, but now you must understand the claim in order to vanquish it.

EXAMPLE 3

Originally discovered in 1897 in southern Russia, ancient gold and silver tubes, approximately three feet long and only an inch in diameter, have puzzled archaeologists. The tubes date back to 3,500 BCE and were found in a burial mound. Although archaeologists initially thought that the tube were meant for architectural support, Viktor Trifonov offered the hypothesis that they are the earliest known drinking straws, used to help filter a drink made from barley.

3. Which finding, if true, would most directly undermine Trifonov's hypothesis?

A) Similarly sized metal tubes are found in locations outside of southern Russia.

B) Viewing the tubes under a microscope reveals barley starch granules attached along the inside walls.

C) Analysis of the tubes suggests that the core was originally filled with wood that had rotted away.

D) Other objects found at the burial mound include ceramic cups, weapons, and jewelry.

SOLUTION

(1) *Read the question to determine the goal*

Which finding, if true, would most <u>directly undermine Trifonov's hypothesis</u>?

*We first need to **find** Trifonov's hypothesis so that we can then disprove it.*

(2) *Read the passage to find the author's claim*

Originally discovered in 1897 in southern Russia, gold and silver tubes, approximately three feet long and only an inch in diameter, have puzzled archaeologists. The tubes date back to 3,500 BCE and were found in a burial mound. Initially thought to be used as architectural support, <u>Viktor Trifonov</u> offered the <u>hypothesis</u> that they are the <u>earliest known drinking straws</u>, used to help <u>filter</u> a drink made from <u>barley</u>.

So Trifonov thinks the tubes were drinking straws, so we should pick a choice that shows that the tube could not be drinking straws.

(3) *Pick the choice with evidence that would best disprove the claim*

A) Similarly sized metal tubes are found in locations outside of southern Russia.

This choice doesn't hurt Trifonov's hypothesis. Finding similar items elsewhere doesn't change what he assumed.

B) Viewing the tubes under a microscope reveals barley starch granules attached along the inside walls.

This would be the strongest <u>support</u> for Trifonov's hypothesis, but we want to <u>undermine</u> the hypothesis.

C) Analysis of the tubes discovers that the core was originally filled with wood that had rotted away.

If the tubes were originally filled with wood, then they wouldn't function as drinking straws. This works!

D) Other objects found at the burial mound include ceramic cups, weapons, and jewelry.

This is additional information, but these additional items do not affect Trifonov's hypothesis.

C

TIP

Typically, the graphs and tables you will see on the SAT are similar to those you might find in a news article.

These figures are generally designed to be data-rich while still being understandable.

Quantitative Command of Evidence Questions

These are some of the easiest questions to spot on the test, as they always have a chart, table, or graph. And if you're worried about really complex graphs and having to find the difference between small values, don't be! Good news about what's actually tested on these questions:

- ✔ Basic line graphs, bar graphs, and tables
- ✘ Complex scatterplots or boxplots
- ✘ Mathematical calculations

You will **not** be expected to interpret confusing graphs or make any calculations. You simply need to choose an option that accurately matches the data in the figure.

Tips for reading graphs and tables

Here are some general tips for reading data figures on the SAT.

Pay attention to any units: The wrong answer choices may mix up the units on the graph, so make sure that you know what they're counting.

Vertical = dependent variable: The vertical axis will be the dependent variable and will represent what happened due to the researcher's choices.

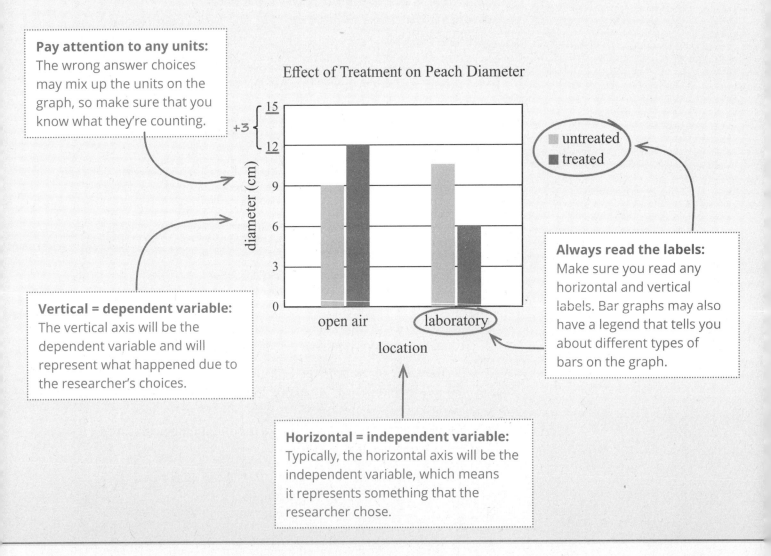

Effect of Treatment on Peach Diameter

Always read the labels: Make sure you read any horizontal and vertical labels. Bar graphs may also have a legend that tells you about different types of bars on the graph.

Horizontal = independent variable: Typically, the horizontal axis will be the independent variable, which means it represents something that the researcher chose.

EXAMPLE 4

Super hot peppers are rapidly becoming a culinary staple, at least among those looking for a spicy thrill. Ghost peppers and their ilk can be found fresh or dried in many markets and are ingredients in all kinds of foods including sauces, chips, and even candies. The demand for super hot peppers (those with a Scoville heat unit above 750,000) is also reflected in their prices: ghost peppers, Trinidad scorpions, and Carolina reapers _____

Scoville ratings and average price per ounce (in dollars)
for different varieties of peppers

Pepper Variety	Scoville Heat Units	Average price per ounce
Bell pepper (green)	0	$0.28
Pimento (red)	100–500	$0.62
Jalapeño (green)	2,500–8,000	$0.11
Habanero (orange)	425,000–577,000	$0.87
Ghost (red)	855,000–1,041,427	$2.19
Trinidad Scorpion (red)	1,200,000–2,000,000	$2.50
Carolina Reaper (red)	1,400,000–2,200,000	$2.65

4. Which choice most effectively uses data from the table to illustrate the claim?

   A) cost more per pepper than their less spicy relatives.
   B) sell for significantly more per ounce than other less spicy peppers.
   C) have some of the highest ratings on the Scoville scale.
   D) are up to three times larger than the size of less spicy peppers.

SOLUTION

(1) *Read the question to determine the goal*

Which choice most effectively <u>uses data</u> from the table to illustrate the claim?

(2) *Read the text to find the author's claim*

...<u>The demand</u> for super hot peppers (those with a Scoville heat unit above 750,000) is also <u>reflected in their prices</u>: ghost peppers, Trinidad scorpions, and Carolina reapers _____

We need to focus on the price of the bottom three rows of the table (ghost, trinidad, and carolina):

Pepper Variety	Scoville Heat Units	Average price per ounce
Ghost (red)	855,000-1,041,427	$2.19
Trinidad Scorpion (red)	1,200,000-2,000,000	$2.50
Carolina Reaper (red)	1,400,000-2,200,000	$2.65

(3) *Pick the answer that provides the conclusion matching the table*

A) cost more per pepper than their less spicy relatives.

This might seem true at first, but the right column measures price per ounce, not price per pepper. We don't have any information on how much each pepper weighs, so this is not supported by the table.

B) sell for significantly more per ounce than other less spicy peppers.

This looks pretty good. Ghost, Trinidad Scorpions, and Carolina Reapers all sell for over $2.00 per ounce, while the less spicy peppers sell for less than $1.00.

C) have some of the highest ratings on the Scoville scale.

While this statement is supported by the table, it does not support the claim about their prices.

D) are up to three times larger than the size of less spicy peppers.

There is no information about the size of the peppers, only their Scoville rating and their price per ounce.

B

TIP

When using data from the graphic, it must be accurate and relevant to the data and the text's main idea. Eliminate answer choices that do not match the data or that are not relevant to the central focus of the text.

Practice Set

1

Genyornis, a two-meter high flightless bird, once roamed across ancient Australia. Its extinction 47,000 years ago seems timed alongside the introduction of humans to the continent. Professor Matthew Collins has proposed that the arrival of humans, and their hunger for *Genyornis'* melon-sized eggs, led to the extinction. There is no evidence that humans directly hunted *Genyornis*, and it is unclear whether early Australian inhabitants had the technology to take down such a formidable bird, but an unwatched nest would provide significant nutrition. Collins proposes that raids on *Genyornis* nests eventually led to a population collapse and the species' eventual extinction.

Which archeological evidence, if true, would most strongly support Collin's hypothesis?

A) Evidence that shows humans inhabited Australia earlier than 47,000 years ago.
B) Evidence that shows stone tools had been used to scrape meat off Genyornis bones.
C) Evidence that shows Genyornis eggshells alongside artifacts from early Australians.
D) Evidence that shows early humans on other continents ate large bird eggs.

2

Isamu Noguchi was a 20th-century Japanese-American modernist sculptor known for the diversity of his work. While many sculptors stick to one physical medium, Noguchi eagerly implemented and blended metal, stone, clay, wood, concrete, and even paper in his works. He designed fine art sculptures and collaborated on set design with dancer Martha Graham. He worked for Herman Miller creating iconic mid-century modernist furniture that is still in production today. He valued public art and applied his skill towards creating inspiring children's playgrounds around the world. ____

What quote by Isamu Noguchi would best reinforce the claim made in the text?

A) "You can find out how to do something and then do it or do something and then find out what you did."
B) "It is weight that gives meaning to weightlessness.
C) "When the time came for me to work with larger spaces, I conceived them as gardens, not as sites with objects but as relationships to a whole."
D) "Everything is sculpture. Any material, any idea without hindrance born into space, I consider sculpture."

"The Spring " is a 17th Century poem by Thomas Carew. In the poem, the speaker compares the changes in the season to the attitude of his beloved: _____

Which quotation from "The Spring" most effectively illustrates the claim?

A) "Now that the winter's gone, the earth hath lost/ Her snow-white robes"
B) "and now no more the frost/ Candies the grass, or casts an icy cream/ Upon the silver lake or crystal stream"
C) "To the dead swallow; wakes in hollow tree/ The drowsy cuckoo, and the humble-bee."
D) "Nor hath the scalding noonday sun the power/ To melt that marble ice, which still doth hold/ Her heart congeal'd, and makes her pity cold"

Top ten foods that contain the most flavonol per gram

Food	(%) of total flavonols consumed
Tea	
Black, brewed	32.11
Black, brewed, decaf	5.70
Onion	
Boiled, drained	3.81
Raw	21.46
Apples	
Raw, with skin	7.02
Beer	
Regular	6.20
Lettuce	
Iceberg, raw	1.93
Coffee	
Brewed from grounds	1.74
Tomato	
Puree, canned	1.45
Red, ripe, raw	1.17

Flavonols are a beneficial nutrient: studies show that flavonol rich diets lower blood pressure and can help prevent blood clots. Flavonol, like many organic compounds, can break down during the cooking process. For example, _____

Which choice most effectively uses data from the table to illustrate the claim?

A) iceberg lettuce is typically eaten raw, as the cellular walls rapidly break down, releasing water and making for an unpleasant mushy texture.
B) tomato puree in a can has more flavonols than fresh ripe tomatoes, as puree is more condensed.
C) raw, unskinned apples have 7.02 percent flavonols per gram while cooked, skinned apples have no flavonols per gram.
D) boiled onions lose a significant amount of their flavonols when compared to their raw counterparts.

5

In his 1871 article, "Americanism in Literature", Thomas Wentworth Higginson argues that American writers, alongside other citizens, need to embrace the American experience, ____

Which quotation from "Americanism in Literature" most effectively illustrates the claim?

A) "The voyager from Europe who lands upon our shores perceives a difference in the sky above his head."

B) "It seems unspeakably important that all persons among us, and especially the student and the writer, should be pervaded with Americanism."

C) "He may still need culture, but he has the basis of all culture. He is entitled to an imperturbable patience and hopefulness, born of a living faith."

D) "The most ignorant man may feel the full strength and heartiness of the American idea, and so may the most accomplished scholar."

6

In 1950 and at the beginning of the Cold War, Paul Nitze wrote the then top secret "National Security Council Paper 68," where he advised the US to not be passive when dealing with the Soviet Union. The paper highlights the difference between the free state and the Soviet state, and while Nitze unequivocally supported the US, he also acknowledged how a free society can be exploited by those looking to undermine it.

Which quotation from the text best illustrates this claim?

A) "The Soviet Union regards the United States as the only major threat to the achievement of its fundamental design."

B) "From this idea of freedom with responsibility derives the marvelous diversity, the deep tolerance, the lawfulness of the free society."

C) "The idea of freedom is the most contagious idea in history, more contagious than the idea of submission to authority. For the breath of freedom cannot be tolerated in a society which has come under the domination of a group of individuals with a will to absolute power."

D) "No other value system is so wholly irreconcilable with ours, so implacable in its purpose to destroy ours, so capable of turning to its own uses the most dangerous and divisive trends in our own society, no other so skillfully and powerfully evokes the elements of irrationality in human nature everywhere"

Dr Lucy McDonald has published an analysis of how "likes" on social media platforms affect interpersonal relationships. Rather than seeing "likes" as a system that brings the best ideas forward, McDonald is concerned that "likes" promote extreme ideas: ____

Which quotation from Lucy McDonald best illustrates this claim?

A) "[Likes are] a form of pseudo-engagement which absolves us of the guilt of not responding to others' posts but creates the bare minimum of human connection."

B) "We should not think of accrued likes as a reliable measure of the esteem in which a person is held."

C) "If our audience has thousands of posts to sift through, we need to say something dramatic to get their (and the algorithms') attention."

D) "In its early days, the internet was heralded for its potential to improve democracy. But the 'like' function has revitalized the age-old worry that vivid rhetoric and emotional appeals will win out over rational deliberation in democracies."

Energy Source	Direct Jobs	Indirect Jobs	Induced Jobs	Total Jobs
Oil & Natural Gas	0.8	2.9	2.3	5.2
Coal	1.9	3.0	3.9	6.9
Building retrofits	7.0	4.9	11.8	16.7
Mass transit/rail	11.0	4.9	17.4	22.3
Smart grid	4.3	4.6	7.9	12.5
Wind	4.6	4.9	8.4	13.3
Solar	5.4	4.4	9.3	13.7
Biomass	7.4	5.0	12.4	17.4

Studies by the International Renewable Energy Agency (IRENA) estimate that job growth is increasing more rapidly in the renewable energy sector than in the fossil fuels sector, and green industries could provide over 16 million jobs within ten years if the world can double the market share of renewable energy technologies. Moreover, estimates by the World Bank indicate that US wind and solar create about 13.3 and 13.7 jobs per million dollars of spending, respectively, and that building retrofits to incorporate sustainable energies create 16.7 jobs per million dollars of spending. ____

Which choice most effectively uses data from the table to illustrate the claim?

A) Interestingly, solar produces only slightly more jobs than wind—a difference of just 0.4 jobs per million dollars of spending.

B) Even better, the mass transit/freight rail system creates the most jobs of all, with 22.3 jobs created per million dollars of spending.

C) Similarly, biomass, a renewable source of stored energy from the sun, has one of the highest ratios at 17.4 jobs created per million dollars of spending.

D) The latter is more than triple the 5.2 jobs per million dollars for oil and natural gas, and more than double the 6.9 jobs per million dollars for coal.

9

Unemployment rates/earnings by educational attainment, 2018

Educational attainment	Unemployment rate (%)	Median usual weekly earnings ($)
Doctoral degree	1.6	1,825
Professional degree	1.5	1,884
Master's degree	2.1	1,434
Bachelor's degree	2.2	1,198
Associate's degree	2.8	862
Some college, no degree	3.7	802
High school diploma	4.1	730
Less than a high school diploma	5.6	553
Total	3.2	932

The U.S. Bureau of Labor Statistics has an answer whether or not education pays off: as workers attain higher levels of education, they are less likely to face unemployment for all levels. As the table shows, workers who have earned less than a high school diploma _____

Which choice most effectively uses data from the table to complete the example?

A) make only $553 per week.

B) need to work more hours per week than those workers with professional or doctoral degrees.

C) have the highest percentage of unemployment when compared to those who have finished high school and/or attained college or other advanced degrees.

D) make significantly less than those with professional or doctoral degrees

Vehicle sales (actual and projected) by automation level

Level of Automation	2019 sales (Millions)	2029 projected sales (Millions)	Percent Change 2019-2029 (projected)
Level 0 (fully manual)	56.1	19.2	-66%
Level 1	33.8	48.1	+42%
Level 2	15.2	76.3	+400%
Level 3	0.1	17.9	+17,800%
Level 4 (fully autonomous)	None available	4.0	N/A
Total (levels 1-4)	49.1	146.3	+198%

A market research outfit (Yole) expects all levels of computer assisted vehicles to see production growth in the coming years. The number of sales of level 2 cars—those with two or more advanced driver assistance systems (ADAS) that can at time control the braking, steering or acceleration of the vehicle—is anticipated to _____

Which choice most effectively uses data from the table to complete the example?

A) have 76.3 million more vehicles available by 2029.

B) generate a 400% increase in vehicle sales from 2019 to 2029.

C) go from no sales in 2019 to at least 4 million in 2029.

D) see a 42% increase in profit from 2019 to 2029.

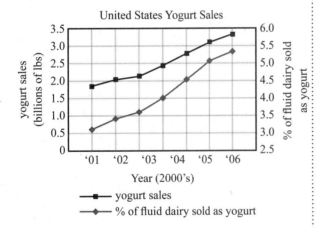

United States Yogurt Sales

Year (2000's)

—■— yogurt sales

—♦— % of fluid dairy sold as yogurt

Yogurt's popularity is due in part to its considerable nutritional value; it is full of protein, calcium, and vitamins. It also contains probiotics, live microorganisms that are thought to boost immune response. Whatever the reason, yogurt has become more popular than ever in the past decade; in 2006, Americans purchased _____

Which choice most effectively uses data from the table to complete the example?

A) over 5 billion pounds of yogurt.

B) over 5% of all yogurt sold globally.

C) under 6% of all dairy products sold as yogurt.

D) over 3 billion pounds of yogurt.

12

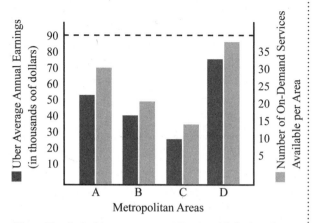

Note: The dashed line represents Uber's published median annual salary in thousands of dollars.

A key question circles around the rise of on-demand services: why are people so eager to pay for someone else to complete their humdrum tasks? Many who use these services do so because they are swamped with their own work. For an overworked computer programmer, outsourced laundry and cleaning may make fiscal sense: the cost of paying someone else is cheaper than taking time away from their job. Acknowledging the practical reasons for the increase of the "on-demand economy" bares a troubling dichotomy. Users have more money than time. However, the "on demand" workers often live below the poverty line. Uber's website published that their drivers make a median annual salary of $90,000, although outside studies have shown that for drivers in many metropolitan areas, ____

Which choice most effectively uses data from the table to complete the example.

A) no Uber driver makes a livable wage working for the service.

B) the number of on-demand services can vary from as low as 15 to as high as 35.

C) the average annual earnings are well below the reported median.

D) the average annual earnings can be as low as $40,000 and as high as $85,000.

13

In his 1870's poem "Has Summer Come without the Rose," Arthur William Edgar O'Shaughnessy contrasts the liveliness of the summer season with the speaker's sullen mood.

Which quotation from "Has Summer Come without the Rose" most effectively illustrates the claim?

A) "HAS summer come without the rose,/Or left the bird behind?"

B) "Where she who said, I love thee,/Now says, I love thee not?"

C) "The skies seem'd true above thee,/The rose true on the tree;"

D) "The seem'd true the summer through/But all prov'd false to me"

14

In his 1925 poem "Weary Blues," Langston Hughes describes a performance by a blues musician. While most of the poem focuses on the musician's attitude and personal struggles, Hughes includes a reference to the greater impact of music.

Which quotation from "The Weary Blues" most effectively illustrates the claim?

A) "Droning a drowsy syncopated tune,/Rocking back and forth to a mellow croon,"
B) "Down on Lenox Avenue the other night/By the pale dull pallor of an old gas light"
C) "With his ebony hands on each ivory key/He made that poor piano moan with melody."
D) "And far into the night he crooned that tune./The stars went out and so did the moon."

15

In her 1921 poem "Wild Peaches," Elinor Wylie focuses on the mixed feelings of a woman moving to rural Maryland. The speaker in the poem not only describes the wonder of the wilderness, but also addresses displeasure with the decision to leave civilization.

Which quotation from "Wild Peaches" most effectively illustrates the claim?

A) "The winter will be short, the summer long,/The autumn amber-hued, sunny and hot,/Tasting of cider and scuppernong;"
B) "The autumn frosts will lie upon the grass/Like bloom on grapes of purple-brown and gold."
C) "Blue plums lie open to the blackbird's beak,/We shall live well — we shall live very well."
D) "Down to the Puritan marrow of my bones/There's something in this richness that I hate."

16

The grammatical rules of Sanskrit, an ancient language from South Asia, were originally codified by Pāṇini around 500 BCE. Linguists analyzing Pāṇini's 4,000 rules for Sanskrit often encountered contradictions where following them would generate nonsense words. This problem has challenged linguists for centuries, but recently, PhD student Rishi Rajpopat was able to crack Pāṇini's algorithm by noticing a pattern in which syllables take precedence over others. This discovery has been a breakthrough in programing artificial intelligence to use Sanskrit: ____.

Which event, if true, would support Rishi Rajpopat's discovery by showing its application?

A) following Rajpopat pattern, artificial intelligence can generate new Sanskrit words with far fewer errors.
B) linguists will continue to refind Rajpopat's discovery and check for any discrepancies with Pāṇini's Sanskrit rules.
C) although Sanskrit is one of the oldest cuneiform languages, only about 25,000 people in India speak Sanskrit today.
D) artificial intelligence has continued to refine its responses in multiple languages and continues to be an advantage for creating low cost communication.

17

When a climate is wetter, the leaves of woody dicot angiosperms become larger, and when the climate is colder, the leaves become toothed around the perimeter. Paleobotanist Aly Baumgartner has been collecting and measuring fossilized leaves across Rusinga Island. She has concluded that the climate of Rusinga Island during the Miocene era varied back and forth between tropical rainforest and temperate woodland.

Which finding, if true, would most directly undermine Baumgartner's conclusion?

A) Woody dicot angiosperms are no longer found on Rusinga Island and therefore her findings cannot be compared to contemporary specimens.
B) Woody dicot angiosperms still grow on Rusinga Island and exhibit large, rounded leaves.
C) The size and shape of woody dicot angiosperms are affected by other environmental conditions besides temperature and moisture.
D) Rusinga Island has had a stable climate for the last 1,000 years and the leaves of woody dicot angiosperms on the island all appear similar.

18

Hormones released by the stomach, such as ghrelin, are an important part of stimulating appetite. A research team at Massachusetts Institute of Technology (MIT) have developed an ingestible capsule that delivers electrical current to the cells responsible for producing ghrelin. Tests on various animals have shown an increase in ghrelin levels and an increase in appetite. The team claims that the capsules will be effective in humans and can be used to increase the appetite of patients with conditions or treatments that reduce the desire to eat.

Which study, if true, would most strongly disprove the research team's claim?

A) A study where new animal species ingest the capsule and gain a significant amount of weight.
B) A study where patients receive behavior therapy to help keep a healthy appetite.
C) A study where patients ingest the capsule and do not have any increase in their appetite.
D) A study where patients ingest the capsule and show an increase in calories consumed.

115

Inference

Tags: Information and Ideas • Inferences

TIP

Puzzle pieces are designed to fit together with their peculiar shapes. Here, it's the specific words in the text and the answer choice that should connect together. You should be able to point to the connection to "prove" the right answer is logical.

Picture two puzzle pieces fitting together

Inference questions ask you to draw conclusions that are not directly stated in the text. These questions are always worded the same:

> *Which choice most logically completes the text?*

To logically complete the text, your answer choice should still "connect" to the rest of the passage like a jigsaw puzzle piece. Earlier sentences set up the tone, claim, and 'vibe,' and only one choice will fit that logic. Correct answers usually reference info from earlier in the text, while wrong choices often bring up a new topic or argument out of nowhere.

TIP

Inference questions often involve finding a statement that best summarizes the information in the text. This skill is closely linked to finding the central idea.

Main Strategy

Your job on inference questions is to first understand the claims being made in the text so you can find the most logical completion.

(1) *Read the text and focus on the key claim.*

(2) *Try to answer the question in your own words.*

(3) *Eliminate answers to find the best choice.*

Read the text and focus on the key claim or idea

Try to answer the question in your own words

Eliminate answers to find the best choice

EXAMPLE 1

A common argument against green or renewable energy is the cost differential between it and conventional fossil-fuel energy. The likely reason for this high cost is that renewable energies are still working with structures and facilities—a power grid, a highway system, a fueling system—built for a world powered by fossil fuels. All of this enormous infrastructure was created through public-sector support including tax credits, low-cost loans, and complete grants from the federal government. Companies designing new energy sources, on the other hand,

_____

1. Which choice most logically completes the text?

A) must advertise directly against fossil fuel-based corporations for consumers to recognize them as direct competitors.
B) avoid incentives for construction and incur the initial operating costs.
C) need to focus on why it's critical for the country to improve its infrastructure.
D) often have to factor in the costs of building their own infrastructure.

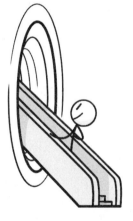

PORTAL

Since we're looking to make a logical connection, we should **focus on logic words** like therefore, because, however, on the other hand, etc.

For more on logic words, check out the *Transitions* chapter on page 216.

SOLUTION

① *Read the text and focus on the key claim*

A common <u>argument against</u> green or renewable energy is the <u>cost differential</u> between it and conventional fossil-fuel energy. The likely <u>reason</u> for this <u>high cost</u> is that renewable energies are still <u>working with structures and facilities</u>—a power grid, a highway system, a fueling system—<u>built</u> for a world <u>powered by fossil fuels</u>. All of this enormous <u>infrastructure</u> was <u>created</u> through <u>public-sector support</u> including tax credits, low-cost loans, and complete grants from the federal government. <u>Companies designing new energy sources,</u> on the other hand,

_____

The text makes a comparison between the support fossil-fuel industries received and what renewable energy companies need now. "On the other hand" tells us we want a contrast with 'public-sector support' of credits, loans, and grants.

Continued on next page →

② *Try to answer the question in your own words*

The phrase "on the other hand," shows us that the choice needs to elaborate on the comparison between fossil fuel companies and renewable energy companies. The fossil fuel industry got widespread support, so it's reasonable to infer that green energy companies should receive similar support.

③ *Eliminate answers to find the best choice*

A̶) must advertise directly against fossil fuel-based corporations for consumers to recognize them as direct competitors.

The text doesn't talk about advertising, so this is not a strong inference.

B̶) avoid incentives for construction and incur the initial operating costs.

It never suggests that green companies want to avoid incentives, so this doesn't work.

C̶) need to focus on why it's critical for the country to improve its infrastructure.

This is a nice sentiment, but it's not continuing the logic of the comparison between the two types of energy companies.

(D)) often have to factor in the costs of building their own infrastructure.

This one addresses why renewable energy can be more expensive than fossil-fuel based energy, which is the main comparison of this passage.

D

Don't assume too strongly!

A common way for the test writer to make an answer choice incorrect is to include an **exaggerated claim**. Whenever you see strong or absolute language in a choice, it's likely there to make that answer choice debatable, and therefore *incorrect*. Bold, exaggerated claims often trick students into picking them because they *sound* confident and decisive. Meanwhile, correct answers may be so logical and simple they fly right under the radar for an easily-distracted student.

EXAMPLE 2

Many of Jean-Luc Godard's early films still appeal to a general film audience, as they playfully reference and subvert Hollywood cliches. For example, his first film, *À Bout de Souffle* (1960), wryly deconstructs the antihero common to the Hollywood crime genre. However, after 1968, Godard's films became more political and require a deep knowledge of French politics and labor disputes to be fully appreciated. Consequently, _____

2. Which choice most logically completes the text?

   A) *À Bout de Souffle* remains Godard's best-loved film.
   B) experts in French politics prefer Godard's post-1968 films.
   C) many filmgoers find Godard's post-1968 films less appealing than his earlier films.
   D) those filmgoers less familiar with French politics are encouraged to avoid all of Godard's films.

SOLUTION

1 *Read the text and focus on the key claim*

Many of Jean-Luc Godard's early films still appeal to a general film audience, as they playfully reference and subvert Hollywood cliches. For example, his first film, *À Bout de Souffle* (1960), wryly deconstructs the antihero common to the Hollywood crime genre. However, after 1968, Godard's films became more political and require a deep knowledge of French politics and labor disputes to be fully appreciated. Consequently, _____

The text makes a comparison between Godard's early films, which many people like, and his later films, which require more political context.

2 *Try to answer the question in your own words*

The last sentence we'll be adding starts with "consequently," so it must follow the logic that Godard's post-1968 films are harder to appreciate without background knowledge.

3 *Eliminate answers to find the best choice*

A) *À Bout de Souffle* remains Godard's best-loved film.

Best is very strong language, which is a non-starter or inference questions. Furthermore, we need an answer that is about his later films, not his first.

B) experts in French politics prefer Godard's post-1968 films.

This assumes that experts all agree, which is too much of a generalization. This is too big of an assumption.

C) many filmgoers find Godard's post-1968 films less appealing than his earlier films.

This answer continues the idea and uses moderate language ("less appealing) versus something more severely ("they hate his later films").

D) those filmgoers less familiar with French politics are encouraged to avoid all of Godard's films.

This language is far too strong. And the advice is to avoid all of his films, which feels far too opinionated.

C

Understanding Claims and Logic

When reading the text as part of an inference question, it's important to understand what kind of **claim** is being made and identify **logic clues** that define it. Here are some common types of **claims** seen in inference texts:

① *Research summary*

These texts summarize some topic of **scientific research**. Use logic words to follow the steps used in the research. Your job will be to <u>state a conclusion or description of the findings</u> that makes sense with what you're told in the summary.

② *Comparison*

These texts will make a **comparison** between two things. Look back at the practice problem about Godard for a perfect example. Your job is to continue the comparison by focusing on a <u>specific piece of information</u> that links the text with the correct answer choice.

③ *Next steps*

These texts are similar to research summaries, but the final conclusion has not yet been reached. Instead, you'll need to pick an answer that determines the **next logical steps** that need to be taken. For this question, you should focus on the <u>obstacles that need to be overcome</u> or the <u>information that is missing</u>.

EXAMPLE 3

Margaret Boone Rappaport and Christopher J Corbally are studying how outer space travel affects neuroplasticity: the brain's ability to adapt to physical changes. Low- or no-gravity space travel puts strain on brains designed to function upright in normal Earth gravity. Studying neuroplasticity, best accomplished by scanning brains while in space, will help create a plan to ease stress on astronauts engaged in long-range missions. The difficulty in studying neuroplasticity in low- or no-gravity conditions is access to those conditions and research subjects. In order to overcome these obstacles, Rappaport and Corbally plan to _____.

3. Which choice most logically completes the text?

A) petition space agencies to restrict human space travel until more research has been completed.

B) interview former astronauts about their experiences in low-or-no gravity

C) work with space agencies to implement brain scans of astronauts while in space.

D) design a long-distance space expedition to see how low-or-no gravity affects the astronauts onboard.

SOLUTION

(1) *Read the text and focus on the key claim*

Margaret Boone Rappaport and Christopher J Corbally are <u>studying</u> how <u>outer space travel</u> affects <u>neuroplasticity</u>: the <u>brain's ability</u> to <u>adapt to physical changes</u>. Low-or-no gravity space travel puts <u>strain on brains</u> designed to function upright in normal Earth gravity. Studying neuroplasticity, <u>best accomplished by scanning brains while in space</u>, will help <u>create a plan</u> to <u>ease stress</u> on astronauts engaged in <u>long-range missions</u>. The <u>difficulty</u> in studying neuroplasticity in low-or-no gravity conditions is <u>access to those conditions and research subjects</u>. In order to overcome these <u>obstacles</u>, Rappaport and Corbally plan to _____.

The words "in order to overcome these obstacles" sets us up to outline the next steps rather than make a big conclusion.

(2) *Try to answer the question in your own words*

The passage mentions that the best thing would be to scan brains while in space, so that would be the most logical next step if we can find it in the choices.

(3) *Eliminate answers to find the best choice*

A) petition space agencies to ~~restrict~~ human space travel until more research has been completed.

They want to study neuroplasticity in space, not restrict space travel.

B) interview ~~former~~ astronauts about their experiences in low-or-no gravity

This might be interesting, but the text says that the best way to study neuroplasticity is to scan brains in space, so this is not the best next step.

C) work with space agencies to implement brain scans of astronauts while in space.

This is the most logical next step for their research.

D) ~~design~~ a long-distance space expedition to see how low-or-no gravity affects the astronauts onboard.

This does not mention anything about scanning brains, so this is not the best fit.

C

Practice Set

1

A botched colonization project on the Isthmus of Panama played a large role in the 1707 union of Scotland with England. The Kingdom of Scotland directed a significant portion of the country's financial resources to establishing the colony, which they named New Caledonia. Their hope was to enter the global trade market by establishing an overland route connecting the Pacific and Atlantic Oceans. However, after numerous obstacles plagued the undertaking, a blockade from the disgruntled Spanish Navy forced the colony to be abandoned after only two years. The failed colony plunged Scotland into economic ruin, ____

Which choice most logically completes the text?

A) which was the goal of Spain at that time, as they controlled most of Central America.

B) making the merger of England and Scotland an economic necessity for Scotland.

C) which revealed that Scotland did not have the naval might to oppose Spain.

D) although the United States would eventually fund and manage the Panama Canal, fulfilling Scotland's ambition.

2

The molars or prehistoric mammoths were huge and took multiple years to grow. While growing, the molars record the chemical signatures of the mammoth's diet. Wouter Bonhof has been analyzing strontium isotopes in mammoth fossils, as those isotopes are affected by changes in soil type. By documenting the differences in strontium isotopes through the layers of a molar, Bonhof ____

Which choice most logically completes the text?

A) can determine the age and weight of the mammoth.

B) gets a better understanding of the different environments the mammoth traversed through its lifetime.

C) can compare the strontium isotopes found in the molars of modern-day animals.

D) better understand how long it takes for a mammoth molar to grow.

3

The Venus of Willendorf is a small stone figurine that dates back to the Gravettian period (30,000-22,000 years ago). Using computer-enhanced tomography, Gerhard Weber has been able to analyze the composition of the limestone carving. He discovered that divots throughout the sculpture were attributed to limonite deposits in the limestone. Although some limonite deposits may have fallen out during carving, others appear to have been intentionally removed to finetune the shape. For example, one of limonite deposits was removed to create the figure's prominent navel, suggesting that _____

Which choice most logically completes the text?

A) the navel indent may have been created by accident.

B) the artist had an idea of how the shape of the figure would look when completed.

C) Gravettian period artists had limited experience with manipulating stone with small tools.

D) the Venus of Willendorf was likely damaged before it was rediscovered.

4

A recent report by a team of economists led by Dr. Matthew Agarwala suggests a potential unforeseen consequence of climate change. Nations that suffer a loss of biodiversity may also suffer a set-back in their credit rating, which affects their ability to borrow as well as the value of their currency. Loss of biodiversity—especially in regards to fisheries, timber production, and wild pollination—will impact a nation's ability to produce and will eventually lead to a net loss of the nation's wealth. However, Agarwala does not see this as an unavoidable outcome and suggests that policymakers should _____

Which choice most logically completes the text?

A) consider other competing economic theories before administering a plan.

B) focus on extracting as much value from natural resources to offset any downturns in the nation's credit rating.

C) invest in sustainability now, which will be more productive and less costly than reacting to any future loss of biodiversity.

D) increase the amount of borrowing now before their creditworthiness declines.

5

The origins of language development in humans are mysterious, as the vocalizations of our closest existing biological relatives, such as chimpanzees, are relatively simple. Lead researcher Dr. Arik Kershenbaum and his colleagues at the University of Cambridge believe that studying the sounds of other intelligent species that use vocal communication for cooperative behavior—such as wolves and dolphins—may provide clues to the earliest evolution of our own use of language. Therefore, they conducted the largest ever study of _____

Which choice most logically completes the text?

A) how dolphins migrate in groups across a wide oceanic range.

B) vocalizations of chimpanzees and other great apes.

C) howling in the 'canid' family, which includes wolves, jackals, and domestic dogs.

D) words used by ancient humans from a wide geographic range.

Varroa Mites are a honeybee parasite native to Asia, but they have spread globally and can cause the collapse of a honeybee hive by physically damaging bees' wings. Beekeepers typically use acaricide treatments to combat varroa mite, but biologist Alexis Beaurepaire has noticed that some Western honeybee populations have adapted through natural or artificial selection to survive mite infestations without beekeeper intervention. While this is a positive development for the often beleaguered honeybee, Beaurepaire is also wary of the potential for co-evolution ____

Which choice most logically completes the text?

A) where varroa mites adapt alongside to counteract the defenses of the mite-resistant Western honeybees.

B) and the potential extinction of varroa mites across North America.

C) which would necessitate more frequent acaricide treatments on healthy hives.

D) which may diminish the quality and quantity of honey a hive can produce.

In the second half of the 20th century, many American cities enacted zoning ordinances that mandated minimum parking requirements for buildings. Many of these zoning ordinances are still in effect today, and according to professors of environmental design Kevin Krizek and John Hersey, they impact urban areas' ability to grow in the 21st century. Krizek and Hersey, in hopes of helping cities to prosper in an environmentally sustainable way, advocate that ____.

Which choice most logically completes the text?

A) zoning ordinances that require parking be eliminated or amended.

B) cities revert back to 20th century building practices.

C) urban areas ban cars from their downtown centers.

D) builders look for new ways to create parking in congested urban areas.

Archaeologists in Egypt have discovered a tunnel beneath Taposiris Magna, a temple dating back to 280 BCE. The 4,300-foot long tunnel appears partially collapsed and archaeologists are still debating its original purpose. Kathleen Martinez, who primarily discovered the tunnel, somewhat controversially hypothesizes that it could be the burial tomb of Cleopatra and Mark Anthony, ____

Which choice most logically completes the text?

A) which will be a career defining moment for Martinez.

B) who are famous from books and movies written about their lives.

C) but more excavation is necessary before this claim can be confirmed.

D) although no other archaeologists support that conclusion.

9

Polyurethanes are commonplace, especially in seat cushions and furniture, durable in a variety of conditions, and versatile. However, they are difficult to recycle and can contain harmful chemicals. Srikanth Pilla and James Sternberg have been researching a bio-based alternative to polyurethane using lignin, a byproduct of the paper pulp industry. Initial tests have been positive and they have created a process to completely recycle their bio-based foams. As their research continues, Pilla and Sternberg will need to determine whether their bio-based foams ____

Which choice most logically completes the text?

A) will be appealing to consumers of furniture.

B) can be as varied and durable as polyurethane foams.

C) will be adopted by the paper pulp industry.

D) can create comfortable cushions for furniture.

10

So-called, green jobs–work involving renewable energy and sustainability–have been a sector for growth, averaging an 8% increase in demand annually. A concern is that the demand for green job workers has already outpaced the supply of those with the necessary skills. Christopher Boone and Karen Seto have studied these concerns and suggest a multi-prong approach to address this imbalance. They advocate that more institutions ____

Which choice most logically completes the text?

A) switch to green energy as it will help create more jobs.

B) consider offering different training options, from college-level degrees to short-term certifications.

C) attempt to slow down the creation of new green jobs.

D) increase funding for green jobs in hopes of making the annual growth greater than 8 percent.

Writing Introduction

Tags: Writing Strategy

....

TIP

Every Standard English Convention question is worded the same way:

"Which choice completes the text so it conforms to the conventions of Standard English?"

When you see this question prompt, you know you've moved from the Reading portion to the Writing portion of the module.

Standard English Conventions

In each Reading & Writing Module, **5-8 questions** test grammar rules.

Boundaries questions test the basic rules of punctuation.	
Comma Basics	Using commas correctly
All About Clauses	Separating independent/dependent clauses with commas, semicolons, and colons

Form, Structure, and Sense questions test rules of agreement.	
Tense Switch	Making sure your verb tenses match up
Subject-Verb Agreement	Making sure plural subjects have plural verbs and singular subjects have singular verbs
Pronoun Error	Matching nouns with the correct pronouns
Possession	Using apostrophes correctly
Misplaced Modifers	Moving modifiers so they are next to the words they are meant to modify

Expression of Ideas

The last **4–6 questions** test your ability to express ideas clearly.

Expression of Ideas questions test your ability to communicate an idea clearly and intentionally.	
Transitions	Picking logical transitions between ideas
Rhetorical Synthesis	Summarizing bullet points to communicate a given idea to an audience

dialect (n.)

a particular form of a language that is peculiar to a specific region or social group.

Some examples of English dialects are Newfoundland English, African American Vernacular English, and Cajun Vernacular English.

Good grammar is all about communication

In relationships, business, diplomacy, and education, ideas are *complicated* and misunderstandings can be *costly*. If everyone spoke according to their own rules, things would get pretty confusing:

There is no universally "correct" grammar...

Communities naturally develop and follow their own sets of grammar rules to make communication go smoothly. This might surprise you, but there are *tons* of different grammars—as many as there are languages and **dialects** in the world—that are equally "correct" *in their own contexts*. You can see this in your own life: you almost certainly use different vocabulary and sentence structure with your friends than you do with your parents, teachers, or employers.

...but there is a correct grammar for the SAT!

On the SAT, you need to use the grammar rules of **Standard English**. This is the grammar that is used in the context of academic, journalistic, and professional work. These rules are taught in most schools and followed by most English speakers around the globe.

If you're a native English speaker, you grew up reading, speaking, and listening to language that follows Standard English conventions. If you can't remember one of the rules you learned in this book, just **trust your ear!** If you're not a native English speaker, then you are likely even *more* familiar with many of the **formal rules** (and strange exceptions) from studying them in class. This will help as you go through this book.

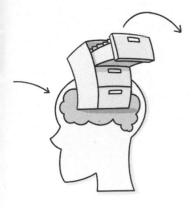

Building a memory bank of grammar rules

Writing questions on the digital SAT test a relatively small list of grammar rules. The best way to increase your score in this section is to **learn the rules one by one**, building up a list of question types in your brain, then practicing with full practice tests to get a feel for the order of questions.

On test day, seeing those familiar question types pop up at the end of the module will trigger memories of this book, like pulling the answer out of a filing cabinet in your head!

Brain Files

Your brain actually has a pretty great, well-organized filing system. If you feed it context clues, it will know which "drawer" to check and which memory to fetch to help answer the question.

Step-by-Step Strategy

Once you've learned and practiced with each of the question types in this section, you'll tackle questions by letting the **answer choices** trigger a memory of the related grammar rule. Here's our step-by-step strategy:

(1) *Check the answer choices & see what's changing*

(2) *Identify the related grammar rule*

(3) *Eliminate wrong answers, choose, and move on*

Check the Choices   Identify the Rule   Eliminate & Choose

TIP

For each question, ask **"What's changing in the answer choices?"** This gives you **context clues** that narrow down the list to just two or three possible topics.

Let's look at an example problem and how we can apply the step-by-step strategy above to quickly find the answer.

EXAMPLE

Recent research by several historians _____ the long-held belief that Marie Antoinette originally said, "Let them eat cake."

A) question
B) questioning
C) questions
D) have questioned

CHECK THE CHOICES

The answer choices are different forms of the same **verb**. You remember two common topics dealing with verbs are **Subject-Verb Agreement** and **Tense Switch**!

A) question
B) questioning
C) questions
D) have questioned

} Verbs

"I should check agreement and tense."

IDENTIFY THE RULE

From the Subject-Verb Agreement chapter, you learn that both the subject and verb must be **singular** or **plural**. So what's the subject?

S   V
Recent **research** ~~by several historians~~ _____ the long-held belief that Marie Antoinette originally said "Let them eat cake."

The subject (research) is singular, which means we need a singular verb to match. Back to the choices!

ELIMINATE & CHOOSE

You need to find a singular verb to match the singular subject. Choice C, "questions", is singular, so you try using it in the sentence:

Recent research by several historians **questions** the long-held belief that Marie Antoinette originally said "Let them eat cake."

That sounds good! You pick choice C and move to the next problem.

That's all there is to it!

If you can keep that small list of rules in your head and cross-reference it with questions using context clues, you will be able to predict the test writers' moves and stay one step ahead of them.

So, let's get started learning and practicing the rules of SAT Writing!

UNIT | Boundaries

Chapters

Overview

This unit covers the basic rules of punctuation. First, we'll learn about the purpose of commas. Next, we'll learn the **punctuation rules** for separating independent and dependent clauses.

Questions covered in this unit have answer choices where the *punctuation* changes from choice to choice.

Comma Basics

Tags: Standard English Conventions • Boundaries • Commas

....

Use your ear to test comma placement

Commas live where you naturally **pause** in your speech. That simple fact means that you can actually hear correct and incorrect comma placement! Read a sentence aloud and **exaggerate the pause** when you see a comma; if it still sounds right, then it's likely in the right spot!

TRY IT OUT

Read the following sentences aloud. Each time you come to a comma, greatly exaggerate the pause before moving on. When there's no comma, blaze ahead without stopping. Which one uses commas correctly?

TIP

Actually say these out loud, pausing at each stop sign. It helps to get a physical "feel" for commas before learning the specific rules.

1. Most students, although, they mean well, overuse, the comma.

2. Most students, although they mean well overuse the comma.

3. Most students, although they mean well, overuse the comma.

SOLUTION

Could you hear the difference? The first option feels like it takes forever to get through. The second option seems to rush at the end. **The third option**, with correct comma placement, sounds and feels best when we *exaggerate the pause*.

TIP

When unnecessary commas force a pause, they break up an idea without introducing a new one. When we have too many ideas and too few commas, it sounds jumbled and rushed.

Commas separate different ideas

Let's look at that third option to see *why* it sounds the best. Notice that we have **two separate ideas**, separated by commas.

> **Most students,** although they mean well, **overuse the comma.**
> Idea 1 —————— Idea 2 —————— Idea 1 (continued)

Commas allow us to put these two related ideas **in the same sentence**. Use your ear to test the comma in the example below. Then check to see if it's separating *two different ideas*.

EXAMPLE 1

Recent showings by two local artists _____ Raleigh's art scene is experiencing a renaissance.

A) suggest, that
B) suggest, that,
C) suggest that,
D) suggest that

TIP

Don't be afraid to remove commas! In about 40% of comma problems, the correct answer is to **cut the commas**.

SOLUTION

The comma after "suggest" sounds awkward because it breaks up a single idea: "that" is connected to "suggest." Try it without:

 D) Recent showings by two local artists <u>**suggest that**</u> Raleigh's art scene is experiencing a renaissance.

D

Commas are the crossing guards of sentences

Without commas (and the pauses they provide in speech), different ideas **crash into each other**. Commas tell us which words in a sentence belong to which idea. Without them, things get a bit jumbled:

Most students although   they mean well overuse   the comma.

TIP

This question is hoping to dazzle you with commas and quotation marks. Don't be distracted! Take it slow and **pause where you see commas**, letting your ear guide you to the right choice.

EXAMPLE 2

Few would dispute that New Orleans is the birthplace of jazz, but some musicologists suggest _____ active in Philadelphia in the 1820s, may have laid the foundation of many of jazz's iconic flourishes and improvisations.

A) that Francis "Frank" Johnson, a horn player
B) that, Francis "Frank" Johnson a horn player
C) that Francis "Frank" Johnson a horn player,
D) that, Francis "Frank" Johnson, a horn player,

SOLUTION

There are two ideas that need to be separated by commas

1. Some musicologists suggest that Francis "Frank" Johnson laid the foundation of many of jazz's flourishes...

2. Francis Johnson was a horn player in Philadelphia in the 1820s.

To insert this second idea into the first without it sounding awkward or rushed, we need a couple of pauses! To get the pauses, we should separate the two ideas with commas:

A) Few would dispute that New Orleans is the birthplace of jazz, STOP but some musicologists suggest that Francis "Frank" Johnson,

a horn player active in Philadelphia in the 1820s, STOP

may have laid the foundation of many of jazz's iconic flourishes and improvisations.

A

TIP

When you see a clause separated by commas on either end:

(1) *Slip out the clause.*

(2) *Read what's left.*

If the main idea is still intact, the commas are doing their job!

Try removing a clause separated by commas

A clause separated by commas on both ends should be **nonessential** to the sentence. If you **slip out the clause**, the main idea should be intact!

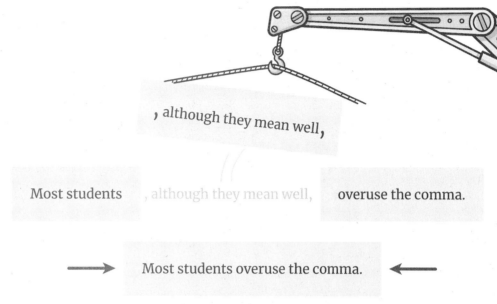

, although they mean well,

Most students , although they mean well, overuse the comma.

⟶ Most students overuse the comma. ⟵

The main idea is intact!

TIP

The SAT will often open a nonessential clause with a comma, but forget to close it! It's your job to finish what they started.

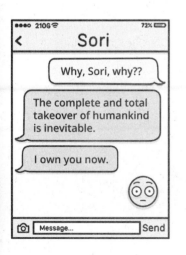

You can use dashes instead of commas

The SAT treats commas and dashes identically, so the same rules apply to both. But be careful! If you open with a comma, close with a comma. If you open with a dash, close with a dash! Never start with a comma and end with a dash, or vice-versa!

EXAMPLE 3

My iPhone 23—a dear _____ out a third mortgage on my house despite our agreement that it would check with me before making any major transactions.

A) friend—and trusted companion took
B) friend, and trusted companion—took
C) friend and trusted companion, took
D) friend and trusted companion—took

The underlined clause has part of an **appositive**: a phrase that **renames** the noun it follows. Because it is not essential to the main idea, we need to separate it with commas—or dashes—on both ends.

D) My iPhone 23—a dear friend and trusted companion—took out a third mortgage on my house despite our agreement that it would check with me before making any major transactions.

D

You don't need a comma before a parenthetical

Occasionally, the SAT will test how you use commas around a parenthetical. The good news is that the rule is simple: **never put a comma before a parenthetical**. However, you *can* put a comma after a parenthetical if that's logical in the sentence.

EXAMPLE 4

A citrus blight from China, known as _____ has been spreading globally by tiny infected insects known as psyllids. In order to save Spain's citrus crop from this disease, the European Union has funded a taskforce to combat the blight.

Which choice completes the text so that it conforms to the conventions of Standard English?

A) Huanglongbing, (HLB)
B) Huanglongbing (HLB),
C) Huanglongbing (HLB)
D) Huanglongbing, (HLB),

SOLUTION

You can **never** put a comma before a parenthetical, so choices A and D are out. The phrase "known as Huanglongbing (HLB)" is an appositive describing the blight, so we need to place a comma <u>after</u> the parenthetical to show that the appositive has ended:

B) A citrus blight from China, known as <u>Huanglongbing (HLB),</u> has been spreading globally by tiny infected insects known as psyllids. In order to save Spain's citrus crop from this disease, the European Union has funded a taskforce to combat the blight.

That works! We didn't commit the grave error of putting a comma before the parentheses, and we remembered to finish what we started by closing the appositive with a second comma. **Choice B is our answer!**

B

How to spot Comma Basics problems:

The giveaway is in the answer choices. You'll see the same sentence with commas (or dashes) changing position:

A) a decent human and even better, Overwatch player
B) a decent human, and even better Overwatch player
C) a decent human, and even better Overwatch player,
D) a decent human, and, even better Overwatch player

Recapping Comma Basics

1. *Exaggerate the pause when you see a comma.*

2. *Commas are used to separate ideas.*

3. *Nonessential phrases, like appositives, can be slipped out without harm.*

4. *Dashes function like commas.*

Quiz

Identify the error (if present) in each of the following sentences.

1. Flying horses, in her opinion were prettier and more intimidating than turtles that knew karate.

2. What had started as a dare during recess had quickly escalated into the town's first annual Hog Olympics.

3. Sally came home, from the salon, with freshly manicured nails and a tightly curled perm that brought back all the glory of the eighties.

4. For as long as he could remember, Johnny had wanted to become a private detective, when he grew up investigating crimes in the fashion of the heroes of film noir.

5. Clancy's over-investment in dryer lint companies, forced him to fire his housekeeper when the stock market took a spill.

Answers

1. *Add a comma after "opinion."*

2. *Correct as written!*

3. *Remove all commas from the sentence. None are needed!*

4. *Remove the comma after "detective," and add a comma after "up."*

5. *Remove the comma after "companies."*

Practice Set

1

Iconoclastic singer David Bowie wrote, sang, and produced _____ releasing 26 full-length albums over his remarkable career.

Which choice completes the text so that it conforms to the conventions of Standard English?

A) records, since 1967
B) records since 1967
C) records, since 1967,
D) records since 1967,

2

Marjane Satrapi's autobiographical graphic novel *Persepolis*, an innovative and gripping work depicting her Iranian family and her teenage _____ received international acclaim and was adapted into an Academy award-nominated animated film in 2007.

Which choice completes the text so that it conforms to the conventions of Standard English?

A) years
B) years–
C) years,
D) years:

3

By adding carbon nanotubes to polymers like kevlar and zylon, scientists can make synthetic materials stronger _____ combined.

Which choice completes the text so that it conforms to the conventions of Standard English?

A) than steel and titanium
B) than steel and titanium,
C) than steel, and titanium,
D) than–steel and titanium–

4

Edmond Thomas Quinn–an American sculptor and _____ is best known for his bronze of Edwin Booth as Hamlet, which was placed in New York City's Gramercy Park in 1919.

Which choice completes the text so that it conforms to the conventions of Standard English?

A) painter,
B) painter–
C) painter;
D) painter

5

The idea of burying biomass in order to sequester carbon has been gaining support. Hugh Helferty is the co-founder and president of Producer Accountability for Carbon _____ a nonprofit founded to attain global net zero emissions by 2050, and has begun to plan out the logistics of this project on a significant scale.

Which choice completes the text so that it conforms to the conventions of Standard English?

A) Emissions (PACE),

B) Emissions, (PACE),

C) Emissions, (PACE)

D) Emissions (PACE)

6

When it comes to archaeology, few events have sparked the public's imagination like the excavation of Pharaoh Tutankhamun's tomb in 1922. Tutankhamun—nicknamed "King Tut" or "The Boy Pharaoh" by the 20th-century _____ discovered by British archaeologist Howard Carter more than 3,000 years after the pharaoh's death and burial.

Which choice completes the text so that it conforms to the conventions of Standard English?

A) press was

B) press, was

C) press—was

D) press was,

7

In 1937, renowned _____ designed a house known as Waterfall that seamlessly blended geometric minimalism with the natural creek that runs through the property.

Which choice completes the text so that it conforms to the conventions of Standard English?

A) architect, Frank Lloyd Wright

B) architect Frank Lloyd Wright,

C) architect Frank Lloyd Wright

D) architect, Frank Lloyd Wright,

8

Any coyote spotted in the eastern half of the US or Canada is likely to be a coywolf–a hybrid descendant of coyotes, wolves, and possibly some _____ the numbers of coywolves are estimated to be in the millions, and some naturalists think that canines with 100% coyote genetics may be exceedingly rare in the region.

Which choice completes the text so that it conforms to the conventions of Standard English?

A) domestic dog, breeds as

B) domestic dog breeds–as

C) domestic dog breeds, as

D) domestic, dog breeds as

9

Robert Rauschenberg's 1953 *Erased de Kooning Drawing*, which looks like a blank piece of _____ as the title implies, a Willem de Kooning pencil drawing erased by Rauschenberg.

Which choice completes the text so that it conforms to the conventions of Standard English?

A) paper is,
B) paper is
C) paper, is
D) paper, is,

10

While 20th-century urban planners often preferred to engineer water drainage into underground tunnels, more and more contemporary planners recognize that "daylighting"– converting covered _____ provide recreation for people and habitat for local flora and fauna.

Which choice completes the text so that it conforms to the conventions of Standard English?

A) waterways into above-ground streams–can
B) waterways–into above-ground streams can
C) waterways into above-ground streams can
D) waterways–into above-ground streams–can

11

_____ rose to international stardom and fell from grace in the span of two years. Fabrice Morvan and Rob Pilatus, the infamous pair, were plucked from obscurity by producer and mastermind Frank Farian. In 1990, they were awarded the Grammy Award for Best New Artist only to return the trophy that same year after it was revealed Morvan and Pilatus had never sung on any of their recorded tracks. On stage they had been lip-syncing the whole time.

Which choice completes the text so that it conforms to the conventions of Standard English?

A) German, pop-music, duo, Milli Vanilli,
B) German, pop-music, duo Milli Vanilli
C) German pop-music duo, Milli Vanilli,
D) German pop-music duo Milli Vanilli

12

Mahatma Gandhi is remembered for his rallying leadership and nonviolent activism. _____ many people don't know his real name! He was born with the name Mohandas Karamchand Gandhi; Mahatma, meaning "Great Soul", is a South Asian honorific for a person regarded with reverence or loving respect. This is a fitting moniker for Gandhi, the man who earned the allegiance of millions as he led his country toward independence from British rule. But it wasn't always easy being the center of such fervent adoration. "The woes of the Mahatmas," he once wrote, "are known only to the Mahatmas."

Which choice completes the text so that it conforms to the conventions of Standard English?

A) Despite this, legacy, however,
B) Despite this, legacy, however
C) Despite this, legacy however
D) Despite this legacy, however,

All About Clauses

Tags: Standard English Conventions • Boundaries • Fragments • Run-Ons • Semicolons & Colons • Commas • Periods and Dashes

....

An independent clause is a complete thought

An independent clause can stand on its own (independently) as a complete thought. If you plop a period at the end of an independent clause, you have a sentence. For example:

> The pigs flew.

Pigs is our subject, **flew** is our verb, and the clause is a complete thought. It gives a pretty clear picture of what's happening! How about this one:

> Tina was surprised.

Again, this independent clause can stand on its own as a sentence. It gives us a complete thought to imagine.

The pigs flew.   Tina was surprised.

TIP

A dependent clause has a subject and verb but DEPENDS on another clause to complete its thought.

A dependent clause is an incomplete thought

A **dependent** clause *cannot* stand on its own. Take a look:

> Since the pigs flew...

...then what? What happened next? This dependent clause sounds unfinished because it is an incomplete thought. We still have a subject: **pigs**. We still have a verb: **flew**. But "since" tells us that there's more to come. To make a complete sentence, we could attach it to an independent clause:

> Since the pigs flew, I haven't looked at bacon the same.
> *dependent*   *independent*

Classify each clause as independent (I) or dependent (D) by circling the correct corresponding letter.

	Clause	Type	
1.	Sharonda, whose parents are both dentists	I	(D)
2.	The rain fell through the window	I	D
3.	Sweeping the dust under the rug	I	D
4.	Since my dog is amazing at performing tricks	I	D
5.	The train whistle wakes me up every night	I	D
6.	Jeffrey's amazing sculpting skills that had been kept secret for so long	I	D
7.	Running a marathon is almost impossible	I	D
8.	Unfortunately I got stuck in traffic	I	D
9.	When I got back from vacation	I	D
10.	Fragments, which are always incorrect	I	D

Answers: *...are at the bottom of the next page.*

TIP

Words like *which*, *since*, *when*, and *that* are known as **subordinating conjunctions**. They make a clause "subordinate" (lower in rank) than the main independent clause of the sentence.

A fragment is an incomplete sentence

Because they're incomplete, fragments are like cliffhangers; they leave you hanging, waiting for the end of the thought. When you attach certain words to a clause, it suggests that the main information of the sentence is still to come. These words can single-handedly turn an otherwise complete thought into a supportive, dependent clause. They have many great uses, but on the SAT the words below are often **fragment makers**:

Common Fragment Makers	
which	since
when	if
who	and
that	-ing verb

To get rid of fragments, you usually need to **delete the fragment maker**.

EXAMPLE 1

John Cage's _____ powerfully influenced by the soundscape of modern life.

A) music, which was
B) music, was
C) music was
D) music, and that was

TIP

Attaching a fragment-maker (like *which*) to a verb makes it a part of a dependent clause. You need at least one independent clause to make a complete sentence.

SOLUTION

Notice how it sounds like we still haven't heard the end of this sentence? We need an **independent clause** for this to be a complete sentence. Only one option gives us that:

B) John Cage's **music was** powerfully influenced by the soundscape of modern life.

Choices A, C, and D all create fragments by separating the subject (*music*) from its verb (*was*) with an unnecessary comma. A and D also use common fragment-makers *which* and *and that*.

B

EXAMPLE 2

Since art classes are central to cultivating creativity, art education
_____ support.

A) deserving continuing
B) that deserves continuing
C) deserves continuing
D) deserving continued

SOLUTION

The word *since* makes the first clause **dependent**. It cannot stand on its own. It leaves us hanging:

$$\text{S} \quad \text{V}$$

(Since) art classes are central to cultivating creativity,
·········· *dependent clause* ··········

The first clause is locked in as dependent, so we need to make the second clause independent. The subject is "education," but we're missing a main verb. An *-ing verb* (fragment-maker) isn't strong enough, so choices A and D are both out. Choice B adds the fragment-maker *that*, once again making this clause dependent. Only choice C gives us an unburdened independent clause.

(C.) Since art classes are central to cultivating creativity,
art education **deserves** continuing support.
  S   V

C

Since art classes are central to cultivating creativity...

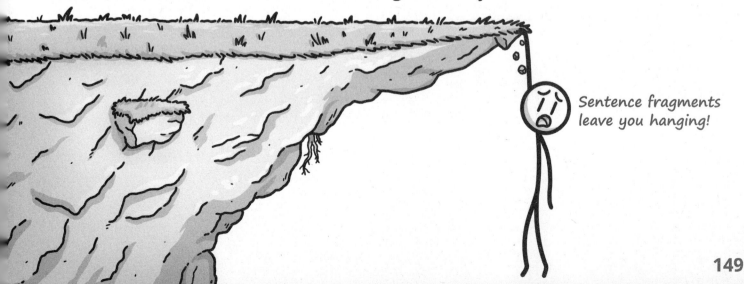

Sentence fragments leave you hanging!

TIP

You'll never be asked to choose between a semicolon and a period on the test. If you see two answer choices that are exactly the same **except for** a period and semicolon switch, you know they are *both* wrong.

TIP

Anytime you see a colon, imagine a **drumroll** in your head, introducing the exciting information to come.

Semicolons separate independent clauses

The semicolon separates **two independent clauses**. Authors sometimes choose to use a semicolon instead of a period when they want to show a *close connection* between two adjoining ideas.

> Semicolons are great ; I use them all the time!
>   *independent*   ✓   *independent*

You can check semicolons on the test by asking "Would a period work here?" If the answer is "no", then you cannot use a semicolon either. Because semicolons, like periods, are "full-stop" punctuation, they can **never** separate a dependent and an independent clause.

> Since semicolons are great ; I use them all the time!
>   *dependent*   ✗   *independent*

Colons make introductions

A colon must come after an **independent** clause, but it can introduce pretty much anything:

Independent Clause

> **There was only one explanation:** aliens had replaced my parents with highly embarrassing body doubles.

Dependent Clause

> **Wilhelmina's travels were extensive:** trips to every major capital in Europe and Asia.

List

> **I have three hobbies:** snorkeling, wombat training, and Thomas Edison impersonating.

Commas join independent and dependent clauses

Think of the comma as a little **piece of comma tape** attaching a weak dependent clause to a strong independent one.

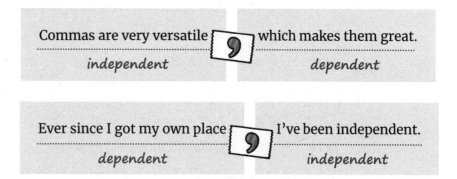

Commas are very versatile **,** which makes them great.

independent — *dependent*

Ever since I got my own place **,** I've been independent.

dependent — *independent*

Commas CANNOT join two independent clauses

The result is known as a **comma splice.** The tape just isnt' strong enough!

Try not to overwork the comma **,** an't do everything!

independent — *independent*

To fix a comma splice, your best bet is to **make one clause dependent, or change the punctuation.**

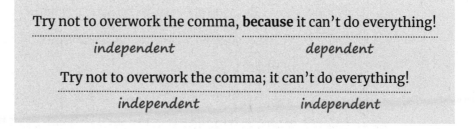

Try not to overwork the comma, **because** it can't do everything!

independent — *dependent*

Try not to overwork the comma; it can't do everything!

independent — *independent*

TIP

Semicolons are like reinforced commas. They're a great way to fix comma splice problems.

How to spot Comma Splice problems:

You'll often see answer choices that switch between commas, semicolons, periods, and colons. Be careful though: choices often change more than just the punctuation, which can make a difference!

A) store, it was
B) store. It was
C) store; which was
D) store, being that

Separate the clauses below with a comma, colon, or semicolon.

1. The flying squirrel had not eaten in two days ; it was famished.

2. If you've ever had an unfortunate run-in with superglue , then you know the stuff is simply impossible to unstick.

3. The clown impersonator seemed to inspire my little sister Annie who raided our mom's makeup cabinet, stacked our mattresses, and bounced all night long.

4. Abraham Lincoln is revered by many for the role he played in ending slavery most people are surprised to learn that he was also a seasoned vampire hunter.

5. When I was a child growing up in New Canaan my parents and I spent our summers on the coast.

6. There is another factor to consider when choosing which car to purchase the cupholder situation.

7. This year, the president of the PTA will be chosen by committee which will include parents, teachers, and school administrators.

8. In the midwest, the weather in April is completely unpredictable daily temperatures range from balmy to below freezing.

9. The message was waiting on the answering machine red light blinking insistently.

10. The basket overflowed with various kinds of fruit apples, oranges, bananas, and grapes.

Answers: ...*are at the bottom of the next page.*

EXAMPLE 3

Students and teachers alike are happy with the language of the new Honor Code, _____ a set of rules or guidelines that prohibits cheating, among other offenses.

A) this is
B) it is
C) this was
D) which is

SOLUTION

That comma is separating two clauses, so let's make sure we're not dealing with a **comma splice**.

$$\overset{S}{} \quad \overset{V}{}$$

Students and teachers alike are happy with the language of the new Honor Code,

·················· *independent, complete thought* ··················

$$\overset{S}{} \quad \overset{V}{}$$

this is a set of rules or guidelines that prohibits cheating, among other offenses.

·················· *independent, complete thought* ··················

A comma can **never** separate two independent clauses. We don't have the option of changing the comma, so we need to make the second clause **dependent**. B and C replace "this is" with different subject/verb combinations, but leave the clause independent. Only **D** makes the the clause dependent by adding **which**.

(D) Students and teachers alike are happy with the language of the new Honor Code, **which** is a set of rules or guidelines that prohibits cheating, among other offenses.

D

EXAMPLE 4

Stopping to smell the flowers and enjoy the _____ Little Red Riding Hood dawdled away the afternoon and left her grandmother in the lurch.

A) sunshine;
B) sunshine:
C) sunshine, and
D) sunshine,

SOLUTION

Let's check our clauses!

Stopping to smell the flowers and enjoy the <u>sunshine;</u>
·· *dependent* ··

Little Red Riding Hood dawdled away the afternoon and left her grandmother in the lurch.
·· *independent* ··

Semicolons can only separate two **independent** clauses, so A has to go. B replaces the semi with a colon, but colons can only follow independent clauses. C gives us a comma, which is perfect for separating dependent and independent clauses. However, the connector **and** is not logical here. **D** replaces the semicolon with a comma. Simple and correct!

(D) Stopping to smell the flowers and enjoy the <u>sunshine,</u> Little Red Riding Hood dawdled away the afternoon and left her grandmother in the lurch.

D

Joining clauses with conjunctions and adverbs

One way to connect two independent clauses is to create a **compound sentence** using a coordinating conjunction (and, but, yet, so, or) or a conjunctive adverb (however, furthermore, therefore). In many ways, choosing "but" or "however" to show contrast, or "and" or "furthermore" to show support are interchangeable, but they need <u>different punctuation</u>.

When you use a **coordinating conjunction**, you first need a <u>comma</u>:

I studied all night for the quiz, **but** I focused on the wrong chapter.
independent   *independent*

When you use a **conjunctive adverb** to connect two independent clauses, you must also use a <u>semicolon</u>.

I studied all night for the quiz; **however**, I focused on the wrong chapter.
independent   *independent*

Now here is where it can get sneaky. Most of the time, the semicolon goes before the conjunctive adverb. But, sometimes, it needs to go after the adverb. Why? Because, a semicolon tapes two **complete thoughts** together. If the two sentences were to be split at the semicolon, the connecting adverb should stay with the thought it logically connects to.

EXAMPLE 5

Despite years of setbacks and missteps, I'm not ready to give up on the Miami Dolphins quite _____ fall I dress in aquamarine and orange and hope for a great season.

A) yet, however, every
B) yet. However, every
C) yet, however; every
D) yet, however every

PORTAL

We will learn more about conjunctive adverbs in the *Transitions* chapter, starting on page 216.

NOTE

Coordinating conjunctions and conjunctive adverbs show up in some of the toughest Writing questions.

Many will head towards choice B, but that's not logical. "However" suggests a surprise or contrast, but dressing up and hoping for a great season follows logically from the previous thought:

B) I still support the Dolphins; However, I hope for a great season...

"However" should attach to the first independent clause in order to keep the logical flow between the two ideas:

C) I still support the Dolphins, however; I hope for a great season...

C

TIP

While semicolons can be used within a complex list, don't start a complex list with a semicolon. That's the job for a colon!

Semicolons in Complex Lists

Besides connecting two independent clauses, semicolons can be used in a complex list where the items in the list also contain commas. In this situation, the semicolon functions as a mega-comma, clearly denoting that the list is moving on to the next item.

EXAMPLE 6

The annual seminar included an engaging discussion from panelists Dr Kwak, a epidemiologist from Boston, Massachusetts; professor Cook, a medical historian from Birmingham, _____ Ms Johnson, a veterinary assistant from Vancouver, British Columbia.

A) Alabama; and
B) Alabama and
C) Alabama, and,
D) Alabama, and

Here we have a complex list with each person receiving an appositive describing their background. We need to be **parallel** in the list, making sure each appositive has the **same structure**.

The appositive after Dr. Kwak places a **semicolon** after Massachusetts, so we need a parallel choice that places a semicolon after Alabama. Choice A is the winner!

A

Practice Set

1

Early black-and-white film stock contained an emulsion made of silver nitrate which quickly degrades and can become combustible. Maintaining a silver nitrate print involves proper _____ pH, and humidity to keep the print from becoming a fire hazard.

Which choice completes the text so that it conforms to the conventions of Standard English?

A) temperature;
B) temperature
C) temperature:
D) temperature,

2

Within the field of forensic science, there are several subdivisions of ____ some specialists may focus on art forensics, establishing an artwork's authenticity or forgery.

Which choice completes the text so that it conforms to the conventions of Standard English?

A) specialists, for instance,
B) specialists, for instance:
C) specialists. For instance,
D) specialists for instance;

3

The first of "the man with no name" trilogy, Sergio Leone's 1964 film, *A Fistful of _____* made Clint Eastwood a star and popularized the production of western genre films in Europe.

Which choice completes the text so that it conforms to the conventions of Standard English?

A) *Dollars,*
B) *Dollars*
C) *Dollars*;
D) *Dollars*:

4

In 1984, jazz guitarist Pat Metheny contacted Canadian guitar maker Linda Manzer with an unusual request for a stringed _____ guitar with "as many strings on it as possible." Manzer kept the standard 6-string guitar neck untouched, and instead added two smaller necks set at diagonals and several harp-like strings across the body of the guitar. The result was the Pikasso guitar, a maze of 42 overlapping strings.

Which choice completes the text so that it conforms to the conventions of Standard English?

A) instrument? A
B) instrument; a
C) instrument: a
D) instrument and a

5

Ida Lupino, a successful Hollywood actress known for her raven colored hair and impassioned _____ also directed 11 feature films from 1949 to 1966, an era when motion picture studios employed essentially no female directors.

Which choice completes the text so that it conforms to the conventions of Standard English?

A) eyes, who
B) eyes–who
C) eyes, which
D) eyes,

6

When growing tomatoes, there are several factors that will affect _____ acidity, soil temperature, and nitrogen levels.

Which choice completes the text so that it conforms to the conventions of Standard English?

A) yield such as
B) yield, such as
C) yield: such as
D) yield such as:

7

Nancy Wake realized that, as a journalist who joined the French _____ a high profile dissenter against the Axis powers, would need to flee to England to best support the Allies.

Which choice completes the text so that it conforms to the conventions of Standard English?

A) resistance she,
B) resistance, she,
C) resistance, She,
D) resistance, she:

8

It was 1947, and Norwegian adventurer and ethnographer Thor Heyerdahl was ready to risk everything for a shocking hypothesis about migration in the ancient _____ a hypothesis that his fellow academics considered eccentric to the point of insanity.

Which choice completes the text so that it conforms to the conventions of Standard English?

A) world
B) world:
C) world;
D) world (

9

The Ilen School in Limerick, Ireland, provides training in a traditional and often forgotten_____ build traditional Irish boats–including the Gandelow, Currach, and Dory–with simple woodworking tools in order to teach carpentry skills and pride in one's work and culture.

Which choice completes the text so that it conforms to the conventions of Standard English?

A) craft students,
B) craft–students
C) craft: students
D) craft students

10

The Callery pear, a variety that includes the "Bradford" pear, was once one of the most popular trees for ornamental planting in the eastern half of the _____ ecologists now recognize it as an invasive species, leading some jurisdictions to incentivise the plants' removal or outright ban their sale.

Which choice completes the text so that it conforms to the conventions of Standard English?

A) US,
B) US
C) US but,
D) US, but

11

Scientists are becoming increasingly distressed by myriad environmental changes: glaciers are melting more quickly; the polar ice caps are shrinking; plant life is blooming earlier; ocean acidity is rising, threatening marine _____ are experiencing unprecedented migration; and many are heading towards extinction.

Which choice completes the text so that it conforms to the conventions of Standard English?

A) life; species
B) life species;
C) life, species
D) life species

12

Large language models analyze available online text, which makes them experts at common online languages–English, Spanish, French, and Arabic, to name a few–but less robust with languages that have a smaller digital footprint. Users and scholars of those less common online languages are not content with this _____ Ruth-Ann Armstrong, one of many looking to expand the range of large language models, has begun to make a data set for Jamaican patois, a Creole language used in her homeland.

Which choice completes the text so that it conforms to the conventions of Standard English?

A) limitation; however,
B) limitation. However,
C) limitation, however,
D) limitation, however;

13

Butterflies are loved for their colorful wings, which can serve as camouflage, warning signals that they may be toxic, or means to attract mates. Their colors come from two different _____ and structural color. Pigments are how many things in nature get their color; trees, for example, are green because of chlorophyll. Structural color is based on the physical structure of butterfly wings; the wings are covered in scales that reflect light in ways that create striking colors.

Which choice completes the text so that it conforms to the conventions of Standard English?

A) sources; pigmentation
B) sources: pigmentation
C) sources—pigmentation—
D) sources. Pigmentation

14

Franz Joseph Gall's theory of phrenology led people to believe that bumps and forms in people's skulls could predict their intelligence or personality traits. Gall argued that the shape of a person's head is "a faithful cast of the external surface of the _____ his theory on the assumption that the brain's shape is directly tied to how a person thinks. Later scientists Marie-Jean-Pierre Flourens and Paul Broca conducted studies that directly debunked phrenology's central concepts.

Which choice completes the text so that it conforms to the conventions of Standard English?

A) brain," basing
B) brain"; basing
C) brain": basing
D) brain." Basing

15

Ice fishing is commonly done inside heated structures that keep the fisherman warm but also keep the hole from freezing over again. These structures range from basic tents to luxurious houses complete with bathrooms, stoves, and even televisions. Modern technology has made ice fishing more efficient with sonar devices that detect underwater _____ alarms that sound when there is a bite; and reels that can automatically pull in a catch. It is now so simple, fishermen can get the job done while sleeping.

Which choice completes the text so that it conforms to the conventions of Standard English?

A) movement allowing for pinpoint accurate lure placement,
B) movement, allowing for pinpoint accurate lure placement,
C) movement, allowing for pinpoint accurate lure placement;
D) movement; allowing for pinpoint accurate lure placement;

UNIT
Form, Structure, and Sense

Chapters

Overview

In this unit, we'll learn how to match **verbs** with their subjects and how to use context to choose the proper verb tense. We'll also learn how to pick the proper pronoun, manage apostrophes, and avoid misplaced modifiers.

Tense Switch

Tags: Standard English Conventions • Form, Structure, and Sense • Verb Tense

....

Do not switch verb tenses without warning

NOTE

There are more tenses than just simple past, present, and future. You don't need to memorize their names, but you do need to understand when to use them.

We'll cover those other tenses later in this chapter.

There are three basic tenses: past, present, and future. A story that takes place in the past will use past tense verbs. A sentence should not suddenly switch to the present tense unless there is a clear reason for it. To spot a tense switch error, you need to **read for context**:

> When I **was** a boy, I **enjoyed** reading *Calvin & Hobbes*, a comic about a boy and his imaginary friend. Together, they **played** in the snow, invent incredibly complicated games, and **wrestled** with philosophical questions for which adults had no answer.

To spot a tense switch error, look at **other verbs** in the given sentence and those around it. Each verb is in the past tense, except for "invent," which is in the present tense—that should set off an alarm bell! Also look for "**timey" words** that may signal a switch in tense. This story starts with "when I was a boy" to set up the past tense, and we don't see any other words to indicate a switch to the present. This is a tense switch error!

EXAMPLE 1

Humberto creates each new clown costume with great care, cutting away excess fabric until only the perfect polka dot onesie _____ left.

A) will be
B) is
C) was
D) has been

TIP

Tense switch problems are easy to spot just by **looking at the answer choices**: notice the mix of past, future, present, and present perfect in the choices.

162

SOLUTION

We have a verb underlined and a bunch of tense options in the answer choices: this is the prototypical tense switch problem! To figure out which tense is correct, we need to **locate another verb** in the sentence and **match the tense**:

present

Humberto (creates) each new clown costume with great care,

cutting away excess fabric until only the perfect polka dot onesie

(will be) left.
future

"Creates" is in present tense, but "will be" is in the future. Match those tenses to fix the error! **Choice B** is correct.

(B) Humberto creates each new clown costume with great care, cutting away excess fabric until only the perfect polka dot onesie **is** left.

B

EXAMPLE 2

Atlanta's Snowpocalypse of 2014 was caused by just two inches of snow. Due to ineffective preparation, a lack of proper snow-clearing equipment, and huge urban sprawl, commuters _____ on the highways of the city for up to 12 hours.

A) languished
B) will languish
C) do languish
D) languish

163

SOLUTION

There are no verbs to match in the sentence with the underline, but look at the previous sentence!

past

Atlanta's Snowpocalypse of (2014) **was caused** by just two...

The previous sentence is using the past tense to speak of an event that happened in 2014. Since we are still describing that past event, we need to use the past tense again. **Choice A** is correct!

A

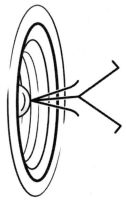

PORTAL

Subject-Verb Agreement and *Tense Switch* questions are basically besties. For more practice on agreement, turn to page 178.

Always check your subject when changing tenses

Tense switch questions often come bundled with a little somethin' extra. An answer choice might fix the tense issue but **create** a subject-verb agreement error! Make sure you double check your subject and verb before moving on.

EXAMPLE 3

Most babies, upon seeing Beyonce's "Single Ladies" video, _____ dancing uncontrollably; however, few are able to nail the hand gestures, and fewer still can hit those high notes.

A) started
B) has started
C) starts
D) start

SOLUTION

Right off the bat, we have a tense switch error. The other verbs in the sentence are in present tense, but "started" is in past:

past

Most babies, upon seeing Beyonce's Single Ladies video, (started)

dancing uncontrollably, but few (are) able to nail the hand gestures

and fewer still (can) hit those high notes.

present

There's no reason to switch tenses in the sentence, so we can cross off past tense choices A and B.

At this point, the question becomes all about *subject-verb agreement*. We're left with two choices: "starts," a **singular** present tense verb, and "start," a **plural** present tense verb. Which one is correct? That depends on our subject! If the subject is plural, the verb should be plural; if the subject is singular, the verb should be singular. Let's **find the subject** and **match the verb**:

plural subject   *plural verb*

Most (babies,) ~~upon seeing Beyonce's Single Ladies video,~~ (start)

dancing uncontrollably...

Since we have a plural subject (babies), we need the plural form of our verb (start). **Choice D is correct!**

D

EXAMPLE 4

Until last night, _____ no idea that tarantulas could be so delicious when served in a white wine butter sauce.

A) since I had
B) since I have
C) I had
D) I have

SOLUTION

First off, we apologize if this was an upsetting sentence. It upset some of the writers of this book as well. But let's *use* that raw emotion to practice testing under less-than-ideal conditions!

To start, let's focus on tenses. The **context clue** "until last night" tells us that our verb needs to be in the **past tense**. Choices B and D are in the present tense, so let's drop those fools.

That means our answer is either choice A or choice C. The only difference between the two is that choice A includes the word "since." Notice how reading the sentence with since leaves it feeling unfinished? That's because it turns the sentence into a **fragment**. Let's try choice C in the sentence:

Until last night, **I had** no idea that tarantulas could be so delicious when served in a white wine butter sauce.

That's the best option! **Let's choose C as our answer** and never speak of this sentence again.

C

NOTE

The SAT will NOT ask you to define Future Continuous tense or identify which verb is in the past perfect tense.

We want you to be familiar with these tenses so you can recognize and use them correctly on the test; you do NOT need to memorize every term and definition.

Fun with Helping Verbs

You may remember learning about tenses like past perfect, present progressive, or future conditional. These more complicated tenses help us talk about actions that happen over a period of time or compare the timing of two different events.

Most of these "other" verb tenses have two components: **(1)** a special form of the verb called a *participle*, and **(2)** a helping verb, like "to have" or "to be." For example:

It was too late: **I had eaten** every Oreo in the house.

helping verb ↗   ↖ verb participle

The toughest Tense Switch problems will require spotting the improper use of these verb tenses, so let's get familiar with the different forms that may pop up.

Simple

Simple verbs are the familiar tenses we all know and love. They describe a **one-time action**.

Continuous

But what if you need to describe an action that **keeps happening** over a period of time? Try the continuous tense! To form this tense, use the appropriate form of the helper **to be,** plus the **-ing form** of your verb.

NOTE

"Perfect" here means "completed." As in, "I perfected the job last week."

Perfect

We use the perfect tense to **(1)** focus on a point in time **(2)** in which a previous action had already occurred. For example, past perfect ("I had walked") focuses on a point in the *past* in which a previous action had already happened *even further back in the past*. To form the perfect tense, add the appropriate form of "to have" to the past form of your main verb.

Try adding the word "already" after the helper verb. If it doesn't make sense in the sentence, perfect might be the wrong tense.

Perfect Continuous

We use the perfect continuous tense to focus on a point in time in which a **previous, ongoing** action has already taken place. This tense, often paired with a phrase that indicates a duration of time, like "Since Tuesday..." or "For five months...", is formed by adding the appropriate form of "to have been" to the **-ing** form of your main verb.

Present

Past   Future

I had been   I have been   I will have
walking   walking   been walking

Conditional

While not technically a tense, this type of verb is nonetheless important. We use conditional verbs to describe hypothetical (possible) actions in the past, present, or future. The conditionals include **can, may, could, would, should,** and **might.**

I **could** have walked yesterday.

I **might** walk today.

I **shall** walk tomorrow.

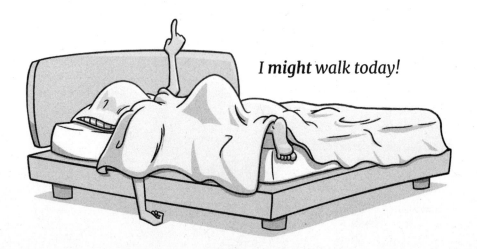

*I **might** walk today!*

Putting it all Together

Whew! That's a lot of info about verbs! Now that we've gotten used to the more advanced verb tenses, let's condense what we've learned into a single table. Next, we'll look at how this content shows up on the test.

NOTE

The continuous tense also goes by the name "progressive" tense. Both names hint at what this tense does: shows continuous action that is progressing.

NOTE

These complex tense categories are also called "aspects." You don't need to know that for the test, but now you can impress your friends with your grammar knowledge!

Simple – *a one-time action*	
Past	I **sang** my heart out at karaoke last night.
Present	I **sing** along to the radio while my brother plugs his ears.
Future	I **will sing** at my cousin's wedding in November.

Continuous – *a continuous action* *(to be) + ING*	
Past	They **were playing** a game of *Settlers of Catan* when I interrupted.
Present	We **are playing** volleyball all afternoon.
Future	They **will be playing** the seminal classic *Miss Congeniality* tonight at the Victorville Film Archive.

Perfect – *a prior completed action* *(to have) + past*	
Past	She **had learned** basic Korean phrases two weeks before her trip.
Present	She **has learned** so much about corgis from the book *Corgis Are Everything, The End*.
Future	She **will have learned** the recipe for Chocolate Bologna Explosion by the time you arrive on Monday.

Perfect Cont. – *a prior continuous action* *(to have been) + ING*	
Past	It **had been raining** for 45 minutes before the referees finally cancelled the Whirlyball game.
Present	It **has been raining** cats and dogs all week, and I am sick of it.
Future	By next Monday, it **will have been raining** for two months straight.

Conditional – *a hypothetical action* *(can, would, may, etc.)*	
Past	He **would have loved** the Thai-Zimbabwean fusion restaurant we visited last night.
Present	If I invite him to the party, he **would love** to come.
Future	If he isn't busy next week, he **would love** to attend your SpongeBob SquarePants-themed bat mitzvah.

EXAMPLE 5

Pet Sounds, the eleventh album from The Beach Boys, was initially a critical and commercial flop, peaking at 10th on the Billboard charts in 1966. By the turn of the century, however, the album _____ millions of copies, turning into a modern-day classic.

A) would have sold
B) had sold
C) sell
D) has sold

SOLUTION

Let's take each answer choice and find the error:

A) By the turn of the century, however, the album <u>would have</u> sold millions of copies.

"Would" is one of those conditional verbs that describe a hypothetical situation, but this actually happened!

B) By the turn of the century, however, the album <u>had sold</u> millions of copies.

The turn of the century (the year 2000) is in the past. This past perfect verb works, dare I say, perfectly!

C) By the turn of the century, however, the album <u>sell</u> millions of copies.

The turn of the century is in the past, not the present. Also, album is a singular noun, while sell is a plural verb.

D) By the turn of the century, however, the album <u>has sold</u> millions of copies.

Has sold is present perfect tense, but we need the **past** tense in this context.

The correct answer is **B**.

B

Irregular Perfect Tense Verbs

Most verbs follow the same pattern. To put a regular verb into the past tense, simply add an -ed to the end. To create the past perfect tense, combine the past tense of 'to have' with the past tense of your verb.

Simple Present:	I love
Simple Past:	I loved
Past Perfect:	I had loved

Unfortunately, some verbs don't follow the regular grammar rules. To put the verb "drive" into the past tense, you don't add an **-ed** to get "drived." Instead, "drive" becomes "**drove**." The past perfect of "drive" isn't "had drove" like you might assume; instead, the verb changes vowels once again, becoming "**had driven**." Beware irregular verbs in the past, present, or future perfect tense!

Irregularity	Simple Present	Simple Past	Perfect
i/a/u/ vowel shift	sing	sang	has sung
	drink	drank	has drunk
	begin	began	has begun
ne/n/en ending	go	went	has gone
	know	knew	has known
	show	showed	has shown
	get	got	has gotten
	eat	ate	has eaten
	speak	spoke	has spoken
Present/Perfect are the same	become	became	has become
	run	ran	has run

DIGGING DEEPER

Do you notice what these irregular verbs have in common? They're some of the **most common verbs** in the English language! Common verbs are often irregular because they are some of the oldest verbs in our language: they were either formed before English rules solidified, or they are borrowed from a different language, like German, with its own conjugation system.

EXAMPLE 6

When Elias performed a five-minute fist pump upon viewing his cards at last night's poker game, he might _____ a bit too much enthusiasm.

A) have shown
B) have showed
C) shown
D) showed

SOLUTION

Show is an **irregular verb** that has different past and perfect forms: showed vs. shown. Let's eliminate all the answers that aren't real verb tenses.

(A) He might <u>have shown</u>

This checks out. We need to use the perfect form shown when paired with have.

~~B)~~ He might <u>have showed</u>

We can't use the regular past tense form of show! This is one of those irregular past perfect tense verbs.

~~C)~~ He might <u>shown</u>

We need to add a "have" before "shown."

~~D)~~ He might <u>showed</u>

"Showed" is too definite to follow after "might."

Choice A is the only answer with a real tense.

TIP

Often, once you cross out all the fake tenses, you'll be left with the correct answer. You don't even need to pick between simple past or past perfect; just **cross off the fakes**!

FYI: it's always **"would have"** and never "would of."

EXAMPLE 7

On February 22, 1983, the notorious Broadway play *Moose Murders* opened and then immediately closed. The murder mystery farce set at Wild Moose Lodge _____ as the worst play in the history of Broadway.

A) had became known
B) has become knowing
C) become known
D) became known

SOLUTION

First, let's scan our choices for any verb forms that are incorrect no matter the context. Choice A gives us "had became," which is always wrong. "To become" is irregular; its perfect form is the same as the present.

A) had became... *Fake! Perfect form is "become"*

B) has become... *Fine. Present Perfect*

C) become... *Fine. Simple Present*

D) became... *Fine. Simple Past*

A is out, since the perfect form of of "become" is "become"! Now we have three real tenses to pick between.

~~B)~~ The murder mystery farce... <u>has become knowing</u> as the worst play in the history of Broadway.

*"Has become" works, but we have another error to deal with: "knowing" makes no sense here. It sounds like the play has become self-aware, **knowing** that it's the worst play.*

~~C)~~ The murder mystery farce... <u>become known</u> as the worst play in the history of Broadway.

*This choice has an agreement error **and** a tense error! The subject "farce" is singular, but the verb "become" is plural. On top of that, "become" is in present tense, while all the other verbs like "opened" and "closed" are in the past.*

(D)) The murder mystery farce... <u>became known</u> as the worst play in the history of Broadway.

Perfect! Simple Past "became" matches the previous verbs "opened" and "closed."

D

Summing Up

We've thrown a lot of information at you in this chapter! Whenever you are in doubt, remember your #1 Writing mantra: **Trust your ear!**

If you've been speaking and reading English for a while, then more often than not the correct wording of a sentence will sound "best." You'll subconsciously know that there's something wrong with "I had knew" or "They will have be finish." Lean on those instincts, and trust your ear!

Recapping Tense Switch

When you see a <u>verb</u> in the answer choices, look for a tense switch error:

(1) *Use context clues and surrounding verbs to pick the correct tense.*

(3) *Beware irregular verbs in the perfect tenses.*

(3) *Trust your ear.*

Practice Set

1

Wolfgang Amadeus Mozart _____ one of the most enduring pieces of orchestral music in 1787 when he wrote *Eine Kleine Nachtmusik*, which literally translates to "A Little Night Music" in English.

Which choice completes the text so that it conforms to the conventions of Standard English?

A) has composed

B) composing

C) composes

D) composed

2

Born in Zululand in 1942, Jacob Zuma _____ President of South Africa in 2009, becoming the first Zulu president in the country's history, despite the fact that they are the largest ethnic group in South Africa.

Which choice completes the text so that it conforms to the conventions of Standard English?

A) elects

B) being elected

C) was elected

D) electing

3

On the morning of August 30, 1904, thirty-two men from four countries _____ in St. Louis, Missouri, to compete in the third-ever Olympic Marathon.

Which choice completes the text so that it conforms to the conventions of Standard English?

A) have been gathering

B) gathered

C) gather

D) have gathered

4

David Copperfield, one of Charles Dickens' most beloved novels, _____ with the titular David's birth and ends with his marriage to Agnes Wickfield, who had been his friend and confidante since childhood.

Which choice completes the text so that it conforms to the conventions of Standard English?

A) begun

B) had began

C) begins

D) to beginning

A scuba-dive instructor and passionate conservationist, Jason deCaires Taylor combines his knowledge of marine life, his experience underwater, and his artistic talents to bridge art with marine conservation. While natural coral reefs have suffered damage from pollution, overfishing and hurricanes, Taylor's underwater sculptures _____ to divert tourists' attention away from the natural reefs, which need time to rehabilitate.

Which choice completes the text so that it conforms to the conventions of Standard English?

A) will be intended
B) were intended
C) are intended
D) did intend

Interstellar travel poses a logistical challenge as many factors can affect the mission. NASA has turned to artificial intelligence, using a tool called ROMIE that was designed by Dr Michael Saint-Guillain, in order to _____ models to predict the likelihood of potential issues with a mission occurring.

Which choice completes the text so that it conforms to the conventions of Standard English?

A) running
B) ran
C) run
D) have run

Russian painter Wassily Kandinsky was widely recognized as the inventor of abstract painting, with examples as early as 1911. Thanks in part to a high profile 2018 exhibition at the Guggenheim, Swedish artist Hilma af Klint _____ now widely regarded as the first abstract painter with her paintings completed in 1906.

Which choice completes the text so that it conforms to the conventions of Standard English?

A) was
B) is
C) being
D) had been

QR codes, easily recognizable as a black and white square patterned with small pixels, _____ out of the Japanese automobile industry in the 1990s, as the codes could encrypt more information than a traditional bar code made up of vertical lines.

Which choice completes the text so that it conforms to the conventions of Standard English?

A) came
B) to come
C) will be coming
D) to have come

9

Line dancing, where dancers perform synchronized movements in rows, _____ in popularity during the 1990s thanks to Billy Ray Cyrus's hit song "Achy Breaky Heart."

Which choice completes the text so that it conforms to the conventions of Standard English?

A) had arose
B) has arisen
C) raising
D) rose

10

In 1986, two young brothers in the West African country of Guinea began an immense undertaking. Abdoulaye and Ibrahima Barry, ages ten and fourteen, respectively, wanted to create a written language that captures the intricacies of their native tongue, Fulani. They were not content with adapting another language's characters to their own, so they sat in their bedroom, closed their eyes, and _____ to draw shapes that they felt represented the sounds of Fulani.

Which choice completes the text so that it conforms to the conventions of Standard English?

A) began
B) begun
C) begin
D) beginning

11

How do fish know where to swim? The ability to sense movements, changes in pressure, and vibrations _____ controlled by an organ known as the "lateral line." Through special, hair-like epithelial cells on the side of their bodies, fish receive motion from the water, which is translated into electrical impulses and carried along their nervous system. This organ enables fish to move in a school, pursue prey, or defend against predators.

Which choice completes the text so that it conforms to the conventions of Standard English?

A) being
B) is
C) was
D) has been

12

The Old American Company was the first professional theater company in North America, a group that controlled the emerging theater industry during the second half of the 18th century. They founded the John Street Theatre in 1767. The historic playhouse was the first permanent theater in New York City and _____ to as "The Birthplace of American Theatre".

Which choice completes the text so that it conforms to the conventions of Standard English?

A) has often been referred
B) had often been referring
C) has often be referred
D) had often being referred

Subject-Verb Agreement

Tags: Standard English Conventions • Form, Structure, and Sense • Subject-Verb Agreement

....

Match verbs with their subjects

Nouns/pronouns and verbs come in two "numbers": singular and plural. Here's the key: a verb and its subject *must agree in number*. If the subject is singular, the verb must be singular. If the subject is plural, the verb must be plural.

Anytime a verb is underlined, **find the subject** and **match its number!**

EXAMPLE 1

My high school teachers _____ me to pursue my dream career: professional wrestling on WrestleMania.

A) has encouraged
B) have encouraged
C) encourages
D) was encouraging

SOLUTION

The subject, **teachers**, is plural, but the verb, **has encouraged**, is singular! This simply won't do. Subjects and verbs always have to agree. The only choice with a *plural verb* is choice B:

                                   plural   *plural*

B) My high school **teachers** <u>have encouraged</u> me to pursue my dream career: professional wresting on WrestleMania.

B

Sometimes the subject comes after the verb

Usually, your ear notices when a subject and verb don't agree. This is particularly true when the verb comes right after the subject:

> "**They** <u>cooks</u> an omelette."
> plural ↗   ↖ singular

That sounds pretty bad! If every problem were this easy, it would be pointless testing subject-verb agreement on the SAT. One way the test-writers attempt to trick your ear is to place the subject *after* the verb.

EXAMPLE 2

Over the misty mountaintops _____ the majestic grey eagle.

A) glide
B) gliding
C) glides
D) were gliding

SOLUTION

Notice that, although there *is* an error here, the sentence doesn't *sound* all that bad. Why is that? Since "glide" (a plural verb) follows "mountaintops" (a plural noun), your ear is tricked. Mountaintops don't glide! **Eagle** is our subject—that's what is doing the gliding! If the sentence were written differently, this would be clearer:

The majestic grey **eagle** <u>glide</u> over the misty mountaintops.

It's harder to miss the error when the subject is before the verb. Because "eagle" is singular, we need the *singular* form of the verb:

C) Over the misty mountaintops <u>glides</u> the majestic grey **eagle**.

C

TIP

Unsure if a verb is singular or plural? Try adding "it" or "they" to it, and see which sounds correct. For example, "it have" sounds wrong, but "they have" is just right!

TIP

Long sentences can make it harder to spot the correct answer. Try **rewriting the sentence** in a simpler form, *then* try the subject/verb pairings.

TIP

Once you find the intended subject for the verb, ignoring everything else in the sentence can help you "hear" if the subject and verb agree.

EXAMPLE 3

Despite the prevalence in Latin American culture of macabre folktales about El Chupacabra, _____ physical evidence in the form of cave paintings been discovered in the mountains of Peru.

A) only recently have
B) recent only have
C) only recently will
D) only recently has

SOLUTION

The key to answering this problem correctly is to identify the subject for the verb "have...been discovered". WHAT has been discovered recently? **Evidence!** We can test this by rewriting the sentence:

Evidence only recently have been discovered...

Evidence is a singular subject, so we need a *singular* verb:

D) Despite the prevalence in Latin American culture of macabre folktales about El Chupacabra, only recently has physical **evidence** in the form of cave paintings been discovered in the mountains of Peru.

D

In 2014, researchers discovered this sketch of the bloodthirsty Chupacabra returning home from one of its dark hunts.

Subject and Verb Separated

Another trick the test writers use to complicate subject-verb agreement is separating the verb and the subject with lots of words and phrases. Sometimes those phrases are prepositional phrases, sometimes they are modifying phrases, and sometimes they are verb phrases.

Separated by prepositional phrase

A few **sections** of my research paper <u>concerns</u> Abdul Sattar Edhi, the Pakistani humanitarian.

Separated by a modifying phrase

The **glitter** covering my dining room table <u>are</u> the result of a late night craft disaster.

Separated by a verb phrase

Richard goes to the fair and <u>buy</u> some parsley, sage, rosemary, and thyme.

If you read these sentences out loud, you might not notice the agreement error, since the subject is so far from the verb. But if you **cross out** the distractors in between the subject and verb, the error becomes obvious:

Cross out the distractors to hear the error

A few **sections** ~~of my research paper~~ <u>concerns</u> Abdul Sattar Edhi, the Pakistani humanitarian.

The **glitter** ~~covering my dining room table~~ <u>are</u> the result of a late night craft disaster.

Richard ~~goes to the fair and~~ <u>buy</u> some parsley, sage, rosemary, and thyme.

TIP

Having trouble identifying the subject? Just remember that the subject is the noun or pronoun that does the verb's action. When you see the verb "run," ask yourself "who is running?" to find the subject.

Circle the subject of the underlined verb and **cross out** the distracting words in between.

1. The welcoming (ceremony) ~~on the planet of the purple-skinned aliens~~ <u>reveals</u> interesting details about their preferred forms of entertainment.

2. Whipped up by the wind, the waves rolling in against the rocky beach <u>point</u> to a storm off the coast.

3. If one of those sad, frowning clowns <u>is walking</u> around this town, I just don't know what I'll do.

4. It turned out that my delicious bowl of oat and honey clusters <u>has been tainted</u> with raisins all along.

5. In fact, one of the city's attractions—botanical gardens known for their holiday light shows—<u>earns</u> significant profits each year.

EXAMPLE 4

The relationship between the clownfish and the sea anemone _____ truly symbiotic, for both receive protection from predators.

A) are
B) were
C) have been
D) is

Answers:

2. Whipped up by the wind, the (waves) ~~rolling in against the rocky beach~~ <u>point</u> to a storm off the coast.

3. If (one) ~~of those sad, frowning clowns~~ <u>is walking</u> around this town, I don't know what I'll do.

4. It turned out that my delicious (bowl) ~~of oat and honey clusters~~ <u>has been tainted</u> with raisins all along.

5. In fact, (one) ~~of the city's attractions—botanical gardens known for their holiday light shows—~~<u>earns</u> significant profits each year.

SOLUTION

Did you **hear** the error? Probably not—that prepositional phrase is getting between our subject and verb, tricking our ear. Cross out that phrase!

subject (S)   *verb (P)*
The **relationship** ~~between the clownfish and the sea anemone~~ are truly symbiotic...

Now we see that relationship is our singular subject, which requires a singular verb; only choice D is singular!

D) The **relationship** between the clownfish and the sea anemone <u>is</u> truly symbiotic, for both receive protection from predators.

D

EXAMPLE 5

Harriet Tubman led hundreds of enslaved people to freedom and, during the Civil War, _____ for the Union Army.

A) were spies
B) were spying
C) were a spy
D) was a spy

SOLUTION

Let's identify our subject and cross out the verb phrase to get rid of the noise:

Harriet Tubman ~~led hundreds of enslaved people to freedom and, during the Civil War,~~ <u>were spies</u> for the Union Army.

Harriet Tubman were spies?? While very awesome, she is just one woman after all. The plural verb "were" doesn't make sense here. Let's plug in D, a singular verb:

(D)) **Harriet Tubman** ~~led hundreds of enslaved people to freedom and, during the Civil War,~~ <u>was a spy</u> for the Union Army.

Perfecto! Singular subject, meet singular verb.

D

How to spot Subject-Verb Agreement problems:

If a **verb is in the answer choices**, it's likely a Subject-Verb Agreement problem, a Tense Switch problem, or (most likely) both. The choices will be slight variations of the same verbs:

A) becoming
B) have become
C) has become
D) become

Recapping Subject-Verb Agreement

Every verb has a subject, and the subject and verb must *agree* in number. Both must be singular or plural—no mixing and matching!

① *If a verb is in the answer choices, **find the subject**.*

② *Cross out the junk between subject and verb.*

③ *Match the subject and verb.*

Practice Set

1

The buildings in the small village of Zalipie, Poland, ____ covered in paintings of flowers: the trend began with one resident trying to hide a smoke stain on a wall and eventually spread all around the village, making it a tourist attraction.

Which choice completes the text so that it conforms to the conventions of Standard English?

A) is
B) are
C) was
D) had been

2

Cinnamon–a common flavor in a variety of foods, candies, and potpourri– ____ actually the bark of several species of evergreen trees indigenous to South Central Asia.

Which choice completes the text so that it conforms to the conventions of Standard English?

A) is
B) are
C) had been
D) were

3

With their two-tone colors in rectangular forms, the paintings of abstract expressionist artist Mark Rothko ____ easy to identify by even inexperienced observers.

Which choice completes the text so that it conforms to the conventions of Standard English?

A) was
B) to be
C) is
D) are

4

Although an icon of the Cold War, only small portions of the Berlin Wall, which once circled all of Western Berlin, ____ standing as a monument to the capital's troubled past.

Which choice completes the text so that it conforms to the conventions of Standard English?

A) remains
B) remaining
C) has remained
D) remain

5

Flavonols are types of antioxidants that are used in the human body to repair and rebuild cells. Cocoa powder, a primary ingredient in ____ especially high in flavonols, which have shown in scientific studies to increase blood flow to the brain and improve memory.

Which choice completes the text so that it conforms to the conventions of Standard English?

A) chocolates are
B) chocolates, are
C) chocolates, is
D) chocolates being

6

Stashes of corn, a favorite treat of baboons, were hidden around Tsaobis Nature Park by scientists eager to see how these animals would react to a surprise meal. Researchers have found that wild baboons, once a tribe has identified a food source, ____ a line and wait their turn.

Which choice completes the text so that it conforms to the conventions of Standard English?

A) forms
B) form
C) are formed
D) formed

7

Cells are composed of compartments called organelles. Temperature change within these organelles ____ cell activity and overall health. Young-Tae Chang has developed a way to better detect any temperature changes by using fluorescent cell imaging.

Which choice completes the text so that it conforms to the conventions of Standard English?

A) signal
B) signals
C) have signaled
D) signaling

8

The Burgess Shale, known worldwide for its pristine preservation of fossils, ____ a plethora of arthropods from the Cambrian era that archeologists are still unearthing.

Which choice completes the text so that it conforms to the conventions of Standard English?

A) preserves
B) preserve
C) have preserved
D) would have preserved

9

Meeting in 1840 at the World Anti-Slavery Convention in London, Lucretia Mott and Elizabeth Cady Stanton became fast friends and allies and ____ crucial in establishing the Seneca Falls Convention in 1848, which began the women's suffrage movement in the United States.

Which choice completes the text so that it conforms to the conventions of Standard English?

A) was
B) were
C) is
D) being

10

Once common in the Indian Ocean, guitarfish, named for their uniquely shaped bodies, ____ quickly becoming endangered due to overfishing.

Which choice completes the text so that it conforms to the conventions of Standard English?

A) is
B) are
C) was
D) has been

11

A 77-square-mile meadow of seagrass on the floor of Australia's Shark Bay holds the distinction of being the largest clone in the world. Through a process known as "horizontal rhizome extension", the plant effectively clones itself by creating genetically-identical offshoots. This sort of asexual reproduction is rare among seagrass species but ____ occurring continuously among this individual plant for almost 4,500 years. In theory, this clone could continue multiplying forever, making this Australian seagrass immortal.

Which choice completes the text so that it conforms to the conventions of Standard English?

A) have been
B) has been
C) have
D) has

12

Guaranteed Rate Field was opened on the South Side of Chicago in 1991 as Comiskey Park, named after the historic ballpark that once stood adjacent to the new stadium. Held at the original Comiskey ____ the 1918 World Series and the 1937 boxing match that saw Joe Louis claim the Heavyweight title for the first time.

Which choice completes the text so that it conforms to the conventions of Standard English?

A) being
B) was
C) were
D) has been

Pronouns

Tags: Standard English Conventions • Form, Structure, and Sense • Pronouns

Subject vs. Object Pronouns

Subjects are the movers, shakers, and doers in a sentence: they **act**. Objects are more like the ball in a pinball machine: they are **acted upon**.

Rachel	launched	the **banana**	at **Geoff**.
subject	verb	object	object

In the above sentence, Rachel is the one **acting**, while the banana and poor Geoff are being **acted upon.** If we want to replace these nouns with pronouns, we keep this distinction in mind. Subjects get subject pronouns, and objects get object pronouns:

She	launched	it	at him.
subject pronoun	verb	object pronoun	object pronoun

Rachel takes the **subject pronoun** "She," not the *object* pronoun "her." Geoff takes the **object prounoun** "him," not the *subject* pronoun "he." On the test, be on the lookout for sentences that mix these up.

Here's a handy-dandy chart to keep subject & object pronouns organized:

_____ do(es) things	Things happen to _____
I	Me
You	You
He, She, It, Who	Him, Her, It, Whom
We	Us
They	Them

EXAMPLE 1

Our tour guide for the day was a friendly young woman <u>whom</u>, after showing us around the main academic buildings on campus, showed us some of her own favorite landmarks.

TIP

If you have trouble remembering when to use *whom*, focus on the **-m**.

He, *they*, and *who* are all subject pronouns with no **-m**.

Him, *them*, and *whom* are all object pronouns that end in **-m**.

SOLUTION

Whom is an object pronoun – but is it being acted upon in the sentence? Looks like "whom" refers to the tour guide, and she is acting all over the place! She **shows** us the buildings, plus her favorite landmarks. We should replace whom with the subject pronoun **who**.

Our tour guide for the day was a friendly young woman <u>**who**</u>, after showing us around the main academic buildings on campus, showed us some of her own favorite landmarks.

189

The (Not So) Difficult Case of I vs. Me

You might notice that people often aren't sure when to say "I" and when to say "me." But the rules are the same as with any other subject and object pronoun. **I** is a subject, and **me** is an object.

> **I** do things. Things happen to **me**.
> *subject*   *object*

TIP

If your pronoun is the object of a preposition, the object pronoun "me" is correct.

EXAMPLE 2

In appreciation of all the hard work we did designing the set, the cast of *You're a Good Man, Charlie Brown* <u>threw a party for Joyce, Steve, and I</u>.

SOLUTION

TIP

When the SAT gives you a long list of names including "I" or "me", cross out everything but the pronoun. It will make it easier for your ear to guide you!

Let's cross out Joyce and Steve and let our ears do all the work:

In appreciation of all the hard work we did designing the set, the cast of *You're a Good Man, Charlie Brown* <u>threw a party for ~~Joyce, Steve, and~~ I</u>.

The cast threw a party for **I**? That doesn't sound right! That's because "I" isn't doing the action in the sentence. The **cast** threw the party, not "I." We need the **object** pronoun **me**.

In appreciation of all the hard work we did designing the set, the cast of *You're a Good Man, Charlie Brown* <u>threw a party for Joyce, Steve, and **me**</u>.

Reflexive Pronouns

There's one more type of pronoun you need to know about: the reflexives. Each personal pronoun (I, you, he/she/it, etc.) has a reflexive pronoun that goes along with it:

	Singular	Plural
1st Person	myself	ourselves
2nd Person	yourself	yourselves
3rd Person	herself / himself /itself	themselves

We use reflexive pronouns for two purposes. First, when the **subject** and the *object* of a sentence are the same. For example:

> **I** love *myself*.
> **Eleazar** bought *himself* a triple scoop ice cream sundae.
> **We** are so proud of *ourselves*!

Second, you can also use reflexive pronouns to intensify a statement and give it an extra bit of emphasis:

> Jordan *himself* told me I could borrow his car.
> I can do this *myself*.

When you use reflexive pronouns to intensify a statement in this way, you should be able to **cut it out of the sentence** entirely and maintain the meaning. Try it with the sentences above to see how the meaning stays.

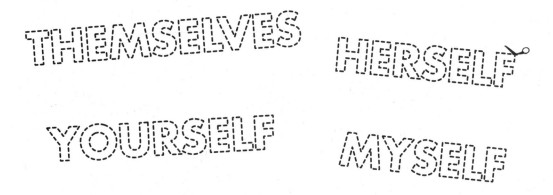

EXAMPLE 3

Much to my chagrin, Shelly informed _____ that my toy poodle was not welcome at Bring Your Daughter to Work Day.

A) myself
B) me
C) I
D) one

SOLUTION

What's the subject of this sentence? It's Shelly!

Shelly informed <u>myself</u>.
Subj.   *Obj.*

The subject and object are not the same person, so we should NOT use a reflexive pronoun: a simple object pronoun will do!

B) Much to my chagrin, **Shelly** informed <u>me</u> that my toy poodle was not welcome at Bring Your Daughter to Work Day.

B

Pronouns must match the nouns they replace

A pronoun's antecedent is the word or words the pronoun replaces. If the antecedent is singular, the pronoun must be too:

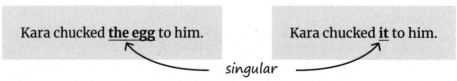

Kara chucked **the egg** to him.   Kara chucked **it** to him.

singular

Simple enough, but be careful: the SAT occasionally uses words that *look* plural but are, in fact, singular. Check the table below for examples.

NOTE

While "team" and "band" are sneaky singular words, a plural team or band *name* (for instance, *The Beatles*) is still plural.

Sneaky Singular Words	
anybody, anyone	nothing, everything
everybody, everyone	nobody, no one
each	none
either, neither	amount, number
group, family	audience, team, band, club

EXAMPLE 4

Every member of the football team <u>shaved their head</u> when the team won the game against its biggest rival.

SOLUTION

Did every member shave **their** head? Do they share one head? **Every** is a singular word, so we can't use the plural pronoun their to replace it. We need the singular pronoun **his** or **her**.

Every member of the football team <u>shaved **his/her** head</u> when the team won the game against its biggest rival.

TIP

Words like *army*, *team*, and *family* are known as **collective nouns**: nouns that denote a group of individuals. When collective nouns act as a single unit, they use singular verbs.

EXAMPLE 5

Because the U.S. Army anticipated only a brief engagement in Fallujah, <u>they only had</u> enough supplies for 24 days of combat.

SOLUTION

The U.S. Army is acting as a singular entity, a thing, an it. **It** takes the place of a singular noun.

Because the U.S. Army anticipated only a brief engagement in Falluja, <u>**it** only had</u> enough supplies for 24 days of combat.

EXAMPLE 6

Meteorologists have been studying comets for years, but they have only recently realized how varied in composition <u>they</u> can be.

SOLUTION

"They" is a plural pronoun, so it must have a plural antecedent. But here's the problem: we have **two** plural nouns in the sentence! Does "they" refer to the meteorologists... or the comets? Pronouns are handy, but not if they make the sentence more confusing. If it's unclear which word is the antecedent to your pronoun, ditch the pronoun altogether and repeat the noun.

Meteorologists have been studying comets for years, but they have only recently realized how varied in composition **<u>comets</u>** can be.

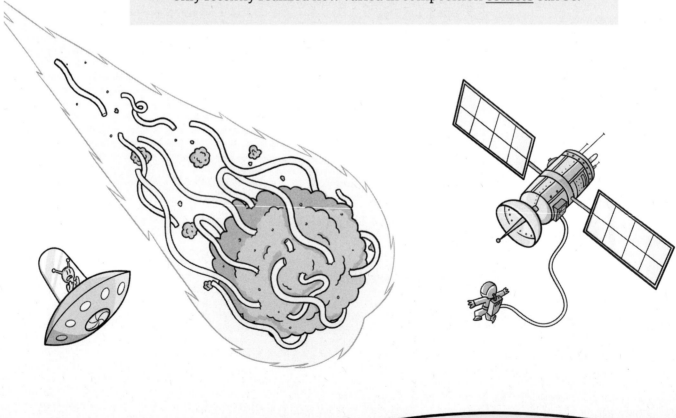

Quiz

Identify the error (if present) in each of the following sentences.

1. Over the course of the 40-week academic calendar, roughly three dozen students will take its turn as Most Popular Kid of the Third Grade.

2. Marjorie gained unlikely celebrity for her "Bouncing On Air" initiative, in which she trained adults whom had never learned to properly pogo.

3. The students in Ms. Odewabe's underwater basket weaving class have discovered working together heightens its creativity.

4. According to our calculations, Millie and me have spent more than $427 on our collection of super bouncy balls.

5. Just between you and I, Eric's new boyfriend is a compulsive liar: I saw that condescending vegetarian stuffing his face at Messy Matt's Rib Shack on Tuesday.

Answers

1. Over the course of the 40-week academic calendar, roughly three dozen students will take **their** turn as Most Popular Kid of the Third Grade.

2. Marjorie gained unlikely celebrity for her "Bouncing On Air" initiative, in which she trained adults **who** had never learned to properly pogo.

3. The students in Ms. Odewabe's underwater basket weaving class have discovered working together heightens **their** creativity.

4. According to our calculations, **Millie and I** have spent more than $427 on our collection of super bouncy balls.

5. Just between **you and me**, Eric's new boyfriend is a compulsive liar: I saw that condescending vegetarian stuffing his face at Messy Matt's Rib Shack on Tuesday.

Practice Set

1

Swedish chemist Alfred Nobel, _____ made a fortune from his invention of dynamite, used his money to establish the Nobel prizes, which honor global achievements in the sciences, arts, and world peace.

Which choice completes the text so that it conforms to the conventions of Standard English?

A) which
B) who
C) whom
D) whose

2

The Environmental Protection Agency reports that food scraps represent 20 to 30 percent of Americans' trash. In 2012, that equaled approximately 35 million tons of food waste—the majority of _____ headed straight to a landfill.

Which choice completes the text so that it conforms to the conventions of Standard English?

A) one
B) them
C) it
D) you

3

Are there any foods that you completely hate and refuse to eat? Recent scientific studies suggest that some of those dislikes may be due to genetics. Specific genes may factor how _____ perceive certain tastes and smells, making foods like cilantro appealing to some and off-putting to others.

Which choice completes the text so that it conforms to the conventions of Standard English?

A) who
B) you
C) them
D) whom

4

Air ionizers designed for home use were heavily marketed in the 1990s and early 2000s and featured ad campaigns promising cleaner household air. While these models did remove some air pollutants, the ionization process also created ozone (O3), which ironically is a harmful pollutant _____

Which choice completes the text so that it conforms to the conventions of Standard English?

A) itself.
B) themself.
C) oneself.
D) themselves.

5

In order to sustainably restore areas alongside highways, botanist Julie Kudzokina needs access to native seeds. She explains, "an abundant quantity of native grasses and shrubs will allow ____ to rebuild areas that will improve drainage and reduce erosion."

Which choice completes the text so that it conforms to the conventions of Standard English?

A) my team and I
B) me and my team
C) my team and myself
D) team's and me

6

The Earth's crust is broken into tectonic plates (regions of land that sink into and rise from the mantle). Plates can move under each other and rotate around the surface in a process is called continental drift. The relative position of the plates remains the same though ____ may shrink or grow in size.

Which choice completes the text so that it conforms to the conventions of Standard English?

A) it
B) them
C) these
D) they

7

Conventional wisdom suggests that second language acquisition – the process of learning and assimilating a foreign language – becomes extremely difficult as an adult, making it hard for people to become multilingual after their twenties. In contrast, consider the case of Kató Lomb, a Hungarian polyglot ____ studied more than two dozen languages and mastered sixteen. Even more impressively, Lomb focused her attention on learning languages in her 40s, which goes against conventional wisdom involving language acquisition.

Which choice completes the text so that it conforms to the conventions of Standard English?

A) she
B) her
C) who
D) whom

8

It was March 12, 1993. Off the coast, in the Western Gulf of Mexico, a storm was brewing, which would become known as the "1993 Superstorm." Even before it made landfall, weather experts knew this was not your average storm. Professionals at the National Weather Service issued storm warnings five days in advance and blizzard warnings two days in advance, unusual at the time. In fact, it was the first time ____ had predicted such a massive storm. Thanks to their warnings, millions of people took precautions and prepared for the storm.

Which choice completes the text so that it conforms to the conventions of Standard English?

A) it
B) they
C) who
D) that

The developing field of paleoclimatology is sending scientists to some of the harshest environments on the globe to research the climates of past epochs. ____ research projects have revealed vast variations in Earth's climate, including glacial periods when much of the Earth was covered in ice, and interglacial periods when temperatures warmed up and the polar ice caps shrunk.

Which choice completes the text so that it conforms to the conventions of Standard English?

A) These
B) Which
C) That
D) Where

In 2011 rebranding, DC announced a campaign called "New 52," which controversially resulted in fewer female creators than before. In rebuttal, fans launched a petition calling on the company to hire more female creators and presented a list of more than 120 experienced female creators ____ DC could consider hiring.

Which choice completes the text so that it conforms to the conventions of Standard English?

A) who
B) whom
C) whose
D) who's

Although Thomas Edison is often ascribed the honor of inventing technology to make recordings of sound, the first relevant innovation was made by Édouard-Léon Scott de Martinville, a French editor. Inspired by the structure of eardrums, Édouard-Léon created a recording device from a trumpet, glass plate, and boar's hair. All of our modern music recordings, as well as many forms of saving data, can be attributed to ____.

Which choice completes the text so that it conforms to the conventions of Standard English?

A) Edison and he
B) Edison and him
C) theirs
D) their

The first Paris Fashion Week was held in 1973 at the Palace of Versailles. The French government was unable to pay for the much-needed restorations of the former royal residence, and the fashion show was meant to raise the necessary funds for ____.

Which choice completes the text so that it conforms to the conventions of Standard English?

A) it
B) them
C) itself
D) that

Possessive

Tags: Standard English Conventions • Form, Structure, and Sense • Apostrophes

NOTE

Depending on which Grammar Guru you ask, you'll get different answers about the best way to make singular nouns that end in s (like *boss*) possessive.

Is it *my boss' desk* or *my boss's desk*?

The SAT avoids this controversy. For test purposes, any possessive noun ending in *s* is likely plural, and should have just an apostrophe—no *s*.

Show possession with an apostrophe

In most cases, you simply add an **'s** to a noun to show ownership. However, when you do this to a **plural noun** that ends in an **s**, like **dogs's**, it can look and sound terrible. So, the rulers of English decided you can just write **dogs'**.

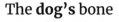

The **dog's** bone   The **dogs'** bone

Notice that these words *sound* the same. The test writers are hoping to trip you up with words that sound similar but have different meaning, such as *family's* (singular possessive), *families* (plural, not possessive) and *families'* (plural possessive). To avoid this trap, anytime you see a noun followed by an apostrophe on the test, just ask yourself two questions:

(1) *Does this noun own something?*

(2) *Should the noun be singular or plural?*

Your answer will be nearby, so be sure to read the whole sentence!

199

EXAMPLE 1

Georgia's minimum sentences are defined by the _____, which are in turn determined by the legislature.

A)   state criminal laws
B)   states' criminal laws'
C)   state's criminal laws
D)   state's criminal law's

SOLUTION

We're dealing with **two** possible possessions, so let's take them one at a time by asking our two questions:

(1) *Does "states" own anything in the sentence?*
Yes! It owns the **criminal laws**, so we need either **state's** or **states'** to show ownership. That lets us cross off A.

(2) *Should "states" be singular or plural?*
Georgia is only one state, so we need a singular possessive — **state's**. That lets us cross off B.

To help us choose between C and D, we only need to ask one question: Does "laws" own anything in the sentence? Nope! So we don't need any apostrophe here. That leaves **C** as the only choice that gets it right:

(C) Georgia's minimum sentences are defined by the <u>state's criminal laws</u>, which are in turn determined by the legislature.

C

TIP

Students often struggle with the possessive form of plural words.

If you're uncertain, try using a prepositional phrase, rather than an apostrophe, to show ownership. For example:

Children's books could be rewritten as **books of the children**. That sounds right.

Childrens' books would be rewritten as **books of the childrens**. That sounds wrong.

Possessive Pronouns

The SAT wants to make sure you know when to use a possessive pronoun and when to use a *contraction*. Possessive pronouns like *its*, *your*, *whose*, and *their* **do not use** an apostrophe. If you see an apostrophe, you've got a contraction on your hands!

Check out the handy-dandy table below to help you keep your possessives and contractions straight.

TIP

If you ever see **its'** on the test, immediately cross it out!

Possessive	Contraction
its	it's (it is / it has)
their	they're (they are)
your	you're (you are)
whose	who's (who is)

EXAMPLE 2

The French horn players have long suspected that the flautist fills their horns with Gatorade before the halftime shows, ruining _____ melodious music.

A) they're
B) their
C) there
D) it's

They're has an apostrophe, so it's a *contraction*. Do we want to say "ruining they are melodious music?" That's nonsense! We need to show **ownership**, since the French horn players own the melodious music. That means we need to use **their**, the possessive pronoun. The answer is **B**:

B) The French horn players have long suspected that the flautists filled their horns with Gatorade before the halftime show, ruining **their** melodious music.

B

201

EXAMPLE 3

Despite _____ long history as a haunted house, the Shrieking Shack has become the most popular venue for high school proms.

A) its
B) it's
C) their
D) they're

PORTAL

Possession questions often get thrown in with *Pronoun Error* questions. For a refresher on pronoun rules, turn to page 188.

SOLUTION

Does "it" own anything? Yes, it owns the "long history!" **Its** shows ownership... but so does **their**. How do we know which to choose? Remember your pronoun rules: singular pronouns refer to singular nouns, and plural pronouns refer to plural nouns. **It** refers to the **Shrieking Shack**; the shack has a long history as a haunted house. Since the antecedent is singular, we need a **singular** pronoun. Our answer is **A**!

A) Despite <u>its</u> long history as a haunted house, the Shrieking Shack has become the most popular venue for high school proms.

A

Quiz

Identify the error (if present) in each of the following sentences.

1. Because of there teachers severe case of the Mondays, the students watched the seminal film *Bring It On* during English class today.

2. It is Jacob's responsibility to clean the microscope's lenses' once a week.

3. Scientific studies have expanded our knowledge about the brains' ability to heal itself after a traumatic injury.

4. Known for their distinctive tuxedos, penguins are the cutest animals in Antarctica.

5. When your at the end of you're rope, try eating your weight in peanut butter and jelly sandwiches.

Answers

1. Because of **their teacher's** severe case of the Mondays, the students watched the seminal film *Bring It On* during English class today.

2. It is Jacob's responsibility to clean the microscope's **lenses** once a week.

3. Scientific studies have expanded our knowledge about the **brain's** ability to heal itself after a traumatic injury.

4. *Correct as written!*

5. When **you're** at the end of **your** rope, try eating your weight in peanut butter and jelly sandwiches.

Practice Set

1

After an initial analysis of the data collected by the biomedical research team, the ____ became all the more apparent.

Which choice completes the text so that it conforms to the conventions of Standard English?

A) relationships complexity
B) relationship's complexity
C) relationships' complexity's
D) relationships complexities'

2

18th-century Europe offered few ____ but this did not stop Dutch painter Rachel Rusych from having a successful career focused on painting still lifes with dramatic lighting.

Which choice completes the text so that it conforms to the conventions of Standard English?

A) opportunities' for female's artists,
B) opportunity's for female artist's,
C) opportunities for female artists,
D) opportunities for female artists',

3

The first African American theater, the African Grove Theatre, was founded in New York City in 1821. The Theatre's founder was William Alexander Brown, a free black man from the West Indies, and ____ initial focus was on adaptations of Shakespeare plays.

Which choice completes the text so that it conforms to the conventions of Standard English?

A) their
B) its
C) it's
D) those

4

The Tesla coil, invented in 1891 by Nikola Tesla, is a device still used in radios today; ____ to wirelessly transmit radio signals served as the foundation for telecommunication research.

Which choice completes the text so that it conforms to the conventions of Standard English?

A) its ability
B) it's ability
C) their ability's
D) their abilities

5

The Indian film industry is often referred to as "Bollywood," a portmanteau that blends Hollywood with Bombay, the home of Indian filmmaking. Although Bombay has changed _____ name to Mumbai, the term Bollywood endures.

Which choice completes the text so that it conforms to the conventions of Standard English?

A) there
B) their
C) its
D) it's

6

The 1914 Italian film *Cabiria*, an adventure film set in Ancient Rome, uses large and extravagant sets to tell its tale of love and war. In order to better show the immenseness of the sets, director Giovanni Pastrone placed the movie camera on a cart and filmed shots while laterally moving across the set. Although these shots may appear amateurish by _____ represented a new way to use space and perspective in films.

Which choice completes the text so that it conforms to the conventions of Standard English?

A) today's standards, they
B) today standard's, they
C) today's standards, it
D) todays' standards, their

7

Ants, which include over 12,000 species worldwide, are famously hard workers. Foraging varieties can travel up to 700 feet from _____ in search of food and coordinate a caravan through pheromones to haul it back.

Which choice completes the text so that it conforms to the conventions of Standard English?

A) its nest
B) their nests
C) it's nest
D) they're nests

8

The reptilian suborder Cryptodira includes freshwater turtles, snapping turtles, tortoises, soft-shelled turtles, and sea turtles. The classification of a specimen occurs by analyzing the various types of scutes or bony plates, found on _____

Which choice completes the text so that it conforms to the conventions of Standard English?

A) a turtle's shell's.
B) a turtles' shell.
C) a turtle shells.
D) a turtle's shell.

Macondo, the fictional Latin American village ____ history comprises the heart of Gabriel García Márquez's acclaimed novel *One Hundred Years of Solitude*, is an imaginary location brought to life by a compelling story and powerful vision. This small town – which is similar in some ways to the Colombian town where Márquez was raised – becomes a microcosm of a larger world.

Which choice completes the text so that it conforms to the conventions of Standard English?

A) whose
B) who's
C) their
D) they're

One way to evaluate the effect of sleep on an athlete's reaction is known as the ruler test, where a research team measures how long participants take to react in order to grab a ruler dropped in front of ____ hands.

Which choice completes the text so that it conforms to the conventions of Standard English?

A) his or her
B) their
C) your
D) one's

Humans have been drinking coffee for centuries, dating back to Ethiopia prior to the 14th century. Trade across the Red Sea brought coffee to the Arabian Peninsula. Soon merchants sailed coffee beans across the Mediterranean to port cities in Europe and Northern Africa. Brazilians first tasted coffee in 1727; upon earning their independence in 1822, they began mass producing the beverage. Today, ____ of coffee are the largest in the world, followed by Vietnam.

Which choice completes the text so that it conforms to the conventions of Standard English?

A) they're export's
B) they're exports'
C) their exports'
D) their exports

The Kingdom of Lovely was created by a British comedian as part of a television series about how to create a country in your own apartment. Christiania, a small neighborhood within Copenhagen, was created by a journalist who called upon young people to take over disused military barracks. These tiny territories are micronations, entities ____ members claim they belong to a sovereign state, even though they lack international recognition from governments.

Which choice completes the text so that it conforms to the conventions of Standard English?

A) whose
B) who's
C) whom
D) who

Misplaced Modifier

Tags: Standard English Conventions • Form, Structure, and Sense • Modifiers

....

When it comes to modifiers, location is everything

A modifying phrase needs to be <u>right next</u> to the word it modifies, or else it is what we call a **misplaced modifier** error. We see misplaced modifiers all the time in the real world and typically just ignore them. That's because we can usually use context clues to figure out what the writer *really* meant to say.

Since you may be so used to forgiving this error, it can be easy to miss on test day. When you have the option of rearranging the words in a sentence, make sure modifiers are touching their intended target!

EXAMPLE 1

Ripping through the street, _____.

A) Emily was terrified by the tornado
B) Emily is terrifying the tornado.
C) the tornado terrified Emily.
D) Emily's terror was heightened by the tornado.

Who or what is ripping through the street? The word immediately after the modifying clause! Which means, as written, this sentence suggests Emily is the one causing the destruction:

Ripping through the street, **Emily** was terrified of the tornado.
          modifier

That's probably not the intended meaning. We need to pick a choice that puts "the tornado" right next to the modifier. The only option that does this is choice C:

Ripping through the street, **the tornado** terrified Emily.
          modifier

C

EXAMPLE 2

A hybrid of chihuahuas and dachshunds, _____ These dogs are beloved for their soft, floppy ears and loyalty to their owners.

A) dog breeders are increasingly breeding "chiweenies."
B) breeders of dogs are gaining popularity towards "chiweenies."
C) dog breeders have been gaining popularity with "chiweenies."
D) "chiweenies" are gaining popularity with dog breeders.

TIP

Even if you don't like the passive way choice D is worded, you MUST fix the modifier error.

SOLUTION

Again, we need to focus on what comes *before* the underlined phrase. Dog breeders are human, and so cannot be a hybrid of chihuahuas and dachshunds. Only **choice D** has the correct modifier placement:

A hybrid of chihuahuas and dachshunds, "chiweenies" are...
modifier

D

EXAMPLE 3

On the coast of South Africa, _____ a type of sea snail prized for its iridescent shell.

A) diving for abalone is a popular pastime,
B) diving for abalone is a popular pastime among divers,
C) a popular pastime is abalone diving,
D) a popular pastime is diving for abalone,

SOLUTION

In this sentence, the modifier is *after* the underlined portion, which means we need to focus on the **last word of each choice**. Which choice ends in a word that could be a type of sea snail?

A) ...pastime, *nope, not a sea snail*

B) ...divers, *those are people, not a snail*

C) ...diving, *that's an activity, not a snail*

D) ...abalone, *that could work!*

Only choice D gives us a suitable neighbor for our modifier!

D

How to spot Misplaced Modifiers:

As usual, glance at the answer choices to identify the problem type. Misplaced Modifier choices simply **move around the same phrase:**

A) my boss has a vintage Mustang that is the talk of the town.
B) the talk of the town is my boss's vintageMustang.
C) the town is talking about my boss's vintage Mustang.
D) my boss's vintage Mustang is the talk of the town.

EXAMPLE 4

Born in Neosho, Missouri, _____. He was at the forefront of the Regionalist art movement, which became popular in the 1930s.

A) painter Thomas Hart Benton used urban and rural laborers as his subjects.
B) Thomas Hart Benton's paintings used urban and rural laborers as his subjects.
C) urban and rural laborers were the subjects of the paintings of Thomas Hart Benton.
D) urban and rural laborers were the subjects of American painter Thomas Hart Benton's paintings.

SOLUTION

Choices A and B seem the most appealing, but **B** uses a possessive to make the subject paintings and not Benton.

B

Timmy found his stray gerbil cleaning his room.

Practice Set

1

Although they are now associated with the music and iconography of Scotland, ____ more than 3,000 years ago.

Which choice completes the text so that it conforms to the conventions of Standard English?

A) ancient Persians invented the bagpipes
B) Persians invented the ancient bagpipes
C) bagpipes were invented by ancient Persians
D) Persians, who were ancient, invented the bagpipes

2

The life cycle of a monarch begins with the birth of the first generation of butterflies in southern Canada and the northern and central United States. Shortly before their deaths, ____

Which choice completes the text so that it conforms to the conventions of Standard English?

A) hundreds, sometimes thousands, of eggs are laid by female monarchs lay on the underside of milkweed leaves.
B) hundreds, sometimes thousands, of eggs on the underside of milkweed leaves are laid by female monarchs lay.
C) female monarchs lay hundreds, sometimes thousands, of eggs on the underside of milkweed leaves.
D) the underside of milkweed leaves are where female monarchs lay hundreds, sometimes thousands, of eggs.

3

Now recognized as a pioneering African American video game programmer, ____ the first console to use cartridges to load different games.

Which choice completes the text so that it conforms to the conventions of Standard English?

A) Jerry Lawson invented the Fairchild Channel F
B) the Fairchild Channel F was invented by Jerry Lawson
C) Jerry Lawson's Fairchild Channel F was invented by him,
D) the invention by Jerry Lawson was the Fairchild Channel F

4

Upton Sinclair's novel *The Jungle*, published in 1905, tells the story of Lithuanian immigrant Jurgis Rudkus and his young wife Ona. Full of ambition and hope for the future, _____

Which choice completes the text so that it conforms to the conventions of Standard English?

A) the newlyweds settle in Chicago where Jurgis gets a job at the meatpacking plant.

B) the meatpacking plant is where Jurgis finds a job, once the newlyweds settle in Chicago.

C) Chicago is where the newlyweds settle and Jurgis gets a job at the meatpacking plant.

D) a job at a meatpacking plant is found by Jurgis once the newlyweds settle in Chicago.

5

Made with the use of high-speed video cameras that capture the movement of fungal spores that occur in microseconds, _____ and movements of mushrooms.

Which choice completes the text so that it conforms to the conventions of Standard English?

A) Nicholas Money makes art that reveals the hidden patterns

B) the art of Nicholas Money reveals the hidden patterns

C) hidden patterns are revealed by the art of Nicholas Money

D) hidden patterns by Nicholas Money are revealed in his art

6

Born in Cuba from a Congolese mother and Chinese father, _____ His childhood was immersed in Afro-Cuban culture, where he learned many folktales of forest spirits and magic, which inspired his later paintings.

Which choice completes the text so that it conforms to the conventions of Standard English?

A) various traditions are blended together in Wilfredo Lam's art.

B) Wilfredo Lam's art is known for blending various traditions.

C) Wilfredo Lam excelled at blending various traditions in his art.

D) blending various traditions was what Wilfredo Lam excelled at in his art.

7

The proliferation of spicy peppers has been a byproduct of globalization. Native to Brazil, _____ New varieties of peppers eventually developed with some becoming culinary icons, such as Hungarian paprika and Thai "bird's eye" peppers.

Which choice completes the text so that it conforms to the conventions of Standard English?

A) European explorers would bring chili peppers back home, where the peppers would quickly disperse and become a staple in many Asian and African cuisines.

B) many Asian and African cuisines would use peppers as a staple once the peppers were brought back home by European explorers and dispersed.

C) peppers were brought back home by European explorers, where the peppers were quickly dispersed and became a staple in many Asian and African cuisines.

D) European explorers would quickly disperse peppers after bringing them back home, and the peppers would become a staple in many Asian and African cuisines.

8

With his newly invented phonautograph, _____ making the first recording of a human voice all the way back in 1860.

Which choice completes the text so that it conforms to the conventions of Standard English?

A) *Au Clair de la Lune* was sung and recorded by Édouard-Léon Scott de Martinville,

B) *Au Clair de la Lune*, recorded and sung by Édouard-Léon Scott de Martinville,

C) the recording of *Au Clair de la Lune* by Édouard-Léon Scott de Martinville,

D) Édouard-Léon Scott de Martinville recorded himself singing *Au Clair de la Lune*,

9

By observing the night's sky and recording their observations, _____ and preserved how those eruptions affected the European climate.

Which choice completes the text so that it conforms to the conventions of Standard English?

A) logs of medieval monks mentioned some of history's largest volcanic eruptions

B) medieval monks' logs mentioned some of history's largest volcanic eruptions

C) medieval monks created logs of some of history's largest volcanic eruptions

D) some of history's largest volcanic eruptions were mentioned in logs created by medieval monks

The oceans naturally absorb carbon dioxide as part of its natural cycle, although many factors, including some that are man-made, can affect that rate. In his hopes to better track the absorption rate in different parts of the ocean, ____

Which choice completes the text so that it conforms to the conventions of Standard English?

A) Peter de Menocal's design is a system of interconnected monitors that can relay information about specific regions.

B) Peter de Menocal has been designing a system of interconnected monitors that can relay information about specific regions.

C) a system of interconnected monitors that can relay information about specific region has been designed by Peter de Menocal.

D) the relaying of information about specific regions occurs through a system of interconnected monitors designed byPeter de Menocal.

A source of national pride and obsession, ____ an island nation in the Caribbean. There is even a park in Havana that serves as the dedicated venue for heated debates about the game and its players. Due to this passion, it is hardly surprising that the country produces some of the best ballplayers in the world.

Which choice completes the text so that it conforms to the conventions of Standard English?

A) baseball is the most popular sport in Cuba,

B) the most popular sport in Cuba is baseball

C) Cuba's most popular sport is baseball

D) baseball is Cuba's most popular sport

Possessing longer than average fingers that allowed him to play three octaves at once, ____ who mesmerized European audiences during the early 19th century. His original compositions were so complex that nearly all other violinists of his time struggled to play them.

Which choice completes the text so that it conforms to the conventions of Standard English?

A) Italy was the home of violinist Niccolò Paganini

B) Niccolò Paganini was an Italian violinist

C) the violin was the instrument played by Niccolò Paganini

D) Italian Niccolò Paganini played the violin

UNIT | Expression of Ideas

Chapters

Overview

In this unit, we'll look at how to logically connect ideas and organize information. We'll get practice with transition/logic words, which are hugely helpful across the Reading & Writing section, and we'll learn a clever strategy for turning the last questions of the section into a breeze.

Transitions

Tags: Expression of Ideas • Transitions

Similar vs. Opposite

Picking the right word to join two ideas depends on whether those ideas are **similar (=)** or **opposite (≠)**. For example, the following ideas are *similar*, since the second idea logically follows from the first:

I followed the recipe exactly, _____**so**_____ the meal came out perfectly!

You would **expect** that following a recipe would lead to a good result. In contrast, *opposite* ideas are unexpected or surprising:

I followed the recipe exactly, _____**but**_____ the end result was a disaster!

Fill in each grey box with "=" if the ideas on either side are similar or "≠" if the ideas are opposite.

1. Most people thought that Auntie Gladys, with her thick cockney accent, was born in London's West End, [≠] she had never even left Kansas!

2. My little brother realized too late that his plastic superhero did not have the power of flight; [=], we watched the red and blue figure plummet into our mother's beet garden two floors below.

3. Four out of five doctors agree that Colgate is the best toothpaste. [ ], Dr. Fluffington prefers brushing his teeth with a mixture of baking soda and sea salt.

4. Katniss and Elmer's meticulously planned outdoor wedding had to be moved inside at the last minute, [ ] it started to rain.

5. According to the review of Guillermo's new novel, the plot was muddled and confusing, [ ] the book was redeemed by its insightful character development.

6. The unseasonably warm winter caused significant thawing in the California mountains. [ ], more counties than usual are under flash flood warnings.

7. Abjit diligently trained for eight months, [ ] he was able to finish all 26 miles of the Boston Marathon.

8. Many people believe that Napoleon was unusually short; [ ], he was 5'7", above average for men at that time.

9. The author Bram Stoker is most famous for his novel *Dracula*, which is set in the Romanian region of Transylvania. [ ], Stoker never travelled to Eastern Europe, and spent most of his life in Ireland and England.

10. Globally, public health campaigns reporting the ill effects of tobacco smoke are having positive effects; [ ], in 2005, Bhutan became the first country to outlaw the sale and use of tobacco products.

Eliminate illogical choices first

When you see answer choices full of connecting words, you should start by figuring out if they are joining similar or opposite ideas:

> (1) *Ask yourself, "are the ideas **similar** or **opposite**?"*
>
> (2) ***Eliminate illogical choices** based on your answer.*
>
> (3) ***Reread the sentence** using each remaining word.*

EXAMPLE 1

There was one thing Wilhelmina knew for sure about lobsters: stay away from the pincers. _____ when a large lobster attempted to share her beach towel, she vacated the area in a hurry.

A) Therefore,
B) Conversely,
C) Nonetheless,
D) Despite this,

SOLUTION

Let's take this problem one step at a time.

(1) *Ask yourself, "are the ideas similar or opposite?"*

First, Wilhelmina learns to **stay away** from lobsters. Next, she **vacates**. We're definitely dealing with **similar ideas**.

(2) *Eliminate illogical choices based on your answer*

Connectors that link **opposite ideas** have to go. That means we can cross off B, C, and D, that just leaves **choice A**!

A

EXAMPLE 2

Jane's obsession with great apes began at an early age. _____ she insisted on celebrating her fifth birthday by dressing up like an orangutan and trying to communicate with her furry friends at the zoo.

A) Finally,
B) Similarly,
C) For example,
D) Although,

SOLUTION

1 *Ask yourself, "are the ideas similar or opposite?"*

Ape obsession and orangutan party are **similar** ideas.

2 *Eliminate illogical choices based on your answer*

We can cross off any connectors that link **opposite** ideas. That eliminates choice D!

3 *Reread the sentence using each remaining word.*

A) Jane's obsession with great apes began at an early age. **Finally,** she insisted on celebrating her fifth birthday by dressing up like an orangutan...

There's nothing **final** about a 5-year-old's birthday party.

~B) Jane's obsession with great apes began at an early age. **Similarly,** she insisted on celebrating her fifth birthday by dressing up like an orangutan...

These two ideas are certainly similar. This connection is okay, but I think we can get more specific. Squiggle it.

C) Jane's obsession with great apes began at an early age. **For example,** she insisted on celebrating her fifth birthday by dressing up like an orangutan...

Jane's fifth birthday at the zoo is an **example** of her early ape obsession. This connector makes a tight, logical connection between these ideas. C is correct!

C

Learn your logical connectors

To help you make logical connections on the SAT, let's get familiar with the connectors you'll see on the test. In the table below, you'll find some of the most common connectors and how they are used.

TIP

When you see a connector on the test, think about its **specific meaning** and whether it works in the **context** of the paragraph. A word isn't right simply because it sounds smart (the same goes for people).

Function	Similar (=)	Opposite (≠)
Showing Logic	Thus Consequently Therefore Hence So Because	However Despite Nevertheless Nonetheless Regardless Although Yet But
Extending Ideas	Additionally In addition Furthermore Moreover Likewise Also	Alternatively On one hand On the other hand In contrast
Giving Examples	For example For instance In fact	
Showing Time	Thereafter Subsequently Next Previously Finally	
Summarizing Ideas	In short In broad terms In other words	

How to spot Transitions questions:

As usual, glance at the answer choices to identify the problem type. Here, you'll see a series of the connector words we see in this chapter:

A) Nevertheless ≠
B) In contrast, ≠
C) Consequently, =
D) On the other hand, ≠

When you see connectors, quickly label them as similar (=) or opposite (≠).

Practice Set

1

Fossil fuel stocks have long been a safe financial bet. With price rises projected until 2040 and governments prevaricating or rowing back on the Paris Agreement, investor confidence is set to remain high. ____ new research suggests that the momentum behind technological change in the global power and transportation sectors will lead to a dramatic decline in demand for fossil fuels in the near future.

Which choice completes the text with the most logical transition?

A) Otherwise,

B) However,

C) Accordingly,

D) Therefore,

2

Face jugs–sometimes referred to as ugly jugs–first appeared in the 1860s in Edgefield County in South Carolina, where they were handmade from locally sourced kaolin clay. ____ they are functional jugs with a narrow opening at the top that can be easily corked; this made them useful in 18th and 19th century America for storing and carrying water. On the other hand, face jugs are intriguing works of art: the sides of the jugs are sculpted to look like faces with exaggerated features.

Which choice completes the text with the most logical transition?

A) Subsequently,

B) Moreover,

C) Eventually,

D) In one sense,

3

The human distal gut hosts a bustling community comprising thousands of different kinds of bacteria. Thankfully, most of these intestinal residents don't cause disease but instead play key roles in nutrition, metabolism, pathogen resistance, and immune response regulation. ____ these beneficial bacteria are just as susceptible to the antibiotics we take to treat disease-causing bacteria.

Which choice completes the text with the most logical transition?

A) Logically,

B) Alternatively,

C) Eventually

D) Unfortunately,

4

Popular television shows like *CSI* and *Law and Order* depict law enforcement agents at the scene of a crime, hunting down clues to help find the culprit. These detectives are the stars of the shows and in reality often receive the public credit for crime-solving. There is another role, ____ that goes unseen. Fulfilling an equally important job, forensic science technicians work behind-the-scenes in criminal justice and law enforcement to assist in the investigation.

Which choice completes the text with the most logical transition?

A) in fact,

B) therefore,

C) accordingly,

D) however,

221

5

The historical value of many older audio-visual productions was not realized at the time, and copies were often thrown out or left to degrade. ____ 90% of the films produced before 1929 are now considered lost; film distributors would trash used film prints because the film stock used at the time was highly flammable and prone to spontaneous combustion.

Which choice completes the text with the most logical transition?

A) Despite this,
B) However,
C) Likewise,
D) For instance,

6

We tend to think of migration in terms of flocks of birds and herds of animals. Humans migrate too, although our movements often go unnoticed among the interwoven chaos of contemporary life. Immigration and emigration between countries are the easiest migrations to notice, ____ they involve visas and border crossing. Within a single country, migrations are less obvious, but determining who migrates and for what reasons can illuminate important social trends.

Which choice completes the text with the most logical transition?

A) yet
B) as
C) and
D) or

7

Peppers gain their spiciness from the chemical capsaicin, which is produced in the seed pods. The plant's genetics, and to a lesser degree its environment, determine how much capsaicin will be in the peppers. Botanists believe that capsaicin originated as a deterrent to herbivores, increasing the chances that seeds would fully ripen. ____ this defense has made the peppers more desirable in many cuisines, and human breeding has created hotter and hotter peppers.

Which choice completes the text with the most logical transition?

A) Ironically,
B) Moreover,
C) Indeed,
D) Subsequently,

8

The 1987 edition of the Pan American Games was complicated by political strife that made some nations unwilling or unable to host the sporting event. After two selected South American capitals withdrew their bids, the Midwestern city Indianapolis eventually took the reins after some encouragement from the US Olympic Committee. Organizers had little time to prepare for the influx of thousands of athletes. ____ the event was thoroughly successful and fostered a reputation that propelled Indianapolis into a sporting destination and likely had a hand in the city hosting the Super Bowl in 2012.

Which choice completes the text with the most logical transition?

A) Besides,
B) Likewise,
C) Nevertheless,
D) Thus,

9

The concept of brainstorming was first advanced in the 1950s by advertising agency executive Alex Osborn, who was convinced that his creative employers would work well together. ____ the allure of brainstorming waned and by 2015, Tomas Chamorro-Premuzic declared, "after six decades of independent scientific research, there is very little evidence for the idea that brainstorming produces more or better ideas than the same number of individuals would produce working independently."

Which choice completes the text with the most logical transition?

A) Abruptly,
B) Regrettably,
C) Gradually,
D) Logically,

10

Fueled by a concern with unwanted persuasion online, Truth Labs for Education has begun to create videos to directly combat misinformation online. The team has created animated videos to teach viewers about how online media can manipulate them. Truth Labs purchases advertising to air before inflammatory videos, ____ "inoculating" viewers to the misinformation they are about to watch. The hope is that the video will act similarly to a vaccine, providing some resistance to those watching.

Which choice completes the text with the most logical transition?

A) thereby
B) however,
C) nevertheless
D) yet

11

The first sculptures created by Rain Jordan were original bronzes made through the lost wax method, ____ as her art developed, she began to enjoy the immediacy and flexibility that other media offer, transitioning to mixed forms that incorporated clay, acrylics, and repurposed vintage glass.

Which choice completes the text with the most logical transition?

A) because
B) but
C) or
D) whereby

12

Many orchids are uniquely specialized to be pollinated by specific insects. Coryanthes, also called bucket orchids, ____ "trick" bees into helping them fertilize because the bucket shape of their petals causes bees to slip into a sticky liquid. Unable to use their wings, the bees are forced to crawl out, distributing pollen as they go.

Which choice completes the text with the most logical transition?

A) as such,
B) consequently,
C) for instance,
D) furthermore,

Rhetorical Synthesis

Tags: Expression of Ideas • Rhetorical Synthesis

TIP

Rhetorical Synthesis questions are easy to spot: they always come at the end of the module, and they are the only question type to present the text as **bullet points**.

Bulleted Information (That You Can Skip!)

Rhetorical Syntehsis questions will give you pieces of information in bullet points and ask you to select a sentence that accomplishes a specific task. **Focusing on that task** is key to answering these questions effectively. Let's look at an example, then talk strategy:

> While researching a topic, a student has taken the following notes:
>
> - The song "Yakety Sax" was recorded by Boots Randolph in 1963.
>
> - "Yakety Sax" was inspired by the saxophone solo in The Coasters' 1958 recording of "Yakety Yak."
>
> - The British television comedy The Benny Hill Show began using "Yakety Sax" as the end credits theme in 1969.
>
> - The version of "Yakety Sax" used on The Benny Hill Show was not the original recording and featured saxophonist Peter Hughes.
>
> - The end credits of The Benny Hill Show would often feature comedic chase scenes with sped up footage, something Hill referred to as "live animation."
>
> The student wants to emphasize the inspiration for "Yakety Sax." Which choice most effectively uses relevant information from the notes to accomplish this goal?
>
> A) Although the song "Yakety Sax" was originally recorded in 1963 by Boots Randolph, a different version was used in the ending credits of *The Benny Hill Show.*
> B) "Yakety Sax," which was featured in comedic chase scene on *The Benny Hill Show*, was originally recorded in 1963 by Boots Randolph.
> C) The 1963 song "Yakety Sax" by Boots Randolph was inspired by the saxophone solo in the 1958 recording of "Yakety Yak,"
> D) The closing credits of *The Benny Hill Show* featured comedic chases scenes and the song "Yakety Sax."

Rhetorical Synthesis Strategy

As usual, we'll jump to the question before reading the text. But this time, we will then **skip right to the answer choices!**

Read the question and determine what it's asking for

This is key, as rhetorical synthesis questions never ask you to pick out the best or most well rounded answer. Rather, they ask you to select an answer that does something specific with the information provided.

Go right to the answer choices

This may seem counterintuitive, but these questions are easier to answer when you don't focus on the text first, because the text likely contains information irrelevant to the question asked.

Eliminate answers that don't match the question asked

For rhetorical synthesis questions, it's easier to see wrong answers when you haven't read the text. So read each answer and determine whether or not it answers the question asked.

Read the text only if needed

Oftentimes, step 3 will lead you to one right answer. If you're not sure between two or more, then read over the text to help you better understand the topic. Then pick the answer that best matches both the text and the question asked.

TRY IT OUT

Check out the example question on the previous page about Yakety Sax and try the strategy.

1. *Read the question and underline the task.*

2. *Jump to the answer choices.*

3. *Eliminate answers that don't address the task.*

4. *Check your answer by reading the bullets.*

EXAMPLE 1

While researching a topic, a student has taken the following notes:

- Marie Antoinette was an Austrian Princess who became the last Queen of France.

- The French monarchy had become unpopular with the French people, which led to the French Revolution.

- When informed that there were widespread bread shortages, the press reported that she replied "let them eat cake."

- There is no historical evidence that she ever said "let them eat cake," and many historians assume it was political propaganda.

- During Antoinette's reign, The French economy suffered due to France's involvement in numerous wars and the deregulation of grain prices.

1. The student wants to emphasize that Marie Antoinette was unfairly blamed for all of France's problems. Which choice most effectively uses relevant information from the notes to accomplish this goal?

   A) The phrase "let them eat cake" is synonymous with Marie Antoinette, but it's likely that she never actually said it.
   B) Political propaganda can dramatically affect political action, as when the story that Marie Antoinette said "let them eat cake" helped fuel the French Revolution.
   C) Marie Antoinette became a symbol for all that was wrong with the French monarchy, but much of the economic suffering was caused by other factors, including wars and deregulated grain prices.
   D) Austrian-born Marie Antoinette, who likely never said "let them eat cake," was the last queen of France.

SOLUTION

(1) *Read the question and determine what it's asking for*

The student wants to <u>emphasize</u> that <u>Marie Antoinette</u> was <u>unfairly blamed for all of France's problems</u>. Which choice most effectively uses relevant information from the notes to accomplish this goal?

You need to pick an answer that directly emphasizes that **Marie Antoinette was unfairly blamed**.

(2) *Go right to the answer choices*

This step may feel weird at first, but it will help you to focus on the task at hand.

(3) *Eliminate answers that don't match the question asked*

A) The phrase "let them eat cake" is synonymous with Marie Antoinette, but it's likely that she never actually said it.

   This choice mentions nothing about her being unfairly blamed.

B) Political propaganda can dramatically affect political action, as when the story that Marie Antoinette said "let them eat cake" helped fuel the French Revolution.

   No mention that she was unfairly blamed.

C) Marie Antoinette became a symbol for all that was wrong with the French monarchy, but much of the economic suffering was caused by other factors, including wars and deregulated grain prices.

   Ah yes, this one mentions alternate reasons for France's problems.

D) Austrian-born Marie Antoinette, who likely never said "let them eat cake," was the last queen of France.

   This answer introduces her, but says nothing about blame.

(4) *Read the text if needed*

Choice C looks pretty good, but if you need to confirm it, then feel free to read over the text.

C

Just to show you that you can answer questions without reading the text, let's practice some rhetorical synthesis style questions **without** any texts.

1. The student wants to emphasize that David Jachowski's research focuses on how small carnivores can best establish the health of an ecosystem. Which choice most effectively uses relevant information from the notes to accomplish this goal?

   A) David Jachowski is an associate professor at Clemson University and studies carnivores.
   B) Small carnivore is a category of predatory mammals that includes foxes, weasels, and skunks.
   C) Rather than focusing on large mammals like panda bears and elephants, David Jachowski believes that small carnivores offer a better indicator of ecosystem health.
   D) The range of black-footed ferrets once including the entirety of the western prairies, but scientists have estimated that fewer than four hundred may be left in the wild.

2. The student wants to establish the initial international influence on 1960s and 70s electric cumbia from Peru. Which choice most effectively uses relevant information from the notes to accomplish this goal?

   A) Cumbia is a traditional Andean dance music defined by a rolling beat played on timbales, although it went through a transformation in the late 1960s and 1970s.
   B) The inventor or electric cumbia is widely considered to be Enrique Delgado Montes, who recorded a seminal 45 rpm single with his band Los Destellos.
   C) Peruvian electric cumbia would eventually evolve into chicha, and would gradually incorporate synthesizers and drum machines throughout the 1980s and 90s.
   D) Electric surf guitar, with its twangy and reverb-drenched tone, would originate in Southern California in the early 1960s, but spread internationally and influenced Peruvian cumbia musicians to switch to electric guitars.

3. The student wants to introduce how blue holes can provide information about the history of hurricanes. Which choice most effectively uses relevant information from the notes to accomplish this goal?

A) Blue holes, a type of sinkhole common around the Bahamas, are formed when carbonate rock dissolved to form underwater caves.

B) By using radiocarbon dating, Tyler Winkler can determine the age of sediment cores removed from blue holes and use changes in sediment composition to uncover the frequency of prehistoric hurricanes in the region.

C) Tyler Winkler, an oceanographer with the Woods Hole Oceanographic Institution, studies the frequency of hurricanes by analyzing ocean sediment from the waters around the Bahamas.

D) Data collected from underwater core samples near blue holes indicate that strong hurricanes have become more frequent around the Bahamas.

4. The student wants to introduce a visual description of the painting "Lucretia" to an audience already familiar with Artemisia Gentileschi. Which choice most effectively uses relevant information from the notes to accomplish this goal?

A) Artemisia Gentileschi was born in Rome in 1593, and became one of the few successful female painters in the Baroque era.

B) "Lucretia" by Artemisia Gentileschi was recently rediscovered and has been acquired by the Getty Museum in Los Angeles.

C) "Lucretia" by Artemisia Gentileschi presents the titular heroine in a dramatic pose, with her eyes cast upward, looking away from the silver knife in her hand.

D) "Lucretia" by Artemisia Gentileschi was likely painted between the years of 1635 and 1645, although an exact date of completion is unknown.

Answers: 1. *C*   2. *D*   3. B   4. *C*

Familiar audiences don't need an introduction

Some rhetorical synthesis questions ask you for a summary tailored to an **audience who is either familiar or unfamiliar** with some part of the topic. When you see "unfamiliar" or "familiar" in the question, that may affect which answer works best.

If you're summarizing for an audience **unfamiliar** with a topic, then you'll need to pick an answer choice that <u>introduces or explains that topic</u>.

- ✓ Do pick a choice that answers the relevant who, what, where, when, how, and why questions
- ✓ Do pick a choice that introduces the topic
- ✗ Don't pick a choice that assumes knowledge of the topic

In contrast, an audience **familiar** with an element of the text does not need an introduction or explanation of that detail. Usually, a familiar audience needs nothing more than a <u>name drop with no explainer</u>.

- ✓ Do pick a choice that focuses on what the question specifically asks about
- ✗ Don't pick a choice that introduces or explains the familiar topic

A look at a previous example

Let's look back at **question 4** from the previous exercise. The question asks to pick an answer for an audience "**already familiar with Artemisia Gentileschi.**" Choice A would be <u>great</u> for an audience <u>unfamiliar</u> with Artemisia Gentileschi as it establishes who she is:

> A) Artemisia Gentileschi was born in Rome in 1593, and became one of the few successful female painters in the Baroque era.

But choice C assumes we already know who she is and instead focuses on the physical details of one of her paintings:

> C) "Lucretia" by Artemisia Gentileschi presents the titular heroine in a dramatic pose, with her eyes cast upward, looking away from the silver knife in her hand.

TIP

We can assume that an audience already familiar with Artemisia knows about her birth and her status as a female painter. We shouldn't waste precious words on a familiar audience.

Choice C simply name drops Artemisia and then focuses on the task at hand: describing the painting "Lucretia." That's perfect for a 'familiar' audience!

Practice Set

1

While researching a topic, a student has taken the following notes:

- The Virginia coast used to provide habitat for beds of eelgrass (*Zostera marina*).
- The eelgrass beds were home to many types of fish and crustaceans.
- In the 1930s, disease and hurricanes wiped out many of the beds, leading to a loss of wildfowl and sealife.
- Starting in 1999, a team led by Robert "JJ" Orth started to reseed the coast with eelgrass.
- By 2020, 9,600 acres across four bays have been reseeded with eelgrass.

The student wants to emphasize the role that Orth played in helping reseed the Virginia coast. Which choice most effectively uses relevant information from the notes to accomplish this goal?

A) Under the guidance of Robert "JJ" Orth, a team started reseeding eelgrass along the Virginia coast in 1999, leading to 9,600 acres being recovered with eelgrass by 2020.

B) Eelgrass was once common on the Virginia coast, but disease and hurricanes destroyed the population in the 1930s; recent efforts have tried to regrow eelgrass in the region.

C) A home to many types of fish and crustaceans, eelgrass (*Zostera marina*) is slowly returning to the Virginia coast.

D) Disease and hurricanes damaged the beds of eelgrass off the coast of Virginia, which were home to many species of birds and crustaceans.

2

While researching a topic, a student has taken the following notes:

- Daan Roosegarde invented a 7 meters high smog-free tower to clean a city's air.
- The smog-free tower uses air ionizers, which negatively charge air molecules.
- Early air ionizers create ozone (O_3) as a byproduct, which is also a pollutant.
- Roosegarde's invention does not create ozone.
- The pollutants collected are compressed into small cubes and sold as jewelry to fund the project.

The student wants to emphasize that the smog-free tower does not produce ozone to an audience already familiar with air ionizers. Which choice most effectively uses relevant information from the notes to accomplish this goal?

A) Daan Roosegaarde has invented a 7-meter tall air ionizer, which converts pollutants into cubes that are used for jewelry.

B) Air ionizers have a reputation for creating ozone as a byproduct, but Daan Roosegaarde's smog free tower does not have that issue.

C) Daan Roosegaarde does not create ozone as a byproduct when producing small cubes of pollutants that are used for jewelry.

D) Air ionizers use negatively charged air molecules to clean air and Daan Roosegaarde has built one 7 meters high.

While researching a topic, a student has taken the following notes:

- A research team at Oxford University tested how singing affects building a group bond.
- The experiment had two groups, one which sang together and the other that did craft projects.
- The groups were asked about their closeness to each other at 1-month, 3-month, and 7-month intervals.
- After 1-month, the singing group felt much closer than the crafting group.
- After 7-months the crafting group felt closer than the singing group.

The student wants to acknowledge the short-term impact of singing to an audience already familiar with the experiment. Which choice most effectively uses relevant information from the notes to accomplish this goal?

A) Researchers at Oxford University split people into two groups, with one singing and the other crafting.

B) Singing can help a group feel closer, but as the Oxford University experiment shows, its significance is most strongly felt early on.

C) Researchers at Oxford University tested how bonded people felt in a group over a 7-month period.

D) Singers feel more socially bonded early on, but often lose interest in each other as time progresses.

While researching a topic, a student has taken the following notes:

- Volcanic eruptions are categorized as either major or minor.
- Major eruptions can cool global temperatures.
- Global temperatures have continued to rise due to the burning of fossil fuels.
- Scientists Dr. Thomas Aubry and Dr. Anja Schmidt study how volcanic particles distribute around the globe.
- Aubry and Schmidt are analyzing computer models to see if volcanic eruptions could offset global warming.

The student wants to introduce the research of Aubry and Schmidt to an audience already familiar with global warming. Which choice most effectively uses relevant information from the notes to accomplish this goal?

A) Volcanic eruptions can range from minor to major and the latter can affect global temperatures.

B) Global warming continues to be a major concern and Dr. Thomas Aubry and Dr. Anja Schmidt are planning a strategy to combat it using volcanoes.

C) Scientists Dr. Thomas Aubry and Dr. Anja Schmidt are using their expertise on how volcanic particles move around the global atmosphere to determine if major volcanic eruptions could mitigate global warming.

D) Scientists are using models to predict how volcanic particles, from minor and major eruptions, can be distributed across the world.

5

While researching a topic, a student has taken the following notes:

- In Gulf Shores, Alabama, a man-made ditch connects Mobile Bay with the Gulf of Mexico.
- Archaeologist Gregory Waselkov thought the ditch was from the 19th century.
- Local historian Harry King investigated the mile-long waterway and charcoal samples dating back to 600 CE.
- The ditch is what remains of a canal built by indigenous people to allow canoe travel between the two bodies of water.
- The waterway is the earliest example of earthwork construction along the Alabama coast.

The student wants to emphasize how King's findings contradicted Waselkov's assumptions. Which choice most effectively uses relevant information from the notes to accomplish this goal?

A) Indigenous people inhabited Gulf Shores, Alabama, where they constructed a canal around 600 CE that connected Mobile Bay with the Gulf of Mexico.

B) The ditch in Gulf Shores, constructed by indigenous people around 600 CE, should really be considered a canal that was designed to allow canoes to pass between two bodies of water.

C) While archaeologist Gregory Waselkov assumed that the ditch in Gulf Shores, Alabama dated back to the 19th century, local historian Harry King determined that it was built by indigenous people as far back as 600 CE.

D) Historian Harry King has investigated the canal in Gulf Shores, Alabama, and used charcoal samples found at the site to determine the age to be much older than was previously thought.

6

While researching a topic, a student has taken the following notes:

- American filmmaking moved to Hollywood after the Edison Motion Picture company lost control of exclusive rights in 1915.
- Films made before 1927 are considered silent era films as they lack synchronized sound, although live music accompaniment in theaters was common.
- Lois Weber was a prolific director, writer, and actor during the Hollywood silent era.
- Weber directed at least 138 films which was uncommon in a male-dominated industry.
- Weber pioneered using split-screen-cinematography, and the films she wrote focused on social issues affecting women.

The student wants to emphasize Lois Weber's contribution to film to an audience unfamiliar with the silent era. Which choice most effectively uses relevant information from the notes to accomplish this goal?

A) Lois Weber was a prolific and innovative filmmaker during the silent film era, which is defined as films before 1927 since films made at that time lacked synchronized sound.

B) An innovative director, Lois Weber made at least 138 films, with many of them focusing on social issues.

C) The American film industry transitioned from the Edison Motion Picture company to Hollywood due to Edison losing exclusive rights in 1915.

D) Lois Weber, active in the silent era, was the first director to use split-screen cinematography.

While researching a topic, a student has taken the following notes:

- High-frequency radio waves were first used to heat food at the 1933 Chicago World's Fair.
- The invention of the cavity magnetron made it possible to produce smaller wavelengths (microwaves).
- Microwaves were initially used to develop radar systems during World War II.
- In 1945, the microwave oven was invented by Percy Spencer while studying radar tubes at Raytheon.
- It was not until 1977, 44 years later, that microwave ovens were provided in models affordable and small enough for residential use.

The student wants to emphasize the large amount of time and effort that goes into refining technologies before they can be made practical for the public. Which choice most effectively uses relevant information from the notes to accomplish this goal?

A) From its initial use in 1933, microwave cooking technology was developed for 44 years before it became available to the average consumer.

B) Microwave ovens provide the modern convenience of heating or cooking food quickly and efficiently.

C) The use of microwaves for cooking was a groundbreaking technology in the 1970s, when it was first provided to the public, but it is now regarded as a simple, common tool.

D) Technological innovations often find their origins in other applications, such as military research that leads to useful devices for common households.

While researching a topic, a student has taken the following notes:

- Glove puppeteering is a form of opera that traces its origins back to China's Fujian province during the 17th century.
- The Huang family has contributed to this tradition of puppet theater for multiple generations.
- The family patriarch Huang Hai-tai was renowned as a national treasure for his traditional puppet shows during the first half of the 20th century.
- His son, Chun-hsiung, is considered the father of television puppet theater, praised for helping the artform adapt to modern entertainment standards during the 1960s.
- Grandsons Chris and Vincent formed Pili in 1983, the world's largest puppet film studio, known for producing the television action series *Thunderbolt Fantasy*.

The student wants to present the Huang family's legacy to an audience unfamiliar with *Thunderbolt Fantasy*. Which choice most effectively uses relevant information from the notes to accomplish this goal?

A) The members of the Huang family who developed *Thunderbolt Fantasy* have a long tradition of performing traditional opera using glove puppeteering.

B) The Pili studio produces films that exhibit the art of glove puppeteering, a traditional Chinese form of theater.

C) Known for his performances with the traditional art of puppet theater, Huang Hai-tai began a family legacy that culminated in the production of *Thunderbolt Fantasy*.

D) The Huang family has dedicated several generations to the traditional Chinese art of glove puppeteering, including their action-oriented television show *Thunderbolt Fantasy*.

9

While researching a topic, a student has taken the following notes:

- Bacteria are pervasive and essential throughout the biological world.
- Many essential biological processes rely on bacteria.
- Human digestive systems rely on bacteria to break down food into nutrients.
- Antibacterial agents, such as hand sanitizer, create an altered microbial environment.
- An altered microbial environment can be ideal for the spread of harmful bacteria.

The student wants to provide an example that emphasizes the negative impact of antibacterial agents. Which choice most effectively uses relevant information from the notes to accomplish this goal?

A) Bacteria is found throughout the biological world and many processes, including human digestion, rely on bacteria.

B) Hand sanitizer is a type of antibacterial agent that can cause an altered microbial environment that can spread harmful bacteria.

C) Antibacterial agents can create a microbial environment that fosters harmful bacteria.

D) Harmful bacteria can thrive in an altered microbial environment that would hinder beneficial bacteria.

10

While researching a topic, a student has taken the following notes:

- "Americana" is a term that describes art with themes around American history and myth.
- In the 1930s and 40s, Americana became popular with ballet and professional dance troupes.
- Americana dance performances often incorporated folk tunes in their musical compositions.
- *Appalachian Spring* was written by Aaron Copeland and starred Martha Graham in 1944.
- *Appalachian Spring* uses dance to tell the story of the wedding of a young couple on the American frontier.
- *Appalachian Spring* was made into a short film directed by Peter Glushanok in 1958.

The student wants to introduce *Appalachian Spring* as an example of Americana dance. Which choice most effectively uses relevant information from the notes to accomplish this goal?

A) Americana became a popular theme in dance in the 1930s and 1940s, including works from Aaron Copeland and Martha Graham.

B) *Appalachian Spring* was originally created in 1944 and was later made into a short film in 1958.

C) Americana ballets would incorporate American history in their stories and folk tunes in their music.

D) 1944's *Appalachian Spring*, with its story about a frontier marriage, is a representative case of how Americana themes became common in dance performances in 1930s and 40s.

Math Overview

Tags: Math Strategy

Structure and Timing

On each of the two math modules, you will have 35 minutes to complete 22 questions testing your skills in algebra, arithmetic, geometry, and a *bit* of trigonometry. While most questions are multiple choices, several will give you a blank text box and ask you to key in the answer.

2	35	22
modules	minutes	questions

Digital Tools

The SAT is taken through the College Board's official testing app: Bluebook. The Bluebook app offers several basic tools to help you mark questions, eliminate answers, pull up a calculator, and more.

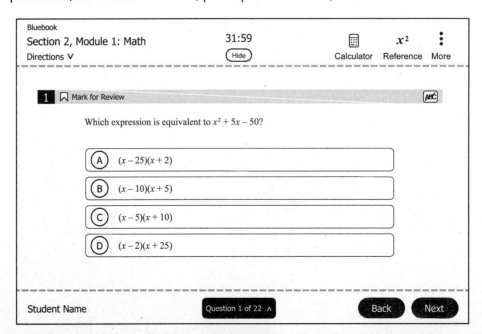

TIP

In each module, the questions start out relatively easy and get harder as you go.

TIP

Keep in mind that, along with these digital tools, you also are given scratch paper during the test. Using this scratch paper in conjunction with the built in calculator is key to success on the Digital SAT

238

TIP

At the bottom middle of the Bluebook app is an index of questions, which will also show the flag symbol for any marked questions.

TIP

Get familiar with the standard SAT directions *before* test day so you can focus on working the problems.

Note particularly the instructions entering fractions, decimals, and negatives. If your answer is **negative one-third**, acceptable answers include:

- ✓ –1/3
- ✓ –.3333
- ✓ –0.333

However, failing to use the full space will <u>NOT</u> give credit:

- ✗ –.33
- ✗ –0.33

If you're unsure, check the directions box for examples at any point in the test.

Digital Tools of the Bluebook App

Let's get familiar with the different buttons & tools in the bluebook app:

- 🖩 **Calculator -** Clicking this button brings up a pop-up window with the built-in Desmos calculator (detailed in the next chapter).

- **A̲B̲C̲** **Answer Eliminator -** Clicking this button allows you to cross out any answer choices that you believe are incorrect.

- ⚑ **Mark for Review -** Clicking the flag button labels the question as one you want to return to after finishing the section.

- x^2 **Reference** – Clicking this button brings up a pop-up window with the SAT math reference formulas.

- **Directions -** Clicking here brings up the standard directions for the Digital SAT math section.

The questions in this section address a number of important math skills. Use of a calculator is permitted for all questions. A reference sheet, calculator, and these directions can be accessed throughout the test. Unless otherwise indicated:

- All variables and expressions represent real numbers.

- Figures provided are drawn to scale.

- All figures lie in a plane.

- The domain of a given function f is the set of all real numbers x for which $f(x)$ is a real number.

For **multiple-choice questions**, solve each problem and choose the correct answer from the choices provided. Each multiple-choice question has a single correct answer.

For **student-produced questions**, solve each problem and enter your answer as described below.

- If you find **more than one correct answer**, enter only one answer.

- You can enter up to 5 characters for a **positive** answer and up to 6 characters (including the negative sign) for a **negative** answer.

- If your answer is a **fraction** that doesn't fit in the provided space, enter the decimal equivalent.

- If your answer is a **decimal** that doesn't fit in the provided space, enter it by truncating or rounding at the fourth digit.

- If your answer is a **mixed number** (such as 3 1/2), enter it as an improper fraction (7/2) or its decimal equivalent (3.5).

- Don't enter **symbols** such as a percent sign, comma, or dollar sign.

Scratch paper is still key to success!

Even with the powerful, built-in calculator, it's crucial that you use the provided scratch paper to keep **organized, helpful notes** as you work to help avoid mistakes and give your short-term memory a break:

- Write down your **goal**: what are you asked to solve for?

- Record **what variables MEAN**, not just what they EQUAL. If a word problem tells you that "x" represents "cars", write that!

- Jot down any **formulas** as soon as you know they are needed.

- In multistep problems, write down any **discoveries** you make (such as variables or factors) to "save" your progress.

- Draw **figures** for any geometry or trigonometry problems.

TIP

Organized notes make it much easier to double-check your work and review questions at the end.

Use scratch paper as you work through problems in this book to practice organization that can nab you precious points on test day.

Organization makes a huge difference

Without a plan, scratch paper can turn into a disorganized mess. Follow the tips below to keep your notes (and thoughts) organized on test day:

- **Number the questions** to make review easier.

- **Draw boxes** to keep your notes for each problem separate.

- **Circle answers** to make double-checking easier.

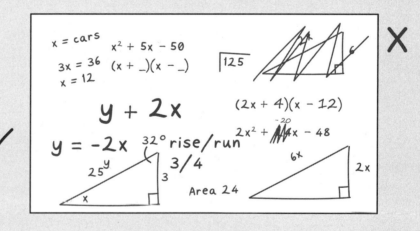

A bit of organization makes a big difference!

TIP

Working in **columns** can help you stay organized and use your space efficiently. Find an organiziation system that works best for you... and stick to it!

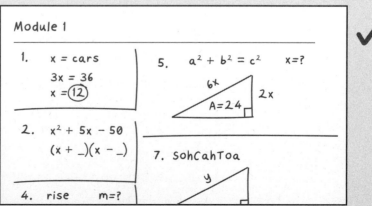

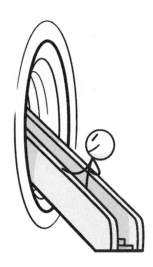

PORTAL

Have you had negative experiences in the past that make you anxious as soon as a math test starts?

This feeling of anxiety or powerlessness can be overcome! With the right tools, you can be **empowered**. To learn about test anxiety, turn to the *Beyond the Content* section on page 715.

Math is a skill you can build with practice

If you feel like a higher score is locked away behind some impenetrable door—it's not! This test measures two things and practice will improve them both. First, it measures your **knowledge** of key math concepts, all of which are covered in the very book you hold in your hands. Second, it measures your **skill** at tackling math problems—and you can build that skill just like you can build the skill of playing guitar or twirling a pen in that fancy way some people do. So here's how we'll raise your score:

① *Learn Key Concepts*

Take each chapter one-at-a-time. Try the examples, read the explanations, complete the practice problems, check your work, and look over the ones you miss the next day. Each time you do this, it's like adding another key to your keyring, unlocking more questions and more points.

② *Practice Using Your Math Tools*

The solutions to example problems will model the **skill** of solving math problems. You will learn to solve problems step-by-step, to tinker with the given information, and to use workarounds when you feel stuck. Along the way, you'll get better at using different tools to quickly work your way toward a correct answer.

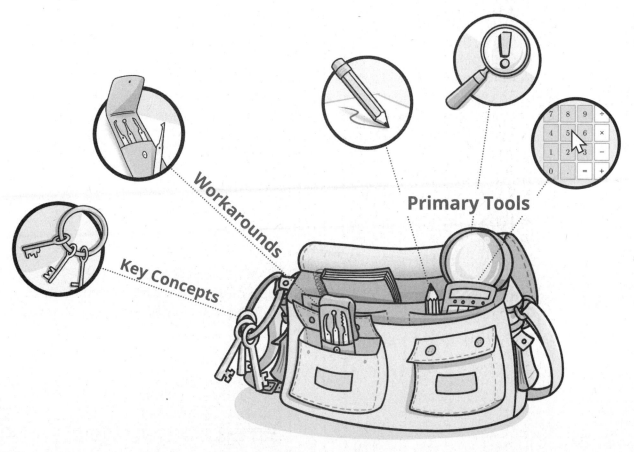

Math Strategy

Tags: Math Strategy

....

Step-by-Step Strategy

Let's sum up your step-by-step approach to answering math questions:

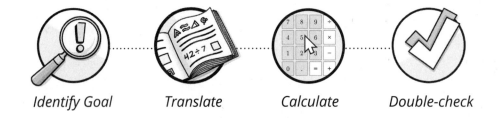

Identify Goal   *Translate*   *Calculate*   *Double-check*

TIP

Translation is extremely important on the SAT. Some questions are almost ALL translation: no calculations needed!

Math is more than just number crunching

Notice that "calculate" is only ONE step of the process! Many students think of "math" as "the stuff calculators do." But there's much more to "doing math" than just solving computations or doing arithmetic. Tackling a math problem involves reading, translating, and experimenting. In future chapters, we'll look at the creative ways you can tinker your way to a solution when you're stuck. For now, let's look at your primary strategy.

IDENTIFY YOUR GOAL

The first step is always to **read the problem actively** and <u>take notes</u> on key information that is given to you, including what variables mean and any related formulas. Before starting your work, answer these questions:

- What is my **goal**?

- What **key concepts** might I need?

- What do I know so far, and what do I need to find?

TRANSLATE

The next step is to **translate the information** in the prompt into math. This bridges the gap between reading the problem and calculating, and it is where many rushing students miss points. After you've identified the given information, use your pencil to:

- Copy any given **equations** (e.g., *Sarah = 2J + 4*).
- Create and define **variables** (e.g., *h = 12, V = ?*).
- Set up **ratios** (e.g., *2x = 3y*).

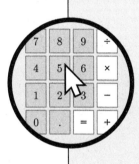

CALCULATE

Now that we've set up our work in steps one and two, it's time to start making calculations. Use a combination of your built-in calculator and scratch paper to record each step of your work. This will keep you on task and make it easier to spot any mistakes in the final step. Remember:

- Record **each step**: no exceptions!
- Work **one calculation** at a time.
- When you get a **result**, write it down!

——— Don't stop here! ———

At this point, we've read the problem, translated the given info to math, and carefully worked out each step, ending with an answer. There's even a multiple choice option with our answer! But are we finished? No! Give yourself a couple seconds to lock in those points by double-checking.

DOUBLE-CHECK

How often has this happened to you on a test: you put in all the hard work of the problem, reach what you think is the answer, and move on... only to realize later you forgot one final step, or gave *x* instead of *y*! Before moving on, save yourself points:

- **Circle** your answer.
- Double check that your solution **matches your goal**.
- Make sure your answer is **reasonable**.

UNIT | Math Toolkit

Chapters

Overview

In order to tackle math problems head-on, you need to identify your goal and carefully translate words into math using the **art of translation**. But if you get stuck, don't give up! Even if you're missing the key to a problem, you can often use the tools of **picking numbers** or **working backwards** to crack a locked problem wide open.

Calculator Overview

Access the calculator at desmos.com/calculator or through the Bluebook App.

....

Get to know the calculator to raise your score!

The built-in graphing calculator is a fantastic tool that is often (though not always) the fastest and most reliable tool for solving problems. You will want to practice with this calculator while studying, so let's learn the core features of the "Desmos" calculator built into the Digital SAT.

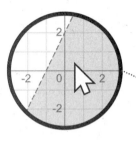

GRAPH

This area allows you to see the graph of equations entered into the inputs.

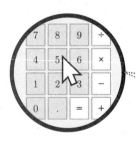

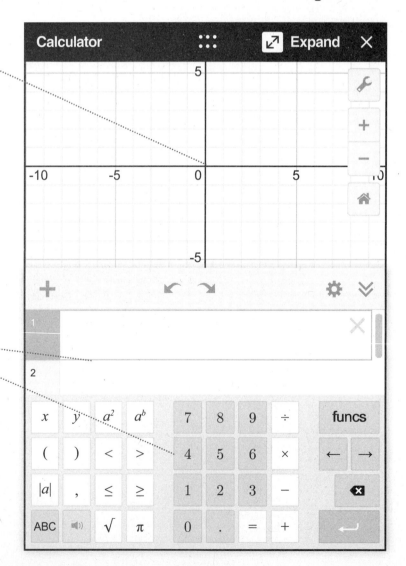

INPUT

This area allows you to enter algebraic equations or carry out simple arithmetic opeartions.

TIP

Scan the QR code above to open up the desmos calculator on your mobile device. Bookmark this page!

Any time you are studying or practicing for the Math section, make sure you have a Desmos calculator pulled up on your phone, laptop, or tablet!

Move the Calculator - You can click and drag here (or in the top bar to the left of the icon) to move the calculator. This can be helpful if the calculator is covering a part of the problem that you want to reference without closing the calculator.

Expand/Collapse - This allows you to switch between a smaller, vertically oriented calculator with the graphing window above the inputs and a larger horizontally oriented calculator with the graphing window to the right of the inputs.

Graph Settings - This has a couple of accessibility settings (larger font, reverse contrast (aka dark mode), and braille mode). It also gives you the opportunity to set the graphing window dimensions.

Zooming tools - There are a few different ways to zoom in and out on the graph depending on what input device(s) you are using. Click these buttons on a desktop, or use two fingers to zoom in and out on a mobile device.

Home - This button is not initially present, but if you have zoomed or moved the graph at all it will appear. Clicking the home button will take you back to the default zoom and location for the graph.

Add Item - This button gives you two options: Add Expression and Add Table. Add Expression is redundant since you can just click the next empty input slot. It isn't common, but if you want to plot a set of points, adding a table might be helpful.

Undo and Redo - These arrows allow you do undo and redo actions. If you accidentally delete a function or expression you weren't done with, this is a fast way to get it back.

Input Settings - Clicking this button opens a mode that gives you a fast way to delete everything if you want to clear the calculator out at the end of a problem. It also gives you tools to duplicate an input or to convert a function to a table.

Hide Expression List - This button lets you hide the expression list, aka, the input section, to allow the graph to take up the entire calculator window. You can restore the expression list by clicking the [double up arrow] icon in the lower right corner (or the [double right arrow] icon in the upper left in the expanded version of the calculator).

Input slots - This is where you type in the expressions you want the calculator to evaluate and the functions you want it to graph. Clicking into an input slot will bring up the calculator key pad. You are welcome to use it or your keyboard, whichever is easier for you on your device.

TIP

Using the calculator will speed you up and raise your score, but only if you familiarize yourself with it to get past any feelings of "clunkiness" on test day.

Practice with these core navigation tools until you get a base comfort level with the interface so you can focus on quickly getting solutions when you need them!

Changing your View and Zooming In/Out

As you graph equations, you may need to change your view in order to find intersections or curves of the graph. Let's look closer at your options:

Zoom In/Out – Clicking the zoom in/out buttons is a foolproof way to change your view until the graph is fully in view. On a mobile device or a touch pad, you can instead use two fingers to pinch-zoom in and out.

Clicking and Dragging – Click (or tap on a mobile device) and drag anywhere on the graph to move your view around the grid.

Home Button – If you ever get lost in the graph, clicking the Home button will reset your view to the default zoom level and location for your screen size.

Adjust Graph Settings – The wrench button in the upper right will allow you to set the boundaries of your graph. Simply change the minimum and maximum for the x-axis and y-axis to get a precise view of your choice.

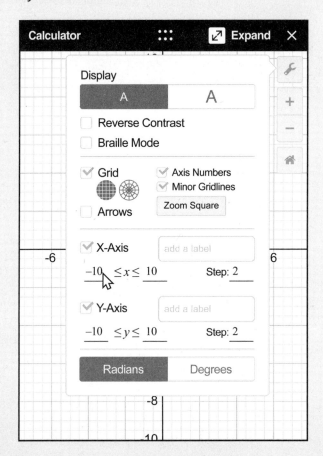

Do NOT use your browser keyboard zoom

Stick to the built-in Desmos tools to zoom in and out. Using your browser keyboard shortcuts for zooming in/out can cause odd scaling of the calculator. Remember to hit that "Home" button if things ever get weird!

Using Desmos to Solve SAT Math Problems

In just about every chapter of this section, you will find clever ways to use the built-in Desmos calculator to solve SAT problems. In the table below, we've listed the pages where you'll find advanced tips that will take your calculator game (and math score) to a whole new level.

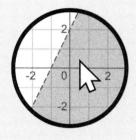

TIP

If you want to focus on building your Desmos calculator skills, turn to the pages listed here and read the calculator callout sections.

To practice each skill with realistic SAT questions, try the examples before and/or after each callout.

Alternatively, just work your way through the chapters of the book, learning the Desmos skills as you go.

Desmos Skills in Context

Art of Translation

Tags: Math Strategy

....

Translate words into math

Wordy problems are very common on the SAT. These problems depend almost entirely on correct translation from *English* into *Math* (or vice versa). For example, the sentence below can be translated into algebra:

The number of cookies	is	12	times	the number of trays.
C	$=$	12	$\times$	T

PORTAL

This chapter will give you the tools for dealing with word problems. We'll dig deeper into this concept in the *Linear Modeling* chapter, starting on page 482.

Translation helps you start on the right foot

Careful translation **bridges the gap** between reading the problem for the first time and starting your written work. When you use your pencil to translate what you're given and what you're asked, you start your work by answering two key questions:

What do I **know?**   What do I **need to find?**

Phrasebook

Notice how specific English words can be translated into specific symbols. We will be working on your ability to translate throughout the book, but here is a basic phrasebook for translating between languages.

English Word	Math Meaning
What, how much, a number	Some variable (? or x or y)
Is, was, equals	Equals (=)
Sum, increase, more/greater than	Add (+)
Subtract, less than, exceeds, difference	Subtract (−)
Of, times, product	Multiply (×)
Divisible by, divided by, out of, per	Divide (÷)
Percent (%)	Multiply by $\frac{1}{100}$

TIP

It is okay (and normal) to not immediately know what to do with every problem. Use the first two steps to reveal things about the problem you didn't notice at first glance:

1) **Circle** your goal
2) **Translate** what you can

Translate wordy sentences before you solve

The SAT writers are really good at finding slightly different ways to ask questions about the same basic concepts. For example, they might cloak a simple algebra equation behind a wordy sentence. These questions test whether you can **play and tinker** with problems as much as they are testing your algebra skills.

Let's practice by focusing on the <u>first two steps</u> of our math strategy: **identify** the goal and **translate** into math.

EXAMPLE 1

The product of two positive integers is 30 and their difference is one. What is the sum of the two numbers?

KEY IDEAS

An **integer** is a number that is not a fraction.

A **positive** number is greater than zero.

Never underestimate the importance of careful reading and translation! Let's work only the first two steps of our strategy.

Step 1: Identify the Goal

The product of two positive integers is 30 and their difference is one. What is the sum of the two numbers?

What's my goal?   the SUM of two numbers

What is given?
1. positive integers
2. difference is one
3. multiply to 30

Step 2: **Translate** the sentences into math equations.

The product of two positive integers	is	30
$a \times b$	=	30

their difference	is	one		what	is	their sum
$a - b$	=	1		?	=	$a + b$

So after the first two steps of our strategy, we have translated this wordy problem into three equations.

The product of two positive integers is 30 and their difference is one. What is the sum of the two numbers?

1. $a \times b = 30$
2. $a - b = 1$
3. $a + b = ?$

For now, we're only interested in translating. We'll practice the skills used to solve this in the **Basic Algebra** chapter.

Translate the following expressions into math using the phrasebook table on the previous page.

1	English	5 more than a number
	Math	$x + 5$
2	English	7 less than three times a number
	Math	
3	English	The square of one more than a number is added to 17
	Math	
4	English	The sum of two consecutive numbers
	Math	
5	English	4 less than the sum of a number and twice its square
	Math	

Translate the following SAT problems into math. Remember, we are not solving the problems yet—just translating!

6	English	If half of a number is equal to 5 more than twice the number, what is the number?
	Math	If $\frac{1}{2}x = 2x + 5$, $x = ?$
7	English	If 7 more than three times a number is equal to 25, what is half the number?
	Math	
8	English	If 6 more than a certain number is tripled the result is 66. What is the number?
	Math	

Answers: *Bottom of next page*

EXAMPLE 1

A painter charges $35 per hour for each hour he works on a house plus a one-time fee of $45. If he charges $220 after painting a house, how many hours did he work?

SOLUTION

This word problem needs some translating! Since we're focusing on correct translation, let's work through **just steps 1 and 2** of our math strategy.

Step 1: Identify the Goal

A painter charges <u>$35 per hour</u> for each hour he works on a house <u>plus a one-time fee of $45</u>. If he charges <u>$220 after painting a house</u>, ⟨how many hours⟩ did he work?

What's my goal? the number of HOURS worked

What is given?
1. $35 per hour
2. plus $45
3. total of $220

Now that we know what's given and what's needed, let's translate.

Step 2: Translate

Since the **number of hours** is unknown, let's make that *x*.

$35 per hour	plus $45	is $220	How many hours did he work?
35x	+ 45	= 220	x = ?

From here, we can do some basic algebra to solve for *x*!

TIP

We have two unknowns here: Levi's age and Maria's age. So we'll need TWO variables. Picking letters that connect to the words in the problem will help you remember what you're solving for.

Make Levi's age "L" and Maria's age "M."

EXAMPLE 2

Levi is twice as old as his sister Maria. Three years ago he was three times as old as she was then. How old is Levi?

Step 1: Identify the Goal

Levi is <u>twice</u> as old as his sister Maria. <u>Three years ago</u> he was <u>three</u> times as old as she was then. **How old is Levi?**

What's my goal?   Levi's current age (L)

What is given?
1. Now: Levi is twice Maria
2. 3 years ago: Levi was 3 times Maria

Step 2: Translate

We have two equations to translate that will lead us to L.

Levi	is	twice Maria		3 years ago, Levi	was	3 times Maria
L	$=$	$2M$		$(L-3)$	$=$	$3(M-3)$

Now we have two equations that we can use to solve for L:

1. $L = 2M$
2. $L - 3 = 3(M - 3)$

Translate the following word problems into math equations. The first one has been completed for you.

1	Levi is twice as old as his sister Maria. Three years ago he was three times as old as she was then. How old is Levi?	
	Goal	$L = ?$
	Equation 1	$L = 2M$
	Equation 2	$L - 3 = 3(M - 3)$
2	Atamari ran 5 more miles in February than she did in January. If she ran one and a half times farther in February than in January, how far did she run in February?	
	Goal	
	Equation 1	
	Equation 2	
3	Vi has a jar of change and has sorted it into piles of quarters, dimes and nickles. The number of nickles is three less than twice the number of quarters. The number of quarters is six more than twice the number of nickles. The number of dimes is two less than four times the number of quarters. How many coins does she have?	
	Goal	
	Equation 1	
	Equation 2	
	Equation 3	

Answers: 1. *given*
2. Goal: $F = ?$ E1: $F = J + 5$ E2: $F = 1.5J$
3. Goal: $Q + D + N = ?$ E1: $N = 2Q - 3$ E2: $Q = 2N + 6$ E3: $D = 4Q - 2$

For each equation, **write a sentence** that it could model. Use the first as an example.

BONUS!

1	Math	$N = 2P + 35$
	English	We need twice as many napkins as people, plus a backup of 35 in case of spills.
2	Math	$a + 5 = 3a$
	English	
3	Math	$2a + 4 = 5(a - 1)$
	English	
4	Math	$a + 3b = 17, \ a + b = 9$
	English	

Answers: We can't imagine what you came up with, but try translating it BACK into math to check your work!

Working Backwards

Tags: Math Strategy

....

When the choices are in order, work backwards

Sometimes it is easier to check whether an answer is correct than it is to solve for the answer directly. In algebra, students are often taught that the last step of a problem is to take the answer they've gotten and substitute it back into the original problem to check their work. On a multiple choice test, you can sometimes skip directly to that step since the answer is right there in the choices!

> John has x pieces of candy in his pocket. He gives half of the candies to Kerri, and one-third of the remaining candies to Lori. If he is left with 10 candies in his pocket, what is the value of x ?

We only have 4 choices.

One of them MUST be the right answer...

A) 60
B) 50
C) 40   *What if we just plug this in for x ?*
D) 30

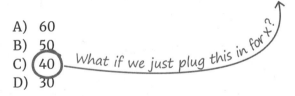

Sometimes the SAT will intentionally design problems so that you can't work backwards - watch out for them asking you for something like the sum of x and y rather than their values - but any time the answer choice is something you have the option of sneaking in through the back door.

EXAMPLE 1

John has x pieces of candy in his pocket. He gives half of the candies to Kerri, and one-third of the remaining candies to Lori. If he is left with 10 candies in his pocket, what is the value of x?

A) 60
B) 50
C) 40
D) 30

SOLUTION

Notice that this question is asking us for the value of a variable in the problem. We can test numbers to see if they work in this context, so this is a problem where we can work backwards. But first, let's actively read the question.

John has x pieces of candy in his pocket. He gives half of the candies to Kerri, and one-third of the remaining candies to Lori. If he is left with 10 candies in his pocket, what is the value of x?

So the answer choices are the number of candies at the start, and we want the one that results in 10 candies at the end. If we start by **plugging in a middle choice**, we get a result that is too high:

Try C		
	Start with 40	*40*
	Give away half (20)	*40 ÷ 2 = 20*
	Give away a third (~7)	*20 − 7 ≈ 13 too high!*

So if he starts with 40 pieces, he ends up with *more* than 10. That means he must need to start with fewer than 40 candies! Even though we only tested one choice, we can cross off **A**, **B**, and **C**! If we **try the next smaller choice**, we find the answer!

Try D		
	Start with 30	*30*
	Give away half (15)	*30 ÷ 2 = 15*
	Give away a third (5)	*15 − 5 = (10) bingo!*

D

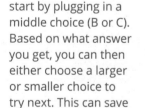

TIP

When working backwards, start by plugging in a middle choice (B or C). Based on what answer you get, you can then either choose a larger or smaller choice to try next. This can save you some time.

TIP

When a question asks you to pick an equivalent expression, that's a sign that working backwards with graphing is an option.

Expressions in the choices? Work Backwards!

You have access to a powerful tool while taking the SAT: the Desmos graphing calculator. This means that working backwards is not limited to just substituting in answer choices to algebra problems - if you can check whether an answer is correct by graphing, you can work backwards!

EXAMPLE 2

Which expression is equivalent to $\dfrac{2}{x+4} - \dfrac{6}{3x+1}$?

A) $\dfrac{-4}{-2x+3}$

B) $\dfrac{6}{(x+4)(3x+1)}$

C) $-\dfrac{2}{(x+4)(3x+1)}$

D) $-\dfrac{22}{(x+4)(3x+1)}$

TIP

When typing fractions into Desmos, you can press the right arrow on your keyboard (→) or the built-in keyboard to exit the numerator or denominator.

SOLUTION

This question is asking you to add two rational expressions and you could do that directly, but if you aren't comfortable doing so, you don't have to! Instead, you can **graph these expressions** and see which answer choice matches the original expression.

When you put "$\dfrac{2}{x+4} - \dfrac{6}{3x+1}$" in an input slot, Desmos will interpret it as "$y = \dfrac{2}{x+4} - \dfrac{6}{3x+1}$" and give you the corresponding graph:

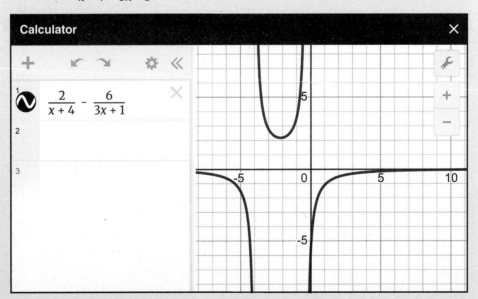

Continued on next page →

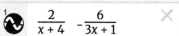

A) $\dfrac{-4}{-2x+3}$

B) $\dfrac{6}{(x+4)(3x+1)}$

C) $-\dfrac{2}{(x+4)(3x+1)}$

D) $-\dfrac{22}{(x+4)(3x+1)}$

You can then also graph each of the corresponding answer choices to find the one where the graph matches:

A)
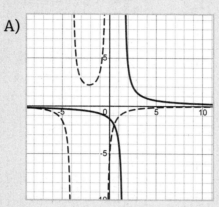

B)
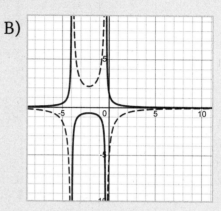

C)
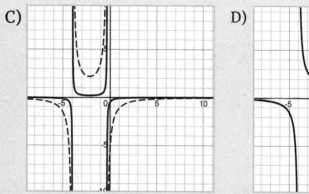

D)
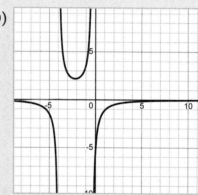

In **choice D** we see that the graph of the expression exactly matches the graph of the original expression, so it must be correct!

Picking Numbers

Tags: Math Strategy

Picking Numbers is a tool for taking questions that feel abstract and making them more concrete. On the SAT, it is particularly useful for some types of modeling problems. If you don't like translating a word problem into an algebraic expression or function, picking numbers can help!

PORTAL

To learn how to solve word problems head-on, check out the *Modeling Unit* on page 481.

Algebra (Head-on)
This method will get you to the answer choice more directly, but requires thinking more abstractly. We will discuss this approach in more detail in the modeling section of the book.

– or –

Picking Numbers (Workaround)
Sometimes it is easier to think through a scenario with actual numbers than with variables. It can also make it easier to catch mistakes since you can evaluate the numbers you get for reasonableness in context.

How to Pick Numbers

First, as usual, identify your goal. Second, **choose a value for x** (or whatever variable is given) that makes sense with the problem. Finally, plug in that value for x in the answer choices, looking for a match.

EXAMPLE 1

The sum of two positive consecutive integers is x. In terms of x, what is the value of the smaller of these two integers?

A) $\frac{x}{2} - 1$

B) $\frac{x-1}{2}$

C) $\frac{x}{2}$

D) $\frac{x}{2} + 2$

Step 1: Identify the Goal
No matter what strategy you're using, the first step is ALWAYS to read the question and identify your goal!

The <u>sum</u> of <u>two</u> <u>positive</u> <u>consecutive</u> <u>integers</u> is x. In terms of x, what is the value of the (smaller) of these two integers?

What's my goal?   The smaller number

What is given?   <u>Two numbers that are:</u>

1. **positive** (greater than zero)

2. **consecutive** (back-to-back)

3. **integers** (no fractions)

4. sum = x

Step 2: Pick Numbers
Now we can pick any numbers that follow the rules above. Let's keep it simple and make the smaller integer **2**. That would make our larger consecutive integer **3**.

Write the equation	x = smaller + larger
Pick "2" and "3"	x = 2 + 3
Find the sum	x = 5

Now we know that when we pick 2 and 3, the sum (x) is 5.

Continued on next page →

Step 3: Plug in and Solve

Now we have a number for x that we can plug into each answer choice. If we **plug in 5 for x**, the correct answer should give us our target: the smaller integer 2.

$x = 5$	target = 2

Plug 5 into Choice **A**   ~~A)~~ $\frac{x}{2} - 1$ $=$ $2.5 - 1 = 1.5$ *Not 2!*

Plug 5 into Choice **B**   ✓ B) $\frac{x-1}{2}$ $=$ $\frac{5-1}{2} = \frac{4}{2} = 2$ *Bingo!*

Plug 5 into Choice **C**   ~~C)~~ $\frac{x}{2}$ $=$ $\frac{5}{2} = 2.5$ *Nope!*

Plug 5 into Choice **D**   ~~D)~~ $\frac{x}{2} + 2$ $=$ $\frac{5}{2} + 2 = 4.5$ *Nope!*

When we plug in one possible sum (5) for x in each choice, only **choice B** correctly spits out the value of our **smaller number**!   **B**

TIP

Go ahead and check each answer, even if you find a match... just in case.

TIP

Notice that once you find that choice C is 2.5, you can just add 2 to get choice D!

Guidelines for Picking Numbers

Here are a couple of best practices when you are picking numbers.

1. **Follow the rules.** This is crucial! If the problem tells you the numbers are less than 15, don't pick 20!

2. **Do NOT pick 0 or 1.** These numbers do strange things to equations and functions. They can cause confusion, so it's (usually) best to steer clear of them.

3. **Solve for the loner.** If you are solving an equation like $x + y = z$, it's better to PICK numbers for the two variables on the same side and SOLVE for the one that's alone.

4. **Repeat if necessary.** If more than one answer choice gives you your target number, don't worry! You've narrowed your choices down, and can now pick different numbers to confirm the best choice (this is rarely required).

EXAMPLE 2

Chris is ordering food for a party. There is a flat $20 delivery fee and each tray of food is an additional $15. Which equation represents the total cost c, in dollars, to have t trays of food delivered?

A) $c = 15(t + 20)$

B) $c = 20(t + 15)$

C) $c = 20t + 15$

D) $c = 15t + 20$

 SOLUTION

Step 1: Identify the Goal
Is picking numbers a resonable approach? Let's start by taking a quick look at the answer choices. They all express one variable, c, in terms of the other, t, and we are looking for an equation that works for a wide range of situations rather than setting up to solve for a specific one. These features mean we can use picking numbers!

Step 2: Pick Numbers
The cost is *determined* by the number of trays, so lets pick a value for t. Suppose we want to order 3 trays of food. Then $t = 3$ and since each tray costs $15, altogether they will cost $3 \cdot 15 = \$45$. Then there is the additional delivery fee, so our total cost is $45 + 20 = \$65$.

Continued on next page →

Step 3: Test the Answer Choices

Now that we have determined the total cost, we can plug in $t = 33$ into each answer choice and see which one gives us $c = 65$.

$t = 33$	target = 65

Plug 33 into Choice A   ~~A)~~ $c = 15(3 + 20) = 345$ ✗

Plug 33 into Choice B   ~~B)~~ $c = 20(3 + 15) = 360$ ✗

Plug 33 into Choice C   ~~C)~~ $c = 20(3) + 15 = 75$ ✗

Plug 33 into Choice D   ✓ D) $c = 15(3) + 20 = 65$ *Yes!*

D

Mixed Practice

*For each problem, choose whether you should use **Picking Numbers (PN)** or **Working Backwards (WB)**.*

1

John is 6 years older than Mark. 6 years ago John was twice as old as Mark. How old is John today?

A) 6
B) 9
C) 12
D) 18

☐ PN ☐ WB

2

Which of the following equations expresses z in terms of x for all real numbers x, y, and z such that $x^3 = y$ and $y^2 = z$?

A) x^6
B) x^5
C) x^3
D) $2x$

☐ PN ☐ WB

3

A kindergarten class wants to buy a $64 aquarium for the classroom. If the teacher and students split the cost such that the teacher pays three times as much as the students, how much, in dollars, should the teacher pay?

A) 16
B) 32
C) 48
D) 56

☐ PN ☐ WB

4

Scott has exactly twice as many trading cards as Todd does. Ryan has exactly four times as many trading cards as Scott does. If the three of them have fewer than 100 trading cards combined, what is the maximum number of trading cards Todd could have?

A) 6
B) 9
C) 10
D) 12

☐ PN ☐ WB

5

If $x = 3z$ and $y = 9z$, what is x in terms of y?

A) $3y$

B) $6y$

C) y

D) $\frac{y}{3}$

☐ PN ☐ WB

6

Jamal has a bag of marbles. He gives exactly 1/3 of his marbles to Isaac, and has 2/3 of his original number of marbles remaining. If Jamal is able to repeat this action at least 3 more times without breaking any marbles into pieces, how many marbles could he have started with?

A) 12
B) 18
C) 24
D) 81

☐ PN ☐ WB

267

7

A Spanish teacher wants to have a party for her students, and she needs to buy candy to put in the piñata. She buys $100 worth of 2 types of candy. One type of candy costs $0.10 a piece and another type costs $0.25 a piece. If she bought 550 pieces of candy in total, how many pieces of the more expensive candy did she buy?

A) 200
B) 240
C) 300
D) 380

□ PN □ WB

8

If a, b, and c are nonzero numbers such that $a = bc$, which of the following must be equivalent to ac ?

A) $\dfrac{b}{a}$

B) b^2c

C) bc

D) $\dfrac{a^2}{b}$

□ PN □ WB

9

Two identical 6-inch deep water buckets drain at uniform rates of 1 inch per hour. If bucket one begins draining at 12 p.m., and bucket two begins draining at 2 p.m., at what time will bucket two have exactly five times as much water as bucket one?

A) 4:00 p.m.
B) 4:30 p.m.
C) 5:30 p.m.
D) 6:00 p.m.

□ PN □ WB

10

The side of a square is d inches longer than the side of a second square. The perimeter of the first square must be how much longer, in inches, than the perimeter of the second square?

A) $\dfrac{d}{4}$

B) d

C) $4d$

D) d^2

□ PN □ WB

11

Train A travels 75 mph less than twice the speed of Train B. If the speed of Train A is k mph, which of the following expressions represents the speed of Train B, in miles per hour?

A) $\dfrac{k + 75}{2}$

B) $\dfrac{k - 75}{2}$

C) $k + 75$

D) $2k + 75$

□ PN □ WB

UNIT | Foundations

Chapters

Overview

In this unit, we'll practice core skills and vocabulary that can be tested in a number of different question types. We'll learn to balance equations, work with exponents, and practice solving equations involving fractions and decimals.

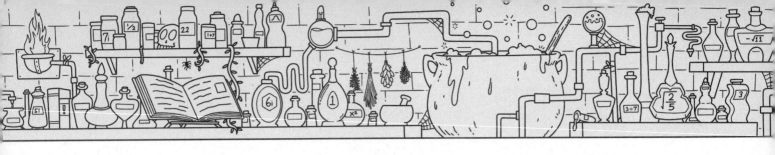

Basic Algebra

Tags: Algebra • Algebra Foundations

NOTE

The letters *a*, *b*, *c*, *x*, *w*, *y*, and *z* are common variable choices. You may have even seen worksheets where an empty box or a "?" is used.

Algebra is all about exploring the unknown

In our art of translation phrasebook, we have the following line:

English	Math
What, how much, a number	Some variable (x)

Anytime there is something we don't know—the number of hours, the price of a hamburger, a person's age, etc.—we stick a symbol in as a placeholder and call that symbol a **variable**. The goal in algebra problems is to figure out what number(s) the variable represents (or, in math terms, what value you can **substitute** for the variable to make the expression true).

You might be able to solve easy problems just by staring at them. For example, you might look at "$7 + x = 13$" and think "Well $7 + 6$ is 13, so x must be 6!" However, as problems get more complicated, this approach brings more and more space for errors. For tougher problems, we need a more concrete, systematic approach. And *that's* where <u>algebra</u> comes in.

TIP

When you see an expression like "2a", that is a short cut for "2 times a" and means that there are two copies of "a" present. So "2a + a" means "two copies of a plus one more" which gives you three copies of "a", so "2a + a = 3a". Note that if you have different letters, like "2a + b" or one term with a variable and one without, like "2x + 1", you can't directly combine them.

TIP

In this example, if we add 7 to the left side of the equation and NOT to the right side, it disrupts the balance and **changes the equation.**

Make balanced changes to each side

Solving basic algebra problems is just a balancing act. The test writers will give you an algebra equation, like:

$$2x - 7 = -21$$

...and then they'll ask you to "solve for x." Which really just means that we need to strategically add, subtract, multiply, or divide until "x" is alone on one side of the equation.

But here's the key: we have to keep the equation **balanced**. Anything we do to the left side of the equal sign we must also do to the right side... otherwise, we throw off the balance and change the equation:

Balanced!

$$2x - 7 = -21$$
$$+7 \quad\quad +7$$
$$2x = -14$$

Not Balanced!

$$2x - 7 = -21$$
$$+7$$
$$2x = -21$$

On the right, we made the mistake of only adding 7 to one side of the equation. We can tell at a glance that something's wrong... after all, how can $2x = -21$ when $2x - 7 = -21$? To avoid this, remember to always make step-by-step, **balanced changes** to each side of the equation.

Write down your work to avoid errors

Making balanced changes is the most basic algebra skill we can cover. But in the rush of the test, it's often these basic skills that suffer. It's not just "careless" students who make "careless errors" – they can result from focusing so much on the tougher topics that you forget to actually work out the simpler steps. As a result, you forget to distribute a negative or you make a basic error of substitution. To avoid these errors, get in the habit of writing out careful, step-by-step work.

Follow the step-by-step instructions to complete the solution below.

If $5x - 6 = 54$, then $x = ?$	
1. *Rewrite equation*	
2. *Add 6 to both sides*	
3. *Write the result*	
4. *Divide both sides by 5*	
5. *Write the result*	

Solve for *x* in the problems below.

Equation	$x = ?$
6. $12x + 12 = 12$	
7. $3x - 7 = 14$	
8. $2x + 3 = 4x - 8$	
9. $-13x = -3x + 30$	
10. $15x - 10 = 12x + 11$	

Answers: 1. $5x - 6 = 54$ 2. $5x - 6 + 6 = 54 + 6$ 3. $5x = 60$ 4. $5x \div 5 = 60 \div 5$ 5. $x = 12$

6. 0   7. 7   8. 11/2   9. –3   10. 7

TIP

"What value of x satisfies the equation" is just a fancy way to say "Solve the equation for x".

You can tinker with problems to find a solution

As long as you follow the rule of making balanced changes to each side (as well as those pesky rules about not dividing by zero, etc.) you are **free** to manipulate the equation as you see fit. If you feel like adding 1,000,000 and then subtracting 1,000,000 to each side, you'd be totally free to do that! We wouldn't recommend it, but, hey, you're the boss. *Experimentation* is a skill that can be a huge help on tougher problems.

EXAMPLE 1

What value of x satisfies the equation $\frac{13}{15}x - \frac{8}{15}x = \frac{3}{5} + \frac{3}{20}$?

Start by combining like terms on the left. Both terms have the same denominators and one x, so let's combine and simplify:

① combine $\qquad \frac{5}{15}x = \frac{3}{5} + \frac{3}{20}$

② simplify $\qquad \frac{1}{3}x = \frac{3}{5} + \frac{3}{20}$

Now clean up the right side. We have two constants. To combine these fractions, we need a common denominator:

③ find C.D. $\qquad \frac{1}{3}x = \frac{3}{5} + \frac{3}{20} \implies \frac{12}{20} + \frac{3}{20} \implies \frac{15}{20} \implies \frac{3}{4}$

so... $\qquad \frac{1}{3}x = \frac{3}{4}$

Finally, make balanced changes to isolate x. To get x by itself, we need to get rid of that fraction by multiplying *both sides* by 3.

④ balance $\qquad (3)\frac{1}{3}x = \frac{3}{4}(3)$

voila! $\qquad x = \boxed{\frac{9}{4}}$

$\frac{9}{4}$

You can also fully solve algebra problems like this one in your Desmos calculator. Let's explore how this works.

PORTAL

When you have fractional coefficients, you add and subtract them following normal fraction rules.

For practice on working with *Fractions*, turn to page 300, but don't forget that you can also use your calculator!

TIP

Desmos treats *x* and *y* differently than it treats all other letters/variables.

PORTAL

For more about working with *Systems of Equations*, turn to page 447.

Desmos: Solving Algebra Problems

There are two main approaches to using Desmos to solve algebra problems with 1 variable. Both options below assume that your variable is *x*. If it isn't, you will need to **replace the variable with *x*** before putting it into Desmos.

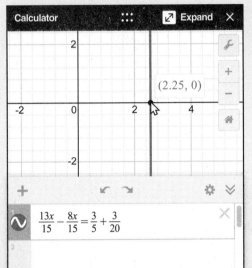

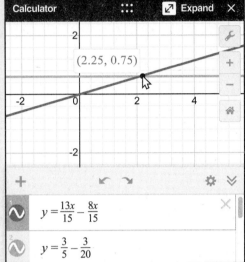

Option 1: If you type the full equation into one input slot, the calculator will graph a vertical line. The *x*-coordinate of that vertical line is the solution to your equation!

Option 2: Turn one equation into a System of Equations by taking each half and setting it equal to *y*. When you do this, the *x*-coordinate of the intersection point is the solution to the original equation.

Try these problems again with Desmos and double check that you get the same answers you did when solving by hand on the previous page.

Equation	$x = ?$
1. $12x + 12 = 12$	
2. $3x - 7 = 14$	
3. $2x + 3 = 4x - 8$	
4. $-13x = -3x + 30$	
5. $15x - 10 = 12x + 11$	

Distributive Property

The distributive property states that for all real numbers a, b, and c:

$$a(\overset{\frown}{b + c}) = ab + bc$$

If we translate this into words, it means that when multiplying an expression where two or more things are added, you can "distribute" that multiplication to each term rather than first simplify the parentheses.

$$2(3 + 5) \ = \ 2(8) \ = \ \mathbf{16}$$
$$2(\overset{\frown}{3 + 5}) \ = \ 6 + 10 \ = \ \mathbf{16}$$

When working with numbers, as in this example, you can go either way, but the distributive property is important once variables get involved.

EXAMPLE 2

If $3(x + 4) = 2(10 - x) + 17$, then $x = ?$

There are balanced changes we could make here, but none of them are particularly nice or helpful. The best first step is to apply the distributive property to both sides:

(1) *Distribute* $\qquad\qquad 3(\overset{\frown}{x + 4}) = 2(\overset{\frown}{10 - x}) + 17$

$\qquad\qquad\qquad\qquad\qquad\qquad 3x + 12 = 20 - 2x + 17$

(2) *Simplify* $\qquad\qquad\qquad 3x + 12 = -2x + 37$

Next, make balanced changes to move all terms with an x to one side. Let's move the x's to the left, and everything else to the right.

(3) *Add* $\mathbf{2x}$ $\qquad\qquad\qquad 3x + 12 + \mathbf{2x} = -2x + 37 + \mathbf{2x}$

$\qquad\qquad\qquad\qquad\qquad\qquad 5x + 12 = 37$

Continued on next page →

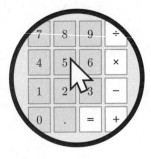

TIP

Try using Desmos to solve this problem! Remember to replace the *m*'s with *x*'s.

TIP

It's completely okay (and often necessary) to multiply both sides of an equation by an **expression**, such as (*m* − 7), rather than just a variable or constant.

Remember, you can do anything you want to the equation as long as you keep it balanced!

④ Subtract **12** $5x + 12 - 12 = 37 - 12$

$$5x = 25$$

⑤ Divide by 5 $\boxed{x = 5}$

5

EXAMPLE 3

If $\frac{4m + 2}{m - 7} = 9$ what is the value of *m*?

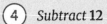

SOLUTION

First, look at the left side. We have a fraction with the variable we're looking for, *m*, in both the numerator and denominator. That's messy. Let's get rid of the fraction by multiplying **both sides** of the equation by the denominator, then make more balanced changes until *m* is all by itself.

① Multiply by (*m* − 7) $(m-7)\frac{4m+2}{m-7} = 9(m-7)$

$$4m + 2 = 9m - 63$$

② Subtract 4m $4m - 4m + 2 = 9m - 4m - 63$

$$2 = 5m - 63$$

③ Add 63 $2 + 63 = 5m - 63 + 63$

$$65 = 5m$$

④ Divide by 5 $\frac{65}{5} = \frac{5m}{5}$

...booyah! $\boxed{13} = m$

13

276

You can substitute equivalent values for variables

Whenever you are given (or discover through work) another "name" for a variable, you can **plug in** that new name anywhere the variable appears. For example, if we have the equation:

$$5k + a = 26$$

...and we learn that **$k = 2$**, we can go back and **substitute** in 2 anywhere we see k, and that will help us move forward in the problem:

$$5(2) + a = 26$$
$$10 + a = 26$$
$$10 - 10 + a = 26 - 10$$
$$a = 16$$

This also works if you are told that **$k = a - 2$**. In this case, we just replace every k with an ($a - 2$):

$$5(a - 2) + a = 26$$
$$5a - 10 + a = 26$$
$$6a - 10 = 26$$
$$6a = 36$$
$$a = 6$$

PORTAL

Balancing and substitution are the most important keys for unlocking algebra problems. You'll use these basic skills to solve even the toughest *Systems of Equations* problems.

Don't believe us? Turn to page 448 to see for yourself!

The name's k, but YOU can call me (a − 2)!

Parentheses

Please use them! We've seen far too many students forget to place parentheses before they substitute, only to accidentally forget a negative and miss easy points.

Solve for _d_ by following each step below.

	$3a - b - c = d$ If $a = -2$, $b = -5$, and $c = 1$, then $d = ?$	
1. Rewrite equation	$3a - b - c = d$
2. Substitute for a	
3. Substitute for b	
4. Substitute for c	
5. Simplify	
6. Solve	$d =$

Substitute the given values to solve each problem below.

	$a = 3$ $\quad$ $b = 4$ $\quad$ $c = -2$
7. $2a + 7 =$	
8. $b - 2c =$	
9. $2a + 3b - 4c =$	
10. $a^2 + 2a + c =$	
11. $ab - bc + ac =$	

Answers:
1. $3a - b - c = d$
2. $3(-2) - b - c$
3. $3(-2) - (-5) - c$
4. $3(-2) - (-5) - (1)$
5. $-6 + 5 - 1$
6. 2
7. 13
8. 8
9. 26
10. 13
11. 14

PORTAL

Occasionally the SAT will dress this kind of problem up in a context. For more practice, turn to *Applied Algebra* on page 534.

TIP

The question tells you that the variables represent distinct positive numbers. For questions where the answer choices are equations, you can generally ignore these qualifications. Sometimes they are there to make sure that you don't end up with undefined points in the answer. Sometimes, like in this problem, they are just there as a distraction.

Solving for one variable in terms of others

Sometimes the SAT will ask you to express a particular variable in terms of others. Your goal here is to use your algebra skills to get the variable they have asked for by itself on one side of the equation.

EXAMPLE 4

$$\frac{a}{4} + 12b = c$$

The given equation relates the distinct positive numbers a, b, and c. Which equation correctly expresses a in terms of b and c?

A) $a = \frac{c}{4} - 3b$

B) $a = 4c - 48b$

C) $a = \frac{c}{4} - 12b$

D) $a = c - 12b$

SOLUTION

Our goal in this problem is to express a in terms of the other variables. This means our goal is to get a by itself. We want to use balanced changes to move all terms that contain a to one side and all terms that don't to the other. Then we can handle any coefficient on the a term.

(1) *Subtract*

$$\frac{a}{4} + 12b = c$$
$$\quad -12b \quad -12b$$
$$\frac{a}{4} = c - 12b$$

(2) *Multiply*

$$4(\frac{a}{4}) = 4(c - 12b)$$
$$a = 4(c - 12b)$$

(3) *Distribute!*

$$\boxed{a = 4c - 48b}$$

B

Practice Problems

Use your new skills to answer each question.

1

Which expression is equivalent to $15s - (3s - 5s)$?

A) $7s$
B) $12s$
C) $17s$
D) $23s$

2

Which expression is equivalent to $(12x - 5) + 3(x - 4)$?

A) $15x - 17$
B) $15x - 9$
C) $15x - 7$
D) $15x + 7$

3

If $x = 32$, what is the value of $x - 8$?

A) 4
B) 24
C) 26
D) 40

4

$$m + 15 = 3m - 5$$

What is the solution to the given equation?

A) 2
B) 5
C) 10
D) 20

5

$$6x - 5 = 23$$

Which equation has the same solution as the given equation?

A) $6x = 115$
B) $6x = 28$
C) $6x = 18$
D) $6x = 4.6$

6

$$3x + 20 = 44$$

What value of x is the solution to the given equation?

7

If $\frac{1}{2}(n - 12) = -5$, what is the value of $4n + 5$?

A) 2
B) 6
C) 13
D) 14

8

If $\frac{10}{4 - n} = -c$, what is the value of n when $c = 10$?

A) −5
B) −3
C) 3
D) 5

9

If $a = kb$ where k is a constant and $a = 12$ when $b = 15$, what is the value of a when $b = 12$?

A) $\frac{4}{5}$

B) $\frac{5}{4}$

C) $9\frac{3}{5}$

D) 12

10

If the points (5, 20) and (3, a) are solutions for the equation $y = kx$, where k is a constant, what is the value of a ?

A) 5
B) 6
C) 12
D) 19

11

If 7 less than 5 times a number is two more than twice that number, what is the result when the number is added to 8 ?

A) $\frac{5}{7}$

B) 3

C) 11

D) 17

12

If $6x + 1$ is 3 more than $3x + 13$, what is the value of 8 subtracted from 4 times x ?

A) 12
B) −5
C) −20
D) −28

282

13

$$6r + 15s = t$$

The given equation relates the numbers r, s, and t. Which equation correctly expresses s in terms of r and t?

A) $s = \dfrac{t - 6r}{15}$

B) $s = \dfrac{6r - t}{15}$

C) $s = \dfrac{t}{15} - 6r$

D) $s = 15t - 6$

14

$$j = \dfrac{3p + 5}{2m - 7}$$

The given equation relates the distinct negative numbers j, p, and m. Which equation correctly expresses $2m - 7$ in terms of j and p?

A) $2m - 7 = 3p + 5 - j$

B) $2m - 7 = j(3p + 5)$

C) $2m - 7 = \dfrac{j}{3p + 5}$

D) $2m - 7 = \dfrac{3p + 5}{j}$

15

$$3j + 4p = 12m - 3p$$

The given equation relates the the numbers j, m, and p. Which equation correctly expresses p in terms of j and m?

A) $p = 12m - 3j$

B) $p = \dfrac{12m - 3j}{7}$

C) $p = 3j - 12m$

D) $p = \dfrac{3j - 12m}{7}$

Exponents

Tags: Algebra • Equivalent Expressions: Exponents and Radicals

Exponents are a shorthand for multiplication

Multiplication is something of a shorthand for **repeated addition**. For example, when we say "2 × 3" it is equivalent to *adding 2 three times*:

$$2 \times 3 = 2 + 2 + 2$$

Similarly, *exponents* can be thought of as **repeated multiplication**.

$$2^3 = 2 \times 2 \times 2$$

In this example, we are multiplying 3 copies of the number 2 together. 2 is called the <u>base</u> and 3 is the <u>exponent</u> (aka the <u>power</u>). Often, the base will be a variable, like x, rather than a number. Any number in front of the base is called the <u>coefficient</u>. All of this together is called a <u>term</u>.

TIP

You can think of even lonely terms like "x" or "y^2" as having a hidden coefficient and power of 1.

For example, $x = 1x^1$.

$$\text{coefficient} \longrightarrow \underbrace{3x^{3}}_{\text{term}} \quad \begin{array}{l} \leftarrow \text{power} \\ \leftarrow \text{base} \end{array}$$

PORTAL

To see what happens when the exponent is a **variable**, like x, check out *Exponential Modeling* on page 522.

Quick Vocab

A **monomial** is an expression consisting of a <u>single</u> term (e.g., $15x^3$)

A **binomial** consists of the sum of <u>two</u> terms. (e.g., $2x^2 + 2x$ or $xy^2 + 5z$)

A **polynomial** is a catchall word for the sum of <u>any number</u> of terms. This includes monomials, binomials, and one-to-infinity-nomials.

Identify the different terms of the polynomials, and for each term identify the coefficient, base, and power.

$5x^4 + 12x^3 + 7x$			
term	coefficient	base	power
1. $5x^4$	5	x	4
2.			
3.			

$6x^5 - 4x^2 + 3y^2 - 2y + 4$			
term	coefficient	base	power
4.			
5.			
6.			
7.			
8.			

Answers: *Bottom of next page*

TIP

Sometimes you can manipulate terms so that they do have like bases, but on the SAT you are unlikely to need to. For now, just remember that if the bases are different, they can't get together.

Exponent rules apply to like bases

Coming up, we'll review the basic rules for combining terms with exponents. But first a blanket rule: **you can only combine terms with like bases**. "Like bases" just means the bases are the same number of variable. This is why we can't further simplify "$(a^2)(x^3)$", but we CAN do something about "$(a^2)(a^3)$."

It just never worked with any of my x's.

285

Exponent Rules	
Any number **raised to zero** is equal to **one**.	$x^0 = 1x^0 = 1(1) = 1$
When you **multiply** like bases, **add** exponents.	$x^2 \cdot x^3 = (x{\cdot}x)(x{\cdot}x{\cdot}x) = x^5$
When you **divide** like bases, **subtract** exponents.	$x^6 \div x^2 = \frac{x^6}{x^2} = \frac{(x{\cdot}x{\cdot}x{\cdot}x{\cdot}x{\cdot}x)}{(x{\cdot}x)} = x^4$
When you **raise** a power to a power, **multiply** exponents.	$(x^2)^3 = (x{\cdot}x)(x{\cdot}x)(x{\cdot}x) = x^6$
When you have a **negative exponent**, take the **reciprocal**.	$x^{-2} = \frac{1}{x^2}$
When you have a **fractional exponent**, make it a **root**.	$x^{\frac{1}{2}} = \sqrt{x}$ or $x^{\frac{1}{3}} = \sqrt[3]{x}$

LIKE TERMS (N.)

Any terms with the same variable and exponent. For example:

- $2a$ and $3a$
- $6a^5$ and $8a^5$
- $4a^2b$ and $-3a^2b$

NOT $3a$ and $3a^2$

Combining Like Terms

The simplest questions that test these exponent rules are basic algebra questions that require you to **combine like terms**. After all, "like terms" just means "terms with the same variable and exponent." Remember: we can combine $x + 2x$, and we can combine $x^2 + 2x^2$, but we can NOT combine $x + x^2$. Got it? Good. Let's get some practice.

EXAMPLE 1

$$4x^2 + 7x - 12$$
$$-2x^2 + 3x - 5$$

What is the sum of the two given polynomials?

Previous Page: 1. *given*   2. $12x^3$; 12 ; x ; 3   3. $7x$; 7 ; x ; 1   4. $6x^5$; 6 ; x ; 5

5. $-4x^2$; -4 ; x ; 2   6. $3y^2$; 3 ; y ; 2   7. $-2y$; -2 ; y ; 1   8. 4 ; n/a ; 4 ; 1

To add these polynomials, we'll need to **combine like terms** (terms where the variables *and exponents* are the same). In this problem, the like terms are conveniently aligned vertically! Let's combine like terms:

$$
\begin{array}{rrr}
4x^2 & +7x & -12 \\
+(-2x^2) & +(+3x) & +(-5) \\
\hline
2x^2 & +10x & -17
\end{array}
$$

And that's it! By adding the like terms in each column, we get our answer: **$2x^2 + 10x - 17$.**

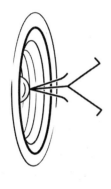

PORTAL

This problem is an example of a special type of problem we'll cover in greater detail in the *Pattern Matching* chapter on page 394.

EXAMPLE 2

$$(4x^2 - 11x + 3) - 3(x^2 + 4x - 5)$$

If the expression above is rewritten in the form $ax^2 + bx + c$, where a, b, and c are constants, which of the following is the value of $b + c$?

A) −35
B) −11
C) −5
D) 18

Watch Signs!

Most students who miss this problem either forget to distribute the negative in **–3** or miss that **b** must be *negative* 23, not just 23. Can you see why that is?

If you made one of these errors, what precautions could you take to avoid making the same mistake again?

SOLUTION

Before we can combine like terms in this problem, we have to take care of the parentheses (remember your order of operations!). The parentheses around **($4x^2 - 11x + 3$)** are just grouping them, so we can safely remove them without changing anything. But before we can combine like terms, we first need to distribute the **–3** across **($x^2 + 4x - 5$):**

(1) distribute $\quad -3\,(x^2 + 4x - 5) = -3x^2 - 12x + 15$

Now we can put it together and find like terms.

(2) combine like terms

$$\frac{4x^2 - 11x + 3 - 3x^2 - 12x + 15}{x^2 - 23x + 18}$$

We have now rewritten the original expression in the exact form we need! If we stack them, we can figure out what a, b, and c are.

(3) stack & spot

$$x^2 - 23x + 18$$
$$ax^2 + bx + c$$

$a = 1$
$b = -23$
$c = 18$

If we match patterns between these two expressions, we see that **$a = 1$, $b = -23$**, and **$c = 18$**. Now we just need to find **$b + c$**

(4) add! $\quad b + c = -23 + 18 = \boxed{-5}$

C

EXAMPLE 3

$$2(a^2 + 2ab - 8ab^2) - (2a^2 + 3ab - 5ab^2)$$

Which of the following is equivalent to the above expression?

A) $3a^2 + 5ab - 13ab^2$
B) $ab - 11ab^2$
C) $ab - 21ab^2$
D) $4a^2 - ab - 3ab^2$

NOTE

Anytime a term has no coefficient, there is secretly a 1 hidden there. That's why **a = 1** in the previous question.

That's also why here you multiply each term by **−1** when you see a minus sign outside of the parentheses.

SOLUTION

When you first look at this problem, the terms with multiple letters might look complicated. But they don't actually make it any harder! The first step is the same as the last problem – **distribute across the parentheses**, being careful with negative signs.

$$2(a^2 + 2ab - 8ab^2) - 1(2a^2 + 3ab - 5ab^2)$$

$$\underline{2a^2} + \underset{\sim}{4ab} - \overset{\cdots}{16ab^2} \quad \underline{- 2a^2} - \underset{\sim}{3ab} + \overset{\cdots}{5ab^2}$$

Now we need to combine like terms. This is just pattern matching.

$$\underline{(2 - 2)a^2} + \underset{\sim}{(4 - 3)ab} + \overset{\cdots}{(-16 + 5)ab^2}$$

$$= 0a^2 + 1ab - 11ab^2$$

$$= \boxed{ab - 11ab^2}$$

B

EXAMPLE 4

For non-zero values of a and b, which of the following expressions is equivalent to $\frac{35a^2b^4}{7ab^2}$?

A) $5ab^2$
B) $5a^2b^2$
C) $5a^3b^6$
D) $28ab^2$

Pick Numbers!

This is a good time to practice a picking numbers workaround! Try picking $a = 3$ and $b = 2$. Plug those values into the original fraction and write down the result. Then do the same for each answer choice until you get a match.

SOLUTION

We could solve this problem directly by using exponent rules to simplify the fraction. Remember that a fraction bar is basically a **division** symbol, so we need to match up like bases and **subtract** exponents.

① *align like bases* $\dfrac{35a^2b^4}{7ab^2} = \dfrac{35}{7} \cdot \dfrac{a^2}{a} \cdot \dfrac{b^4}{b^2}$

② *subtract exponents* $= 5 \cdot a^{2-1} \cdot b^{4-2}$

③ *simplify* $= 5 \cdot a^1 \cdot b^2$

Our answer is $\boxed{5ab^2}$.

A

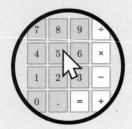

TIP

Remember how we have to change variables to x and y to get Desmos to graph them? You can't get sliders for x or y. Desmos also reserves e for the irrational number $e \approx 2.718$, but you can get a slider for any other letter.

TIP

You can select values in the slider by moving the dot on the slider, but you can also select the expression (eg "$a = 1$") and change the value by typing. Selecting the expression will also allow you to set your own bounds for the slider and the step, which is how you want it to increment.

Desmos: Introduction to Sliders

We can use Desmos to try different values by using a combination of working backwards, picking numbers, and a feature called 'sliders.'

① **Input the expression you are given into the calculator.** When you do, you will initially see a caution sign next to the expression and buttons to add sliders for a, b, or "all" under the expression. Press the all button. You should get something that looks like the image on the right.

② **Input the 4 answer choices** in lines 4-7. The calculator will evaluate each answer choice with the values selected for a and b in the sliders.

③ **Try different values** and look for which choices matches the original. With the default values of $a = 1$ and $b = 1$, the original expression and choices A-C all evaluate to 5. The correct answer will match the value of the original expression regardless of the values chosen for a and b. Use the sliders to try something different. If we try $a = 2$ and $b = 3$, the only answer choice that has the same value as the original expression is **choice A!**

Changing the sliders tries out different values for the variables. If the answer choices are equivalent to the original equation, this solution should match the top input!

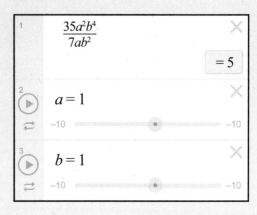

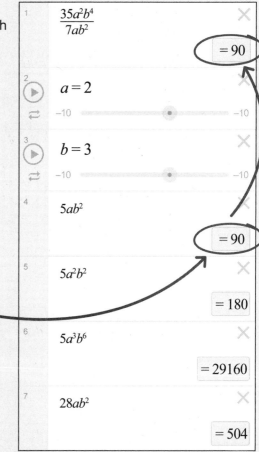

Roots and Fractional Exponents

You may have noticed that arithmetic operations come in pairs. **Subtraction** undoes <u>addition</u> and **division** undoes <u>multiplication</u>. The operation that lets you undo **exponentiation** is <u>taking roots</u>.

When we use the root symbol, $\sqrt{\ }$, we mean the positive *square root* if we don't otherwise specify. If we want a root for undoing a power other than 2, you can tuck a little number into the front of the root symbol. For example, $\sqrt[3]{\ }$ is the *cube root*.

$$\sqrt{16} = \sqrt{4^2} = 4$$
$$\sqrt{x^2} = x$$
$$\sqrt{x^4} = \sqrt{(x^2)^2} = x^2$$

$$\sqrt[3]{x^3} = x$$
$$\sqrt[3]{x^2} \text{ cannot be simplified}$$

Desmos: Working with Roots

The **square root symbol** is available directly in the keypad.

To get other roots you have **three options**:

1. **Type "*nthroot*"** into the entry box and it will bring up a root symbol that will prompt you to specify what kind of root you want.

2. **Click the *funcs* button** to open the "functions" menu, then scroll all the way to the bottom to find the *n*th-root ($\sqrt[n]{\ }$) symbol.

3. **Use fractional exponents** and bypass needing the root entirely.

Fractional exponents are roots

When you are adding and want to undo a "+2" you can either subtract 2 or you can add –2. Taking the square root is like subtracting 2. The equivalent to adding –2 is raising the expression to a *fractional power*. To understand what is happening with fraction exponents, let's play with an example. We know that raising a power to another power means we multiply exponents. That means raising x^2 to the power of ½ **undoes** the squaring. This is the same exact operation as taking the square root.

$$(x^2)^{\frac{1}{2}} = x^{\frac{2}{2}} = x$$

$$(x^2)^{\frac{1}{2}} = \sqrt{x^2} = x$$

The same thing happens with cubed roots and powers of $\frac{1}{3}$:

$$(x^3)^{\frac{1}{3}} = x^{\frac{3}{3}} = x$$

$$(x^3)^{\frac{1}{3}} = \sqrt[3]{x^3} = x$$

As a general rule, raising to the $\frac{1}{n}$ power is equal to taking the nth root:

$$x^{\frac{1}{n}} = \sqrt[n]{x}$$

You can split and combine roots as needed

You can **split roots** across multiplication. For example:

$$\sqrt{12x} = \sqrt{4} \cdot \sqrt{3x} = 2\sqrt{3x}$$

NOTE

You cannot combine roots of different orders, such as:

$$\sqrt{2} \cdot \sqrt[3]{3}$$

When multiplying, you can **combine** two roots of the same order:

$$\sqrt{2} \cdot \sqrt{3} = \sqrt{6}$$

EXAMPLE 5

$$\frac{2}{\sqrt{6}} + \frac{3}{\sqrt{15}} = ?$$

A) $\dfrac{5}{\sqrt{6} + \sqrt{15}}$

B) $\dfrac{5}{\sqrt{21}}$

C) $\dfrac{2\sqrt{15} + 3\sqrt{6}}{\sqrt{21}}$

D) $\dfrac{2\sqrt{15} + 3\sqrt{6}}{3\sqrt{10}}$

TIP

If none of the answer choices had roots in the denominator, you would have to **clear the square root from the denominator**.

To do this, multiply the numerator and denominator by that root, then simplify:

$$\frac{2}{\sqrt{10}} \cdot \frac{\sqrt{10}}{\sqrt{10}} = \frac{2\sqrt{10}}{10} = \boxed{\frac{\sqrt{10}}{5}}$$

SOLUTION

To combine fractions, we need a **common denominator**. The *product* of the denominators is always an option... It might not be the least common denominator, but that's fine for now:

(1) *rewrite the equation* $\dfrac{2}{\sqrt{6}} + \dfrac{3}{\sqrt{15}}$

(2) *make common denominators* $\dfrac{\sqrt{15}}{\sqrt{15}} \cdot \dfrac{2}{\sqrt{6}} + \dfrac{3}{\sqrt{15}} \cdot \dfrac{\sqrt{6}}{\sqrt{6}}$

$$\dfrac{2\sqrt{15}}{\sqrt{90}} + \dfrac{3\sqrt{6}}{\sqrt{90}}$$

(3) *combine fractions* $\dfrac{2\sqrt{15} + 3\sqrt{6}}{\sqrt{90}}$

This isn't an answer choice, so let's see if we can simplify:

(4) *simplify* $\dfrac{2\sqrt{15} + 3\sqrt{6}}{\sqrt{9 \cdot 10}}$

$$\dfrac{2\sqrt{15} + 3\sqrt{6}}{\sqrt{9} \cdot \sqrt{10}}$$

$$\boxed{\dfrac{2\sqrt{15} + 3\sqrt{6}}{3\sqrt{10}}}$$

Working Backwards with Desmos:

Desmos won't give you a simplified root expression, but you *can* ask it to evaluate each expression in the answer choices, then look to see which matches the original expression.

The only choice that evaluates to the same value as the original is **choice D!**

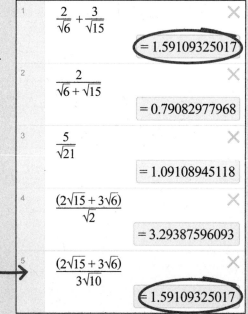

D

EXAMPLE 6

If $r = 2\sqrt[3]{5}$ and $3r = \sqrt[3]{5s}$, what is the value of s?

TIP

You could also replace r and s with x and y and just type this problem into Desmos.

TIP

Remember your fractional exponent rules:

$$x^{\frac{1}{n}} = \sqrt[n]{x}$$

We can split roots into their component pieces by following exponent rules:

$$(5s)^{\frac{1}{3}} = (5)^{\frac{1}{3}}(s)^{\frac{1}{3}}$$

SOLUTION

We are told that $r = 2\sqrt[3]{5}$, so the first thing we do is plug in:

(1) *plug in for r* $\qquad 3(2\sqrt[3]{5}) = \sqrt[3]{5s}$

$\qquad\qquad\qquad\qquad\qquad 6\sqrt[3]{5} = \sqrt[3]{5s}$

From here we have **two options** for how to solve for s.

Option 1: We see cube roots on both sides and both sides are connected by multiplication, making it easy to **cube both sides**.

(2) *cube both sides* $\qquad (6\sqrt[3]{5})^3 = (\sqrt[3]{5s})^3$

$\qquad\qquad\qquad\qquad\qquad (216)(5) = 5s$

(3) *divide by 5* $\qquad\qquad \boxed{216} = s$

Option 2: We can **split cube roots** across multiplication if it makes it easier for us to reach our goal:

(2) *split the cube root* $\qquad 6\sqrt[3]{5} = \sqrt[3]{5s}$

$\qquad\qquad\qquad\qquad\qquad 6\sqrt[3]{5} = (\sqrt[3]{5})(\sqrt[3]{s})$

(3) *divide by $(\sqrt[3]{5})$* $\qquad\qquad 6 = \sqrt[3]{s}$

(4) *cube both sides* $\qquad\quad (6)^3 = (\sqrt[3]{s})^3$

$\qquad\qquad\qquad\qquad\qquad \boxed{216} = s$

Practice Problems

Select the best answer choice for each equation.

1

Which expression is equivalent to $8x^4 - 3x^4$?

A) $5x^4$
B) $11x^4$
C) $5x^8$
D) $11x^8$

2

Which expression is equivalent to $5x^2 + 6x^2 + 5x$?

A) $30x^4 + 9x$
B) $5x^2 + 11x$
C) $16x^5$
D) $11x^2 + 5x$

3

$$3(x^2 - 2x + 4) - 2(x - 7)$$

Which of the following expressions is equivalent to the one shown above?

A) $x^2 - 9x + 4$
B) $x^2 - 3x - 3$
C) $3x^2 - 8x + 26$
D) $3x^2 - 3$

4

$$3a^2 - 6a + 7$$
$$7a^2 + 9a - 13$$

Which of the following is equivalent to the sum of the two expressions above?

A) $10a^2 + 15a - 6$
B) $10a^2 + 3a + 6$
C) $10a^2 + 15a + 20$
D) $10a^2 + 3a - 6$

5

$$2(ab^2 + a^2b + ab) - (4ab - 3a^2b - 2ab^2)$$

Which of the following expressions is equivalent to the expression above?

A) $-2a^2b - 2ab^2 - ab$
B) $-2ab - 2a^2b - ab^2$
C) $4ab^2 + 5a^2b - 2ab$
D) $-ab + 3a^2b - 3ab^2$

6

Which of the following is equal to the sum of $5a^5 + 3a^3 - 7$ and $-2a^4 - 4a^3 - 5a^2 + a$?

A) $3a^5 - 2a^3 - 6$
B) $5a^5 - 2a^4 + 3a^2 - 7$
C) $5a^5 - 2a^4 + 7a^3 - 5a^2 - 7a$
D) $5a^5 - 2a^4 - a^3 - 5a^2 + a - 7$

7

$$(6x^2 + 5) - (-3x^2 + 7)$$

The given expression is equivalent to $ax^2 - 2$, where a is a constant. What is the value of a ?

8

$$f(x) = 3x^2 - 2x + 4$$
$$g(x) = -x^2 + 7x - 2$$

For the functions given above, $f(x) + g(x) = h(x)$. If $h(x)$ is given by the equation $h(x) = ax^2 + bx + c$, where a, b, and c are constants, what is the value of ab ?

A) -20
B) -10
C) 0
D) 10

9

Which expression is equivalent to $(a^3b^{-2}c^4)(a^2b^3c)$, where a, b, and c are positive?

A) $a^6b^{-6}c^4$

B) a^5bc^5

C) $a^5b^5c^5$

D) $ab^{-5}c^3$

10

$$\left(\frac{x^4x^{-2}}{x^6}\right)$$

The given expression is equivalent to x^k, where k is a constant. What is the value of k?

11

Which expression is equivalent to $\sqrt[11]{x^6y^{-6}}$, where x and y are positive?

A) $\left(\frac{x}{y}\right)^{\frac{6}{11}}$

B) $\left(\frac{x}{y}\right)^{\frac{11}{6}}$

C) $(xy)^{11}$

D) $(xy)^{-11}$

12

If $\sqrt{108}$ is equal to $2x\sqrt{3}$, and x is greater than zero, what is the value of x?

A) 3
B) 18
C) 27
D) 54

13

$$2\sqrt{9a^3b^4c}$$

Which of the following is equivalent to the expression above?

A) $6ab^2\sqrt{ac}$
B) $\sqrt{18ab^2c}$
C) $18abc\sqrt{a^2b^3}$
D) $6a^2b^2\sqrt{ac}$

14

If $\sqrt{ab} = \sqrt{bc}$, $\sqrt{ac} = \sqrt{4c^4}$, and a, b, and c are greater than zero, what is the value of c?

A) $\dfrac{1}{4}$

B) $\dfrac{1}{2}$

C) 2

D) 4

15

$$\left(\frac{27}{a^6b^{12}}\right)^{-\frac{2}{3}}(12a^5b)^{\frac{1}{2}}$$

Which of the following is equivalent to the above expression?

A) $\dfrac{2a^8b^{12}\sqrt{3ab}}{27}$

B) $\dfrac{2a^8b^{12}\sqrt{3ab}}{3}$

C) $\dfrac{12a^6b^8\sqrt{b}}{9}$

D) $\dfrac{2a^6b^8\sqrt{3ab}}{9}$

Fractions

Tags: Algebra • Algebra Foundations

....

Many high schoolers are error-prone when working with fractions. Perhaps it's because they learned these rules way back in elementary and middle school, and haven't gotten much practice since. So, let's review!

- The **numerator** is the quantity above the bar (top bunk).

- The **denominator** is the quantity below the bar (bottom bunk).

- In **improper fractions**, the numerator is larger than the denominator (e.g., 3/2).

- Improper fractions can be rewritten as a **mixed number**: a combination of an integer and a proper fraction.

    Example: $\dfrac{12}{5} = \dfrac{10}{5} + \dfrac{2}{5} = 2\dfrac{2}{5}$

- The **reciprocal** of a fraction is what you get if you flip the numerator and denominator (switch bunks).

    Example: $\dfrac{2}{3}$ and $\dfrac{3}{2}$ are reciprocals.

NOTE

Fractions are not **integers**. Integers include all of the whole numbers, including zero and negative versions of the counting numbers.

Together, fractions and integers are sometimes referred to as *rational numbers*.

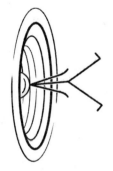

PORTAL

If you multiply a fraction by its reciprocal, it will always equal one.

Negative reciprocals show up later when we talk about lines with **perpendicular slopes** on page 329.

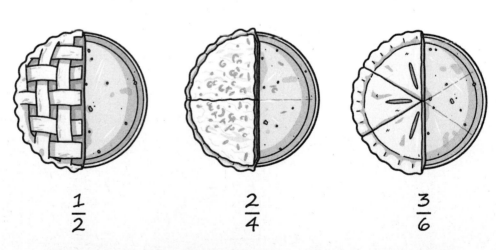

$$\dfrac{1}{2} \qquad \dfrac{2}{4} \qquad \dfrac{3}{6}$$

The same quantity displayed with different denominators

Desmos: Working with Fractions

Throughout this chapter we are going to review how to work with fractions and there are problems on the SAT where it is very helpful to be comfortable dealing with fractions by hand. However, There are *also* a lot of problems where Desmos can handle the fractions for you. There are two keys to remember for putting fractions **into** Desmos:

- A fraction bar is a division sign—you can either type "/" or press the ÷ key.

- Pay attention to where the cursor is so that you don't put more in the denominator than you meant to.

TIP

In the exercises throughout this chapter, try using Desmos to check your work

This means that to input $\frac{1}{2} + \frac{3}{4}$ with a keyboard, you would type "1 / 2", press the right arrow to move the cursor out of the denominator and then type "+ 3 / 4". If you don't have a separate keyboard or prefer to use the build in calculator buttons, you would press [1] [÷] [2], click/tap next to the fraction to move the cursor out of the denominator, and then press [+] [3] [÷] [4].

If your **answer is a fraction**, the button that lets you switch between fractions and decimals is your friend.

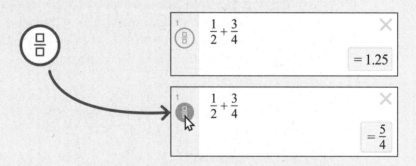

Use the LCM to find the LCD!

TIP

You can also break the numbers down into their prime factor "building blocks" (like 2, 3, 5, etc).

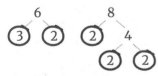

Think of the LCM as a room *just* big enough to fit all the building blocks of each number. We can use the three 2's we need for 8 and the one 3 we need for 6 to get:

$3 \times 2 \times 2 \times 2 = 24$

You can't add or subtract fractions until they have the *same denominator*. Usually, this requires finding the **least common denominator** (LCD), by finding least common multiple (LCM) of their denominators.

If we wanted to add or subtract $\frac{1}{6}$ and $\frac{1}{8}$, we'd need the LCM of 6 and 8.

We could list all the multiples of 8 and look for the first one divisible by 6, as below, but often there's a faster way, as we'll see in the next example.

	×1	×2	×3	×4
6	6	12	18	(24)
8	8	16	(24)	32

EXAMPLE 1

What is the least common denominator of the fractions $\frac{1}{12}$, $\frac{2}{15}$, and $\frac{4}{27}$?

A) 3
B) 150
C) 540
D) 1,620

SOLUTION

Option 1: Solve head-on with factor trees
The least common denominator will be the LCM of 12, 15, and 27. We could list out the multiples of each looking for a match, but it's faster to find the prime factorization:

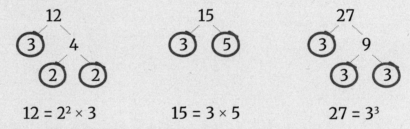

$$12 = 2^2 \times 3 \qquad 15 = 3 \times 5 \qquad 27 = 3^3$$

So our LCM needs to have at least two 2's, three 3's, and one 5.

$$LCM = 2^2 \times 3^3 \times 5 = \boxed{540}$$

Option 2: Work backwards!
We can **use our calculator** to divide each answer choice by 12, 15, and 27. If any choice leads to a decimal, it's not a multiple!

~~A)~~ 3 – This is a factor, not a multiple!

~~B)~~ 150 ÷ 12 = 12.5. ✗ 150 is not a multiple of 12.

Ⓒ 540 ÷ 12 = 45 ✓   540 ÷ 15 = 36 ✓   540 ÷ 27 = 20 ✓

NOTE

Usually, we want to start from the middle when we work backwards. In this case, we're looking for the **SMALLEST** number, so starting with A is safer.

302

Use common denominators to add fractions

When we add fractions with the same denominator, we just add the numerators. Pretty simple:

$$\frac{1}{3} + \frac{1}{3} = \frac{2}{3}$$

But let's look at what we're doing when we add the fractions $\frac{2}{3}$ and $\frac{1}{2}$.

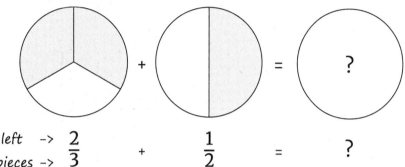

Pieces left -> $\frac{2}{3}$ + $\frac{1}{2}$ = ?
Total pieces ->

Exactly how much total pie do we have in the picture above? In order to figure this out, we need to find a **common denominator** for our fractions. Or, in tastier terms, cut the pies into **pieces of equal size**. The smallest common multiple of 2 and 3 is 6, so cut each pie into sixths:

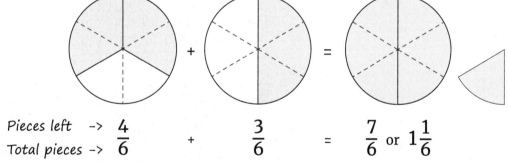

Pieces left -> $\frac{4}{6}$ + $\frac{3}{6}$ = $\frac{7}{6}$ or $1\frac{1}{6}$
Total pieces ->

Notice that for each pie we changed both the **total number of pieces** (denominator) and the **number of pieces remaining** (numerator). This is why we multiply the top and bottom of a fraction by the same number when changing denominators.

TO ADD FRACTIONS:

(1) *Find a common denominator*

(2) *Rewrite each fraction as an equivalent fraction with that denominator.*

(3) *Add the numerators.*

Subtraction works just like addition

We can always think of subtracting as **adding a negative value**. The process for subtracting fractions is the same as for adding them except, in the last step, you **subtract** numerators instead of add!

Multiply across the numerator and denominator

Let's start by thinking about what it means when we multiply fractions. Remember that when we translate between math and English, " *of* " means multiplication:

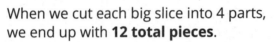

$$\frac{2}{4} \times \frac{2}{3} = ? \qquad \frac{2}{4} \ of \ \frac{2}{3} = ?$$

Now say we have <u>a pie where two-thirds is left</u>. If we eat two-fourths of the *remaining* two-thirds, we need to divide up the pie into smaller pieces. A logical approach would be to take **two-fourths of each big piece.**

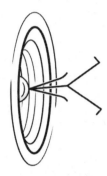

PORTAL

The processes for combining fractions continue to work even when variables get involved. To see this in action, check out the *Advanced Algebra* chapter on page 406.

When we cut each big slice into 4 parts, we end up with **12 total pieces**.

If we take 2 small slices from the two 2 original pieces, we eat **4 small pieces**.

In other words, we did the following:

$$\frac{2}{4} \times \frac{2}{3} = \frac{2 \cdot 2}{4 \cdot 3} = \frac{4}{12}$$

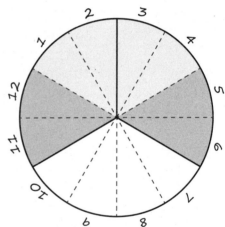

TO MULTIPLY FRACTIONS:

① *Multiply across the numerators*

② *Multiply across the denominators*

③ *Simplify*

TIP

A number doesn't change if you divide by 1, so you can always write integers as fractions with 1 as a denominator.

e.g., $2 = \frac{2}{1}$

To divide by a fraction, multiply by the reciprocal

Remember that the reciprocal of a fraction is what you get when you switch (or "flip") the numerator and the denominator. So if you are asked to divide by a fraction, **flip the fraction** and **multiply** as usual:

$$\frac{2}{3} \div \frac{3}{4} = \frac{2}{3} \times \frac{4}{3}$$

flip and multiply

$$2 \div \frac{1}{5} = \frac{2}{1} \times \frac{5}{1}$$

flip and multiply

Fractions within fractions (aka fractionception)

When the numerator and/or denominator of a fraction contains another fraction, just treat it as a division problem:

$$\frac{\frac{7}{8}}{\frac{3}{4}} = \frac{7}{8} \div \frac{3}{4} = \frac{7}{8} \times \frac{4}{3}$$

Use your fraction skills to rewrite each expression as a single fraction.

1. $\frac{3}{4} + \frac{2}{3} = \underline{\qquad \frac{17}{12} \qquad}$

2. $\frac{1}{2} + \frac{3}{7} = \underline{\qquad\qquad}$

3. $\frac{5}{8} - \frac{1}{4} = \underline{\qquad\qquad}$

4. $\frac{1}{3} + \frac{4}{3} - \frac{1}{6} = \underline{\qquad\qquad}$

5. $3 + \frac{3}{8} = \underline{\qquad\qquad}$

6. $5 - \frac{12}{7} = \underline{\qquad\qquad}$

7. $\frac{2}{5} + \frac{1}{3} + \frac{3}{4} = \underline{\qquad\qquad}$

8. $\left(\frac{3}{5}\right)\left(\frac{2}{7}\right) = \underline{\qquad\qquad}$

9. $\left(\frac{4}{3}\right)\left(\frac{1}{8}\right) = \underline{\qquad\qquad}$

10. $\frac{4}{3} \div \frac{1}{2} = \underline{\qquad\qquad}$

11. $\frac{15}{7} \div \frac{3}{2} = \underline{\qquad\qquad}$

12. $\dfrac{\frac{2}{3} + \frac{1}{4}}{\frac{5}{7} - \frac{1}{3}} = \underline{\qquad\qquad}$

13. $\dfrac{\frac{1}{2}\left(\frac{5}{8} - \frac{1}{4}\right)}{3} = \underline{\qquad\qquad}$

Answers: *Bottom of next page.*

Translating with Fractions

Let's revisit our Art of Translation phrasebook to check two new fraction-specific terms:

- "A number **per** a number" translates into a **fraction**. The first number is the numerator, per is the fraction bar, and the second number is the denominator.

Example:

Harriet walked	13 miles	per	2 hours
H =	13 mi	/	2 hr

- The word **of** still means **multiply**.

Example:

x	is	one-half	of	y
x	=	$\frac{1}{2}$	×	y

EXAMPLE 2

The school band is selling packs of candy for $2 each as a fundraiser. The band earns $3 profit per $10 of candy sold. If a case of candy has 75 packs in it and Shania sells two-thirds of a case, how much profit did the band earn from the candy sold by Shania?

A) $ 0.30
B) $ 22.50
C) $ 30.00
D) $ 45.00

Last Page: **1.** *given*   **2.** $\frac{13}{14}$ **3.** $\frac{3}{8}$ **4.** $\frac{3}{2}$ **5.** $\frac{27}{8}$ **6.** $\frac{23}{7}$ **7.** $\frac{89}{60}$

8. $\frac{6}{35}$ **9.** $\frac{1}{6}$ **10.** $\frac{8}{3}$ **11.** $\frac{10}{7}$ **12.** $\frac{77}{32}$ **13.** $\frac{1}{16}$

SOLUTION

First, establish our goal: We want to know the **profit** based on the amount of candy sold by Shania.

The school band is selling packs of candy for $2 each as a fundraiser. The band earns $3 profit per $10 of candy sold. If a case of candy has 75 packs in it and Shania sells two-thirds of a case, how much profit did the band earn from the candy sold by Shania?

So we want to first find the amount sold by Shania, *then* the profit. From here, let's write what we know and use that to translate toward our goal.

  1 *write what you know*

        1 pack = $2

        1 case = 75 packs

  2 *translate Shania's sales*

        $Sold = \frac{2}{3}$ of a case

        $Packs\ sold = \frac{2}{3}(75) = 50\ packs$

        $Amount\ sold = 50(\$2) = \mathbf{\$100}$

Now that we know Shania sold **50 packs** for **$100**, let's figure out how much profit that earned for the band. The band's earned profit is $3 **per** $10 of candy sold. We can write that as a fraction.

  3 *translate profit to fraction*

        $profit = \frac{3}{10} \times (sold)$

So if we multiply $100 by $\frac{3}{10}$, we find the band's profit:

  4 *apply to Shania's sales*

        $profit = \frac{3}{10} \times (\$100)$

        $profit = \$30$

C

Decimals, powers of 10, and scientific notation

Our number system is based around **powers of 10**. Look at the three-digit number **324**. Each digit represents a multiple of a power of 10.

$$324 = 300 + 20 + 4$$
$$324 = (3 \times 100) + (2 \times 10) + (4 \times 1)$$
$$324 = (3 \times 10^2) + (2 \times 10^1) + (4 \times 10^0)$$

Now let's expand the decimal number **324.56** in the same way:

$$324.56 = (3 \times 10^2) + (2 \times 10^1) + (4 \times 10^0) + (5 \times 10^{-1}) + (6 \times 10^{-2})$$

TIP

Some questions will ask you to **round** your answers. Pay close attention to whether you're being asked to round to the nearest **hundred** or **hundredth**!

The position to the left or right of the decimal point tells you which power of 10 that digit is multiplied by. This is how we get our place value names:

$$
\begin{array}{ccccccc|cccc}
1 & , & 3 & 4 & 6 & , & 2 & 0 & 5 & . & 7 & 2 & 8 \\
10^6 & & 10^5 & 10^4 & 10^3 & & 10^2 & 10^1 & 10^0 & & 10^{-1} & 10^{-2} & 10^{-3}
\end{array}
$$

millions, hundred thousands, ten thousands, thousands, hundreds, tens, ones, tenths, hundredths, thousandths

Scientific notation is a useful shorthand

Notice we can write 200 as **2×10^2** and we can write 0.02 as **2×10^{-2}**. This shorthand is called **scientific notation**, and it helps shorten some numbers with an annoying amount of zeroes:

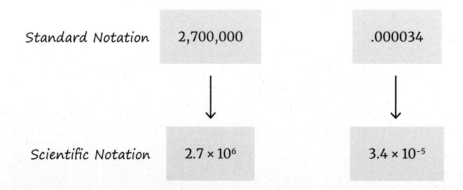

	Standard Notation		Standard Notation
	2,700,000		.000034
Scientific Notation	2.7×10^6	Scientific Notation	3.4×10^{-5}

Scientific notation consists of a decimal number between 1 and 10 multiplied by a power of 10. The power of 10 tells you **how far to move the decimal**, and **which direction** to move it.

TIP

Positive exponents hop the decimal to the right.

Negative exponents hop the decimal to the left.

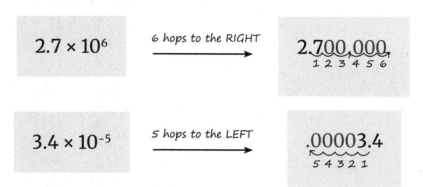

Convert the numbers into scientific notation (and vice versa).

	Number	Scientific Notation
1		2.53×10^5
2	57,400,000,000	
3	.000103	
4		7.203×10^{-8}
5	1,000,000,000,000,000	

TIP

When you see a line over decimal places, it means those numbers repeat:

$.7\overline{5} = .7555555555...$

Repeating decimals are harder to convert to fractions; luckily, the test won't ask this of you!

Converting decimals to fractions

Converting a decimal to a fraction is as simple as putting any numbers to the right of the decimal in the numerator. In the denominator, put a 1 followed by as many zeroes as there are digits in the decimal.

.755 has three digits so it converts to $\frac{755}{1000}$.

If the resulting numerator and denominator have any factors in common then you can **simplify** the fraction:

In $\frac{755}{1000}$, 5 is a common factor. This simplifies to $\frac{151}{200}$.

Answers: 2. 253,000   3. 2. 5.74×10^{10} 4. 3. 1.03×10^{-4} 5. 4. .00000007203   6. 5. 1.0×10^{15}

Converting fractions to decimals

An easy way to convert a fraction to a decimal is to treat the fraction bar as a **division** symbol. When you can, just plug it into your calculator!

Convert fractions to decimals and decimals to fractions. Once converted, simplify fractions and round decimals to the nearest hundredth.

1. $\frac{3}{4}$ = <u>.75</u>

2. 0.8 = _____

3. $\frac{5}{3}$ = _____

4. $\frac{3}{7}$ = _____

5. 0.34 = _____

6. 4.62 =

7. $\frac{2}{9}$ = _____

8. $2\frac{7}{8}$ = _____

9. .125 = _____

10. .501 = _____

Comparing Fractions/Decimals

There are several ways you can approach situations when you need to determine which of two decimals or fractions is larger.

NOTE

Watch out for **negatives**! The direction for these comparisons switches if you are comparing negative numbers.

342.61 > 342.16

but...

–342.61 < –342.16

1. **Convert both of the numbers to decimals.** When you are comparing two decimal numbers, find the first digit from the left where the two numbers differ. The larger number will have the larger digit.

Example: 3 4 2 . 1 6
3 4 2 . 6 1

6 is bigger

2. **Convert to fractions with common denominators.** Once the fractions have a common denominator, the larger number will have the larger numerator.

3. **Subtract with your calculator (when able).** If you are comparing A and B, try plugging in "A − B". If the result is positive, A is bigger. If it is negative, B is bigger.

Answers: 4. *given*   1. $\frac{4}{5}$ 2. 1.67   3. 0.43   4. $\frac{17}{50}$

5. $4\frac{31}{50}$ 5. 0.22   6. 2.88   7. $\frac{1}{8}$ 8. $\frac{501}{1000}$

Fill in the blanks by following the instructions below.

1. Place the following numbers in **ascending order**:

$$\frac{1}{3}, 0.3, \frac{2}{5}, 0.33, \frac{1}{4}$$

__ __ __ __ __

2. Place the following numbers in **descending order**:

$$-\frac{2}{3}, -\frac{3}{2}, 2.783, 15.4, \frac{26}{4}, \frac{7}{8}$$

__ __ __ __ __ __

Scratch Work

Answers: 1. $\frac{1}{4}$, 0.3, 0.33, $\frac{1}{3}$, $\frac{2}{5}$ 2. 15.4, $\frac{26}{4}$, 2.783, $\frac{7}{8}$, $-\frac{2}{3}$, $-\frac{3}{2}$

Fractions Practice 1

Select the best answer choice for each equation.

Build the skills before you test!

The following practice set tests the fraction skills underlying many SAT practice problems. Work this set to test the skills you just learned, then try the following practice set to see how fractions are tested on the SAT.

1

Which of the following numbers has the greatest value?

A) 0.125
B) 0.12$\overline{5}$
C) 0.1$\overline{25}$
D) 0.$\overline{125}$

2

Which of the following is the least common denominator of the fractions $\frac{5}{33}$, $\frac{7}{18}$, and $\frac{7}{24}$?

A) 3
B) 66
C) 198
D) 792

3

If the sum of $2\frac{1}{3}$ and $3\frac{1}{2}$ is written as an improper fraction in lowest terms, what is the sum of the numerator and denominator?

A) 12
B) 19
C) 25
D) 41

4

Which of the following expressions is equal to 16.3 billion?

A) 1.63×10^{12}
B) 1.63×10^{11}
C) 1.63×10^{10}
D) 1.63×10^{9}

5

Lucy has a craft kit with 1,200 beads. If $\frac{1}{3}$ of the beads are made of glass and 2 out of every 5 beads made of glass are blue, how many blue glass beads are in the kit?

A) 80
B) 160
C) 240
D) 400

6

In which of the following are $\frac{2}{3}$, $\frac{4}{9}$, and $\frac{1}{2}$ arranged in descending order?

A) $\frac{2}{3} > \frac{1}{2} > \frac{4}{9}$

B) $\frac{2}{3} > \frac{4}{9} > \frac{1}{2}$

C) $\frac{4}{9} > \frac{2}{3} > \frac{1}{2}$

D) $\frac{4}{9} > \frac{1}{2} > \frac{2}{3}$

7

Which of the following expresses the answer to 0.000094 − 0.000017 in scientific notation?

A) 77×10^{-4}
B) 77×10^{-5}
C) 7.7×10^{-4}
D) 7.7×10^{-5}

8

On a number line, which of the following numbers is exactly halfway between $\frac{1}{3}$ and 0.8 ?

A) 0.23
B) $0.5\overline{6}$
C) 0.56
D) 0.73

9

$$\frac{2}{15} \text{ ———— } -\frac{3}{7}$$

Which of the following operations will produce the smallest result when placed in the blank in the expression above?

A) plus
B) minus
C) multiplied by
D) divided by

10

Suppose a is a positive integer, b is 2 times a, and c is 3 times a. What is the least common denominator, in terms of a, of the fractions $\frac{1}{a}$, $\frac{1}{b}$, and $\frac{1}{c}$?

A) $2a$

B) $\frac{1}{6}a$

C) $6a$

D) $6a^3$

11

Which of the following is the decimal equivalent of $\frac{7}{22}$?

A) 0.3181818

B) $0.31\overline{8}$

C) $0.3\overline{18}$

D) $0.\overline{318}$

12

Let p, q, and r be distinct prime numbers and suppose

$a = pq^2$, $b = p^2q^3$, and $c = pq^2r^2$. If $\frac{1}{a} + \frac{1}{b} + \frac{1}{c} = \frac{n}{abc}$, what is the

greatest common factor of n and abc ?

A) pq^2

B) p^2q^4

C) pqr

D) $p^2q^3r^2$

13

When $-2 \le a \le 3$ and $4 \le b \le 10$, the largest possible value for

$\frac{3}{2b - a}$ is:

A) $\frac{1}{2}$

B) $\frac{3}{5}$

C) $\frac{3}{10}$

D) $\frac{3}{17}$

Fractions Practice 2

Select the best answer choice for each equation.

See how fractions show up on the SAT

The questions below are modeled after actual SAT problems, which test fraction skills along with other core algebra skills.

14

If $\frac{x}{6} = 7$, what is the value of $\frac{6}{x}$?

15

$$\frac{4}{7}x - \frac{1}{2} = \frac{2}{7}x + \frac{13}{14}$$

What is the value of x in the equation above?

16

If $\frac{x}{y} = 5$ and $\frac{12x}{ky} = 5$, what is the value of k?

17

$$m = 6 + \frac{5}{k}$$

The given equation relates the numbers m and k, where k is not equal to 0 and $m > 6$. Which equation correctly expresses k in terms of m?

A) $k = \frac{m - 6}{5}$

B) $k = \frac{5}{m - 6}$

C) $k = 5(m - 6)$

D) $k = \frac{m}{5} - 6$

18

If $\frac{m}{m + n} = \frac{5}{7}$, what is the value of $\frac{3n}{m}$?

A) $\frac{10}{7}$

B) $\frac{6}{5}$

C) $\frac{1}{2}$

D) $\frac{15}{2}$

UNIT | Functions

Chapters

Overview

In this unit, we'll learn about the connection between basic algebra, linear equations, and their illustrations: *graphs*. We'll also practice thinking of equations and graphs as *functions* built on inputs and outputs.

Linear Equations

Tags: Algebra • Equation of a Line

Graphs are Illustrations

Every line on a graph is attached to a certain mathematical equation that tells you how to find points on that line. You can think of the graph of a line as simply an **illustration** of all the possible solutions to an equation. We can illustrate "$y = 2x + 1$" or "$y = -2x + 1$" just like we can illustrate "Marian Rejewski" or "Tobi the dog."

Marian Rejewski

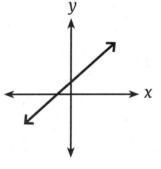

$y = 2x + 1$

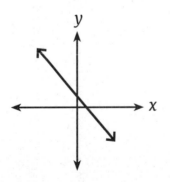

$y = -2x + 1$

Tobi the Dog

Slope-Intercept Form

Before we can illustrate a linear equation, however, it helps to put the equation into the **slope-intercept form**.

$$y = mx + b$$

We call it the slope-intercept form because that's exactly what it tells us about the line. Just by looking at an equation in this form, we can see the line's **slope (*m*)** and its **y-intercept (*b*)**. And if you know these two things, you know exactly how to draw the line!

(*b*) y-intercept

Every line drawing's gotta start somewhere, and there's no better place than the point where the line crosses the *y*-axis, a.k.a. the **y-intercept**. This is the point where *x* is zero.

(*m*) slope

The slope of a line is the relationship between two of its points. It tells us whether the line goes uphill or downhill, and just how steep of a hill we're talking. A **positive** slope runs uphill from left to right, while a **negative** slope runs downhill from left to right.

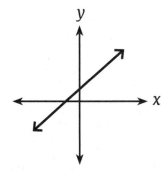

Positive Slope

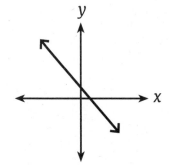

Negative Slope

NOTE

Sometimes, instead of a slope, you have a flat ground or a sheer cliff. When a line is a flat, horizontal line, it has a **slope of zero**. When a line is a straight, vertical line, its slope is **undefined**.

TIP

Remember, *x* comes before *y* in the alphabet, and *x* comes before *y* in the ordered pair!

Key things to know about the coordinate plane

- Horizontal and vertical gridlines are **perpendicular**.

- The center point at (0, 0) is called the **origin.**

- Up/right from the origin is **positive**; down/left is **negative.**

- Every point is named by its **ordered pair**; first, write the *x*-coordinate for the point, then write the *y*-coordinate.

TIP

Equations will not always be in slope-intercept form.

Whenever a line's equation is not in the form $y = mx + b$, rearrange it!

Reading Slope-Intercept Form

Before we try some test problems, let's get used to reading the slope-intercept form. The table below contains a number of linear equations. For problems 1–5, make sure the equation is in the $y = mx + b$ form and determine the slope (m) and y-intercept (b). For problems 6–8, you are told the slope and y-intercept of a line and must write its equation in slope-intercept form.

Fill in the empty entries in the table below.

Equation	m	b
1. $y = -5x + 4$	-5	
2. $y = \frac{2}{7}x - 3$		
3. $6 = 3x - y$		
4. $-32 = -8x + 4y$		
5. $8x + y = 0$		
6.	$\frac{1}{3}$	7
7.	-4	2
8.	$\frac{5}{13}$	-4

Answers: 1. $m = -5, b = 4$ 2. $m = 2/7, b = -3$ 3. $m = 3, b = -6$ 4. $m = 2, b = -8$

5. $m = -8, b = 0$ 6. $y = (1/3)x + 7$ 7. $y = -4x + 2$ 8. $y = (5/13)x - 4$

TIP

On the test you might not be given the two points in coordinate form. Sometimes you will have to pull them from a graph, table, or word problem.

Calculating Slope

We calculate slope as **rise over run**, or change in y over change in x:

$$\text{Slope } (m) = \frac{rise}{run} = \frac{y_2 - y_1}{x_2 - x_1}$$

If you're given two points on a line—(x_1, y_1) and (x_2, y_2)—you can find the slope just by plugging them into the slope formula above.

Find the slope of the lines containing the following pairs of points.

Points		Slope
1. $(2, 7)\,(9, 3)$ $\dfrac{y_2 - y_1}{x_2 - x_1} = \dfrac{3-7}{9-2} =$		$-\dfrac{4}{7}$
2. $(10, -8)\,(6, 7)$		
3. $(2, 4)\,(1, 9)$		
4. $(-7, 0)\,(-9, -10)$		
5. $(-45, 2)\,(31, -21)$		
6. $(3, a)\,(4, 7)$		
7. $(s, t)(0, 5)$		
8. $(-2, 15)(x, 6)$		

Answers:

1. $-\dfrac{4}{7}$ 2. $-\dfrac{15}{4}$ 3. -5 4. 5

5. $-\dfrac{23}{76}$ 6. $7 - a$ 7. $-\dfrac{5-t}{s}$ 8. $\dfrac{-9}{x+2}$

323

EXAMPLE 1

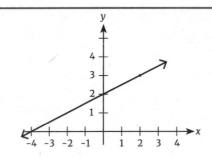

Which of the following represents the relationship between x and y?

A) $x = 2y$

B) $y = 2x + 2$

C) $y = 2x + \frac{1}{2}$

D) $y = \frac{1}{2}x + 2$

SOLUTION

Asking for the relationship between x and y is another way of asking for the equation of the line. Imagine that you wanted to text information about this line to your friend so they could recreate it. You could accomplish that in just three questions:

Where does the line cross the y-axis?   (0 , **2**)

Is the line going uphill or downhill?   uphill

How much does the line go up for every unit it goes over?   1/2

Finding Slope

We can find the slope by looking at the graph or by plugging two points on the graph, **(–4, 0)** and **(0, 2)**, into the slope formula:

$$m = \frac{2 - 0}{0 - (-4)} = \frac{2}{4} = \frac{1}{2}$$

So our y-intercept (**b**) is **2**, and our slope (**m**) is **positive** $\frac{1}{2}$. We can plug that into the slope-intercept equation to find our answer:

① *write line equation* $y = mx + b$

② *plug-in* $y = \frac{1}{2}x + 2$ **D**

EXAMPLE 2

A line in the xy-plane passes through the origin and has a slope of $\frac{2}{3}$. Which of the following points lies on the line?

A) $(2, 3)$
B) $(3, 2)$
C) $(4, 6)$
D) $(-2, 3)$

SOLUTION

In this problem, they give us a slope of $m = \frac{2}{3}$. They don't come right out and say "the y-intercept is...", but they do tell us that the line **passes through the origin**, or point $(0, 0)$. That's a y-intercept! So $b = 0$. Now, we can write the equation of this line:

① *write line equation* $\qquad\qquad y = mx + b$

② *plug-in* $\qquad\qquad\qquad\qquad y = \frac{2}{3}x$

Now we can find a point on this line in many ways.

Option 1: Working Backwards
First, let's try a trick that works in multiple situations: **test points with our equation**. Since we have the equation of the line, we can plug each point from the answer choices into our equation. If plugging in the given x-value gives the given y-value, then that point is on the line!

Ⓐ *Try $(2, 3)$* $\qquad\qquad y = \frac{2}{3}(2) = \frac{4}{3} \neq 3$ ✗

Ⓑ *Try $(3, 2)$* $\qquad\qquad y = \frac{2}{3}(3) = 2$ ✓

Bingo! By testing points, we can see that point $(3, 2)$ is on the line.

Option 2: Draw and Plot
There's another way to find a point on this line. Since we have a point $(0, 0)$ and we know that the slope goes **up 2** and **right 3**, we can **draw the line** and find our own points one-by-one.

Continued on next page →

TIP

Once you know the equation of a line, you can do **almost** anything! Find that equation!

TIP

There are two things you need to know to draw a line:

1) one point
2) the slope

Any time you know these two things, you can start at the point and use the slope to find more points.

So let's use what we know about slope to **find our own points**:

(1) *start at y-intercept*

(2) *move up 2, right 3*

$$m = \frac{2}{3}$$

And voila! The first point we find in this way happens to be our answer: (3, 2).

Option 3: Adding with Slope
We could do this same general idea without even drawing a graph. By applying "rise 2, run 3", you can generate as many points as you fancy:

(1) *first point*   (0, 0)

                                                  +3, +2

(2) *second point*   (3, 2)

                                                  +3, +2

(3) *third point*   (6, 4)

                                                  +3, +2

(4) *fourth point...*   (9, 6)

We could keep going forever! But we won't. We can just add points until we see one that is an answer choice, so we can stop at **(3, 2)**.

B

TIP

A table of values displays points in a compact and organized way.

Notice how the table below makes it easy to see that as *x* goes up by **1**, *y* goes up by **2**, so the slope must be equal to 2!

x	y
1	5
2	7
3	9

TIP

If you click any of the *x*-values in this table and change the value, Desmos will automatically solve for a corresponding *y*-value! And vice-versa!

Not only that, but each of these points will show up on the graph of the equation. Very useful!

Desmos: Creating Tables of Values

Sometimes we want to talk about several points that are on the same line (or function). We *could* just list the points, but putting the information in a table can help us stay organized and spot patterns. Let's say we had the equation $y = 2x + 5$ and wanted to see different (x,y) points on that line.

We could plug in values for *x* (1, 2, 3...) and record the *y*-values one by one... *or* we could have the Desmos calculator do it for us!

① *Input an equation and click the gear symbol*

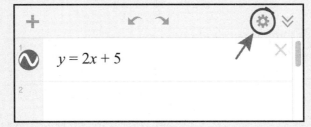

② *Click the table button.*

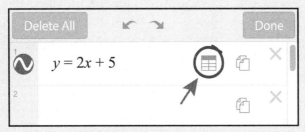

③ *View your table (and add points!)*

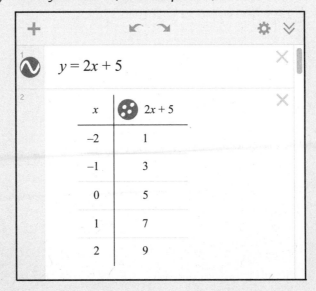

By default, Desmos gives you the five points with *x*-coordinates between −2 and 2, but you can **change or add additional values** in the *x* column and it will automatically calculate the corresponding *y*-values!

EXAMPLE 3

The graph of the linear function f has intercepts at $(a, 0)$ and $(0, b)$ in the xy-plane. If $ab < 0$, which of the following must be true about the slope of the graph of f?

A) It is positive
B) It is negative
C) It equals zero
D) It is undefined

NOTE

Neither a nor b could be 0, because then ab wouldn't be less than zero… it'd just be zero.

SOLUTION

This problem is a little abstract, but don't let that scare you. Let's pick out what we have to work with:

- The function is "linear", so it's **a line**.

- The graph has both an x-intercept $(a, 0)$ and a y-intercept $(0, b)$. The fact that the question gives us points on the xy-plane suggests that **drawing a sketch** might be helpful.

- **$ab < 0$**

This last bit tells us that either a or b (but not both!) is negative. Which means, if we're **sketching a line**, there are two different ways we could draw our points:

① *if a were positive…*
then b would be negative.

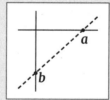

② *if a were negative…*
then b would be positive.

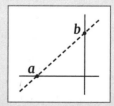

If you imagine "sliding" any of these points toward or away from zero, the steepness of the slope changes, but the fact that it's *positive* never does. Therefore, the answer is **A**— and we just **proved** that if only one of the intercepts is positive, the **slope** must be positive! That's pretty cool.

A

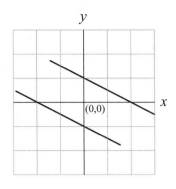

Parallel lines have identical slopes

By definition, two lines are **parallel** if they <u>never</u> intersect. This happens when they go in the same direction and are always a fixed distance from each other.

Since the slope tells you the direction of a line, any two lines that are parallel have the same slope. The reverse is true as well: any two lines that have the same slope are parallel. If you have two equations in the form $y = mx + b$ and they have the same m but different values for b, then you know the two lines are parallel!

Same slopes? → $y = 3x + 1{,}000{,}000$
Parallel lines! → $y = 3x - 5{,}000{,}000$

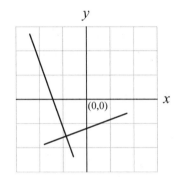

Perpendicular lines have opposite slopes

Two lines that are perpendicular (meet at a 90° angle) have slopes that are **negative reciprocals** of one another. To find the negative reciprocal of a fraction, flip the fraction and then flip the sign:

$$+\frac{1}{2} \implies -\frac{2}{1} \qquad -\frac{3}{4} \implies +\frac{4}{3} \qquad +\frac{5}{12} \implies -\frac{12}{5}$$

So if a line has a slope of $\frac{1}{2}$, then a perpendicular line has a slope of **−2**.

opposite slopes? → $y = \frac{1}{2}x + 1{,}000{,}000$
perpendicular lines! → $y = -2x - 5{,}000{,}000$

TIP

Don't forget to flip the sign when flipping the fraction! There will often be a wrong answer choice that will look perfect if you make this mistake.

329

EXAMPLE 4

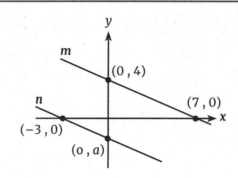

In the xy-plane above, line m is parallel to line n. What is the value of a?

SOLUTION

Here's a tip: if you see parallel lines in a coordinate plane, there is a good chance you are going to be working with **slope**—especially if there are two points marked on each line. So let's find the slope of each line:

① *find **slope** of line m* $slope_m = \frac{0-4}{7-0} = -\frac{4}{7}$

② *find **slope** of line n* $slope_n = \frac{a-0}{0-(-3)} = \frac{a}{3}$

And since our lines are **parallel**, we know that these slopes must really be the **exact same**. So...

③ *set slopes equal to each other* $slope_m = slope_n$

$$-\frac{4}{7} = \frac{a}{3}$$

④ *cross multiply* $-12 = 7a$

⑤ *solve for a* $\boxed{-\frac{12}{7}} = a$ $-\frac{12}{7}$

EXAMPLE 5

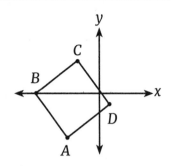

In the xy-plane above, ABCD is a square. The coordinates of points A and B are (-3, -4) and (-6, 0), respectively. Which of the following is the equation of the line that passes through points A and D ?

A) $y = -\frac{4}{3}x - \frac{7}{4}$

B) $y = \frac{3}{4}x - \frac{7}{4}$

C) $y = -\frac{3}{4}x - \frac{7}{4}$

D) $y = \frac{3}{4}x + \frac{4}{7}$

SOLUTION

Let's start by **going over what we know**. We know that ABCD is a square, which means each side is *perpendicular* to its adjoining sides. That may help later, so let's keep it in mind.

We also know we are looking for the **equation of a line** that passes through points A and D. So before we do anything else, let's just jot down the slope-intercept form to start us off:

(1) *write slope-intercept form* $y = mx + b$

Okay! To fill out this equation, we'll need to find the **slope (m)** of line $\overline{AD}$. To do that, we need two points on the line. We don't have that... but we *do* have two points on line $\overline{BA}$: **(-3, -4)** and **(-6, 0)**. Since we can, let's go ahead and find the slope of $\overline{BA}$.

(2) *find slope of $\overline{BA}$* $m_{BA} = \frac{y_2 - y_1}{x_2 - x_1} = \frac{-4 - 0}{-3 - (-6)} = -\frac{4}{3}$

Continued on next page →

Aha! And remember how we know that line $\overline{AD}$ is *perpendicular* to line $\overline{BA}$? That means their slopes are **negative reciprocals** of each other! If the slope of line $\overline{BA}$ is $-\frac{4}{3}$, then the slope of our line is $\frac{3}{4}$. Let's update our equation:

③ *update equation* $\qquad\qquad\qquad y = \frac{3}{4}x + b$

Now we just need to find **b**. We can do that with our old trick: plugging in a point we know to be on the line. Let's use point **A** **(–3, –4)** to help us find **b**:

④ *plug in (–3, –4)* $\qquad\qquad\qquad y = \frac{3}{4}x + b$

$$-4 = \frac{3}{4}(-3) + b$$

$$-4 = -\frac{9}{4} + b$$

⑤ *solve for b* $\qquad\qquad -\frac{16}{4} + \frac{9}{4} = b$

$$-\frac{7}{4} = b$$

At last, we have the last piece of the line equation! Let's plug *m* and *b* back into the equation for our answer:

⑥ *finalize equation* $\qquad\qquad\qquad y = mx + b$

$$y = \frac{3}{4}x - \frac{7}{4}$$

B

Slope shows up in word problems all the time!

Any time you have a word problem where something is **changing at a fixed rate**—such as the cost of buying more and more items, or the distance you travel each hour—you have a situation that can be modeled with linear growth. The equation you get from this kind of word problem will be an equation of a line, where the **rate of change is the slope**.

PORTAL

To see how rates of change can show up in word problems, check out the *Linear Modeling* chapter on page 482.

Standard form provides another shortcut

NOTE

The *b* in standard form is **not** the same as the *b* in slope-intercept form.

It'd be nice if standard form used different letters to make that clear, but that's just not the world we live in.

So far we have been focusing on equations in the **slope-intercept** form of the equation of a line ($y = mx + b$). Sometimes, the test will give you equations for lines in **standard form** ($ax + by = c$). You can always use your basic algebra skills to rewrite the equations in slope-intercept form:

$$ax + by = c \longrightarrow by = -ax + c \longrightarrow y = -\frac{a}{b}x + \frac{c}{b}$$

But notice that when you convert to the standard form, the slope of the line is represented by **-a/b** and the *y*-intercept by **c/b**. That will be true no matter what values are in place for *a*, *b*, and *c*! That can be a helpful shortcut on the test, so let's get some practice with it.

Fill in the empty entries in the table below.

Equation	Slope	y-intercept
6. $ax + by = c$	$-\dfrac{a}{b}$	$\dfrac{c}{b}$
7. $2x + 4y = 8$		
8. $x - 12y = 3$		
9. $7x + \dfrac{1}{2}y = 35$		
10. $\dfrac{2}{3}x - \dfrac{4}{3}y = 12$		

Answers 1. *given*   2. $-\frac{1}{2}$, 2   3. $\frac{1}{12}$, $-\frac{1}{4}$ 4. -14, 70   5. $\frac{1}{2}$, -9

EXAMPLE 6

$$y = \frac{2}{3}x + 5$$

Which of the following lines is parallel to the line represented by the equation above?

A) $2x + 3y = 6$
B) $4x - 6y = 10$
C) $9x + 6y = 4$
D) $-6x + 4y = 5$

SOLUTION

We want to find a line that is parallel to $y = 2/3x + 5$, which means we need a line with the <u>same slope</u> (2/3) but a different y-intercept. The equations in the answer choices are all in **standard form**. We *could* rewrite each choice in slope-intercept form, but that would be pretty time-consuming. Let's try to use our shortcut.

Remember that a line in standard form looks like $ax + by = c$ and has slope $-a/b$. Let's use that to pull the slope from each choice:

A) $2x + 3y = 6 \longrightarrow a = 2, b = 3, c = 6 \longrightarrow -a/b = -\frac{2}{3}$

B) $4x - 6y = 10 \longrightarrow a = 4, b = -6, c = 10 \longrightarrow -a/b = \frac{4}{6} = \boxed{\frac{2}{3}}$

Choice B matches! Just to make sure it's not the same exact line, we should check the y-intercept. That would be c/b, which simplifies to $-5/3$. This means that we have a line with the same slope and a different y-intercept—also known as a parallel line!

B

Practice Problems

Use your new skills to answer each question.

1

$$y = \frac{3}{2}x - 5$$

Which table gives three values of x and their corresponding values of y for the given equation?

A)

x	y
–5	0
–7	3
–9	6

B)

x	y
–2	–2
0	–5
2	–2

C)

x	y
0	5
3	7
6	9

D)

x	y
0	–5
2	–2
4	1

2

A line in the xy-plane has a slope of $\frac{2}{3}$ and passes through the point (0, –6). Which equation represents this line?

A) $y = -\frac{2}{3}x - 6$

B) $y = -\frac{2}{3}x + 6$

C) $y = \frac{2}{3}x - 6$

D) $y = \frac{2}{3}x + 6$

3

A line in the *xy*-plane passes through the origin and the point (2, 3). Which of the following is the slope of the line?

A) $\frac{2}{3}$

B) $\frac{3}{2}$

C) 2

D) 3

4

The line $y = mx - 7$, where m is a constant, is graphed in the *xy*-plane. If the line contains the point (6, –3), what is the value of m?

5

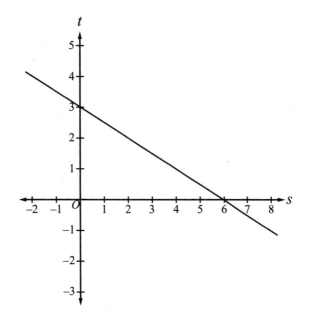

What is an equation of the graph shown?

A) $t = 3s - \frac{1}{2}$

B) $t = -\frac{1}{2}s + 3$

C) $s = 2t + 3$

D) $s = -\frac{1}{2}t + 3$

6

The graph of a particular line contains the points $(-1, -3)$ and $(1, 3)$. What is the equation of the line?

A) $y = x + 3$

B) $y = \frac{1}{3}x$

C) $y = 3x$

D) $y = 3x + 1$

7

x	y
0	12
1	9
2	6

The table shows three values of x and their corresponding values of y. There is a linear relationship between x and y. Which of the following equations represents this relationship?

A) $y = 12x + 9$
B) $y = 12x - 3$
C) $y = -3x + 9$
D) $y = -3x + 12$

8

x	15	20	25
y	17	11	5

The table shows three values of x and their corresponding values of y. There is a linear relationship between x and y that is defined by the equation $y = mx + 35$ where m is a constant. What is the value of m?

9

$$y = \frac{5}{3}x - 2$$

Which of the following equations represents a line that is parallel to the line given by the equation above?

A) $5x - 3y = 12$
B) $2y - 6x = 5$
C) $5y - 3x = 12$
D) $3x - 5y = 6$

10

$$ax + 6y = 3$$
$$bx + 5y = 2$$

If the system of equations above is parallel, which of the following must be a true statement?

A) $5b = 6a$
B) $5a = 6b$
C) $a + b = 11$
D) $ab = 30$

11

$$7x + 3y = 4$$
$$-14x + ny = 10$$

The equations above are parallel and n is a constant. If $(1, c)$ is a solution to the second equation, what is the value of c?

A) -4

B) $-\dfrac{2}{3}$

C) 0

D) 4

12

The graph of the linear function f passes through the quadrants I, II, and IV. Which of the following is true about the slope of the function f?

A) The slope is undefined.
B) The slope is positive.
C) The slope is negative.
D) There is not enough information provided.

13

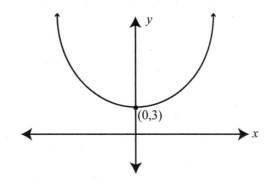

(0,3)

The graph of the parabola $f(x)$ is shown above. If $g(x)$ is a non-vertical linear function which intersects $f(x)$ at exactly one point, which of the following must be true?

A) The slope of $g(x)$ is 0.
B) The slope of $g(x)$ is undefined.
C) $g(x) = 3$
D) The y intercept of $g(x)$ is less than or equal to 3.

14

The line $2ax - by = 2$, where a and b are constants, is graphed in the xy-plane. If the line contains the point (2, -4), what is the slope of the line in terms of b?

A) $-b$

B) $2b$

C) $b + \frac{2}{b}$

D) $\frac{1 - 2b}{b}$

Function Machines

Tags: Algebra • Functions • Graphs of Functions

Inputs & Outputs

A function is something that **takes an input** and **returns an output**. In the last chapter, we worked with lines and their equations, which actually illustrate this exact idea. A line equation can be thought of as a function that lets you **put IN** an x-coordinate to **get OUT** the y-coordinate at that point on the line.

Line Equation:

$y = 3x + 5$
$y = 3(3) + 5 = \mathbf{14}$

- put IN x–value
- get OUT y–value

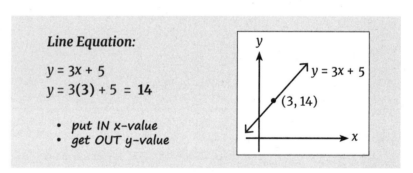

So we can think of the line equation as a perfectly built **function** for finding points on a line. As we dive deeper, however, we sometimes want to graph multiple lines at once, or work with equations where the graph isn't particularly relevant. For those reasons, it helps to use a different notation that emphasizes the connection between inputs and outputs. And *that's* where **function notation** comes in!

Reading $f(x)$

We read $f(x) = 3x + 5$ as:

"f of x is three times x plus five."

f on its own is NOT a variable, and those parentheses do NOT mean multiplication.

The equals sign here means something like "is defined to be."

Function Notation & The Machine

Instead of writing an equation in terms of y, we can write in terms of $f(x)$:

line equation	$y = 3x + 5$
function notation	$f(x) = 3x + 5$

Function notation makes it clear that the left side of the equation **changes** based on what you plug in for x on the right side. You can think of the $f(\ )$ on the left as the input chute for the **function machine**. Anything you plug into the chute for x replaces the x's on the right. If you plug in a different input, you'll get a different output:

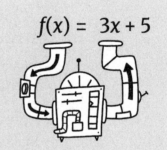

Function Machine:

$$f(2)\ = 3(2) + 5\ = 11$$
$$f(-4) = 3(-4) + 5 = -7$$
$$f(90) = 3(90) + 5 = 275$$

$f(x) = 3x + 5$

- put IN value for x
- get OUT a value for $f(x)$

EXAMPLE 1

If $f(x) = -4x + 3$, what is $f(-2a)$ equal to?

A) $8a + 3$
B) $-8a + 3$
C) $-2a - 1$
D) $8ax + 3$

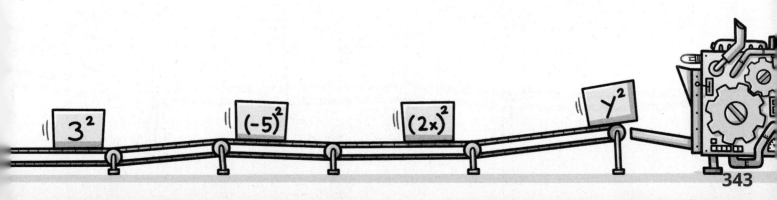

TIP

It's a good, nay, a GREAT idea to keep the parentheses whenever you make a substitution.

Any time you see an equation whose left side is a letter followed by another letter in parentheses, such as $f(x)$, you should assume you are working with a function. In this problem we have a function $f(x)$ to evaluate when $x = -2a$. This means we need to replace each x on the right hand side with $(-2a)$:

① Copy equation		$f(x) = -4x + 3$
② Plug in $(-2a)$ for x		$f(-2a) = -4(-2a) + 3$
③ Simplify		$f(-2a) = \boxed{8a + 3}$

A

Functions and Graphs

Function equations and graphs of those equations are two sides of the same coin. As we saw earlier, we can think of the equation of a line as a specific type of function machine that gives us a y-coordinate when we plug in an x-coordinate. As we plug more and more x-coordinates into that function machine, we collect points on that line. We can talk about those points in terms of xy-coordinates or in terms of function notation:

> If point $(2, 3)$ is on the graph of $f(x)$, then $f(2) = 3$.
>
> If point $(0, 4)$ is on the graph of $g(x)$, then $g(0) = 4$.

In the next few examples, we'll see how we can be flexible with our understanding of functions as both machines and graphs to solve a number of different types of problems.

NOTE

When we plot all of the input-output pairs of function $f(x)$ in a graph, we call that line (or parabola) simply "$f(x)$".

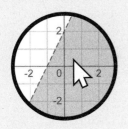

TIP

Not only can you get specific values using function notation, you can also click the gear to get a table of values for the function just as we did for linear equations.

Desmos: Using Function Notation

You can also use function notation in Desmos! If the test gives you a function you can type it straight into an input field to see its graph. In addition, you can simply plug in any number for x in $f(x)$ to see it's corresponding y-value.

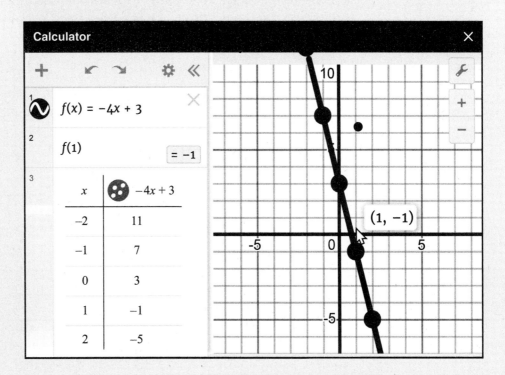

EXAMPLE 2

z	1	2	3	4
$g(z)$	3	1	−1	−3

The table above shows some values of the linear function g. Which of the following defines g ?

A) $g(z) = z + 2$

B) $g(z) = 3z − 2$

C) $g(z) = −2z + 5$

D) $g(z) = -\frac{1}{2}z + 5$

NOTE

Look at the table again. Notice how the values for *g* are going *down* as the values for *z* go *up*?

If you think about it, this tells you that the slope of the line must be negative. With that clue, you can eliminate choices that do not have a negative slope, making it even easier to work backwards.

We can solve this problem in two ways. We can think of the function graphically and use our equation of a line skills... or we can think of the function like a machine, and plug-&-chug.

Option 1: Thinking with Graphs

We are told that $g(z)$ is a **linear** function. This is just a fancy way of telling us that the graph of $g(z)$ is a **line**. Each column in the table tells us the coordinates of *points* on that line:

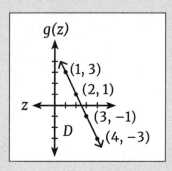

To find the equation of this line, we'll need a slope. We can find that by using any two points on this graph, such as (1, 3) and (2, 1):

① *find slope of* $g(z) = \dfrac{1-3}{2-1} = -\dfrac{2}{1}$

So the **slope** of the line equation is **–2**. If we look at our answer choices, we see that only **choice C** has the correct slope!

Option 2: Thinking with Functions

Alternatively, we could work backwards to solve this problem. Each column in the table tells us what we should get OUT of the correct equation for different inputs. In the correct equation, $g(1) = 3$, $g(2) = 1$, $g(3) = -1$, and $g(4) = -3$. Just like we can "test" line equations by plugging in points, we can also test each answer choice by plugging in z values from the table. The only choice that works with **every value in the table** is choice C:

C) $g(z) = -2z + 5$

$g(1) = -2(1) + 5 = 3$ ✓

$g(2) = -2(2) + 5 = 1$ ✓

$g(3) = -2(3) + 5 = -1$ ✓

$g(4) = -2(4) + 5 = -3$ ✓

C

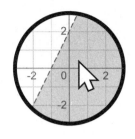

Desmos Tip

You can put points, such as $(-4, 3)$, in an entry field in Desmos to help you visualize what is going on. If you also graph the lines in the answer choices you can see which line goes through the given points!

EXAMPLE 3

$$h(x) = \frac{5}{2}x + k$$

In the function defined above, k is a constant. If $h(-4) = 3$, what is the value of $h(2)$?

A) -2

B) $-\frac{13}{2}$

C) 13

D) 18

SOLUTION

Our goal is to find $h(2)$. To do that, we'll first need to figure out what k is. Luckily, we're given that **$h(-4) = 3$**. We can plug in this solution in order to **find k**.

(1) *Copy equation* $h(x) = \frac{5}{2}x + k$

(2) *Plug-in $h(-4) = 3$* $3 = \frac{5}{2}(-4) + k$

(3) *Solve for k* $3 = -10 + k$

                                   $13 = k$

So now that we know what k is, we can **find $h(2)$**:

(4) *Update equation* $h(x) = \frac{5}{2}x + 13$

(5) *Plug-in $h(2)$* $h(2) = \frac{5}{2}(2) + 13$

(6) *Simplify* $h(2) = 5 + 13$

                      $h(2) = \boxed{18}$ **D**

PORTAL

For more on inequalities, check out the *Inequalities* chapter on page 438.

EXAMPLE 4

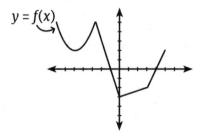

The complete graph of the function f is shown in the xy–plane above. For which of the following values of x is $f(x) > x$?

     I. $x = -5$
     II. $x = -1$
     III. $x = 5$

A) I only
B) II only
C) I and II only
D) I, II, and III

SOLUTION

This problem might look complicated at first, but it's really just asking us to **find the points on the line** at $x = -5$, $x = -1$, and $x = 5$. So let's find the y-value for each one:

   (I) **(−5, 2)**

   (II) **(−1, 0)**

   (III) **(5, 2)**

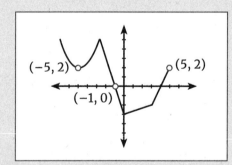

Our three points are **(−5, 2)**, **(−1, 0)**, and **(5, 2)**.

We're asked for which of these points is $f(x) > x$. We know that here $f(x) = y$, so we just need to find the choices where the y-coordinate is greater than the x-coordinate. Since **2 > −5** and **0 > −1**, choices I and II are correct. III doesn't work because **2 < 5**.

That means **choice C is the answer!**   **C**

Compound Functions

Sometimes you'll come across functions-within-functions. These are simply **multistep function problems** where you need to *focus on the inside function first* and work your way out.

EXAMPLE 5

A function f satisfies $f(2) = 4$ and $f(5) = 7$. A function g satisfies $g(5) = 2$ and $g(7) = 3$. What is $f(g(5))$?

A) 2
B) 3
C) 4
D) 7

SOLUTION

We want to evaluate $f(g(5))$, so let's **start with the inside function**, $g(5)$. We are told that $g(5) = 2$, so we can substitute 2 in:

(1) *substitute* $f(g(5)) = ?$

                                       $f(2) = ?$

Once we resolve the inside function, we see that what's left is just $f(2)$, which the problem tells us is **equal to 4**!

C

Use the table to answer the questions below.

x	♥	💣	◐	✳	☆
f(x)	☺	⚡	💬	☹	♥

1. What is f(💣)? _____

2. What is f(✳)? _____

3. If f(a) = 💬, what is a? _____

4. If f(k) = ☹, what is k? _____

5. What is f(f(☆))? _____

Use the graphs to find or estimate information about each function.

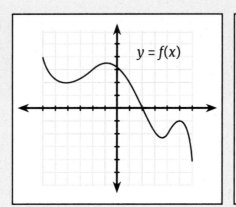

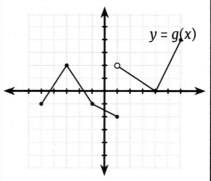

NOTE

Whenever you see two points for the same *x*-value, a hollow circle (O) is NOT considered a point on the line, while a solid point (●) is.

6. What is f(−4)? _____

7. What is g(−1)? _____

8. What is f(4)? _____

9. What is g(1)? _____

10. What is g(4)? _____

11. If f(a) = 3 and −3 < a < 0, what is a? _____

Answers: 1. ⚡   2. ☹   3. ◐   4. ✳   5. ☺
6. 2   7. −1   8. −2   9. −2   10. 0   11. −2

Use the functions to complete the problems below. The first one has already been completed for you because we are generous!

$f(x) = 3x - 4$ $\qquad$ $g(x) = x^2 - 2x + 7$ $\qquad$ $h(x) = -x + 5$

1. $f(100) = 3(100) - 4 = 296$

2. $g(-3) =$

3. $h(17) =$

4. $f(x + 5) =$

5. $h(2x - 3) =$

6. $g(-7a) =$

7. $f(2) + f(4) =$

8. $h(f(4)) =$

Answers:
1. *given* 2. 22 3. –12 4. $3x + 11$
5. $-2x + 8$ 6. $49a^2 + 14a + 7$ 7. 10 8. –3

Practice Problems

Use your new skills to answer each question.

1

The function f is defined by the equation $f(x) = 3x - 5$. What is the value of $f(x)$ when $x = 6$?

2

The function f is defined by the equation $f(x) = 12 - 3x$ and $f(a) = -6$, where a is a constant. What is the value of a?

A) 2
B) 6
C) 22
D) 30

3

x	0	2	4
$f(x)$	15	27	39

For the linear function f, the table shows three values of x and their corresponding values of $f(x)$. Which equation defines $f(x)$?

A) $f(x) = 6x + 15$
B) $f(x) = 12x + 15$
C) $f(x) = 15x + 27$
D) $f(x) = 27x + 15$

4

The function $f(x) = 3x^2 - 5$. What the value of $f(7)$?

A) 16
B) 58
C) 142
D) 436

5

The function f is defined by $f(x) = \sqrt{6x}$. For what value of x does $f(x) = 12$?

6

The function g is defined by $g(n) = 5n^3$. What is the value of n when $g(n) = 135$?

A) 3
B) 5
C) 9
D) 27

7

$$f(x) = 3x^2 + bx$$

For the function f defined above, b is a constant and $f(2) = 18$. What is the value of $f(-2)$?

A) −6
B) 0
C) 6
D) 3

8

A function satisfies $g(1) = -2$ and $g(3) = 4$. If the function is linear, which of the following defines g ?

A) $g(x) = x - 3$
B) $g(x) = 2x - 4$
C) $g(x) = 3x - 5$
D) $g(x) = 4x - 6$

9

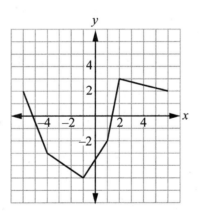

The complete graph of the function g is shown in the xy-plane above. If $g(a)$ gives the maximum value of the graph, what is the value of a ?

A) 3
B) 2
C) −1
D) −5

10

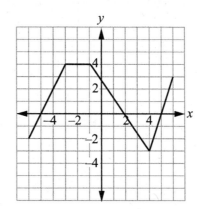

The complete graph of the function f is shown in the xy-plane above. Which of the following is equal to 4?

      I. $f(-2.5)$
      II. $f(-1)$
      III. $f(4)$

A) I only
B) II and III only
C) I and II only
D) I, II and III

11

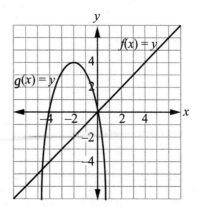

Graphs of functions f and g are shown in the xy-plane above. For which of the following values of x does $f(x) + g(x) = 0$?

A) −5
B) −3
C) −2
D) 1

12

If $f(x) = -7x - 4$, what is $f(-5x)$ equal to?

A) $35x^2 - 4$
B) $-35x - 4$
C) $35x - 4$
D) $35x^2 + 20x$

13

A function f satisfies $f(2) = 3$ and $f(4) = 5$. A function g satisfies $g(3) = 4$ and $g(6) = 2$. What is the value of $f(g(3))$?

A) 2
B) 3
C) 4
D) 5

14

x	2	3	4
$f(x)$	3	7	11

The table above shows values for the function f. If the function is linear, which of the following defines f ?

A) $f(x) = -2x + 7$
B) $f(x) = 3x - 3$
C) $f(x) = 4x$
D) $f(x) = 4x - 5$

15

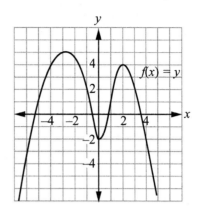

The graph above is a representation of the function $f(x)$. If $f(3) = f(b)$, which of the following could be b ?

A) −2

B) −1

C) 1

D) 2

16

If $f(x - 2) = 3x^2 - 5x + 4$, what does $f(-3)$ equal?

A) 46

B) 12

C) 2

D) −3

UNIT | Polynomials

Chapters

Overview

In this unit, we'll learn how we can use the distributive property and factoring to work with non-linear polynomials (a.k.a., equations with x^2 and larger exponents).

Just as basic algebra helped us work with the equation of a line, the skills we learn in this chapter will help us to understand the graphs of parabolic equations.

Factoring Basics

Tags: Advanced Math • Equivalent Expressions, Factoring and Polynomials

Distributive Property

One of our tools for working with algebraic expressions is the distributive property. When we use parentheses as a shorthand for multiplication, this property tells us what to do.

$$3(2x - 5) \quad \longrightarrow \quad 6x - 15$$

*The outside term gets multiplied (distributed) to **every term** inside.*

Factors & Factoring

factoring (v.)

Rewriting an expression as the product of its components, or "factors".

Now, since we multiplied **3** and **(2x – 5)** to get $6x - 15$, we say 3 and (2x – 5) are each *factors* of $6x - 15$, in the same way that **3** and **5** are *factors* of 15. When we "factor" an expression, like $6x - 15$, or a number, like 15, we are just working in the opposite direction from before:

$$6x - 15$$
$$3 \quad (2x - 5)$$

$$15$$
$$5 \quad 3$$

*Factors work the same whether they are **expressions** or **integers**.*

NOTE

In the exponents chapter, we learned that we can call $2x - 5$ a **binomial** factor since it has **two terms**.

When we look for a factor that **all** of the terms have in common, like the 3 in this problem, it's called a **monomial** factor.

A monomial factor can include a variable (e.g., "$3x$").

Factoring Polynomials

In this chapter, we'll be distributing and factoring with *polynomials*. We'll start off simple, then try tougher and tougher problems. If you understand how we can go from an expression, like $6x - 15$, to its factors, then you already understand the core concept behind even the toughest problems. So before we dive in, let's review the steps:

(1)	look at the expression	$6x - 15$
(1)	see that 3 is a factor of both $6x$ <u>and</u> -15	$6x - 15$ $(3)(2x) - (3)(5)$
(3)	"factor out" a 3	$3(2x - 5)$

Fill in the blanks to complete the solutions below.

1. *distribute*	$2x(3x^2 + 4x + 5) =$	
2. *think...*	The common term in $12x^2 + 15x + 3$ is _____.	
3. *factor*	$12x^2 + 15x + 3 =$	
4. *distribute*	$7(2a + 3b + c) =$	
5. *factor*	$20ab + 28a^2 + 8a =$	

Answers: **(1)** $6x^3 + 8x^2 + 10x$ **(2)** 3 **(3)** $3(4x^2 + 5x + 1)$ **(4)** $14a + 21b + 7c$ **(5)** $4a(5b + 7a + 2)$

Multiplying Expressions

Sometimes we need to multiply two **expressions** together, such as:

$$(x + 3)(x - 2) = ?$$

The Distributive Property still applies! We need to multiply **every term** in the first expression with **every term** in the second expression. While this might look new and complicated when you first see it, it's actually as simple as doing **two** distributions and adding them together:

$$(x + 3)(x - 2) = x(x - 2) + 3(x - 2)$$

If we rewrite the multiplication this way, we can see how plain ol' distribution gives us the answer:

$$x(x - 2) + 3(x - 2)$$

$$x^2 - 2x + 3x - 6$$

$$\boxed{x^2 + x - 6}$$

NOTE

If the first term had been **(x − 3)** instead of (x + 3), then we would be **subtracting** the two distributions:

$$x(x - 2) - 3(x - 2)$$

And *then* we'd have to remember to **distribute the negative** along with the 3.

Pencil Skills

And that's it! So what's the main difference between multiplying two expressions and standard, one-term distribution? Simply the number of steps involved. But we need to be careful! When we're working so many steps at once, the chances of making an error (such as forgetting to distribute a negative) increases.

To help us avoid such errors, we will need to carefully write out each step. Luckily, we have one or two tricks to help us cleanly multiply two expressions together: the **FOIL Method** and the **Box Method**.

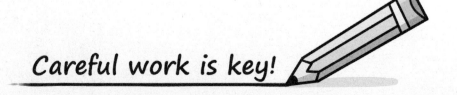

Careful work is key!

FOIL Method

In school you likely learned the FOIL method for multiplying two expressions. FOIL stands for First-Outer-Inner-Last, and it simply gives us an order in which to carry out these four multiplications:

$(x + 3)(x - 2)$

F O
I L

1	*First terms*	$(x + 3)(x - 2) = x^2$
2	*Outer terms*	$(x + 3)(x - 2) = x^2 - 2x$
3	*Inner terms*	$(x + 3)(x - 2) = x^2 - 2x + 3x$
4	*Last terms*	$(x + 3)(x - 2) = x^2 - 2x + 3x - 6$
		$(x + 3)(x - 2) = \boxed{x^2 + x - 6}$

Visualizing with the Box Method

We can also visualize this multiplication using the **box method**. To use the box method with two binomials, we draw a two-by-two box, labeling the columns with the terms from one factor and the rows with the terms from the other. Then, for each cell, multiply the row label by the column label. Once you're done, add up each result:

$(x + 3) \times (x - 2)$

1	Draw box
2	Label rows & columns
3	Fill–in products
4	Add products

	x	$+3$
x	x^2	$3x$
-2	$-2x$	-6

$= x^2 + 3x + (-2x) + (-6)$

$= \boxed{x^2 + x - 6}$

FOIL the given factors to complete the table below.

Factors	F	O	I	L
1. $(2x + 1)(x + 5)$ =	$2x^2$ +	$10x$ +	x +	5
2. $(x + 3)(x - 7)$ =	+	+	+	
3. $(a + 2)(2a + 3)$ =	+	+	+	
4. $(t - 1)(t - 8)$ =	+	+	+	

Use the BOX method to combine the factors below.

5. $(x + y)(x - y)$

6. $(2a + 2)(3a - 1)$

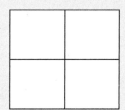

= _____

= _____

7. $(3x + 2)(x - 5)$

8. $(3x^2 - 5x + 1)(2x + 4)$

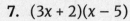

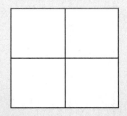

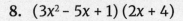

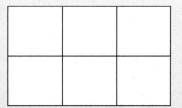

= _____

= _____

TIP

The box method extends nicely if you need to multiply more complicated polynomials. Just make sure you have a row/column for each term!

Answers:

1. *given*   2. $x^2 - 7x + 3x - 21$ 3. $2a^2 + 3a + 4a + 6$ 4. $t^2 - 8t - t + 8$

5. $x^2 - xy + xy - y^2$ 6. $6a^2 - 2a + 6a - 2$ 7. $3x^2 - 15x + 2x - 10$

8. $6x^3 - 10x^2 + 12x^2 + 2x - 20x + 4$

PORTAL

How might you be able to use Desmos to solve this problem or to check your work? Consider the tools we learned for equivalent expressions on pag 258.

EXAMPLE 1

$$5(3s + 1)(2s - 1)$$

Which of the following is equivalent to the above expression?

A) $20s$

B) $30s^2 - 5$

C) $30s^2 - 5s - 5$

D) $150s^2 - 25s + 25$

In this problem we have 3 expressions multiplied together. When we multiply 3 numbers, say 2, 3, and 4, we know that it doesn't matter what order they are multiplied in. For example:

$$2(3 \times 4) = 4(3 \times 2)$$

The same is true when we multiply expressions. That means we can work this problem in whichever way is easiest for us. Let's start by multiplying the two binomials together:

(1) *FOIL the binomials* $(3s + 1)(2s - 1) = 6s^2 + 2s - 3s - 1$

$$= 6s^2 - s - 1$$

Now we can multiply the result by 5, remembering to distribute:

(2) *multiply by 5* $5(6s^2 - s - 1) = \boxed{30s^2 - 5s - 5}$

C

365

FOIL in reverse to factor polynomials

We can use what we know about FOIL to go the other direction: start with a polynomial, and then **figure out its factors**. The trick is to write out empty factors and think backwards from the quadratic.

$$(\quad)(\quad) = x^2 + 2x - 8$$

Let's start by focusing on the **first term**. What two "first" terms would multiply to equal x^2? Two x's would work!

$$(?\quad)(?\quad) = x^2 + 2x - 8$$
$$(x\quad)(x\quad) = x^2 + 2x - 8$$

What multiplies to x^2?

Next, we need think of both the middle and last term of the quadratic. What two numbers will **add to equal +2** and **multiply to equal −8**?

$$(x\ \underline{?}\ )(x\ \underline{?}\ ) = x^2 + 2x - 8$$

What adds to +2 and multiplies to −8?

The best way to do that is to **list the factors** of −8, keeping an eye out for two that add to equal positive 2.

Factors of −8		
+1	×	−8
+2	×	−4
+4	×	−2

Once we find a match, we drop them into our factors, and we've done it:

$$(x + 4)(x - 2) = x^2 + 2x - 8$$

INTERACTIVE EXAMPLE

Factor: $x^2 + 3x - 18 = ($ $)($ $)$

Q1) What are the **first** terms of the factors?

SOLUTION

To end up with an x^2, the first terms must simply be x:

$$x^2 + 3x - 18 = (x \quad)(x \quad)$$

Q2) To end up with **negative** 18 as a constant, what must the **signs** be in the two factors?

A) both are positives
B) both are negatives
C) one is positive, one is negative

SOLUTION

If the "Last" terms in our factors multiply to be a negative, like –18, then one must be negative and the other positive:

A) (positive #)(positive #) = positive number
B) (negative #)(negative #) = positive number
C) (positive #)(negative #) = **negative** number

TIP

Studies show that looking at a drawing of a dragon can increase cognitive ability.

This is a pretty dry chapter, so here, have a dragon!

INTERACTIVE EXAMPLE (continued)

Factor: $x^2 + 3x - 18 = (x +)(x -)$

Q3) What are the **factors of −18**?

SOLUTION

Let's write out the different factors of −18:

Factors of −18					
+ 1	+ 2	+ 3	+ 6	+ 9	+ 18
×	×	×	×	×	×
− 18	− 9	− 6	− 3	− 2	− 1

Q4) Which pair of factors of −18 will give us a +3x as a middle term?

Think

If the original polynomial had "−3x" as its middle term instead of "+3x", what would the factors be?

SOLUTION

We need factors of −18 that add up to positive 3. Looking at our table of factors, it looks like +6 and −3 are our best bet:

Factors of −18					
+ 1	+ 2	+ 3	**+ 6**	+ 9	+ 18
×	×	×	×	×	×
− 18	− 9	− 6	**− 3**	− 2	− 1

Which means our finished factors are:

$$x^2 + 3x - 18 = (x + 6)(x - 3)$$

TIP

Any time you come across a quadratic, factoring is a good option to consider! In this problem, a glance at the answer choices tells us that we should **definitely** try factoring!

Try working backwards!

This problem is a great candidate for **working backwards**! Instead of factoring, simply multiply out each answer choice and see which one lands you back at the given expression.

EXAMPLE 2

$$3n^2 - 6n - 45$$

Which of the following is equivalent to the above expression?

A) $(n - 3)(n + 5)$
B) $3(n + 3)(n - 5)$
C) $3(n - 3)(n + 5)$
D) $3(n - 15)(n + 3)$

SOLUTION

The answer choices hint to us that we need to factor the original expression. A good place to start is to **look for a common factor**:

(1) *identify any common factor* $3n^2 - 6n - 45$

multiples of 3!

(2) *factor out (3)* $3(n^2 - 2n - 15)$

Now to **factor the quadratic** in the parentheses. Since the coefficient of n^2 is **1**, the first term in each factor will just be n:

(3) *set up the first term* $3(n^2 - 2n - 15) = 3(n\ \ )(n\ \ )$

Next, we need to **factor the –15** at the end. To end up with a negative, we know that one factor *must* be negative:

(4) *place signs* $3(n^2 - 2n - 15) = 3(n -\ \ )(n +\ \ )$

Next, we need two numbers that **multiply to 15**. Our options are:

(5) *factor 15* $3(n^2 - 2n - 15)$ $3(n - 15)(n + 1)$
                                                     or
                                                   $3(n + 3)(n - 5)$

Of these two options, only **–5** and **+3** also **add to –2**. So...

(6) *bring it home!* $3n^2 - 6n - 45 = 3(n + 3)(n - 5)$

B

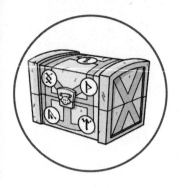

Factoring with the Box Method

The **box method** can be particularly useful when factoring a polynomial where the coefficient of the x^2 term isn't 1 and when you can't just factor that coefficient out like we did in Example 2.

$$6x^2 - 11x - 10 = 0$$

TIP

There are no common terms in this example, but it never hurts to check!

(1) *Factor out any common terms.*

(2) *Draw a box and identify your terms.*

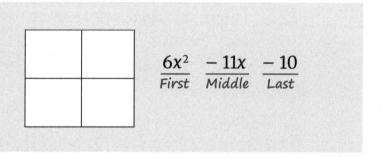

$$\underset{First}{6x^2} \quad \underset{Middle}{-11x} \quad \underset{Last}{-10}$$

(3) *Put the **first** and **last** terms in opposite corners...*

(4) *then find the **product** of these terms.*

First $6x^2$	
	Last -10

$$\underset{First}{6x^2} \quad \underset{Middle}{-11x} \quad \underset{Last}{-10}$$

$(6x^2)(-10) = \boxed{-60x^2}$
product

$-60x^2$ factors		
x	×	$-60x$
$+2$	×	-30
$+3$	×	-20
$+4$	×	-15 — *Bingo!*

This is the only tricky step. A foolproof method is to **list the factors** until you find a pair that adds to the middle term.

(5) *Find factors of this product that **add to the middle term**.*

If we list the factors of $-60x^2$, we find **4x and −15x.**

$$(4x)(-15x) = -60x^2$$

$$(4x) + (-15x) = -11x \quad \checkmark \ \textit{Checks out!}$$

(6) *Put the factors you found in the **empty corners**.*

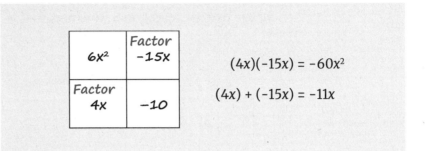

$(4x)(-15x) = -60x^2$

$(4x) + (-15x) = -11x$

(7) ***Factor out common terms** from each row and each column*

TIP

When factoring out a common term, **take the sign of the closer box**.

Here, for example, the "–5" takes the sign of "–15x" and the "2" takes the sign of "4x".

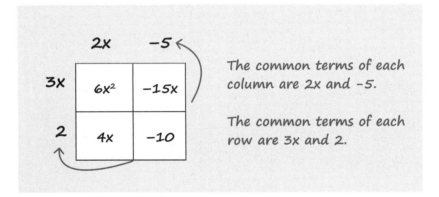

The common terms of each column are 2x and –5.

The common terms of each row are 3x and 2.

(8) *Find the sum of the common factors for the columns and the sum of the common factors for the rows.*

Those are the factors of the polynomial!

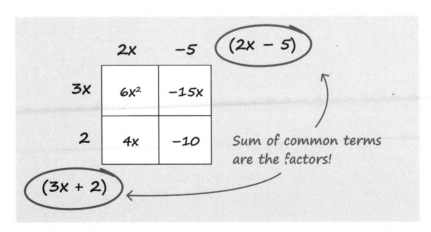

Sum of common terms are the factors!

$$6x^2 - 11x - 10 = (2x - 5)(3x + 2)$$

Thanks box method!

371

Remember

When factoring out a common term, **take the sign of the closer box**.

HINT

If there are no common terms, factor out a **1** or **–1**.

Remember

Before you start filling in the box, make sure there are no common terms to factor out!

TRY IT OUT

Use the box method to factor the polynomials below. You can also choose to draw a dragon in the margin if you need a little boost.

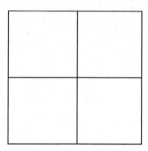

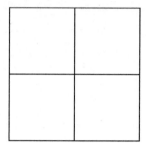

1. *factor:* $3x^2 - x - 30$

2. *factor:* $6x^2 - 7x + 2$

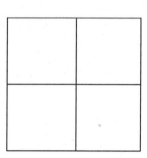

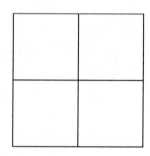

3. *factor:* $6x^2 + 5x - 6$

4. *factor:* $8x^2 - 32x + 30$

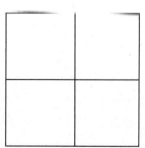

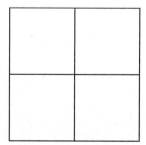

5. *factor:* $5x^2 + 34x + 24$

6. *factor:* $3x^3 + 10x^2 + 3x$

Answers: *See next page.*

Practice Problems

Use your new skills to answer each question.

1

Which expression is equivalent to $3x^2y + 24xy^2$?

A) $27x^3y^3$
B) $3x(xy + 24y^2)$
C) $3x^2y(8y)$
D) $3xy(x + 8y)$

2

$$4(3x^2 + 6)(5x^2 + 1)$$

Which of the following is equivalent to the expression above?

A) $60x^4 + 24$
B) $32x^4 + 28$
C) $60x^4 + 132x^2 + 24$
D) $216x^4$

3

Which of the following is a simplified version of the equation $(x + 3a)(x - 4b) = 0$?

A) $x^2 - 12ab = 0$
B) $x^2 - x(3a - 4b) - 12ab = 0$
C) $x^2 - x(3a + 4b) + 12ab = 0$
D) $x^2 + x(3a - 4b) - 12ab = 0$

4

$$12x^2 + 2x - 24$$

Which of the following is equivalent to the expression above?

A) $2(3x - 4)(2x + 3)$
B) $(4x - 3)(3x + 8)$
C) $12(x - 2)(x + 1)$
D) $12(x - 1)(x - 2)$

Last Page: 1. $(3x - 10)(x + 3)$ 2. $(3x - 2)(2x - 1)$ 3. $(2x + 3)(3x - 2)$

4. $2(2x - 3)(2x - 5)$ 5. $(5x + 4)(x + 6)$ 6. $x(3x + 1)(x + 3)$

5

Which of the following expressions is (are) a factor of $5x^2 + 31x - 28$?

  I) $x + 7$
  II) $5x + 4$

A) I only
B) II only
C) I and II
D) Neither I nor II

6

Which expression is equivalent to $x^2 - 7x - 60$?

A) $(x + 10)(x - 6)$
B) $(x + 6)(x - 10)$
C) $(x + 12)(x - 5)$
D) $(x + 5)(x - 12)$

7

$$(x - 6)(x + 1) + 10$$

Which of the following is equivalent to the expression above?

A) $x^2 + 5x + 16$
B) $(x + 5)^2 + 10$
C) $(x + 4)(x + 1)$
D) $(x - 4)(x - 1)$

8

The polynomial $18x^2 + 27x - 56$ has $(6x - 7)$ as a binomial factor. Which of the following is another binomial factor of the polynomial?

A) $(3x + 8)$
B) $(3x - 8)$
C) $(3x + 6)$
D) $(12x + 8)$

9

$$x^2 + 12x + 25$$

Which of the following is equivalent to the expression above?

A) $(x + 5)^2$
B) $(x + 6)^2 + 11$
C) $(x + 6)^2 - 11$
D) $(x - 6)^2 + 11$

10

Which of the expressions below is a factor of the polynomial $6x^3 + 24x^2 + 30x$?

   I) x
  II) $3x - 5$
 III) $x + 3$

A) I only
B) II and III only
C) I and II only
D) I, II, and III

11

If $(x + 4)(x - 2) = (x + 1)^2 + b$, what is the value of b ?

A) 8
B) −7
C) −8
D) −9

If $u = x + y$ and $v = x + 5y$, which of the following is equivalent to $uv + (\frac{v - u}{2})^2$?

A) $(x + y)(x + 5y)$
B) $(x + 3y)^2$
C) $(x - 3y)^2$
D) $(x - 3y)(x + 3y)$

If $20x^2 - 23x - 21$ factors as $(ax + b)(cx - d)$ where a, b, c, and d are all positive numbers, what is c ?

If $4x^2 - y^2 = 20$ and $2x + y = 2$, what is the value of $2x - y$?

A) -4
B) 3
C) 10
D) 40

The expression $ax^2 + bx + 26$ where a and b are constants can be rewritten as $(hx + k)(mx + 1)$, where h, k, and m are integer constants. Which of the following must be an integer?

A) $\dfrac{h}{k}$

B) $\dfrac{b}{h}$

C) $\dfrac{a}{h}$

D) $\dfrac{a}{k}$

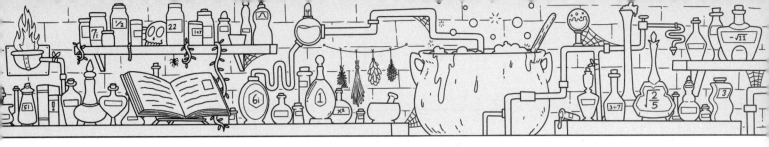

Zeros, Solutions, and Roots

Tags: Advanced Math • Equivalent Expressions: Factoring and Polynomials • Quadratic Equations

....

Set a polynomial equal to zero to find solutions

If you multiply two (or more) numbers together and the result is **zero**, then one or both of those numbers must have been zero! We can use this fact to solve polynomials. Say you are given the equation below:

$$x^2 + 5x + 6 = 0$$

We can use our reverse FOIL-ing skills to **factor** the left side:

$$(x + 2)(x + 3) = 0$$

TIP

If you have a polynomial set equal to zero, **factor and solve**. If it's not equal to zero, make balanced changes until it is!

Now, the above equation is true if either factor equals zero. To solve for the possible values of x, we just **set each factor equal to zero**:

$$x + 2 = 0$$
$$x = -2$$

$$x + 3 = 0$$
$$x = -3$$

If you go back and plug in -2 or -3 for x, the original equation will be true! Behold, the true power of factoring!

PORTAL

If you can't get it to factor, you could also use the quadratic formula. We learn to use it in *Non-Linear Systems* on page 468.

EXAMPLE 1

If $x^2 + 4x = 32$ and $a > 0$, then $x = ?$

SOLUTION

Option 1: Solving Algebraically

In order to use the true power of factoring, we need the polynomial to be equal to 0. This means that the first step is to **move everything to one side** of the equation.

(1) *rewrite equation* $\qquad$ $x^2 + 4x = 32$

(2) *gather to one side* $\qquad$ $x^2 + 4x - 32 = 0$

If we factor the polynomial on the left, we will end up with the product of two things that equal zero. We can then use reverse FOIL to find what those factors are.

(3) *prepare to factor!* $\qquad$ $(\ ? \ )(\ ? \ ) = 0$

(4) *what times what is x^2?* $\qquad$ $(x \quad)(x \quad) = 0$

(5) *what multiplies to –32 and adds to +4?* $\qquad$ $(x + 8)(a - 4) = 0$

If **either** of these factors equaled zero, then the equation would be true. That means x is **either** −8 or +4. But.... look at the original problem. We're given an additional constraint that $x > 0$.

(6) *solve for x* $\qquad$ $x = \boxed{4} \text{ or } \cancel{-8}$

Option 2: Solving by Graphing

You can put the equation into Desmos directly!

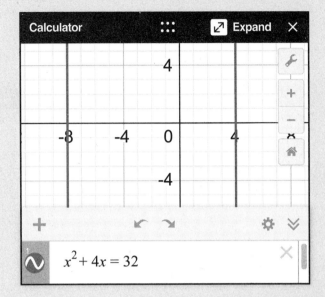

The vertical lines you see at −8 and 4 tell you that the solutions to this problem are $x = -8$ and $x = 4$. The additional constraint that $x > 0$ means that the answer is **4**.

379

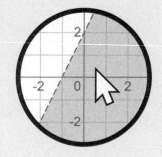

Desmos: Factoring Equations

We saw in the previous problem that we can either solve by factoring or we can get the answer by graphing in Desmos. If we take these two approaches and blend them together, we can use Desmos to help us factor!

Consider the polynomial $x^2 + 8x + 15$. Let's set it equal to y and graph it:

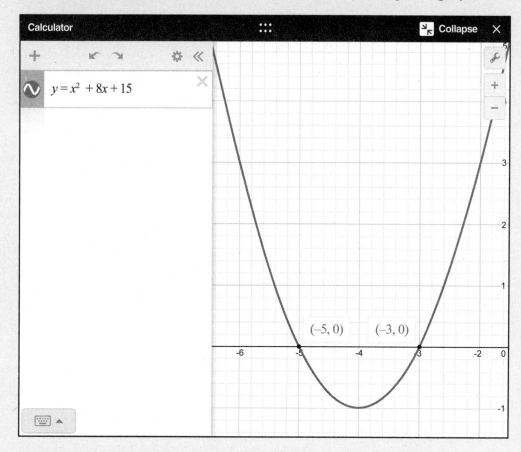

TIP

If you get a solution like $x = \frac{3}{4}$, this process will give you $(x - \frac{3}{4})$ as a factor. This is a valid factor, but we usually want the constants and coefficients to be integers. To achieve this, multiply the factor by the denominator of the fraction to get $4(x - \frac{3}{4}) = (4x - 3)$.

TIP

This process will only give you linear factors: factors of the form $(x - s)$ for some constant s. If your polynomial has a constant factor or a quadratic factor that can't be broken down into linear factors then this process won't find them directly.

When we have a polynomial set equal to 0, if we factor it we can set each factor equal to 0 to get the solutions. This time we are going to work **backwards** through this process to get <u>factors</u> from the <u>solutions</u>.

The points where $y = 0$ are the x-intercepts of the graph: $(-3, 0)$ and $(-5, 0)$. This means that the solutions to $x^2 + 8x + 15 = 0$ are $x = -3$ and $x = -5$. There are two ways to think about getting factors from these solutions:

Option 1: Treat each solution as an equation and rearrange it so that it equals 0. If we add 3 to both sides of $x = -3$ we get $x + 3 = 0$ and similarly we get $x + 5 = 0$. These two equations give us the factors $(x + 3)$ and $(x + 5)$, so we have $x^2 + 8x + 15 = (x + 3)(x + 5)$.

Option 2: If the solution is $x = s$ then the corresponding factor will be $(x - s)$. Here, this gives us $(x - (-3))$ and $(x - (-5))$, which simplifies to $(x + 3)$ and $(x + 5)$.

TIP

The maximum number of potential solutions for an equation is equal to the highest power of the variable.

This means a quadratic equation (x^2) can have up to 2 solutions and a cubic equation (x^3) can have up to 3.

TIP

To solve this problem by graphing remember that you would need to switch to using x and y. Try graphing the equation $y = 3x^2 - 13x - 10$ and see if you can find the solutions that way!

EXAMPLE 2

$$3t^2 - 13t = 10$$

What is a value of t that satisfies the above equation?

SOLUTION

This problem starts the same exact way as the previous one.

1. *rewrite equation* $\qquad 3t^2 - 13t = 10$

2. *gather to one side* $\qquad 3t^2 - 13t - 10 = 0$

Since we have a coefficient in front of the quadratic, our best bet is to use the **box method** for factoring.

3. *Draw a box*

4. *Fill in first and last terms*

$3t^2$	
	-10

5. *multiply $3t^2$ and -10* $\qquad (3t^2)(-10) = -30t^2$

Next, we need to find factors of $-30t^2$ that **add up to -13**.

4. *find factors with coefficients that add up to -13.*

-15 and 2 works!

Factors of $-30t^2$		
$-30t$	×	t
$-15t$	×	$2t$
$-10t$	×	$3t$

Continued on next page →

⑤ *add factors to open boxes.*

⑥ *factor out common terms, keep sign from closer box*

	$3t$	$+ 2$
t	$3t^2$	$2t$
-5	$-15t$	-10

⑦ *write your factors out* $(3t + 2)(t - 5) = 0$

⑧ *solve for t* $t = \left(-\dfrac{2}{3}, 5\right)$

Exercise

Use the graph to answer the questions below.

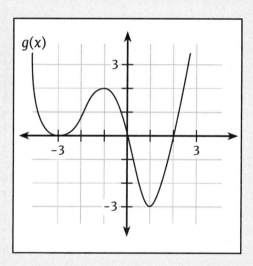

1. How many y-intercepts are there?

   _____

2. What is/are the y-intercept(s)?

   _____

3. How many x-intercepts are there?

   _____

4. What is/are the x-intercepts?

   _____

5. What is/are the zeros of the function g?

   _____

6. If the polynomial g were factored, what factors must it have?

   _____

Key Idea: Different Names for the Same Thing

We've looked at how we can use **factoring** to find solutions to quadratic equations. We've also looked at how we can **graph** quadratic equations and use the **zeros** on the graph to find factors and solutions. The connection between all of these ideas is one of the <u>keys</u> to mastering the SAT Math section. So let's pause to let that connection sink in:

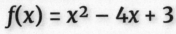

$$f(x) = x^2 - 4x + 3$$

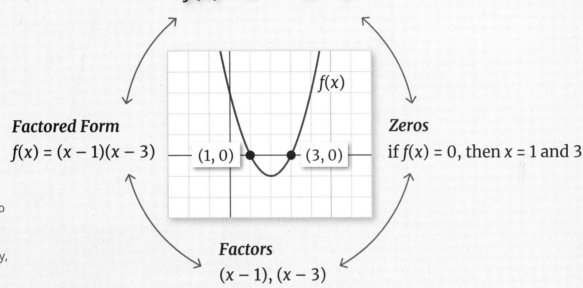

Factored Form
$$f(x) = (x - 1)(x - 3)$$

Zeros
if $f(x) = 0$, then $x = 1$ and 3

Factors
$(x - 1), (x - 3)$

TIP

If you graph a function $f(x)$, the x-intercepts also give you the solutions to the equation $f(x) = 0$. These are, unsurprisingly, also called the zeros of the function.

When the function is a polynomial, they are also known as <u>roots</u> and (as we have seen) can be used to factor the polynomial.

The more comfortable you are with the connection between zeros, graphs, and solutions, the easier you will find many SAT Math problems. If you're not feeling comfortable yet, that's okay! Keep practicing, bookmark this page, and play with the Desmos calculator: each practice problem, struggle, and success is building up that understanding.

EXAMPLE 3

Which of the following is a factor of $2x^3 - 10x^2 - 4x + 48$?

A) $(x - 3)$
B) $(x - 1)$
C) $(x + 1)$
D) $(x + 3)$

SOLUTION

Let's look at two different ways to solve this problem!

Option 1: Graphing

Let's treat the polynomial as a function and graph it:

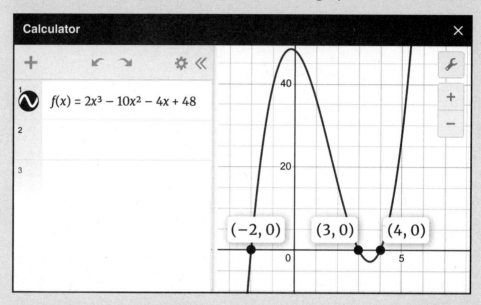

We see that we have **x-intercepts** at $(-2, 0)$, $(3, 0)$ and $(4, 0)$. Each of these intercepts corresponds to a **factor** of the original polynomial: $(x + 2)$, $(x - 3)$, and $(x - 4)$. Comparing these to the answer choices, we see that $(x - 3)$ is **choice A**.

Option 2: Working Backwards

If something is a factor of a polynomial, then the solution that results from setting the factor equal to 0 will also be a solution to setting the polynomial equal to zero. Setting each answer choice here equal to zero, we get the potential solutions 3, 1, –1 and –3. Let's test the result of plugging each of these back into $2x^3 - 10x^2 - 4x + 48$.

A) $(x - 3)$ $x = 3$ $2(3)^3 - 10(3)^2 - 4(3) + 48 = 0$

B) $(x - 1)$ $x = 1$ $2(1)^3 - 10(1)^2 - 4(1) + 48 = 36$

C) $(x + 1)$ $x = -1$ $2(-1)^3 - 10(-1)^2 - 4(-1) + 48 = 40$

D) $(x + 3)$ $x = -3$ $2(-3)^3 - 10(-3)^2 - 4(-3) + 48 = -84$

The only answer choice that gives a solution that makes the original polynomial equal to zero is A, so that is our answer.

A

TIP

If you fully factor this polynomial you get:

$2x^3 - 10x^2 - 4x + 48$

$\downarrow$

$2(x + 2)(x - 3)(x - 4)$

EXAMPLE 4

If the function g has six distinct zeros, which of the following could represent the graph of g in the xy-plane?

A)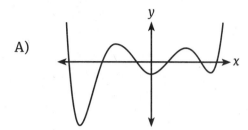

B)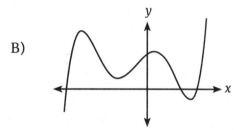

C)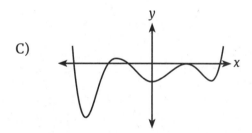

D)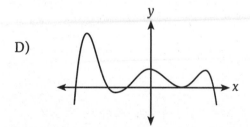

385

SOLUTION

Since the function has six distinct zeros, that means it **has six different x-intercepts**. All we have to do is count how many times the graph in each answer choice crosses the *x*-axis.

 count x-intercepts

Choice A:
6 *x*-intercepts

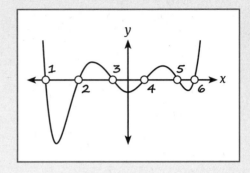

Choice B:
3 *x*-intercepts

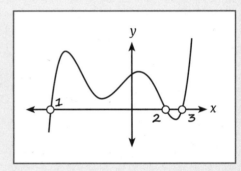

TIP

The word "distinct" in the question is important. In choices C and D the point labeled 4 is at a point where the graph hits the *x*-axis and bounces. When this happens the function has a *double root* at that point. This means that the factor corresponding to that zero would show up an even number of times in the factorization. On the SAT, the factor would most likely be squared.

Choice C:
5 *x*-intercepts

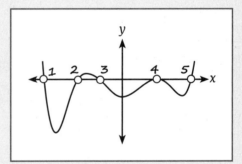

Choice D:
5 *x*-intercepts

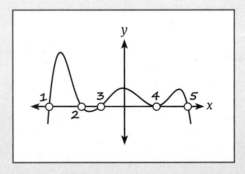

Only **choice A** has a graph that has six different *x*-intercepts, so it could be the graph of a function with 6 solutions.

A

ZEROS, SOLUTIONS, AND ROOTS

EXAMPLE 5

TIP

If you prefer, you could **work backwards** by graphing each answer choice and checking which has the correct x-intercepts.

In the xy-plane, the graph of function f has x-intercepts at -5, 0, and 3. Which of the following could be the function?

A) $f(x) = (x - 5)(x + 3)$
B) $f(x) = x(x - 5)(x - 3)$
C) $f(x) = (x + 5)(x - 3)$
D) $f(x) = x(x + 5)(x - 3)$

SOLUTION

We know that x-intercepts of a function have a y-coordinate of 0. That means if we plug -5, 0, and 3 into the function **equation**, it will spit out a result of **zero**. The simplest way to solve this problem is to do just that: test each answer choice by plugging in the given x-values. If the function doesn't spit out a zero for every single one, then it's not the right equation. It turns out that only choice D works for every single value:

plug-in to test choice D

$$x(x + 5)(x - 3) = ?$$
$$0(0 + 5)(0 - 3) = 0$$
$$-5(-5 + 5)(-5 - 3) = 0$$
$$3(3 + 5)(3 - 3) = 0$$

SHORTCUT: Thinking with Factors

We don't *have* to trial-and-error this problem. When a function is factored out, you can **see** the solutions clearly. If the graph has an x-intercept of k, then one factor would be:

$$f(x) = (x - k)...$$

That means that just knowing the x-intercepts, we can write the factors out and then compare our equation to the answer choices. If there are intercepts at 0, -5, and 3, then the factors are:

$$f(x) = (x - 0)(x - (-5))(x - 3)$$
$$f(x) = x(x + 5)(x - 3)$$

And that matches choice D! This is a great example of how we can **save time** if we understand the connection between solutions, factors, and graphs.

387

EXAMPLE 6

x	−5	−2	0	3	6
f(x)	10	6	4	0	2

The function f is defined by a polynomial. Some values of x with the corresponding values of $f(x)$ are shown in the table above. Which of the following must be a factor of $f(x)$?

A) $x + 3$
B) $x − 3$
C) $x − 4$
D) $x + 4$

TIP

Trap Alert: Notice that the table gives you both an x-intercept, (3, 0), and a y-intercept, (0, 4). The test writers know how easy it can be to pick the wrong intercept if you are rushing, so the answer choices will reflect that. As always, taking the time to read carefully is key—even if what you are reading is a table!

SOLUTION

In this problem, we're not told what the equation is for $f(x)$, but we are still asked for one of its factors. The table must be important. It gives us a series of inputs & outputs, or (x, y) pairs if you're feeling graphy. How can a point tell us a factor of the equation?

Well, every **x-intercept** of a polynomial's graph tells us one of its factors. An x-intercept is **any x input that spits out a zero** for $f(x)$. Do we see one in the table? Yes! In the fourth column:

x	−5	−2	0	3	6
f(x)	10	6	4	0	2

This tells us that when $x = 3$, the polynomial $f(x) = 0$. Which means if we factored whatever that polynomial is, one of its factors must be $(x − 3)$. So the answer is B!

B

Practice Problems

Use your new skills to answer each question.

1

If $s > 0$ and $s^2 + 3s - 28 = 0$, what is the value of s?

A) -7
B) 3
C) 4
D) 7

2

Which of the following polynomial equations has 8 and -2 as solutions?

A) $(x - 8)(x - 2) = 0$
B) $(x + 8)(x + 2) = 0$
C) $(x - 8)(x + 2) = 0$
D) $(x + 8)(x - 2) = 0$

3

$$x^2 - 6x - 27 = 0$$

What is the sum of the two solutions of the equation above?

A) 9
B) 6
C) 0
D) -3

4

$$x^2 - x - 30 = 0$$

If r is a solution of the equation above and $r > 0$, what is the value of r?

5

The equation $ax^2 + bx + c = 0$, has two solutions: $x = \frac{3}{4}$ and $x = \frac{1}{2}$. Which of the following could be factors of $ax^2 + bx + c$?

A) $(4x - 3)$ and $(2x - 1)$
B) $(4x - 1)$ and $(2x - 3)$
C) $(4x + 1)$ and $(2x + 3)$
D) $(4x + 3)$ and $(2x + 1)$

6

What is the value of a if $x + 1$ is a factor of $2x^3 + x^2 - ax + 4$?

A) −4
B) −3
C) 0
D) 2

7

What is the product of all values of k that satisfy $4k^2 - 3k = 7$?

A) −7

B) $-\frac{7}{4}$

C) $-\frac{4}{7}$

D) $\frac{7}{4}$

8

The function g has roots at $x = -4, 1,$ and 5. Which of the following could be the definition of g?

A) $g(x) = (x - 4)(x - 1)(x - 5)$
B) $g(x) = (x + 4)(x + 1)(x + 5)$
C) $g(x) = (x + 4)(x - 1)(x - 5)$
D) $g(x) = (x - 4)(x + 1)(x + 5)$

9

Particular values of the function g are given in the following table:

x	$g(x)$
–3	5
–1	0
0	1
2	8

Which of the following is a factor of g ?

A) $(x - 1)$
B) $(x + 1)$
C) $(x - 2)$
D) $(x + 3)$

10

The graph of the function $f(x)$ has 3 distinct zeros. Which of the following could be the graph of $f(x)$?

A)

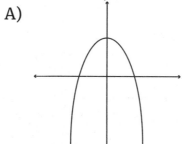

B)

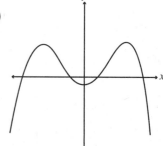

C)

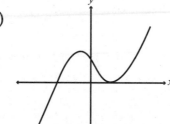

D)

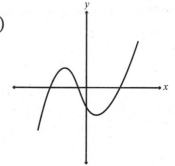

11

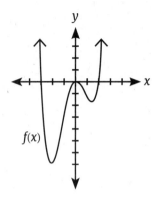

A portion of the graph of the function $f(x)$ is shown. Which of the following functions could be $f(x)$?

A) $f(x) = x(x - 2)(x + 3)$
B) $f(x) = x(x + 2)(x - 3)$
C) $f(x) = x^2(x - 2)(x + 3)$
D) $f(x) = x^2(x + 2)(x - 3)$

12

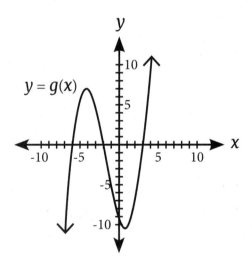

The graph of the function g is shown. Which of the following is a value of x for which $g(x)=0$?

A) 0
B) –2
C) –3
D) –9

13

The functions f and g are defined by $f(x) = 6x^2 + x + 5$ and $g(x) = 2x^2 - 15x - 2$. For what set of x values does $f(x) + g(x) = 0$?

A) $\frac{1}{4}$ and $\frac{3}{2}$

B) $\frac{2}{3}$ and 4

C) $-\frac{1}{4}$ and $-\frac{3}{2}$

D) 2 and 3

14

Functions f and g intersect at the points $(-3, 5)$, $(2, 8)$, and $(11, -17)$. Which of the following could define the function $h(x) = f(x) - g(x)$?

A) $h(x) = (x + 3)(x - 2)(x - 11)$
B) $h(x) = (x - 5)(x - 8)(x + 17)$
C) $h(x) = (x + 2)(x - 6)(x + 6)$
D) $h(x) = (x - 3)(x + 2)(x + 11)$

Pattern Matching

Tags: Advanced Math • Factoring and Polynomials • Polynomial Functions

Pattern Matching

Occasionally, you are asked to find multiple unknowns using a single equation. The trick to discovering their values is **pattern matching**. For example, say we are asked find a, b, and c, in the following equation:

$$5x^2 + 3x + 7 = ax^2 + bx + c$$

It would actually be impossible for us to "solve" for each of these unknown variables... but we don't need to! Notice how each side follows the exact same **pattern**:

same pattern! $\longrightarrow$
$$ax^2 + bx + c$$
$$5x^2 + 3x + 7$$

There's an x^2 with a coefficient (5 or a), an x with a coefficient (3 or b), and a constant at the end (7 or c). Since they are in the same form, we can simply match a, b, and c with the numbers on the left!

$$a = 5, \quad b = 3, \quad c = 7$$

Before we look at some test questions, let's get some practice using pattern matching to figure stuff out!

Use **pattern matching** to complete the table below. You may need to rearrange the equation first! Use the bottom of the page for work.

Equation		a	b	c
1.	$8x^2 + 2x - 15 = ax^2 + bx + c$	8		
2.	$5x^2 - 7x + 12 = ax^2 + bx + c$			
3.	$99x^2 - \frac{1}{99}x + 5 = ax^2 + bx - c$			
4.	$-x^2 - x = ax^2 + bx + c$			
5.	$7x^2 + \frac{1}{3}x + 4 = ax^2 + \frac{1}{b}x + c$			
6.	$x^2 + 2x - bx + 2 = ax^2 + c$			
7.	$3x^2 + 6 = ax^2 + bx + 3x + c$			
8.	$3x^2 - 17x - 5 = ax^2 + bx + 3x + c$			

Answers: 1. 8, 2, –15   2. 5, –7, 12   3. 99, $-\frac{1}{99}$, –5   4. –1, –1, 0   5. 7, 3, 4

6. 1, 2, 2   7. 3, –3, 6   8. 3, –20, –5

EXAMPLE 1

$$3x(2x - 3) + 2(4x + 5) = ax^2 + bx + c$$

In the equation above, a, b, and c are constants. If the equation is true for all values of x, what is the value of b?

TIP

Anytime you see "**true for all values of x...**", it's likely you are dealing with a simple pattern matching problem.

SOLUTION

Our goal is to **simplify the left side** of the equation until it matches the pattern on the right side. So let's start by distributing:

① *copy the left side* $3x(2x - 3) + 2(4x + 5)$

② *distribute* $6x^2 - 9x + 8x + 10$

③ *simplify* $6x^2 - x + 10$

Now we have both sides of the equation in a matching pattern. We want the value of b, which is the coefficient of x on the right side. That means our answer is the **coefficient of x** on the left:

④ *match pattern* $6x^2 - x + 10 = ax^2 + bx + c$

                                        $6x^2 - (1)x + 10 = ax^2 + bx + c$

So b must equal **–1**.

EXAMPLE 2

$$\frac{30x^2 - 52x - 12}{kx + 7} = -6x + 2 - \frac{26}{kx + 7}$$

The above equation is true for all values of $x \neq -\frac{7}{k}$, where k is a constant. What is the value of k?

A) -6

B) -5

C) 5

D) $\frac{52}{6}$

SOLUTION

Since we see "for all values of x" (except the one that makes the fraction undefined), we are likely dealing with a pattern matching problem. The two sides look nothing alike, though, so we'll need to do some simplifying. Since they make things tricky, let's start by **moving the fractions to one side** and combining:

$$\frac{30x^2 - 52x - 12}{kx + 7} = -6x + 2 - \frac{26}{kx + 7}$$

$$\frac{30x^2 - 52x - 12}{kx + 7} + \frac{26}{kx + 7} = -6x + 2$$

$$\frac{30x^2 - 52x + 14}{kx + 7} = -6x + 2$$

Now we can multiply both sides by the denominator, **$kx + 7$**, in order to **clear those pesky fractions**:

$$(kx + 7)\frac{30x^2 - 52x + 14}{kx + 7} = (-6x + 2)(kx + 7)$$

$$30x^2 - 52x + 14 = -6kx^2 - 42x + 2kx + 14$$

Now we *almost* have an exact pattern match. The only problem is we have **two** x terms on the right... but we can fix that!

Continued on next page →

Let's **move −42x to the left side**. It'll be happier there anyway

$$30x^2 - 52x + 14 = -6kx^2 - 42x + 2kx + 14$$

$$30x^2 - 10x + 14 = -6kx^2 + 2kx + 14$$

— match! —

Now we're talking! Both sides of the equation now follow the same $ax^2 + bx + c$ pattern. To solve for k, we can either match the x^2 coefficients or the x coefficients. Either way gives us the answer:

$$
\begin{aligned}
30x^2 &= -6kx^2 \\
30 &= -6k \\
\boxed{-5} &= k
\end{aligned}
\qquad\qquad
\begin{aligned}
-10x &= 2kx \\
-10 &= 2k \\
\boxed{-5} &= k
\end{aligned}
$$

Bonus Solution: Picking Numbers

We're told that the equation is true "for all values of x." This is often a big sign that we could make things easier for ourselves by **picking numbers**. If it's true for all values of x, then it should be true for $x = 1$. Try plugging 1 in for x right from the start, and simplify until you find k. This technique is not always useable, but when it is, it can save you a lot of time and heartache.

B

EXAMPLE 3

If $(mx + 3)(nx - 5) = -6x^2 + rx - 15$ is true for all values of x and $m + n = 1$, what are the two possible values of r?

A) −15 and −6
B) −2 and 3
C) −10 and 9
D) −21 and 19

SOLUTION

We're told that the equation is "true for all values of *x*", and we have way too many unknowns: these are signs that we need to use pattern matching! To do that, we'll need to FOIL the left side:

(1) *rewrite the left side* $(mx + 3)(nx − 5)$

(2) FOIL $mnx^2 − 5mx + 3nx − 15$

Let's pause here and look for a pattern that can help us:

$$mnx^2 − 5mx + 3nx − 15 = −6x^2 + rx − 15$$

If we focus on the **x^2 coefficients**, we can see that **$mn = −6$.** Let's combine that with what we already know about *m* and *n*:

$$mn = −6$$
$$m + n = 1$$

Later, we'll talk formally about how to solve "systems of equations" like this, but for now we can just look at it. We need **two numbers** that **multiply to –6** and **add to 1**.

If we play around with it, we find that **$m = 3$** and **$n = −2$** would work. Let's try plugging that into our equation and do some pattern matching:

$$(3)(−2)x^2 − 5(3)x + 3(−2)x − 15 = −6x^2 + rx − 15$$
$$−6x^2 − 15x − 6x − 15 = −6x^2 + rx − 15$$
$$−6x^2 − 21x − 15 = −6x^2 + rx − 15$$

— match! —

Bingo! Now that we have a **pattern match**, we see that **$r = −21$.** If we check the answer choices, we see that we don't even need to find a second possible value: only **choice D** has –21 in it!

D

PORTAL

To see how to solve systems of equations, turn to the *Linear Systems* chapter on page 448.

EXAMPLE 4

What is the sum of all values of x that satisfy $3x^2 - 18x + 21 = 0$?

A) 6

B) −6

C) $3\sqrt{6}$

D) $6\sqrt{3}$

This looks like it's asking us to solve a quadratic. The first thing to try when solving a quadratic is always **factoring.** All of the coefficients are multiples of 3, so we can **pull 3 out:**

(1) *copy equation* $3x^2 - 18x + 21$

(2) *factor out 3* $3(x^2 - 6x + 7)$

Now, ordinarily, we would just factor the quadratic and get two answers. But there's a problem. We would need to find two numbers that multiply to 7 and add to −6. But our only choices are 1 and 7 (which add to 8) or −1 and −7 (which add to −8). So neither option works! This doesn't mean there are no solutions... just no solutions that are **whole numbers.**

We can solve *this* problem in two different ways: the "hard work" way or the "hard thinking" way.

Option A: "Hard Work" Way
Since we can't factor this quadratic, we'll have to turn to our old, bulky friend: **the quadratic formula.**

(3) *quadratic formula* $x = \dfrac{-b \pm \sqrt{b^2 - 4ac}}{2a}$
     $(x^2 - 6x + 7)$

   $a = 1,\ b = -6,\ c = 7$ $x = \dfrac{6 \pm \sqrt{(-6)^2 - 4(7)}}{2(1)}$

                                      $x = \dfrac{6 \pm \sqrt{8}}{2}$

                                      $x = \dfrac{6 \pm 2\sqrt{2}}{2}$

                                      $x = 3 \pm \sqrt{2}$

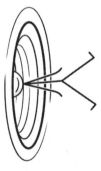

PORTAL

Forget the quadratic formula? Flip to page for a reminder 472.

Continued on next page →

Now we have two solutions: $(3 + \sqrt{2})$ and $(3 - \sqrt{2})$. Since the question asks for the sum of all solutions, we just add these:

④ *add solutions* $\qquad\qquad 3 + \sqrt{2} + 3 - \sqrt{2} = ⑥$

Option B: "Hard Thinking" Way

Let's think about this a little bit abstractly. We wish we could factor $x^2 - 6x + 7$ to find the solutions. Let's pretend we can do that and use variables to stand in for the factors. Say our solutions to the quadratic were **r** and **s.** What would that look like?

pretend to factor $\qquad x^2 - 6x + 7 = (x - r)(x - s)$

$\qquad\qquad\qquad\qquad x^2 - 6x + 7 = x^2 - rx - sx + rs$

$\qquad\qquad\qquad\qquad x^2 - 6x + 7 = x^2 - (r + s)x + rs$

Now we can do some pattern matching! For this factoring to work out, it must be true that those last two terms, **r** and **s** , multiply to equal 7... and **add to equal 6**. Otherwise, FOILing wouldn't produce the right quadratic! So:

$$r + s = 6$$

And look! This is exactly what the question asked for. If "**r**" and "**s**" are the solutions to this quadratic, then we've shown just from how factoring works that the solutions must add to equal 6!

A

Practice Problems

Use your new skills to answer each question.

1

$$4x(7x + 2) + 5(x - 4) = ax^2 + bx + c$$

In the equation above, a, b, and c are constants. If the equation is true for all values of x, what is the value of b?

A) -20
B) 5
C) 8
D) 13

2

$$\frac{2y^2 + 11y + 12}{y + 4} = ay + b$$

In the equation above, a and b are constants. If the equation is true for all values of y, what is the value of a?

A) $-\dfrac{3}{2}$

B) 2

C) 3

D) 11

3

If $(ax - 3)(2x + b) = -2(5x^2 + 8x + 3)$ for all values of x, what is the value of ab?

A) -16
B) -10
C) 10
D) 15

4

What is the sum of all values of x that satisfy
$3x^2 + 17x - 2 = 0$?

A) -2

B) $-\frac{2}{3}$

C) $-\frac{17}{3}$

D) 17

5

The equation $\frac{15x^2 + 21x - 32}{ax - 3} = 3x + 6 - \frac{14}{ax - 3}$ is true for all

values of $x \neq \frac{3}{a}$, where a is a constant. What is the value of a ?

A) 3
B) 5
C) 14
D) 15

6

The equation $\frac{x^2 + 8x - 9}{x - b} = x + 3 - \frac{24}{x - b}$ is true for all values of

$x \neq b$, where b is a constant. What is the value of b ?

A) -5

B) $\frac{11}{3}$

C) 5

D) 8

$$(x - 3)(x - 2)(x + 4) = ax^3 + bx^2 + cx + 24$$

The above expression is true for all values of x. What is the value of c?

A) −1
B) −14
C) 14
D) 24

The expression $6ax + b(x + a) = 14x + 4$ is true for all values of x. If $a \neq b$, what is the value of a?

A) $\frac{1}{3}$

B) 3

C) $\frac{7}{3}$

D) 12

The expression $(3x + 2y)(x - 4y) = ax^2 + bxy + cy^2$ is true for all values of x and y. What is the value of b?

A) −10
B) −8
C) −2
D) 14

UNIT

Advanced Functions

Chapters

Overview

In this unit we will continue to build on the algebra skills we have been working on. We will practice solving more complicated equations and study the graphs of a wide variety of functions. We will also explore how to work with inequalities.

Advanced Algebra

Tags: Advanced Math • Equivalent Expressions: Rational Expressions • Absolute Value • Rational Functions

PORTAL

We talked about how to find the number of solutions to a **system** of equations in *Linear Systems* on page 472 and we talked about how to turn a single equation into a system in *Basic Algebra* on page 270. You can combine those skills to solve questions that ask how many solutions an equation has.

A problem can have zero or infinite solutions

One of the main premises of algebra is that if you are given a single equation with a single variable, you can solve for that variable. Occasionally, however, something goes wrong (even if you don't make any mistakes!). Let's look at two examples where simplifying and combining like terms leads to an interesting situation. First up:

$$4(x+3) - 2(2x+2) = 6$$
$$4x + 12 - 4x - 4 = 6$$
$$8 = 6 \text{ ?!}$$

In this case, simplifying the equation led to a **false** statement ($8 = 6$). That means that no matter what we plug in for x it is <u>always</u> going to result in a false statement. There are **zero** valid solutions! Now look at *this* situation:

$$3(2y+5) = 6(y+4) - 9$$
$$6y + 15 = 6y + 24 - 9$$
$$6y + 15 = 6y + 15$$
$$0 = 0$$

In the second case, simplifying leaves us with a patently **true** statement. This means that no matter what we plug in for y it is <u>always</u> going to be true. This equation has **infinitely many** valid solutions.

Vocabulary: Unknowns, Variables, & Constants

In algebra, we spend a lot of time solving for "unknowns." Sometimes, these unknowns are called *variables* and sometimes they are called *constants*. In many cases the words are interchangeable.

In the generic model for a linear equation, $y = mx + b$, the input (x) and output (y), are considered **variables** because they can be multiple values. The symbols m and b are **constants**; we might have to solve for them, but for any given model, there is one fixed value for m and one for b.

If we are looking at a specific model, say, $y = -3x + 5$, we say that -3 and 5 are the constant values and y and x are the variables.

TIP

This is secretly another type of **pattern matching** problem!

EXAMPLE 1

$$a(x + 5) - 3 = 4x + 7$$

In the above equation, a is a constant. If the equation has no solution, what is the value of a?

Since we are told that the equation has no solution, we need to find the value of a that makes the x's all cancel when we solve. Start by simplifying the expression:

$$a(x + 5) - 3 = 4x + 7$$

$$ax + 5a - 3 = 4x + 7$$

We need a value of a that makes $ax = 4x$ (so they cancel). Well that's straightforward: $a = 4$ should work! Let's plug that in to make sure we end up with a false statement:

$$(4)x + 5(4) - 3 = 4x + 7$$

$$4x + 17 \neq 4x + 7$$

$$a = 4$$

EXAMPLE 2

$$y(k - 7) + 2 = k - 5$$

If k is a constant and the equation above has infinitely many solutions, what is the value of k?

SOLUTION

When the question says there are infinitely many solutions, it means there are infinitely many values of y that make it true. If we simplify the expression, we need the y's to all cancel out into a true statement.

Right now there is only one y and it's being multiplied by the expression $(k - 7)$. For the y to go away, it must be the case that $k - 7 = 0$, or $k = 7$. Let's confirm that:

$$y(k - 7) + 2 = k - 5$$

$$y((7) - 7) + 2 = (7) - 5$$

$$y(0) + 2 = 2$$

$$2 = 2$$

It worked! Plugging in 7 for k makes all the y's disappear, leaving us with a true statement. For this equation to have infinitely many solutions, k must be 7.

$$k = 7$$

Infinity... what a concept.

Working with variables in the denominator

If you know how to work with fractions and how to work with variables, **you can** deal with both at the same time! Recall that if you want to add or **subtract** fractions, you need to find a **common denominator**. This is still **true when** there are variables in the denominator.

	No Variables	Variables
Uncommon denominators	$\frac{2}{5}+\frac{3}{4}$	$\frac{2}{x+3}+\frac{3}{x+4}$
Multiply by 1 to convert	$\frac{2}{5}\cdot\frac{4}{4}+\frac{3}{4}\cdot\frac{5}{5}$	$\frac{2}{x+3}\cdot\frac{x+4}{x+4}+\frac{3}{x+4}\cdot\frac{x+3}{x+3}$
Common denominators	$\frac{8}{20}+\frac{15}{20}$	$\frac{2x+8}{(x+3)(x+4)}+\frac{3x+9}{(x+3)(x+4)}$
	$\downarrow$	$\downarrow$
Combine	$\frac{23}{20}$	$\frac{5x+17}{(x+3)(x+4)}$

TIP

Try to get the left side of the equation into the same form as the right side, *then* see what you can learn about a and b.

EXAMPLE 3

$$\frac{4}{(x+2)}-\frac{6}{(x+3)}=\frac{(ax+b)}{(x+2)(x+3)}$$

The equation above is true for all $x > 0$ where a and b are constants. **What** is the value of $a + b$?

A)   0
B)   −2
C)   22
D)   26

PORTAL

For instruction on *Pattern Matching*, turn to page 394.

SOLUTION

We are told the equation is true for all $x > 0$, and there are two additional variables (a and b). This tips us off that we can use the same skills used in the **Pattern Matching** chapter. To use pattern matching, we first need to put the left and right sides of the equation into the same form. This means we need to combine the fractions on the left by finding a **common denominator**.

(1) Multiply each fraction by 1 $\qquad \dfrac{4}{x+2} \cdot \dfrac{x+3}{x+3} - \dfrac{6}{x+3} \cdot \dfrac{x+2}{x+2}$

(2) Distribute $\qquad \dfrac{4x+12}{(x+2)(x+3)} - \dfrac{6x+12}{(x+2)(x+3)}$

(3) Combine $\qquad \dfrac{-2x}{(x+2)(x+3)}$

(4) Compare to right side $\qquad \dfrac{-2x}{(x+2)(x+3)} = \dfrac{(ax+b)}{(x+2)(x+3)}$

Now that both sides of the equation are a single fraction with the same denominator, we can focus on the numerators.

(5) Compare numerators $\qquad -2x = ax + b$

(6) Put into the same form $\qquad -2x + 0 = ax + b$

Pattern matching tells us that $a = -2$ and $b = 0$, so $a + b = \boxed{-2}$.

Numerator

Denominator

Yup, looks like you've got a bunch of variables down here! No sweat, we'll clear em out for ya.

Use factoring skills to simplify fractions

A **rational function** is when you find a polynomial in the denominator of a fraction. Questions involving rational functions are often factoring and polynomial multiplication questions in disguise. Sometimes you can **factor the numerator** (or denominator) and cancel expressions. Other times you have to **find a common denominator**.

EXAMPLE 4

$$\frac{x^2 + 5x + 6}{x + 2} + \frac{x - 4}{x + 1}$$

Which of the following expressions is equivalent to the above sum when $x \neq -1$ and $x \neq -2$?

A) $\dfrac{x^2 + 6x + 2}{2x + 3}$

B) $\dfrac{x^2 + 6x + 2}{x^2 + 3x + 2}$

C) $\dfrac{x^3 + x^2 - 14x - 24}{x^2 + 3x + 2}$

D) $\dfrac{x^2 + 5x - 1}{x + 1}$

SOLUTION

This question is asking us to add two rational functions (fractions with polynomials in the denominator). Eventually, we'll need to find some common denominators... but first let's simplify. The second fraction is as simple as it'll get, but if we **factor** the numerator of the first fraction, we can **cancel the expression in the denominator**:

(1) *rewrite the equation*
$$\frac{x^2 + 5x + 6}{x + 2} + \frac{x - 4}{x + 1} = ?$$

(2) *factor the numerator*
$$\frac{(x + 3)(x + 2)}{x + 2} + \frac{x - 4}{x + 1} = ?$$

(3) *cancel the denominator*
$$\frac{(x + 3)}{1} + \frac{x - 4}{x + 1} = ?$$

Now that we've simplified, let's **find a common denominator**. We can do this by converting the first fraction's denominator to $x + 1$:

(4) *multiply first fraction by 1*
$$\frac{(x + 3)}{1} \cdot \frac{(x + 1)}{(x + 1)} + \frac{x - 4}{x + 1} = ?$$

$$\frac{(x + 3)(x + 1)}{x + 1} + \frac{x - 4}{x + 1} = ?$$

(5) *add the fractions*
$$\frac{(x + 3)(x + 1) + (x - 4)}{x + 1} = ?$$

This doesn't look like any of our answer choices yet, so let's **simplify the numerator**.

(5) *simplify the numerator*
$$\frac{(x^2 + 4x + 3) + (x - 4)}{x + 1} = ?$$

$$\frac{(x^2 + 5x - 1)}{x + 1} = ?$$

At long last, we have a match! Using our factoring and fraction skills, we've discovered the answer is **choice D**.

D

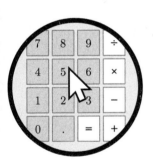

TIP

Now that we've solved it the head-on way, let's try a work around. This is an an equivalent expressions problem, so you can use your Desmos skills if you prefer!

TIP

Often, problems with restricted domains might lead to multiple possible solutions. Always remember to check back for a domain restriction in these instances!

Some problems put limits on what x can be

Many SAT math problems contain **traps** for students who are trying to go too quickly through the section. One such trap is an algebra problem that features an equation or expression with a **restricted domain**. In this context, **domain** is a fancy math word for "what values of x are allowed".

Often, domain restrictions are stated outright in the problem statement. These problems wil ask you to solve an equation, but then add an extra rule like one of the examples below:

| "where x is positive" | "if $x > 9$" | "when $x \neq -3$" |

Some problems naturally have limits on x

A domain restriction is can happen just by the nature of the function. This happens when there are values for which the function would be **undefined**. On the SAT there are two key things to watch out for:

① **Fractions** are not allowed to have 0 in the denominator

② **Negative square roots** ($\sqrt{-1}$) are not allowed either!

EXAMPLE 5

$$\frac{(3x-1)}{(x+2)} - \frac{(2x+4)}{(x+5)} = \frac{(13x+5)}{(x+2)(x+5)}$$

What is the solution to the equation above?

SOLUTION

Let's start by finding a **common denominator** for the left side:

$$\frac{(3x - 1)}{(x + 2)} - \frac{(2x + 4)}{(x + 5)}$$

$$\frac{(3x - 1)}{(x + 2)} \cdot \frac{x+5}{x+5} - \frac{(2x + 4)}{(x + 5)} \cdot \frac{x+2}{x+2}$$

$$\frac{(3x^2 + 15x - x - 5)}{(x + 2)(x + 5)} - \frac{(2x^2 + 4x + 4x + 8)}{(x + 2)(x + 5)}$$

$$\frac{(x^2 + 6x - 13)}{(x + 2)(x + 5)}$$

Now let's plug that back into the left side of the equation:

$$\frac{(x^2 + 6x - 13)}{(x + 2)(x + 5)} = \frac{(13x + 5)}{(x + 2)(x + 5)}$$

Now that we have the same denominator on each side of the equation, we can **focus on the numerators**.

$$x^2 + 6x - 13 = 13x + 5$$

$$x^2 - 7x - 18 = 0$$

$$(x + 2)(x - 9) = 0$$

From here, we can see that **x = −2 or 9**.

But we aren't done! If we look back at the original problem, we see that **(x + 2)** is a factor in the denominator in the very first fraction. If we plug −2 in for x, we'd get a **zero in the denominator**:

$$\frac{(3x - 1)}{(x + 2)} = \frac{(3(-2) - 1)}{((-2) + 2)} = \frac{-7}{0}$$

It's impossible to divide by zero. That means that **x = −2** is NOT a valid answer. The answer is **9**.

9

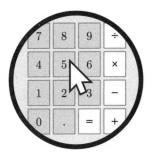

TIP

It's good to try solving this problem by hand because it uses important skills, but, as usual, you can also just put the equation as is into Desmos as an alternate solving option!

TIP

If you find yourself in a situation with multiple absolute value expressions to get rid of, take them one at a time. The first one will give you two equations, and then each of those will split into two (for a total of 4).

Absolute Value

You likely learned that absolute value signs turn negatives positive:

$|-4|$	=	4
the absolute value of −4	is	4

But what does absolute value MEAN? The absolute value of a real number is its **distance from zero** on the number line. That's why the absolute values of negative 4 and positive 4 are the same thing. Just like positive 4, negative 4 is *four away from zero*.

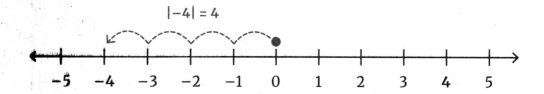

$$|-4| = 4$$

To see why we have to simplify the expression inside first, consider $|-6 + 2| = |-4| = 4$. You **cannot** distribute the absolute value over addition: $|-6| + |2| = 6 + 2 = 8$, which is not the same as 4! Similarly, if you have an expression inside the absolute value, like $|x - 5|$, you cannot distribute the absolute value, even if you cannot simplify the expression further. We'll look at how to proceed with this kind of situation in Example 7.

If you have two copies of the same absolute value expression, you can combine them like you would combine any other like terms. For example: $2|x - 3| + 3|x - 3|$ is the same as $5|x - 3|$.

EXAMPLE 6

If $y = |7 - 3x|$, what is the value of y when $x = 3$?

SOLUTION

We know that $x = 3$; let's plug in and **simplify the absolute value**:

ⓘ	*identify goal*	$y = ?$
①	*rewrite the equation*	$y = |7 - 3x|$
②	*plug in 3 for x*	$y = |7 - 3(3)|$
③	*simplify*	$y = |7 - 9| = |-2|$

Once the absolute value is simplified, we just **drop the negative**.

④	*drop the negative*	$y = |-2| = ②$

Solving with Absolute Values

When you need to solve for a variable **inside** of an absolute value, there are <u>two</u> possible solutions to the equation. Notice that in the equation below, x could be 4 or -6. Both solutions would be correct! To reflect this in our work, we'll create an **evil twin** of the original equation by **multiplying the contents of the absolute value by -1**.

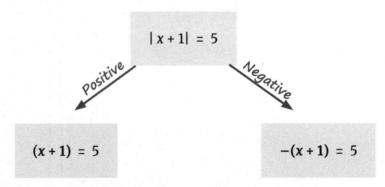

EXAMPLE 7

What are all of the solutions for $|5x - 3| = 8$?

SOLUTION

Since we are solving for a variable inside absolute value bars, we need two equations and two solutions. Let's rewrite our original equation and split it into its positive and negative forms:

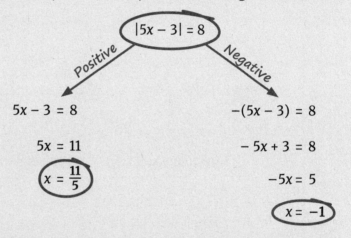

$|5x - 3| = 8$

Positive

$5x - 3 = 8$

$5x = 11$

$x = \frac{11}{5}$

Negative

$-(5x - 3) = 8$

$-5x + 3 = 8$

$-5x = 5$

$x = -1$

By splitting the original equation, we end up with our two possible solutions to the absolute value equation!

Absolute Value Twins

Positive $(x + 1)$

Negative $-(x + 1)$

417

Practice Problems

Use your new skills to answer each question.

1

$$\frac{x}{12} = \frac{3}{x}$$

If $x > 0$, what is the solution to the equation above?

2

$$5(2x - 1) - 4(3x + 2) = -2x - 13$$

How many solutions does the equation above have?

A) 0
B) 1
C) 2
D) Infinitely many

3

$$7(8x + 3) + 2(3x - 4) = 98x + 49$$

How many solutions does the given equation have?

A) -1
B) 1
C) 0
D) Infinitely many

4

$$\frac{6x + b}{2} = 3x + 4$$

In the equation above, b is a constant. If the equation has infinitely many solutions, what is the value of b?

5

$$a(x + 4) - 7 = 3x + 6$$

In the equation above a is a constant. If the equation has no solutions, what is the value of a?

6

$$\frac{4x - 24}{x - 6} = x$$

What is the solution to the equation above?

7

$$\frac{3x + 10}{x^2 - 4} + \frac{1}{x + 2} = \frac{2}{x + 2}$$

What is the solution to the given equation?

A) −6
B) −2
C) 2
D) 6

8

$$\frac{32}{x^2 - 16} = \frac{4}{x - 4} + \frac{x + 3}{x + 4}$$

Which of the following gives all of the solutions to the given equation?

A) 4
B) −7
C) −7 and 4
D) −4 and 4

9

$$\frac{1}{2x+3} - \frac{1}{x-2} = 1$$

Which of the following gives all of the solutions to the given equation?

A) $-\frac{3}{2}$ and 2

B) 2 and $\frac{\sqrt{2}}{2}$

C) $-\frac{\sqrt{2}}{2}$ and $\frac{\sqrt{2}}{2}$

D) $\frac{\sqrt{2}}{2}$

10

$$5x - 3 = k(x + m)$$

In the given equation, m and k are constants. The equation has infinitely many solutions. What is the value of m?

A) -3

B) $\frac{5}{3}$

C) $-\frac{3}{5}$

D) $\frac{3}{5}$

11

If $x > 3$, which of the following is equivalent to $\dfrac{1}{\frac{1}{x+3} - \frac{1}{x+4}}$?

A) $x^2 + 7x + 12$

B) $\dfrac{1}{x^2 - 7x - 12}$

C) $\dfrac{2x + 7}{x^2 - 7x - 12}$

D) $\dfrac{x^2 - 7x - 12}{2x + 1}$

12

What is the value of $4(6 - 8) - 7|3 - 5|$?

A) -29
B) -22
C) 2
D) 6

13

If $x = 11$, then $|7 - x| = ?$

A) -18
B) -6
C) -4
D) 4

14

$$|x - 6| = 13$$

What is the negative solution to the given equation?

15

$$6|x + 2| - 2|x + 2| = 32$$

What is one possible solution to the given equation?

All About Graphs

Tags: Advanced Math • Graphs of Functions • Quadratic Equations • Polynomial Functions • Exponential Functions • Rational Functions

TIP

For most functions you encounter on the SAT the **domain** is all real numbers, but there are a few situations where this isn't true. For example, the domain of $f(x) = \sqrt{x}$ is $x \geq 0$.

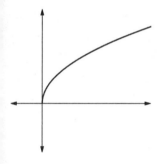

Parabolas have a vertex that restricts the **range** of the function. For example, the function $f(x) = x^2 + 3$ has a minimum value at the vertex, $(0, 3)$, so all outputs are at least 3 and the range is $y \geq 3$.

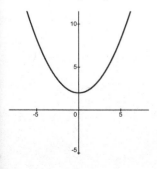

Key Graph Features

When you are looking at a graph of a function, there are a few key features you might be asked about.

(Y) The **y–intercept** of a graph is the point where it crosses the y-axis. This occurs when $x = 0$, so you can graph to see the answer or plug in zero for x.

(X) The **x–intercept(s)** of a graph are the points where it crosses the x-axis. This occurs when $y = 0$. If a test asks for a when $f(a) = 0$, they are asking you to find an x-intercept.

(d) The **domain** of a graph is the set of x-values that are valid inputs. If the line seems to go off infinitely to the left and right, the domain is all real numbers.

(r) The **range** of a graph is the set of y-values that are valid *outputs*. If a graphed function has a global <u>minimum</u> or <u>maximum</u> value, that is going to restrict the range.

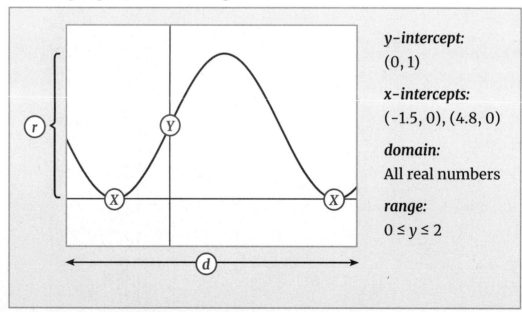

y–intercept:
$(0, 1)$

x–intercepts:
$(-1.5, 0), (4.8, 0)$

domain:
All real numbers

range:
$0 \leq y \leq 2$

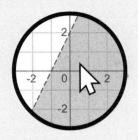

TIP

If the direction of horizontal shift feels counterintuitive, picture functions as **machines** with an input chute, (x), and an output product, $f(x)$ or y.

When you **add** a constant to the x-value, you need less input to get the same output. It's like getting a donation of fuel, so now you need less fuel to get the same amount of production from your function machine.

OR you can just embrace that it's counterintuitive! If you deep down in your gut expect ($x-h$) to shift left, just remember to do the opposite.

Graph Transformations

Sometimes a question will test your undertsanding of **transformations** of a function. These questions ask you to explain how changing the algebraic equation of a function will affect the graph.

Let's test your instincts by considering a change to the function $f(x)$, graphed here. *One* of the changes below would shift the graph to the **right**, and the *other* would shift the graph **up**. Which is which?

$$f(x-3) \qquad f(x)+3$$

Circle which change shifts f(x) to the right.
Underline which change shifts f(x) up.

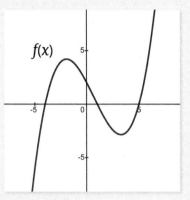

Horizontal Shift: $f(x \pm h)$

We can shift, or translate, a graph left or right by **adding or subtracting a constant from x**, the input to the function.

($+$) **Adding shifts left.**
If we plug in ($x + h$), then the graph shifts h to the left.

($-$) **Subtracting shifts right.**
If we plug in ($x - h$), then the graph shifts h to the right.

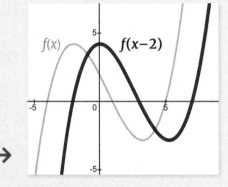

Vertical Shift: $f(x) \pm k$

We can shift, or *translate*, a graph up (by adding) or down (by subtracting) a constant k to the function.

($+$) **Adding shifts up.**
If we add k to $f(x)$, then the graph shifts k units up.

($-$) **Subtracting shifts down.**
If we subtract k from $f(x)$, then the graph shifts k units down.

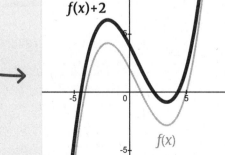

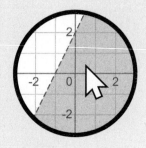

TIP

If any of these transformations feel hard to remember, we recommend you bring up your Desmos calculator and plug in the functions as written here. You can toggle lines on and off to make comparisons and change the constants to see how it changes the graph.

Getting hands-on experience can be invaluable for understanding math. **When in doubt, play around!**

TIP

Multiplying the whole function by a constant less than 1, say 0.5, reduces the y-value of each point by that much, <u>compressing</u> the graph.

When we multiply just the input (x) by a number less than 1, again say 0.5, we have to go much further along the x-axis to get the same y-value as before, <u>stretching</u> the graph like a rubber band.

Flipping/reflecting over the x-axis and y-axis

Multiplying the input or output of a function by −1 flips positive and negative values, reflecting the graph across the x or y axis.

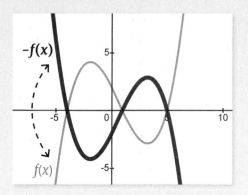

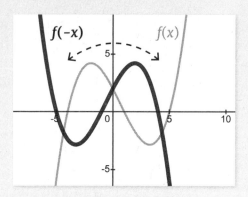

Reflect over x-axis: −f(x)

Multiply the whole function by −1 to make positive outputs negative and negative outputs positive, flipping/reflecting over the x-axis.

Reflect over y-axis: f(−x)

Multiply x by −1 to make positive inputs negative and negative inputs positive, flipping/reflecting the graph over the y-axis.

Stretching/compressing vertically or horizontally

Multiplying the input or output of a function by a **constant** (a) will cause the graph to stretch or compress vertically or horizontally.

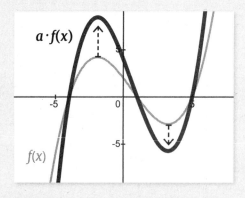

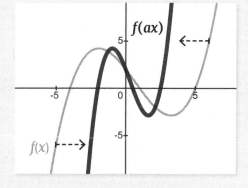

Vertical stretch/squish: a · f(x)

Multiply the whole function by a constant (a) to vertically stretch the graph (if a > 1) or compress the graph (if a < 1).

Horizontal stretch/squish: f(ax)

Multiply just the input, x, by a constant (a) to horizontally stretch the graph (if a < 1) or compress the graph (if a > 1).

EXAMPLE 1

The function f is defined by $f(x) = (x - 4)(x + 2)^2$. In the xy-plane, the graph of $y = g(x)$ is the result of translating the graph of $y = f(x)$ to the left by 3 units. What is the value of $g(0)$?

TIP

You can save a little bit of work by doing this process in Desmos:

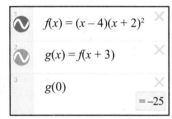

SOLUTION

Our goal in this problem is to find $g(0)$, but we are not directly given $g(x)$.

Option 1: Create $g(x)$

When you read this question, a key word that should jump out at you is *translating*. This tells us that we are dealing with a function transformation problem. In particular, we are translating the graph *to the left* by 3 units. This is a horizontal shift, so to form g we need to shift the input. Since we are shifting f to the left, our new input for f is $(x + 3)$. This gives us:

$$g(x) = f(x + 3) = ((x + 3) - 4)((x + 3) + 2)^2$$

Simplifying this a little, we get

$$g(x) = (x - 1)(x + 5)^2$$

Now we have a definition for g that we can just plug into to find $g(0)$:

$$g(0) = (0 - 1)(0 + 5)^2 = -25$$

Option 2: Translate back to $f(x)$

We are told that $g(x)$ is the result of translating the graph of f to the left by three units. You can also think of this as f being the same as g, just translated 3 units to the *right*. So when we are asked for what the value of g is at 0, we can move 3 units to the right and ask what f is doing at 3.

$$f(3) = (3 - 4)(3 + 2)^2 = -25$$

PORTAL

For a review of linear functions, flip back to *Linear Equations* on page 320.

Types of Functions

Functions and their graphs come in many varieties. You'll want to know the difference between **constant** functions, **linear** functions, and **quadratic** functions. Let's review the differences, then focus on the different <u>forms</u> of quadratic functions.

Constant Functions

Constant functions are horizontal lines. If the line crosses the y-axis at c, it can be described by the function $f(x) = c$. You might also see a horizontal line given by an equation of the form $y = c$. Note that the equation $x = c$ gives a vertical line that crosses the x-axis at c, but this isn't a function.

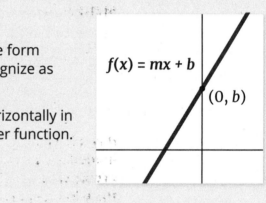

Linear Functions

Linear functions on the test take the form $f(x) = mx + b$, which you should recognize as the **equation of a line**.

You can shift lines vertically and horizontally in the same way you can shift any other function.

TIP

For a relationship to be a function, every input has to have a unique output. In graph terms, any vertical line you could draw on the graph must intersect the function no more than once. This is sometimes called the "vertical line test".

Quadratic Functions

The most basic quadratic function is $f(x) = x^2$, which is an upward facing parabola with its vertex at the origin. If we shift this parent graph h units to the right and k units up, we get $f(x - h) + k = (x - h)^2 + k$.

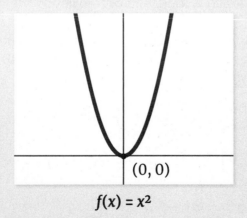

$$f(x) = x^2$$

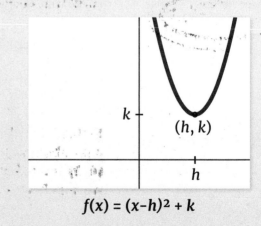

$$f(x) = (x-h)^2 + k$$

TIP

The vertex is the minimum value of the function when the graph opens up and the maximum value if it opens down, so vertex form is useful for questions that ask about the **minimum** or **maximum**.

Vertex Form

If we take our quadratic function $f(x) = (x - h)^2 + k$ and add a factor to control the <u>width</u> of the parabola we get the **vertex form**:

$$\textbf{Vertex Form} \qquad y = a(x - h)^2 + k$$

When you have the equation in this form, the coordinates of the vertex are at **(h, k)**. So, for example, a parabola with the equation $y = (x - 2)^2 + 3$ would have a vertex at point **(2, 3)**.

TIP

If you have a quadratic in standard form, the x-coordinate of the vertex is $-b/2a$.

Standard Form

Note that vertex form includes a squared binomial. If you multiply this out and combine like terms, you can convert vertex form to standard form.

$$\textbf{Standard Form} \qquad y = ax^2 + bx + c$$

If you have the equation of a parabola in standard form you can immediately determine the y-intercept: by definition, the y-intercept occurs when $x = 0$. If you plug in $x = 0$ everything except c drops out, so the y-intercept is $(0, c)$.

Intercept Form

Any parabola that intersects the x-axis (not all do!) can be written in a form that easily lets us see **where** those intersections occur:

$$\textbf{Intercept Form} \qquad y = a(x - r)(x - s)$$

In this form, the x-intercepts happen at **(r, 0)** and **(s, 0)**. So, for example, a parabola with the equation $y = 2(x - 4)(x + 5)$ would have x-intercepts at **(4, 0)** and **(-5, 0)**. To transform the standard form to the intercept form, we simply factor the polynomial.

PORTAL

To get from the standard form to the intercept form, we use **factoring**.

For a refresher on *Factoring Basics*, turn back to page 360.

EXAMPLE 2

When the quadratic function $f(x) = a(x - 2)^2 + 5$, where a is a constant, is graphed in the xy-plane, one of its x-intercepts is $(\frac{25}{3}, 0)$. What is x-value of the other x-intercept of the graph?

TIP

Warning: This is an approximation, but it is a close enough approximation for your answer. However, if you approximated the value of a you might end up far enough off to miss the question. For example, if you used $a = 0.124$ you would get $x = -4.35$ which is incorrect.

Option 1:

We are given a function with an unknown constant and are given a point on that function. We can plug in the point:

$$0 = a(\tfrac{25}{3} - 2)^2 + 5$$

...and solve to get $a = -\frac{45}{361}$.

Now that we have a, we can solve the equation. You have options for this, but the easiest one is to toss the function into Desmos to find that the other x-intercept occurs where $x = -4.333$.

Option 2:

Parabolas are nicely *symmetric*, so the x-coordinate of the vertex is centered between the two x-intercepts. The value of our unknown constant a doesn't affect the vertex, so we know that it is at $(2, 5)$. You can get this either by recognizing the vertex form of the parabola or by graphing it in Desmos.

The x-coordinate of the vertex is 2 and the x-coordinate of the intercept we know is $\frac{25}{3}$, which is $\frac{19}{3}$ bigger than 2. To get the other x intercepts we need to go $\frac{19}{3}$ smaller than 2, which is $-\frac{13}{3}$, or $-4.\overline{3}$. You can enter this answer as $-13/3$ or as -4.333.

PORTAL

You might remember exploring the relationship between factors and x-intercepts in *Zeros, Solutions, and Roots*. If you want a refresher, turn to page 377.

Higher Order Polynomial Functions

Sometimes you will encounter functions with exponents higher than 2 or with more than 2 factors. There are a few key things to keep in mind when considering the graphs of polynomial functions:

- $f(0)$ tells you the *y*-intercept and vice versa.

- The solutions to $f(x) = 0$ tell you the *x*-intercepts and factors and vice versa.

- The number of *x*-intercepts is at *most* the highest power of *x* in the function. If that highest power is odd then it will always have *at least* 1 *x*-intercept. If the highest power is even, it is *possible* for it to have no *x*-intercepts

- If the function is given in factored form, form, *x*-intercepts that come from factors with even powers will touch the *x*-axis and bounce off whereas *x*-intercepts that come from factors with odd powers will cross the axis. For example:

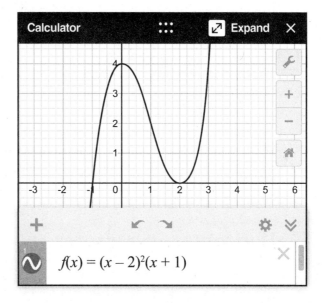

The factor $(x - 2)$ has an even power, 2, so the graph bounces off at $x = 2$ and the factor $(x + 1)$ has an odd power, 1, so the graph crosses the *x*-axis at $x = -1$.

429

Rational Functions

A *rational function* is a function that can be written as a fraction of polynomials. The simplest rational function is $f(x) = \frac{1}{x}$

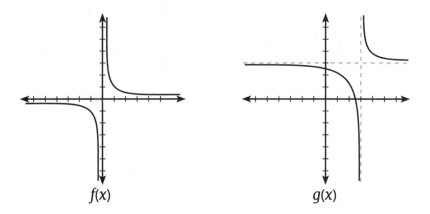

$f(x)$ $\qquad\qquad\qquad\qquad\qquad\qquad$ $g(x)$

In addition to the x- and y-intercepts that we always look for, key features to pay attention to in rational functions are any *asymptotes*. An asymptote is a line that the graph gets very close to but never quite reaches.

Vertical Asymptotes

In general, rational functions have vertical asymptotes where the denominator would be 0 and the numerator would not be.

In the figures above, $f(x) = \frac{1}{x}$ has a vertical asymptote at $x = 0$ and $g(x) = \frac{1}{x-h} + k$ has a vertical asymptote at $x = h$.

Horizontal Asymptotes

In general, rational functions have horizontal asymptotes when the denominator has a higher power of x than the numerator.

In the figures above, $f(x) = \frac{1}{x}$ has a horizontal asymptote at $y = 0$ and $g(x) = \frac{1}{x-h} + k$ has a horizontal asymptote at $y = k$. Think about what happens in $f(x) = \frac{1}{x}$ when x gets really large (or is a negative number with a large absolute value). As x gets bigger, $\frac{1}{x}$ gets smaller. You can get as close to zero as you want by making x big enough, but you will never quite get to zero. On the graph this looks like the function leveling out into an almost-but-not-quite horizontal line at zero.

Exponential Functions

An *exponential function* is a function where the *variable* is in the exponent. The number (or expression) being raised to the power is the base.

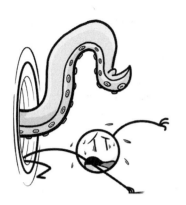

PORTAL

We will explore exponential functions and how to interpret them in more detail in *Exponential Modeling* on page 522.

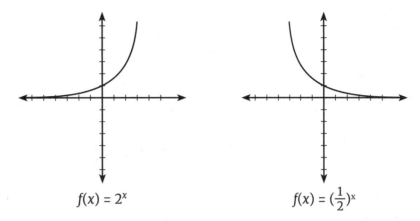

$$f(x) = 2^x \qquad\qquad f(x) = \left(\tfrac{1}{2}\right)^x$$

There are a few key things to keep in mind when considering the graphs of exponential functions:

- Exponential functions have a horizontal asymptote that they only approach in the negative OR positive direction, not both.

- As usual, you find the *y*-intercept by plugging in $x = 0$. Remember that any number (other than 0) raised to the power of 0 is 1.

- Exponential functions grow very quickly, so at first glance it can sometimes look like the function is approaching a vertical line, but exponential functions generally do not have vertical asymptotes.

- The base of the exponential function should always be positive. If the base of the function is between 0 and 1, the function will approach zero as *x* gets large. When an exponential function approaches 0 as *x* gets large, it is called *exponential decay*. If the function base of the function is greater than 1, the function will approach zero as *x* becomes a large negative number. In this situation, as *x* gets large the value of the function also gets large. This is called *exponential growth*.

431

Practice Problems

Use your new skills to answer each question.

1

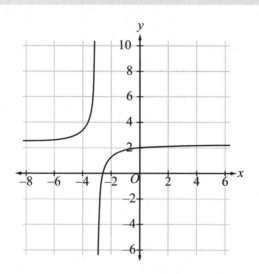

The graph of $y = f(x)$ is shown in the xy-plane. What is the value of $f(0)$?

2

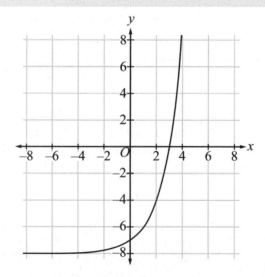

The x-intercept of the graph shown is $(x, 0)$. What is the value of x?

A) −8
B) −7
C) 0
D) 3

3

The graph of $7x + 8y = 15$ is translated 5 units to the left in the xy-plane. What is the x-coordinate of the x-intercept of the resulting graph?

4

$$h(x) = 15(\tfrac{2}{3})^x$$

If the given function h is graphed in the xy-plane, where $y = h(x)$, what is the y-intercept of the graph?

A) $(0, \tfrac{2}{3})$

B) $(0, 1)$

C) $(0, 15)$

D) $(0, 30)$

5

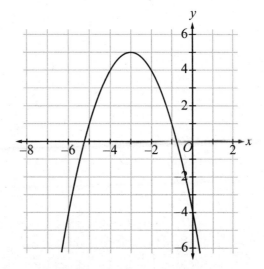

What is the y-intercept of the graph shown?

A) $(0, 0)$
B) $(0, -4)$
C) $(-4, 0)$
D) $(-3, 5)$

6

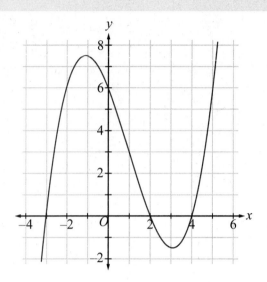

The graph of $y = g(x)$ is shown, where the function g is defined by $g(x) = ax^3 + bx^2 + cx + d$ and a, b, c, and d are constants. For how many values of x does $f(x) = 0$?

A) One
B) Two
C) Three
D) Four

7

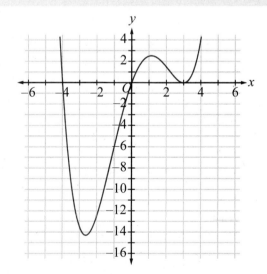

Which of the following could be the equation of the graph shown in the xy-plane?

A) $y = \frac{1}{8}x^2(x - 3)(x + 4)$

B) $y = \frac{1}{8}x(x - 3)^2(x + 4)$

C) $y = \frac{1}{8}x(x - 3)(x + 4)^2$

D) $y = \frac{1}{8}x(x - 3)(x + 4)$

8

$$y = 5x^2 + 16x - 30$$

The given equation relates the variables x and y. For what value of x does the value of y reach its minimum?

9

$$f(x) = 3x^2 - 18x + 23$$

The function g is defined by $g(x) = -f(x - 3)$. For what value of x does $g(x)$ reach its maximum?

A) −3
B) 0
C) 3
D) 6

10

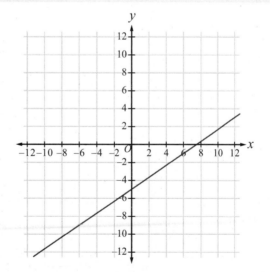

The graph of $y = f(x) - 8$ is shown. Which equation defines function f?

A) $f(x) = \frac{2}{3}x + 3$

B) $f(x) = \frac{2}{3}x - 5$

C) $f(x) = \frac{2}{3}x - 8$

D) $f(x) = \frac{2}{3}x - 13$

11

$$f(x) = 8(3)^x$$

The function f is defined by the given equation. If $g(x) = f(x - 1)$, which of the following functions defines the function g?

A) $g(x) = \frac{8}{3}(3)^x$

B) $g(x) = 24(3)^x$

C) $g(x) = 8(\frac{1}{3})^x$

D) $g(x) = 8(9)^x$

12

The function f is defined by $f(x) = (x - 4)(x + 1)(x + 3)$. In the xy-plane, the graph of $y = g(x)$ is the result of translating the graph of $y = f(x)$ down 3 units. What is the value of $g(0)$?

13

When the quadratic function f is graphed in the xy-plane, where $y = f(x)$, its vertex is $(2, -5)$. One of the x-intercepts of this graph is $(-\frac{5}{3}, 0)$. What is the other x-intercept of the graph?

A) $(\frac{11}{3}, 0)$

B) $(\frac{17}{3}, 0)$

C) $(\frac{5}{3}, 0)$

D) $(-\frac{16}{3}, 0)$

14

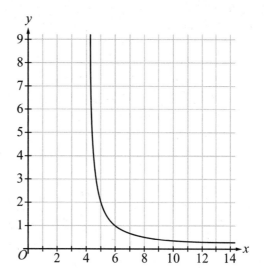

The rational function f is defined by an equation of the form $f(x) = \frac{a}{x+b}$ where a and b are constants. The partial graph of $y = f(x)$ is shown. Which of the following could be b?

A) -8
B) -4
C) 0
D) 4

Inequalities

Tags: Algebra Foundations • Advanced Math • Systems of Inequalities

Words	Symbols
x is **less than** *y*	$x < y$
x is **greater than** *y*	$x > y$
x is **less than or equal to** *y*	$x \leq y$
x is **greater than or equal to** *y*	$x \geq y$

TIP

Draw a number line when working with **negative numbers** or **fractions**. It makes it easier to see why **–3 < –1** if you look at their position on the line.

Inequality signs show that two numbers or expressions are **not equal**: one side is greater than/less than the other. When in doubt on the test, draw a **number line**. *Greater than* means *further to the right*, while *less than* means *further to the left*.

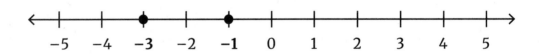

Fill in the blanks with the appropriate inequality symbol.

1. 4 ___<___ 7

2. –2 _____ –2.5

3. $\frac{3}{8}$ _____ $\frac{5}{11}$

4. 2×10^3 _____ 3×10^4

1. 1.5×10^{-6} _____ 3×10^{-7}

2. $\frac{23}{4}$ _____ 5.2

3. –7.3 _____ –7.6

4. –15 _____ –12

Answers: 1. *given* **2.** > **3.** < **4.** < **5.** > **6.** > **7.** > **8.** <

If you multiply/divide by a negative, flip the sign

The rules of algebra for equations are the same for inequalities; you can add, subtract, multiply, and divide around the inequality sign as if it were an equal sign, with one key difference: if you **multiply** or **divide** by a **negative**, **FLIP** the inequality sign.

To solve for x... $-2x \; < \; 4$

(1) *divide by –2...* $\dfrac{-2x}{(-2)} \; < \; \dfrac{4}{(-2)}$

(2) *...and flip the sign* $x \; > \; -2$
     flip!

Numerals flip across zero on the number line

We can see why this happens by looking at a number line. Multiplying by a negative number flips (or reflects) the numbers across zero. This changes which number is farther to the **left** and **right**.

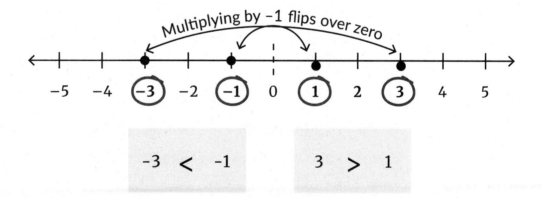

Multiplying by –1 flips over zero

$-3 \; < \; -1$ $3 \; > \; 1$

GATORS

If the > and < symbols were alligator mouths, they'd always be chomping at the **bigger** number or expression.

When you divide or multiply by a negative, **flip that gator!**

439

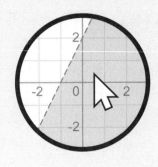

Desmos: Graphing Inequalities

Just as we have been graphing functions, you can also graph inequalities. In Desmos you can find the <, >, ≥, ≤ symbols in the built-in Desmos keypad. You can also use the < and > keys on your keyboard, and if you type "< =" or "> =" with your keyboard, Desmos will automatically convert them to ≤ or ≥ respectively.

When we have been talking about graphing linear equations (or functions more generally) the points on the line are the solutions to the equation, the pairs of x and y that make the equation true. With inequalities, the solutions are no longer represented by a line. So what happens graphically when we swap the = sign for a ≤ sign?

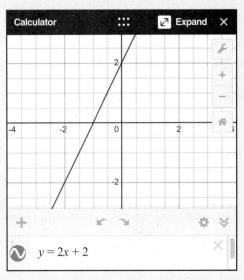

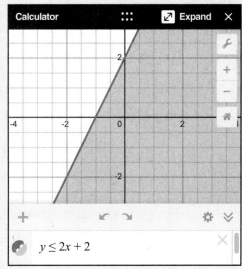

NOTE

If we were graphing

$y < 2x + 2$

...we would draw the line as **dashed** as if to say "Hey, please don't count the points on the line."

How is the graph of $y \leq 2x + 2$ different? First, since the ≤ sign means less than or equal to, every point that made the equation true before still makes this inequality true. So the graph starts with the line $y = 2x + 2$. However, for each x-coordinate, we also need to count every single y-value that is less than (below) the line. To show this graphically, the part of the xy-plane that contains the solutions is shaded.

We can also use graphing to solve systems of inequalities. With systems of equations, the solutions are the points of intersection. With a system of inequalities, the solutions to the system are where shading overlaps. So for the system consisting of $y \geq -2x + 3$ and $y < \frac{1}{2} + 1$ we get the graph:

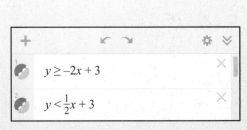

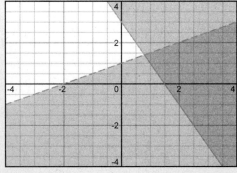

EXAMPLE 1

$$y \geq x + 1$$
$$y \geq -x + 3$$

In the xy-plane, if a point with coordinates (a, b) is a solution to the system of inequalities above, what is the minimum possible value of b ?

SOLUTION

Let's graph this in Desmos:

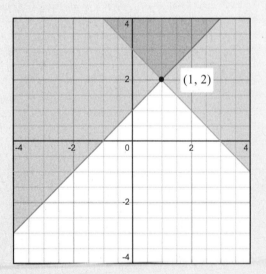

We are asked to find the minimum possible value for b, which we are told is our y-coordinate. That means we need the y-value at the lowest shared point in the overlap region. Notice that the lowest shared point in this case is just the intersection of the two lines. From the graph, we see that this intersection is (1, 2), so the minimum possible value for b is 2.

2

Practice Problems

Use your new skills to answer each question.

1

$$y \le 3x + 7$$

Which of the following points is NOT a solution to the given inequality?

A) $(-4, -4)$
B) $(-1, 2)$
C) $(2, 10)$
D) $(6, 20)$

2

$$y > 3x - 4$$

For which of the following tables are all the values of x and their corresponding values of y solutions to the given inequality?

A)

x	y
2	2
4	8
6	14

B)

x	y
2	0
4	10
6	20

C)

x	y
2	4
4	8
6	16

D)

x	y
2	4
4	10
6	16

3

The maximum value of x is 5 more than 7 times another number a. Which inequality shows the possible values of x?

A) $x \geq 7a + 5$
B) $x \leq 7a + 5$
C) $x \geq 5a + 7$
D) $x \leq 5a + 7$

4

$$2x + 5 > -3x + 4$$

The inequality above is equivalent to an inequality of the form $x > a$. What is the value of a?

5

$$y \leq 2x - 3$$
$$y > -\frac{1}{2}x - 5$$

Which point (x, y) is a solution to the given system of inequalities in the xy-plane?

A) $(-0.8, -4.6)$
B) $(-0.8, 4.6)$
C) $(0.8, 4.6)$
D) $(0.8, -4.6)$

6

$$x + 3y > 5$$
$$y < 12$$

The point $(32, y)$ is a solution to the system of inequalities in the xy-plane. Which of the following could be the value of y?

A) -15
B) -9
C) 10
D) 12

7

$$2y - m > 3x$$
$$3y + n > 2x$$

The origin in the xy-plane is a solution to the system of inequalities above. Which of the following must be true?

A) m is greater than zero.
B) n is greater than m.
C) m is greater than n.
D) m is equal to $-n$.

8

$$y \leq -x(x + 6)$$
$$y \geq x$$

In the system of inequalities above, what is the y-coordinate for the solution that has the smallest value for x ?

9

$$y < -\frac{1}{2}x + a$$
$$y > 2x - a$$

If the value of a is 7, which of the following is a possible solution to the system of inequalities above?

A) $(2, 6)$
B) $(4, 5)$
C) $(5, 4)$
D) $(5, 3)$

10

Which of the following is equivalent to the expression
$\frac{2-4x}{3} + 2 > 0$?

A) $x > 0$

B) $x > \frac{1}{2}$

C) $x < 1$

D) $x < 2$

UNIT | Systems of Equations

Chapters

Overview

In this chapter, we'll learn how to work with systems of equations. We will use strategies like **stack n' smash** and **substitution** to solve for variables, and study the connection between equations, their solutions, and their graphs.

Linear Systems

Tags: Algebra • Systems of Linear Equations

Systems of Equations

Intersections

The solutions for a system of equations are also the *points* where the graphs of the equations **intersect**.

A **system of equations** has multiple equations with multiple variables. These equations are often (but not always) given to you stacked:

$$x + y = 12$$
$$2x + 10y = 40$$

Systems of equations show up all the time on the test. To "solve" a system of equations, we need to find the values for each variable that make both equations true *at the same time*. For example, the solutions to the system above are **x = 10** and **y = 2**, because plugging those values in makes both equations true.

$$(10) + (2) = 12$$
$$2(10) + 10(2) = 40$$

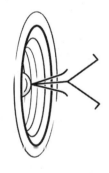

How to solve a system of equations

PORTAL

In this chapter, we learn the tools for solving systems. Many SAT problems ask you to first *create* the system from a word problem. Check out the *Modeling Systems* chapter on page 499.

To solve a system of equations, we will need to **combine** the equations into a single equation in a way that makes one of the variables disappear. There are two main techniques that we can use to combine equations: *stack-and-smash* and *substitute-and-solve*.

TIP

Whenever you see one variable that has the **same coefficient in each equation** (like *y* in this system), try the *stack-and-smash* approach.

Try solving systems by "stacking and smashing"

Sometimes, the systems of equations are set up so that we can combine them by adding or subtracting like terms. For example, say we were told **2x − 2y = 5** and **4x + 2y = 13**. We can "stack" these equations and "smash" them by adding corresponding terms:

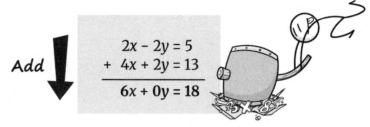

Add
$$2x - 2y = 5$$
$$+ \ 4x + 2y = 13$$
$$\overline{6x + 0y = 18}$$

Notice that this cancelled out the *y*'s, making it easy to solve for *x*. Once we have *x*, we can plug that value into one of the original equations to find *y*.

You may need to change one equation first

In more advanced problems, the systems are good candidates for stacking & smashing but need a little work first. You'll need to make **balanced changes** to one equation to make smashing as effective as possible. For example, neither *a* nor *b* will cancel if we "smash" the system below. But what if we multiply the whole first equation by 2?

Multiply WHOLE equation by 2 ⟶
$$2a + 3b = 12$$
$$-4a - 8b = 40$$

Notice that if we **multiply** the top equation by 2 (or **divide** the bottom equation by 2) we'll be set up for a smashing good time!

Balance

Remember, you are free to experiment with the equation. Just remember to **keep it balanced!**

Add
$$4a + 6b = 24$$
$$+ \ -4a - 8b = 40$$
$$\overline{0a - 2b = 64}$$

Substitute and solve

Other times, a more subtle approach is best. When you have one equation with an easily-isolated variable, it can be best to solve using **substitution**. Just look for x or y with a coefficient of 1. For example:

$$x - y = 2$$
$$3x + 2y = 26$$

Notice how easy it is to get x or y alone in the top equation? Let's try using that to our advantage. If we add y to both sides of the top equation, we get "$x = y + 2$". We can **substitute** that for x in the bottom equation:

Plug in new "name" for x →

$$3(y + 2) + 2y = 26$$
$$3y + 6 + 2y = 26$$
$$5y = 20$$

From here, we can solve for y, and plug that value back into either equation to find x. Boom! Problem solved. Remember, you can pretty much always use substitution if it helps you solve an algebra problem; just be sure to carefullly write out each step.

PORTAL

To see the FIRST time we used this joke, turn to the *Basic Algebra* chapter on page 270!

The name's x, but YOU can call me (y + 2)!

Desmos: Solving Systems with Graphing

Often, the fastest way to solve systems of equations is using the built-in Desmos graphing calculator. This is especially true if you don't have matching coefficients for the same variable or coefficients that are nice multiples. You *could* solve for *x* or *y* in either equation, but in all cases you would end up with fractions, as with the system below:

$$-3x + 5y = 9$$
$$2x + 3y = 13$$

Let's try graphing instead! The graph of a linear equation shows all the (*x,y*) pairs that are solutions to the equation. So what happens when we graph both lines in a *system* of equations? It actually shows us the answer! The solution to a system of linear equations is the **point where the lines intersect** on the graph:

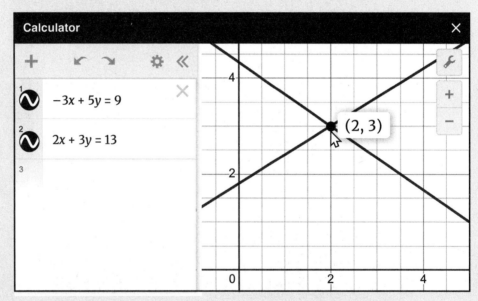

Just by copying the equations into Desmos and clicking on the intersection point, we can see that the solution is (2, 3)! We can double check this by plugging this point back into both equations:

$$-3(2) + 5(3) = 9 \quad \checkmark$$
$$2(2) + 3(3) = 13 \quad \checkmark$$

Yep, it works! This can be a huge time-saver on the test, so make sure to practice using the Desmos calculator when working systems of equations problems in your SAT practice.

TIP

Knowing how to solve systems algebraically is a useful skill and there will be times that it is the more efficient option. However, Desmos can be a *powerful* tool for solving systems problems quickly.

TIP

Remember that you can always go to **desmos.com** to practice with the type of calculator you'll use on the test.

EXAMPLE 1

$$x - 2y = -31$$
$$x + 3y = 59$$

What is the value of x in the solution of the system of equations given above?

SOLUTION

Option 1: Stack & Smash

Looking at these two equations, we see that x has the same coefficient, 1, in both equations. This means that if we **subtract** the equations, the **x's will disappear**.

①	*stack equations*	$x - 2y = -31$
		$-\ \ x + 3y = \ \ 59$
②	*subtract*	$0 - 5y = -90$
③	*simplify*	$-5y = -90$
④	*solve for y*	$y = \boxed{18}$

We're not done yet! We were asked to **solve for x**, not y. But we can simply **plug-in 18 for y** in either equation to find x:

⑤	*plug-in 18 for y*	$x - 2y = -31$
		$x - 2(18) = -31$
⑥	*solve for x*	$x - 36 = -31$
		$x = \boxed{5}$

Smash!

Continued on next page →

Option 2: Solve & Substitute

Let's pick an equation to solve for one of the variables. We can easily **solve the first equation for x** by adding $2y$ to each side:

  (1) *solve for x in first equation* $x - 2y = -31$

                                      $x = -31 + 2y$

Now we can **substitute** $(-31 + 2y)$ for x in the second equation:

  (2) *substitute* $x + 3y = 59$

                               $(-31 + 2y) + 3y = 59$

                                     $-31 + 5y = 59$

  (3) *solve for y* $5y = 90$

                                      $y = \boxed{18}$

Substitute!

Once again, once we find that **$y = 18$**, we're almost done. We just need to **substitute** that into one of the equations and solve for x. This time, for the heck of it, let's use the second equation:

  (4) *plug-in 18 for y* $x + 3y = 59$

                                 $x + 3(18) = 59$

  (5) *solve for x* $x + 54 = 59$

                                      $x = \boxed{5}$

Pretty great! But let's see how much time we can save if we try the third route, *graphing*...

Continued on next page →

Option 3: Graphing

Let's try graphing! You can enter the equations into the first two entry slots in Desmos as they were given to you:

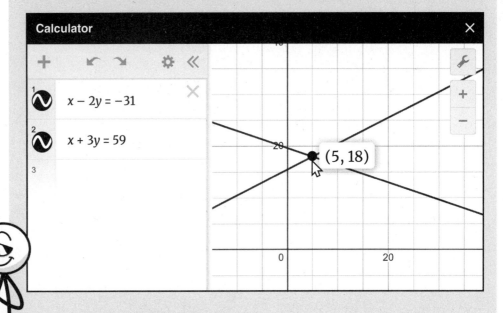

The two lines intersect at (5,18), so the solution to the system is $x = 5$ and $y = 18$. The question asked for the value of x in the solution, so the answer is 5.

Desmos: Using Decimal Points

Graphing is a great solution for solving systems of equations on the SAT. However, notice that in the past couple of examples, the solutions have been nice integers. If the solution is NOT integers, the calculator will give you decimal <u>approximations</u> that may not match the choices exactly.

For example, if the solution was $(3, \frac{1}{7})$, it may be labeled $(3, 0.1428)$.

If you ask Desmos to convert that decimal into a fraction, it will return $\frac{357}{2500}$. This is a decent approximation of $\frac{1}{7}$, but not *quite* the same. Desmos is a powerful tool, but be aware of its limitations!

PORTAL

For more on determining the number of solutions for an equation, see *Advanced Algebra* on page 534.

Numbers of Solutions

As we've seen, the number of solutions can be determined simply by **counting intersection points** on the graph. Occasionally, however, the SAT will give you a system of equations and not the graphs, and ask you to determine how many solutions the system has. So let's think about the different possibilities.

One, None, or a Ton

With a pair of lines, it turns out there are **three possibilities**, and it all depends on the the *slopes* of the lines.

One solution: When two lines have *different slopes*, they have one point of intersection and the system has one solution.

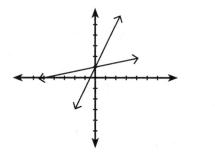

$$y = 2x + 1$$
$$y = \frac{1}{5}x + 1$$

Different slopes, one solution

No solutions: When two lines have the *same slope* and different y-intercepts, they are **parallel** and never intersect. Thus, the system has no solutions.

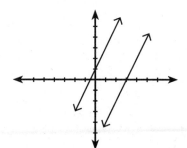

$$y = 2x + 1$$
$$y = 2x - 6$$

Parallel lines, no solutions

Infinite solutions: When two lines are actually the **same exact line**, then the system has infinitely many solutions. In this situation, you're given a system that appears to be two separate equations. But when you put the equations into slope-intercept form, you end up with identical equations.

NOTE

The "∞" symbol means "infinite".

Identify the # of solutions to each system by writing "1", "0", or "∞".

System of Equations	# of Solutions
1. $f(x) = \frac{3}{4}x + 7$ *and* $g(x) = -\frac{3}{4}x + 7$	
2. $f(x) = 2x + 3$ *and* $g(x) = 2x + 7$	
3. $f(x) = \frac{2}{3}x + 3$ *and* $g(x) = \frac{4}{6}x - 4$	
4. $3x + 4y = 16$ *and* $-6x + 8y = 2$	
5. $y = -2x + 3$ *and* $6x + 3y = 9$	
6. $5x + 7y = 2$ *and* $3x - 4y = -13$	

Answers: 1. 1   2. 0   3. 0   4. 1   5. ∞
6. 1

EXAMPLE 2

$$ax + by = 15$$
$$4x + 3y = 75$$

In the system of equations above, a and b are constants. If the system has infinitely many solutions, what is the value of $\frac{a}{b}$?

SOLUTION

Option 1: Stack & Solve

If the system has infinitely many solutions, then these equations must be **exactly the same**, other than some balanced changes that don't alter the graph of the line. Our job, then, is to reverse engineer those balanced changes. Since these equations look pretty similar to one another, we might try a hand at **stacking.**

Notice that $75 = 15 \times 5$. This gives us a good idea of where to start:

(1) *multiply top equation by 5*
$$5(ax + by = 15)$$
$$4x + 3y = 75$$

$$5ax + 5by = 75$$
$$4x + 3y = 75$$

Now we can use **pattern matching** to determine that **$5a = 4$** and **$5b = 3$**. Then we can solve for our answer:

(2) *pattern matching*
$$5a = 4$$
$$5b = 3$$

(3) *solve for $\frac{a}{b}$*
$$\frac{a}{b} = \frac{5a}{5b} = \boxed{\frac{4}{3}}$$

continue →

457

All is one

This is yet **another** opportunity to stop and reflect on the connectivity of all things algebra.

Slope, solutions, factors, functions, graphs, ... they're all connected!

Option 2: Thinking with Slope

If there are infinitely many solutions, then these "overlapping" lines must have the **exact same slope**. We can use that! Let's put the equations in slope-intercept form, and **match their slopes**.

① rewrite equations

$$ax + by = 15$$
$$4x + 3y = 75$$

② slope–intercept form

$$by = -ax + 15$$
$$3y = -4x + 75$$

$$y = -\frac{a}{b}x + \frac{15}{b}$$

$$y = -\frac{4}{3}x + 25$$

Behold, the power of thinking with slope! By putting both equations in **y = mx + b** form, and knowing that their slopes must be identical, we can easily see our answer.

③ pattern match

$$\frac{a}{b} = \left(\frac{4}{3}\right)$$

EXAMPLE 3

$$7x - ry = -17$$
$$-3x - 2y = 13$$

In the system of equations above, r is a constant and x and y are variables. For what value of r will the system have no solutions?

A) $-\frac{7}{3}$

B) $-\frac{14}{3}$

C) $\frac{14}{3}$

D) $\frac{3}{14}$

SOLUTION

The question asks us to find a value of r so that the system has no solutions. If a system of lines has no solutions, then we must be dealing with parallel lines. And what do we know about parallel lines? They have the **exact same slope**. So let's start by getting these lines into the slope-intercept form.

(1) *rewrite equations*

$$7x - ry = -17$$
$$-3x - 2y = 13$$

(2) *change to $y = mx + b$ form*

$$-ry = -7x - 17$$
$$-2y = 3x + 13$$

$$y = \frac{7}{r}x + \frac{17}{r}$$

$$y = -\frac{3}{2}x - \frac{13}{2}$$

(3) *set slopes equal to each other*

$$\frac{7}{r} = -\frac{3}{2}$$

(4) *cross multiply*

$$3r = -14$$

(5) *solve for r*

$$r = \boxed{-\frac{14}{3}}$$

PORTAL

If you need a refresher on parallel lines and slope, turn to *Linear Equations* on page 320.

Digging Deeper: Number of Solutions

Occasionally, a question will ask you to find the **number of solutions** for a quadratic equation. For example:

> How many real solutions (a, b) are there to the system of equations $y = (x - 2)^2$ and $y = -x + 3$?

As we've seen in this chapter, graphing the equations and counting their points of intersection will give you the number of solutions. But what if the equations are not easily graphed, or if you're given a quadratic that does not easily factor? In that case, you can use the quadratic formula and a special formula called the **discriminant**, which will tell you at a glance how many solutions there are for a given equation. We will dig into this further in the next chapter.

EXAMPLE 4

$$3x - 2y = -54$$
$$5x + 4y = -68$$

If (x, y) is the solution to the system of equations above, what is the value of y?

SOLUTION

The first thing to notice is that we are solving a system of equations. The coefficients of x are 3 and 5... it will be difficult making these add or subtract in a way that clears the x's, so let's look at y.

The coefficients of y in the two equations are –2 and 4. That has potential! Do you see why? If we **multiply the top equation by 2**, then we set up the equations for a clean **stack & add** maneuver:

(1) *multiply first equation by 2*

$$2(3x - 2y = -54)$$
$$5x + 4y = -68$$

$$6x - 4y = -108$$
$$5x + 4y = -68$$

(2) *add equations*

$$6x - 4y = -108$$
$$5x + 4y = -68$$

$$11x = -176$$

(3) *solve for x*

$$x = \boxed{-16}$$

(4) *substitute –16 for x*

$$5(-16) + 4y = -68$$

$$-80 + 4y = -68$$

(5) *solve for y*

$$4y = 12$$

$$y = \boxed{3}$$

EXAMPLE 5

$$x + 2y = -11$$
$$5x + y = 8$$

If (x, y) is a solution to the system of equations above, what is the value of $2x + y$?

SOLUTION

This question asks for $2x + y$ rather than just x or y alone. Usually, when the SAT asks you for an expression like this (rather than just x or y), there is some tricky or clever way to find the answer without fully solving for all the variables.

Let's keep "$2x + y$" in mind and try **adding** the two equations:

(1) *keep "$2x + y$" in mind*

(2) *add equations*

$$x + 2y = -11$$
$$5x + y = 8$$
$$6x + 3y = -3$$

Notice anything familiar about the result? Hidden inside it is the very same expression we were asked to find:

(3) *simplify*

$$3(2x + y) = -3$$

(4) *solve for $2x + y$*

$$2x + y = \boxed{-1}$$

Of course, you don't have to see this shortcut. You can **always** solve systems of equations the old-fashioned way by Solving & Substituting. Remember: algebra is just a tool you use to reach your goal! As long as you **keep things balanced**, you're free to manipulate as you see fit!

EXAMPLE 6

$$\frac{x+1}{y-1} = 1$$

$$3(y + 2) = x$$

If (x, y) is a solution to the system of equations above, what is the value of y?

SOLUTION

Since we see two equations with the same two variables, we know we're in systems of equations land. First things first: let's clean up that fraction in the first equation:

(1) *clear fraction*

$$\frac{x+1}{y-1} = 1$$

$$x + 1 = y - 1$$

(2) *simplify*

$$x = y - 2$$

That's better! Let's look at our newly cleaned system.

$$x = y - 2$$

$$3(y + 2) = x$$

Well whaddya know! Now we have two equations that are solved for *x*. That means we can just set them equal to each other and solve for *y*.

(3) *set equal*

$$3(y + 2) = y - 2$$

(4) *solve for y*

$$3y + 6 = y - 2$$

$$2y = -8$$

$$y = \boxed{-4}$$

Practice Problems

Use your new skills to answer each question.

1

$$5x = 30$$
$$-5x + 2y = -16$$

The solution to the given equations is (x, y). What is the value of y?

A) −8
B) 6
C) 7
D) 14

2

$$4x + 5y = -19$$
$$y - 2x = -15$$

What is the solution (x, y) to the system of equations above?

A) $(-6, 1)$
B) $(4, -7)$
C) $(3, -7)$
D) $(5, -2)$

3

$$x + 3y = 27$$
$$3x + 2y = 11$$

Which ordered pair (x, y) is a solution to the given system of equations?

A) $(0, 9)$
B) $(-1, 7)$
C) $(-3, 10)$
D) $(1, 18)$

4

$$5x + 7y = 2$$
$$2x + 3y = 0$$

In the system of equations above, what is the value of $x + y$?

A) −1
B) 0
C) 1
D) 2

5

$$4x + 8y = -32$$
$$7x - 3y = 29$$

In the system of equations above, what is the solution (x, y)?

A) (2, −5)
B) (−2, −3)
C) (−2, 5)
D) (−13, 2)

6

$$3x - 5y = 11$$
$$-2x + 4y = -13$$

In the system of equations above, what is the value of $x - y$?

A) −4
B) −2
C) 2
D) 4

7

$$x + 24y = 80$$
$$x + 40y = 70$$

The solution to the given system of equations is (x, y). What is the value of y?

8

$$3x - 7y = 35$$
$$x - y = 9$$

The graphs of the equations in the given system of equations intersect at the point (x, y) in the xy-plane. What is the value of x?

9

$$2x + 3y = 5$$
$$3x + 2y = 0$$

How many solutions does the system above have?

A) Zero
B) Exactly one
C) Exactly two
D) Infinitely many

10

$$y = 5x + 4$$
$$6x - y = -1$$

Which of the following is a solution to the system given above?

A) $(-3, -11)$
B) $(1, 9)$
C) $(3, 19)$
D) $(4, 24)$

11

$$y = -\frac{2}{5}x + 7$$
$$5y + 2x = 35$$

How many solutions are there to the system of equations given above?

A) Exactly one
B) Exactly two
C) Infinitely many
D) Zero

12

$$ax - by = -2$$
$$6x - 4y = 4$$

In the system of equations above, a and b are constants and x and y are variables. If the system of equations has exactly one solution, what can $\frac{a}{b}$ NOT equal?

A) $-\frac{3}{2}$

B) $-\frac{2}{3}$

C) $\frac{2}{3}$

D) $\frac{3}{2}$

13

$$ax + by = 15$$
$$4x + 3y = 75$$

In the system of equations above, a and b are constants. If the system has infinitely many solutions, what is the value of $\frac{a}{b}$?

14

$$7x - ry = -17$$
$$-3x - 2y = 13$$

In the system of equations above, r is a constant and x and y are variables. For what value of r will the system have no solutions?

A) $-\frac{7}{3}$

B) $-\frac{14}{3}$

C) $\frac{14}{3}$

D) $\frac{3}{14}$

Nonlinear Systems

Tags: Advanced Math • Systems of Nonlinear Equations

....

Curves, Intersections, and Solutions

In the previous chapter we looked at how to solve systems of linear equations. Now we are going to look at what happens when one or more of the equations in a system is nonlinear.

Let's start by looking at a single nonlinear equation and its graph.

INTERACTIVE EXAMPLE
....

The function $f(x) = x^5 - 3x^4 - 5x^3 + 15x^2 + 4x - 17$ is graphed in the xy-plane below. Now we're going to ask a bunch of questions about it!

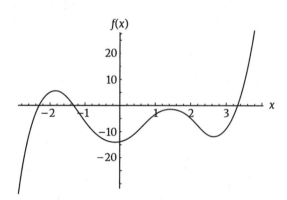

Q1) How many solutions are there to the equation $f(x) = 0$?

Q2) How many solutions are there to the equation $f(x) = -10$?

Q3) If k is a constant such that the equation $f(x) = k$ has 3 real solutions, which of the following could be the value of k ?

    A) 20

    B) 5

    C) −20

    D) −40

PORTAL

We talked about this concept in *Zeros, Solutions and Roots*. Turn to page 377 for a refresher.

Q1) How many solutions are there to the equation $f(x) = 0$?

As we have previously discussed, if we set a polynomial equal to zero, the solutions are the values of x where the y-value is zero. In other words, the solutions to $f(x) = 0$ are the values of x where the y-value is **zero**. That means the *number* of solutions is the *number* of x-intercepts. Simply counting them tells us that there are **3 solutions** to $f(x) = 0$.

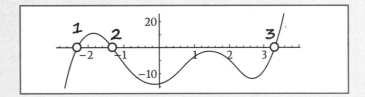

Q2) How many solutions are there to the equation $f(x) = $ -10 ?

On the surface, this just looks like a functions problem, but we can also approach it as a system of equations problem. In the previous question, where we wanted to solve $f(x) = 0$, it was convenient that we had a line, the x-axis, at $y = 0$. This time, we don't have a convenient line at $y = -10$ already built in, but nothing is stopping us from adding one!

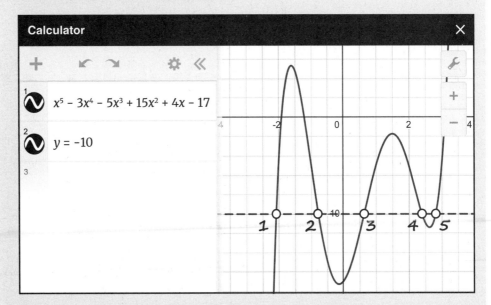

We can see by plotting the point in Desmos that there are 5 points of intersection, and therefore **5 solutions**, at $f(x) = -10$.

Continued on next page →

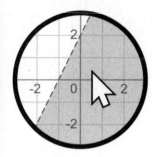

TIP

You might need to play with the graph window on this one if you use Desmos. Don't forget the zoom buttons in the upper right!

Q3) If k is a constant such that the equation $f(x) = k$ has 3 real solutions, which of the following _could_ be the value of k?

In the previous question we wanted to know how many solutions there are for $f(x) = -10$, so we added the line $y = -10$ and counted the intersection points. This question is essentially asking the same kind of thing, only backwards: where can we add a horizontal line that intersects the graph of $f(x)$ exactly 3 times? Since this is a multiple choice question you can work backwards and check each option. You take it from here:

Solve Q3 by completing the table below. Draw lines for each choice and record the number of intersections with the curve of $f(x)$.

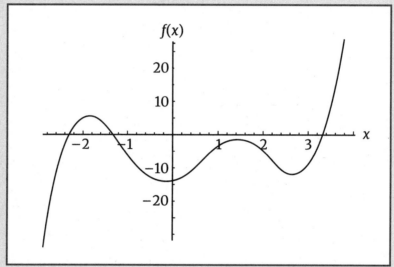

Choice	Line	Number of Intersections
A	$y = 20$	
B	$y = 5$	
C	$y = -20$	
D	$y = -40$	

Use the below graphs to count the number of solutions.

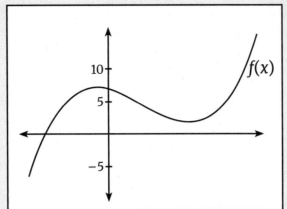

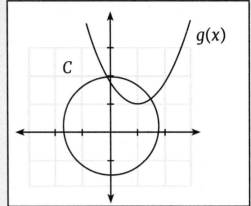

How many solutions are there to...	# of Solutions
1. $f(x) = -3$	*1*
2. $f(x) = 5$	
3. $f(x) = 0$	
4. $f(x) = 10$	
5. $g(x) = 0$	
6. $g(x) = 1$	
7. $g(x) = 3$	
8. The system with circle C and line $y = 0$	
9. The system with circle C and line $y = 2$	
10. The system with circle C and $g(x)$	

Answers:
1. *given*	2. 3	3. 1	4. 1	5. 0
6. 1	7. 2	8. 2	9. 1	10. 2

The quadratic formula shows the # of solutions

Most of the time you can solve non-linear systems by graphing them. But occasionally, there is a faster algebraic approach, **the quadratic formula**, which you can always use to solve a quadratic equation:

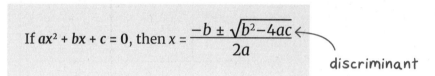

$$\text{If } ax^2 + bx + c = 0, \text{ then } x = \frac{-b \pm \sqrt{b^2 - 4ac}}{2a}$$

discriminant

If we put a quadratic equation into the correct form, we can find a, b, and c and plug into the formula. Doing so lets us quickly see the number of solutions by focusing on the stuff beneath the root: $b^2 - 4ac$. The fancy name for this expression is the **discriminant**, and whether it simplifies to be positive, negative, or zero, tells us how many solutions there are:

Discriminant	# of real solutions
Positive	Two
Equal to Zero	One
Negative	None

When would you want to use this funny-looking formula on the SAT? There are <u>two indications</u> that the quadratic formula is going to be useful:

- You are asked to solve a quadratic and are told/can see from the answer choices that there are square roots in the answer, OR

- You are given a quadratic equation and an unknown constant.

Let's look at an example.

EXAMPLE 1

$$y = 5x(\tfrac{1}{9}x - k)$$
$$y = -20$$

In the system above, k is a constant. If the system has only one solution, what is that solution?

THINK

Can you figure out WHY the discriminant tells us the number of real solutions?

Here's a hint: it has to do with that plus or minus symbol, and the fact that you can't talk about the square root of negative numbers without using imaginary numbers (i).

Imaginary numbers are outside of the scope of the SAT, so we don't have to worry about them.

SOLUTION

We could try to solve this by graphing the equations in Desmos and creating a slider for k, but the answer is not an integer, so it could be tricky to find the right value. Instead, let's use the quadratic formula to answer this question.

(1) *rewrite the equations*

$$y = 5x(\tfrac{1}{9}x - k)$$
$$y = -20$$

(2) *subtitute -20 for y*

$$5x(\tfrac{1}{9}x - k) = -20$$

(3) *solve for zero*

$$5x(\tfrac{1}{9}x - k) + 20 = 0$$

(4) *rearrange for quadratic formula*

$$ax^2 + bx + c = 0$$
$$\tfrac{5}{9}x^2 - 5kx + 20 = 0$$

We know that we want the equation to have **exactly one** solution, so we need the discriminant to equal zero ($b^2 - 4ac = 0$). If we plug in the coefficients for b, a, and c, we'll be set up to solve for k:

(5) *find discriminant*

$$b^2 - 4ac = 0$$
$$(-5k)^2 - 4(\tfrac{5}{9})(20) = 0$$

(6) *solve for k*

$$k = \tfrac{4}{3}$$

(7) *plug $\tfrac{4}{3}$ in for k*

$$\tfrac{5}{9}x^2 - 5kx + 20 = 0$$
$$\tfrac{5}{9}x^2 - \tfrac{20}{3}x + 20 = 0$$

(8) *use quadratic formula*

$$\frac{-\tfrac{20}{3} \pm \sqrt{(\tfrac{20}{3})^2 - 4(\tfrac{5}{9})(20)}}{2(\tfrac{5}{9})}$$

This, believe it or not, simplifies nicely to an even 6. One of the initial equations tells us that $y = -20$, so when $k = 4/3$, the system has the solution $(6, -20)$.

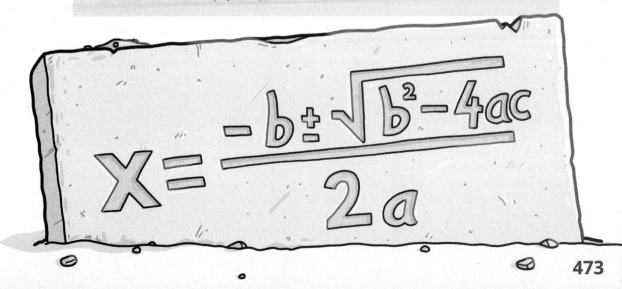

Practice Problems

Use your new skills to answer each question.

1

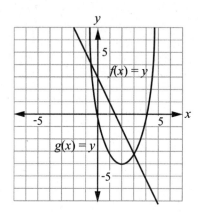

The graphs of $f(x)$ and $g(x)$ are shown above. If the point (u, v) is a solution of the system, which of the following could be u?

A) -3

B) 0

C) 1.5

D) 3

2

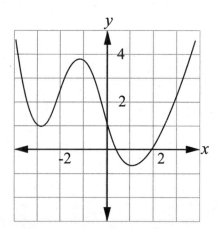

The graph of $f(x)$ is shown above. How many solutions does the equation $f(x) = 3$ have?

3

If $f(x) = 3x - 4$ and there is no solution to the system consisting of $f(x)$ and $g(x)$, which of the following could be $g(x)$?

A) $g(x) = -\frac{1}{3}x + 4$

B) $g(x) = x - 12$

C) $g(x) = 3x^2 - 4$

D) $g(x) = x^2$

4

$$y = 104$$
$$y = x^2 - 5x$$

The graphs of the given equations in the xy-plane intersect at the point (x, y). What is a possible value of x ?

A) −13
B) −8
C) 4
D) 8

5

$$y = (x + 3)(x - 4)$$
$$y = 2x + 6$$

Which ordered pair (x, y) is a solution to the given system of equations?

A) (−3,0)
B) (0,−3)
C) (0,6)
D) (18,6)

6

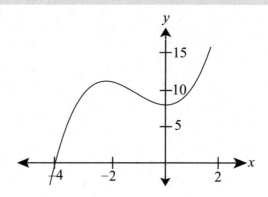

The function $f(x) = x^3 + 3x^2 - x + 7$ is graphed above. If k is a constant and $f(x) = k$ has 3 real solutions, which of the following could be k?

A) 0
B) 6
C) 10
D) 15

7

$$y = u$$
$$y = 2x^2 + v$$

In the system of equations above, u and v are constants. For which of the following values of u and v does the system of equations have exactly two real solutions?

A) $u = 2, v = 3$
B) $u = -2, v = -2$
C) $u = 4, v = 1$
D) $u = 0, v = 2$

8

$$y = (x - 3)^2 + 2$$
$$y = x - 3$$

How many solutions does the given system have?

A) 0
B) 1
C) 2
D) Infinitely many

9

$$y = x^2 + 3x - 4$$
$$y = 2x + 4$$

How many solutions does the given system have?

A) 0
B) 1
C) 2
D) Infinitely many

10

$$f(x) = -x + 4$$
$$g(x) = 3(x + 2)^2 - 4$$

How many solutions does the system above have?

A) 0
B) 1
C) 2
D) 3

11

Which of the following is a solution to the equation $x^2 + 3x - 2 = 0$?

A) 17

B) $3 + \sqrt{17}$

C) $-3 + \dfrac{\sqrt{17}}{2}$

D) $-\dfrac{3}{2} + \dfrac{\sqrt{17}}{2}$

12

How many real solutions does the equation $3x^3 + 5x^2 + x = 0$ have?

A) 1
B) 2
C) 3
D) 4

13

$$x^2 + 2sx = t + 2$$

In the quadratic equation above, s and t are constants. What are the solutions for x?

A) $s \pm \sqrt{s^2 + t + 2}$

B) $-s \pm \sqrt{s^2 + t + 2}$

C) $-s \pm \dfrac{\sqrt{4s^2 + t + 2}}{2}$

D) $-s \pm \sqrt{4s^2 + 4t + 8}$

14

$$y = -3x^2 + 25x - 40$$
$$y = -17x + k$$

In the given system of equations, k is a constant. The graphs of the equations in the given system intersect at exactly one point (x,y) in the xy-plane. What is the value of x?

A) −12
B) 7
C) 84
D) 107

15

$$-x^2 + 28x + c = 0$$

In the given equation c is a constant. The equation has no real solutions if $c < n$. What is the greatest possible value of n?

UNIT | Modeling

Chapters

Overview

In this unit, we practice the **art of translation**: using math equations to model real-world contexts. This skill will not only net you a lot of points on the test, it will also improve your understanding of many problem types throughout this book!

Linear Modeling

Tags: Algebra • Linear Models

....

Equations can "model" real-world situations

Sometimes, it's easy to forget that there is actually a POINT to all of this math. People use algebra **all the time** to learn things they didn't already know about their daily lives.

A new hire could use algebra to determine whether he'll make enough at his position to move to a better apartment; a car factory owner might use algebra to figure out how many tons of steel she needs to order for a busy month; or a college student might use algebra to tackle a major, existential question, like:

> "Wait... how many cookies did we eat last night?!"

The trick to answering such important questions is to **create an equation** using variables and constants that accurately *models* the specific situation. If you can master this skill, not only will you be a better worker, business-owner, and baker, but you'll also be able to gain a *lot* of easy points on the SAT. So let's use that last question about cookies to practice the fundamentals of **basic modeling**.

The Chocolate Chip Conundrum

Last night, you and your college roommates lost track of how many cookies you consumed. Excited by finally having a kitchen all to yourselves, the four of you spent the evening baking and consuming chocolate chip cookies from a giant tub of cookie dough. When you awaken the next morning, a disagreement breaks out over exactly how many cookies were eaten during that wild night. You decide to put an end to the debate the only way you know how: by using some good, old-fashioned algebra.

PORTAL

The second paragraph is an example of how to use semicolons to create complex lists. Boundaries questions on the R&W section can test this usage, so head over to page 146 in *All About Clauses* to review.

What is our Target Variable?

The first step is easy: pick a letter to represent what we're looking to find! We want to know how many cookies we ate... We could pick anything, but let's be honest, C is for Cookie (and that's good enough for me).

$$C = ?$$

"The number of cookies eaten, C, is equal to what?"

What Does it Depend On?

Now, how are we going to figure out how many cookies we ate? The key is to identify some other variable that the number of cookies depends on. We bake cookies in groups – one **tray** at a time. If we knew the number of cookies that fit on a tray AND how many trays we baked, we could figure out the number of cookies we made!

Since we don't yet know how many trays we made, let's make it a **variable**, like t. We know that our cookie tray comfortably fits 12 cookies at a time. If we made one tray, we'd have 12 cookies. If we made two trays, we'd have 24 cookies. In other words, the number of cookies is equal to twelve times the number of trays we baked. Let's write that in math terms:

$$C = 12t$$

"12 cookies per tray...
...times the number of trays"

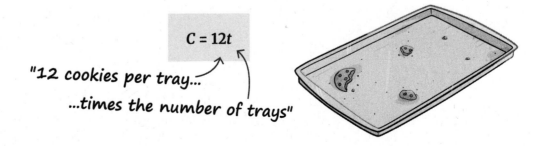

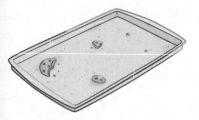

Tray Size: Coefficients & Slope

Let's think about this 12 in front of the *t* in our equation. It tells us the *rate* at which we are making cookies. What if we used a smaller sheet (or made bigger cookies) so that **only 4 fit on the tray**? To show that, we can just change the coefficient in front of *t*:

$$C = 12t$$

$$C = 4t$$

12 cookies per tray

4 cookies per tray

TIP

If a model has the form $y = mx + b$, the units of the rate should always be the units from the *y*-axis per units from the *x*-axis.

So this coefficient tells us the **rate** at which the number of cookies changes when the number of trays changes. Sound familiar? This is our rate of change, *a.k.a.* rise over run, *a.k.a.* slope, *a.k.a.* "*m*" in the equation of a line! If we graphed the two equations above, the lines would have different slopes:

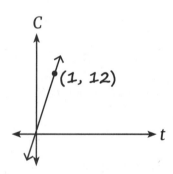

12 cookies per tray
Slope (m) = 12

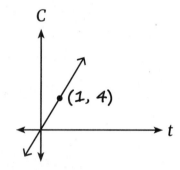

4 cookies per tray
Slope (m) = 4

Labeling Points

Notice how, when we are working with a word problem, a point on the line graphs above has a real-world meaning. The horizontal axis in the graph is the number of trays, and the vertical axis is the number of cookies. That means point (1, 12) can be read (1 tray, 12 cookies), and point (1, 4) can be read (1 tray, 4 cookies). We can read equations in the same way, but we'll come back to that.

Leftovers: Constants & Intercepts

Let's get back to building our equation. Eventually, everyone agrees that you did, in fact, make regular-sized cookies such that 12 cookies fit on each tray. BUT you realize that there are **8 cookies left over** (shocking!). How can we add that information to our equation? Well, no matter how many trays of cookies were baked, we know we'll need to **subtract 8** from that total number to show how many were eaten.

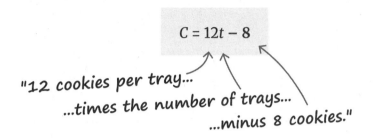

$$C = 12t - 8$$

"12 cookies per tray...
...times the number of trays...
...minus 8 cookies."

Now we've got a pretty great-looking equation of a line in the slope-intercept form. Notice that the constant we just added to model the leftovers, **– 8**, matches the "+ b" (intercept) part of the equation of a line. Sure enough, when we graph this cookie equation, we see that –8 is the y-intercept.

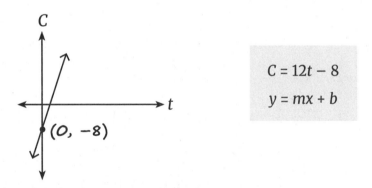

$$C = 12t - 8$$
$$y = mx + b$$

Conundrum Modeled, Cookie Crumbled

And just like that, we have modeled our cookie conundrum into a linear equation, and (bonus!) even shown how we can graph it. Now all we would have to do to determine the number of cookies eaten is figure out the number of trays baked and plug that number in for t.

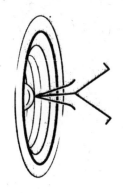

PORTAL

If you haven't completed the *Art of Translation* chapter, turn to page 250.

The Art of Translation

So far, we've seen how we can go from a real-world situation to an algebraic equation. In the process, we saw how we can actually **read** that equation using the real-world context, translating the math into words:

C	=	12	t	– 8
The # of cookies	is	12 cookies per tray	times the # of trays	minus 8 cookies.

The connection between math and words might start out feeling sluggish or rusty, but once it "clicks," many questions on the SAT will instantly become *much* easier! So, let's build up some flexibility by working a number of different questions about the same context.

INTERACTIVE EXAMPLE 1

Ali always gets her hair cut to the same length. She has found that the current length of her hair can be modeled by the equation

$$l = 0.25w + 33$$

Where l is the length measured from the top of her head down her back in centimeters and w is the number of weeks since her latest haircut.

Q1) Which of the following is the meaning of the number 0.25 in the given equation?

A) The length in centimeters of Ali's hair after a haircut.
B) The amount of time she waits between haircuts.
C) The length in centimeters her hair reaches before each haircut.
D) The number of centimeters her hair grows each week.

S1) Let's start by noticing that the equation is in the slope-intercept form $y = mx + b$. The coefficient **0.25** is the **slope** of the line (m). Slope (a.k.a, rise over run) shows us a rate of change. So our answer should tell us the *rate* something is *changing*. From just that information, choice D is looking good. Since l stands for the length of her hair, that's what is changing. .25 is the amount, in centimeters, that her hair is changing. And w, the number of weeks, tells us what causes l to change.

$$l = 0.25w + 33$$

Length of hair is 0.25cm per week plus 33cm.

D

Q2) Which of the following is the meaning of the number 33 in the given equation?

A) The length in centimeters of Ali's hair after a haircut.
B) The amount of time she waits between haircuts.
C) The length in centimeters her hair reaches before each haircut.
D) The number of centimeters her hair grows each week.

S2) Since w is the number of weeks since her haircut, $w = 0$ tells us how long Ali's hair is immediately after getting her hair cut. We can see this if we compare the equation $l = 0.25w + 33$ to the slope-intercept form $y = mx + b$. We see that the number 33 tells us the **y-intercept** of the line. That means the line crosses the y-axis at (0 weeks, 33 centimeters). In other words, when it's been 0 weeks since her hair cut, Ali's hair is 33 centimeters long.

A

Creative Exercises

The same equation could model a number of different situations. One of the best ways to get used to this idea is to try to come up with multiple contexts for the same equation. For example, for the equation below, we've come up with three plausible (if slightly odd) contexts that it could represent. We're sure that you could come up with some better ones, so on the next page you'll have an opportunity to do just that!

$$r = 4t + 5$$

"The cost of entering a raffle (r) is equal to 4 dollars per ticket (t) plus a 5 dollar bribe to the officials."

"Richard (r) drinks 5 cups of coffee a day, plus 4 cups per hour of overtime (t)."

"The length of rope (r) to pack is 5 meters plus another 4 meters for each expected snake trap (t)."

Complete the tables by coming up with contexts that might be modeled by the each equation. This is a creative exercise, so let your imagination run wild. We've come up with one of our own to get you started.

$c = 1.5d + 7$	
Context 1	The total weight, in pounds, of my Calico cat named Cali (c) is at least 7 pounds plus an additional 1.5 pounds per day off her diet (d). c = weight of cat 1.5 = pounds per day d = days off diet +7 = starting weight
Context 2	c = 1.5 = d = +7 =
Context 3	c = 1.5 = d = +7 =

$f = 1,000 - 13p$	
Context 1	f = −13 = p = 1000 =
Context 2	f = −13 = p = 1000 =
Context 3	f = −13 = p = 1000 =

Complete the table by matching each context with the equation that best models it. We have completed the first one for you.

Match	Context	Equation
E	The profit Martha earns from a bakesale is $5 per brownie sold, minus the $45 she spent on supplies.	A) $a = -3b + 60$
	The perceived temperature on a –6°C day drops 3°C for every additional mile per hour of wind.	B) $a = 6b + 3$
	In a psychology study, the average time it takes to finish a particular task alone is 60 minutes. Every added team member cuts that time down by 3 minutes.	C) $a = -3b - 6$
	The amount of hard drive space taken up by Ty's work project is 3mb for a single instructions file, plus 6mb per video she creates.	D) $a = 3b + 60$
	A scientist is studying the effects of a particular "diet" on a 60cm tall plant. She discovers that the plant grows 3cm every week that it is on the diet.	E̶) $a = 5b - 45$

Answers: E, C, A, B, D

489

INTERACTIVE EXAMPLE 2

Morgan is following a strength training exercise plan that claims anyone following it can increase the number of consecutive pushups they can do by 13 pushups per week. Morgan can do 12 consecutive pushups before starting the plan.

Q1) Which of the following expressions gives the number of pushups Morgan should be able to do after following the plan for *t* weeks?

A) $12t + 13$

B) $13t + 12$

C) $13t - 12$

D) $(12)(13)t$

S1) The number of pushups is supposed to change by a constant amount each week, so the model should be linear and look like $y = mx + b$.

- **y** stands for the thing we are interested in – the total number of pushups Morgan can do.

- **m** stands for the slope, so it's the rate at which the number of pushups Morgan can do changes each week (13 per week).

- **b** stands for the y-intercept, so the number of pushups Morgan starts out being able to do (12 pushups).

If we bring that information in, we get:

$$y = 13t + 12$$

The # of pushups Morgan can do (y) equals 13 pushups per week (t) plus 12 pushups.

B

PORTAL

For information about place values and rounding, turn to *Fractions* on page 300.

Q2) After how many weeks will Morgan be able to do 50 consecutive pushups, rounded to the nearest tenth of a week?

A) 2

B) 2.7

C) 2.9

D) 3

S2) We want to know **when** Morgan will be able to do 50 pushups. To figure that out, we can use the formula we built in the previous questions! Since t is our time variable and y is the number of push-ups, we can set the equation equal to 50 pushups and solve for t:

$$50 \text{ pushups} = 13t + 12$$
$$38 = 13t$$
$$2.9 \text{ weeks} \approx t$$

We can check this in another way. If we start at 12 pushups and increase by 13 each week, then we can just add 13 each week and look for when we hit 50 pushups.

Week	0	1	2	3
Pushups	12	25	38	51

C

Write an equation to model each scenario in the blank provided.

Context	Model
Lucy can use a total of 1024 MB of data. Streaming a video uses 1.6 MB every minute. Model data left (d) in terms of minutes streamed (t).	$d = 1024 - 1.6t$
A taxi charges a base fare of $10.50 and an additional $.45 per mile. Model taxi fare (f) in terms of miles driven (m).	$f =$
Jose runs 2 miles to a race track, runs 6 miles per hour while he races on the track, then runs the 2 miles home. Model total miles run (m) in terms of race length in hours (h).	$m =$
Tobi the corgi has a rope that was originally comprised of 350 strings twisted together. He rips out 4 strings a day. Model strings left (s) in terms of days (d).	$s =$
Proper clown shoe length starts at 15 inches, with a half-inch added for every year the clown has been a part of the clown union. Model shoe length (c) in terms of years in the union (y).	$c =$

Answers: 1. *given*   2. $f = .45m + 10.50$ 3. $m = 6h + 4$

4. $s = 350 - 4d$ 5. $c = 15 + .5y$

INTERACTIVE EXAMPLE 3

Luis works as a caterer. He charges a setup fee plus an additional amount for each guest expected at the event. The equation $c = 12g + 55$ gives the total amount Luis charges in dollars (c) in terms of the expected number of guests (g).

Q1) A client calls and informs Luis that there are going to be 8 more guests for an event than originally expected. How much will Luis increase the amount he charges for the event?

A) $8
B) $96
C) $151
D) $440

S1) Since c is the total cost and g is the number of guests, the number 12 in the equation (our rate of change coefficient) tells us that it costs **$12 per guest**. This means that he will charge $12 for each of the 8 additional guests. So if we simply multiply, we can find the cost:

$$12(8) = 96 \text{ dollars}$$

So it will cost $96 to fund an additional 8 guests.

B

Q2) Luis discovers that people are frequently underestimating the number of guests for events that he caters, so he decides to adjust his pricing model. In the updated model, he assumes there will be 4 more guests than the number g that the client gives him. Which of the following equations could be Luis's new model?

A) $c = 16g + 55$
B) $c = 12g + 59$
C) $c = 12(g + 4) + 55$
D) $c = 12(g - 4) + 55$

NOTE

Another possible correct answer would **distribute the 12**.

$c = 12g + 48 + 55$
$c = 12g + 103$

S2) We are told that Luis is assuming there will be **4 more guests than the number g** that is provided. Translating this into math means that we want to replace "g" with "$(g + 4)$". This gives us:

$$old \quad c = 12g + 55$$
$$new \quad c = 12(g + 4) + 55$$

So the answer is **choice C**.

C

Modeling with Graphs

As we discussed earlier, we can think of the rate of change in a model as the **coefficient** in an equation and as the **slope** of the line in the graph of the equation. Sometimes the SAT will give you your model as a graph and ask you to interpret it. Let's look at an example.

INTERACTIVE EXAMPLE 4

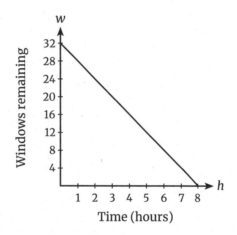

Seana has a job as a window cleaner for a particular office building. The above graph models her work on a typical day, where w is the number of windows she has left to clean that day and h is the number of hours she has worked so far that day (not counting breaks).

Q1) What does the w–intercept in the graph represent?

A) The total number of windows she washes in a typical day.
B) The exact number of windows she washes every day.
C) The number of windows she can typically wash per hour.
D) The time it typically takes her to wash one window.

SOLUTION

To understand the w-intercept, we first need to understand what each axis tells us. The axis labels and the description below the graph help us out. The vertical (w) axis tells us the **number of windows remaining**, and the horizontal (h) axis tells us the **number of hours worked**. That means we could read the point (0, 32) as (0 hours, 32 windows remaining).

Since the w-intercept occurs where $h = 0$, we know that it must tell us the **total number of windows remaining** at the beginning of the work day. That narrows it down to A or B. The problem tells us that the graph models a *typical* day, so A is the better answer.

A

Q2) Which of the following is the best interpretation of the slope of the line?

    A) The total number of windows she washes in a typical day.
    B) The exact number of windows she washes every day.
    C) The number of windows she can typically wash per hour.
    D) The time it typically takes her to wash one window.

SOLUTION

The slope of a line is always the rate of change, so our answer needs to be a **rate**. This means we can immediately eliminate A and B. Recall that:

$$slope = \frac{change\ in\ y}{change\ in\ x}, \text{ or } \frac{change\ in\ w}{change\ in\ h}$$

This means that our answer should be in terms of windows (w) per hour (h). This corresponds with answer choice C.

C

Q3) What does the h-intercept in the graph represent?

    A) The number of windows she washes by the end of the day.
    B) The number of windows she washes each hour.
    C) The earliest she can finish her work.
    D) The number of hours she typically needs to finish her work.

SOLUTION

The h-intercept is the point on the line where w, the number of windows remaining to be washed, is zero. This means it is the point where she finishes her work. Since h is the number of hours she has worked, that means the h-intercept tells us the amount of hours she works before her work is finished on a typical day.

D

Practice Problems

Use your new skills to answer each question.

1

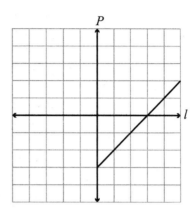

The graph above displays the total profit P, in dollars, after selling l cups of lemonade. What does the l-intercept represent in the graph?

A) The initial cost of starting a lemonade stand
B) The total cups of lemonade sold
C) The total profit the lemonade stand makes in a day
D) The number of cups of lemonade sold that earn a zero dollar profit

2

The total price, in dollars, that a jet-ski rental company charges a group of over five people can be calculated by the expression $10px - 24$, where $p > 5$ is the number of people in the group and x is the number of hours the group will be using the jet-skis. Which of the following is the best interpretation of the number 10 in the expression?

A) The company charges $10 per hour for each individual.
B) A maximum of 10 people can be in each group.
C) The price each member in the group will pay is $10.
D) Each member of the group will spend a maximum of 10 hours renting the jet-skis.

3

$$M = 250 - 20d$$

The equation above gives the number of miles, M, a backpacker still has to travel before reaching her destination, where d is the number of days it has been since she started her trip. What is the meaning of 250 in the equation?

A) The backpacker will hike for 250 days.
B) The backpacker must hike for 250 miles every day.
C) The backpacker's destination is 250 miles from her starting location.
D) The backpacker hiked 250 miles on her first day of the trip.

4

$$T = 45 + 15r$$

The equation above gives the number of tickets T sold, in millions, for a movie with an average movie critic rating of r, where r must be between 0 and 10. If movie theaters sold a total of 105 million tickets for a certain movie, what was the average movie critic rating of that movie?

A) 10
B) 8
C) 7
D) 4

5

$$P = 264.50 + 20m$$

Last year, Fabio bought a piggy bank to hold all of his savings. Ever since then, Fabio has been putting a fixed amount of money into his piggy bank every month. The equation above gives the amount of money P, in dollars, Fabio now has in his piggy bank after m months. If the equation was graphed in the xy-plane, with P on the y-axis and m on the x-axis, what would be the meaning of the y-intercept?

A) Fabio deposits $264.50 every month.
B) Fabio now has $264.50 in his piggy bank.
C) Fabio put $264.50 in his piggy bank the day he bought it.
D) Fabio can only put a maximum of $264.50 in his piggy bank.

6

The equation $S = 14 + 3.5t$ gives the speed S of a ball, in feet per second, t seconds after it was kicked down a hill. After how many seconds will the ball be rolling down the hill at 42 feet per second?

A) 16
B) 12
C) 8
D) 4

7

Elmer works at a call center, and the number of people Elmer still needs to call on a given day can be modeled by $C = 150 - 20h$, where h is the number of hours Elmer has worked that day. What is the meaning of 20 in the equation?

A) Elmer must call 20 people every day.
B) Elmer still has 20 more people to call that day.
C) Elmer will work 20 hours this week.
D) Elmer calls 20 people every hour.

8

At a fast food restaurant, the price of a value meal is three times the price of a kid's meal. If the price of a kid's meal is 4 dollars and the price of a value meal is n dollars, which of the following is true?

A) $\frac{n}{3} = 4$

B) $4n = 3$

C) $3n = 4$

D) $n + 4 = 3$

9

Avery and Patrick work in the telesales department of a company. Last Friday, Avery made x phone calls each hour for 6 hours and Patrick made y phone calls each hour for 8 hours. Which of the following expressions represents the total number of phone calls Avery and Patrick made last Friday?

A) $6x + 8y$
B) $6y + 8x$
C) $48xy$
D) $14xy$

497

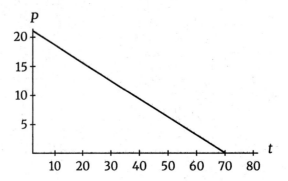

Lorraine is doing her math homework and the above graph shows the number of homework problems, *P*, she has left after working on her homework for *t* minutes. What does the *P*-intercept represent?

A) The time it takes her to do one question
B) The amount of time it will take her to finish the assignment
C) The total number of homework problems she needs to complete
D) The number of problems in the section her class is currently working on

Modeling Systems

Tags: Algebra • Linear Models

In the previous chapter we looked at models where we wanted to find one variable (an output) in terms of the other (an input). Sometimes, however, you will have a scenario where the two variables don't depend on each other directly. In this case your model might look a little bit different; let's look at an example.

INTERACTIVE EXAMPLE 1

Suppose Sasha is playing a game that involves rolling a standard 6-sided die several times. When he rolls a number that is even, he earns 5 points. When he rolls a number that is odd, he earns 2 points. His total score when the game finishes is 38 points.

Q1) How could you model this scenario?

There are two unknown quantities in this scenario, so let's define a variable for each of them:

x = the number of times he rolls an even number
y = the number of times he rolls an odd number

We have a rate associated with **both** of these unknowns.

- He earns 5 points per even roll, which happens x times, so the total number of points earned from even rolls is $5x$.

- He earns 2 points per odd roll, which happens y times, so the total number of points earned from odd rolls is $2y$.

To get his total score (38), we add these two expressions together to get $5x + 2y = 38$.

PORTAL

If you need to learn or review how to solve *Systems of Equations*, turn to page 447.

TIP

The SAT might give you the full scenario and ask how many times he rolled an even number, how many times he rolled an odd number or how many **more** times he rolled an even number than an odd number. When you think you have finished a problem, you should always double check that you are answering the correct question!

INTERACTIVE EXAMPLE 2

....

Suppose that we are also told that in each game Sasha rolls the die exactly <u>10 times</u>.

Q2) How many times did Sasha roll an even number? How many times did he roll an odd number?

SOLUTION

From our work so far, we have defined x and y as the number of times that Sasha rolls an even and odd number respectively. We can use those variables to model the new information about how many times he rolls alongside our equation for his points:

$$5x + 2y = 38$$
$$x + y = 10$$

Now that we've modeled this scenario, we have a familiar systems of equations to solve! Let's use our Desmos calculator to find the intersection of these systems:

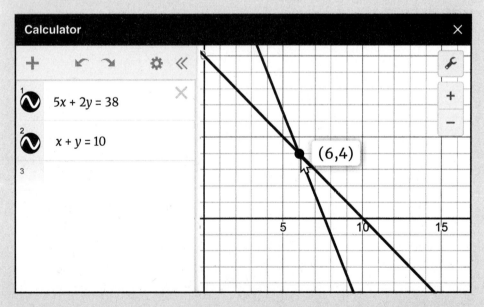

Since the lines intersect at $(6, 4)$, the solution to this system is $x = 6$ and $y = 4$. Let's interpret that answer with our model: Sasha rolled an even number (x) a total of <u>6 times</u>, and he rolled an odd number (y) a total of <u>4 times</u>.

EXAMPLE 3

Mary is designing a quilt that uses two different sizes of squares. The smaller squares have 5 inch sides and the larger squares have 10 inch sides. If Mary wants the finished quilt to have an area of 4800 square inches and contain 120 total squares, how many of the smaller squares will she use?

A) 24
B) 48
C) 96
D) 10

TIP

There are often multiple ways to think about a problem. Sometimes you'll have to stop and ask yourself "What else could I figure out?" or "How else could I think about this scenario?" and then play with things.

Here, we thought in terms of *area*, even though it wasn't immediately obvious to do that. Can you think of other ways to set up this problem?

If the quilt were entirely made of small squares, how many would there be? If you wanted to take out small squares to fit just one large square, how many would you need to take away?

SOLUTION

Let s be the number of smaller squares and l be the number of larger squares. Before we do anything else, let's establish our goal. We're asked to find the number of small squares, so:

 establish your goal $s = ?$

We know we need a total of **120 squares**, so let's model that:

① *write first equation* #small + #large = #total

$$s + l = 120$$

From the side lengths, we can figure out that the small squares are 25 square inches and the larger ones are 100 square inches. We also know the finished quilt will be **4800 square inches**. So we can show how each type of square contributes to the total area in a second equation:

② *write second equation* (area)s + (area)l = total area

$$25s + 100l = 4800$$

And now we have a system we can use to solve for s!

③ *write system* $s + l = 120$

$$25s + 100l = 4800$$

Continued on next page →

It looks like **substitution** will serve us well here. If we use the first equation to get something we can plug in for l in the second equation, we'll be able to solve for s.

(4) *solve for l in 1st equation* $\qquad\qquad l = 120 - s$

(5) *substitute into 2nd* $\qquad\qquad 25s + 100(120 - s) = 4800$

(6) *simplify* $\qquad\qquad 25s + 12{,}000 - 100s = 4800$

$$-75s = -7200$$

$$\boxed{s = 96}$$

C

EXAMPLE 4

A mad scientist has designed two kinds of robots that both utilize a certain kind of widget. The hopping robots, h, require 2 widgets each and the flying robots, f, require 3 widgets each. The scientist wants to produce no less than 5 of each type of robot, and at least 20 robots total. If she has a stash of 100 widgets, which of the following systems models the possible numbers of robots she can create?

A) $h = 5$
    $f = 5$
    $h + f < 20$
    $2h + 3f = 100$

B) $h \geq 5$
    $f \geq 5$
    $h + f \geq 20$
    $3h + 2f < 100$

C) $h > 5$
    $f > 5$
    $h + f = 20$
    $2h + 3f = 100$

D) $h \geq 5$
    $f \geq 5$
    $h + f \geq 20$
    $2h + 3f \leq 100$

TIP

Eliminate choices as you go! Notice that we can narrow our choices down to either B or D by step 2. The only difference between the two are the coefficients of *h* and *f* in the last inequality, which saves us from having to write the equation from scratch.

At this point, we only have to check the problem for how many widgets each robot type gets.

SOLUTION

This problem asks us to *model* four different **inequalities**. Looking at the choices, we can see that getting the less than, greater than, equal to distinction will be important, so let's take it slow:

(1) *"No less than 5 of each type of robot"* $h \geq 5$
$f \geq 5$

(2) *"at least 20 robots total"* $h + f \geq 20$

(3) *"No more than 100 widgets, using 2 per hopping and 3 per flying"* $2h + 3f \leq 100$

D

Practice Problems

Use your new skills to answer each question.

1

The sum of four numbers is 765. The sum of the first two numbers is 25% more than the sum of the other two numbers. What is the sum of the first two numbers?

A) 170
B) 340
C) 425
D) 530

2

$$a = 1.5x + 1.50$$
$$b = 1.25x + 4.50$$

In the system of equations above, a and b represent the cost, in dollars, of buying x buffalo wings at two different restaurants. What amount of money will get you the same number of buffalo wings at both restaurants?

A) $12
B) $19.50
C) $20
D) $29.50

3

A semi-trailer truck is carrying exactly 20,000 kg of cargo consisting of 300-kg crates and 400-kg crates. If the truck is carrying eight 300-kg crates, how many 400-kg crates is the truck carrying?

4

$$P(t) = 2t + 10$$
$$A(t) = 40 - t$$

Function $A(t)$ models the speed, in meters per second, of Aaron's car t seconds after passing a police car. Since Aaron was driving over the speed limit, the police officer sped up to Aaron's car to pull him over. Function $P(t)$ models the speed, in meters per second, of the police officer's car t seconds after Aaron passed it. At 8 seconds after the police officer caught Aaron speeding, by how much had the speed of the police car changed?

A) The speed of the police car increased by 4 meters per second.

B) The speed of the police car decreased by 16 meters per second.

C) The speed of the police car decreased by 26 meters per second.

D) The speed of the police car increased by 16 meters per second.

5

A landscaper has bought 140 plants for a flower bed. The equation $8x + 12y = 300$ represents this situation, where x is the number of trays of pansy plants and y is the number of trays of petunia plants he bought. How many more petunia plants are there per tray than pansy plants?

6

An artist sold x small prints and y large prints at a festival, earning a total of $360. The equation $18x + 45y = 360$ represents this situation. Which of the following is the best interpretation of 45 in this context?

A) The artist earned $45 per small print sold.

B) The artist earned $45 per large print sold.

C) The artist sold 45 small prints.

D) The artist sold 45 large prints.

7

A college professor assigns a class of 105 students a group project. If each group has either 3 or 4 students and there are 31 groups, how many of the students are in a group of 3?

8

Fernando and Lizzie bought notebooks and pens at the store. The price of each notebook was the same and the price of each pen was the same. Fernando bought 6 notebooks and 3 pens for $24.75 and Lizzie bought 5 notebooks and 4 pens for $22.50 . Which of the following systems of linear equations represents the situation, if x represents the price in dollars of each notebook and y represents the price in dollars of each pen?

A) $6x + 3y = 24.75$
    $5x + 4y = 22.5$
B) $6x + 3y = 22.5$
    $5x + 4y = 24.75$
C) $6x + 4y = 24.75$
    $5x + 3y = 22.5$
D) $6x + 5y = 24.75$
    $3x + 4y = 22.5$

9

Lauren is in charge of coordinating tour buses for an historic city. There are large tour buses that seat 60 people and smaller tour busses that seat 40 people. If Lauren sent 50 tour busses one week to pick up 2,300 people, what is the minimum number of large tour busses that Lauren sent?

A) 10
B) 15
C) 25
D) 35

10

If Julian's height h is within 4 inches of the average height, a, of an 18-year-old male, which of the following inequalities MUST be true?

I. $h + a < 4$
II. $-4 < h - a < 4$
III. $|h - a| < 4$

A) III only
B) II and III only
C) I and III only
D) I, II, and III

Quadratic Modeling

Tags: Advanced Math • Quadratic Equations • Nonlinear Models

....

Modeling a ball tossed up into the air

The SAT loves to give you models—mathematical equations that you can use to compute real world information. So far, we've been looking at **linear** models, meaning they have the form $y = mx + b$. Now let's look at what it means when the test describes a **quadratic** model. The most common scenario modeled by a quadratic equation is projectile motion (e.g., throwing a ball up in the air and watching it fall back down).

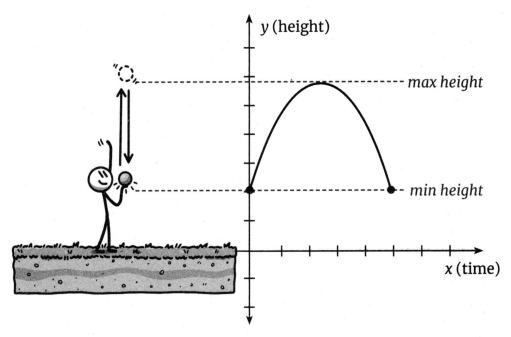

The graph above models the illustrated scenario: the ball is thrown up into the air, reaches a maximum height, falls back down, and is caught. To help understand the model, consider the questions below:

1. Why doesn't the curve start at the origin?

2. Why does the curve stop before crossing the x-axis?

3. If the ball is thrown straight up into the air, why does the curve travel along the x-axis?

508

Throwing a ball and letting it drop off a cliff

Now let's look at the same model in a slightly different scenario. In this situation, you're standing on a cliff side and you throw the ball straight up into the air. Rather than catch the ball, you let it drop far below you. How will the model change? How will the graph change?

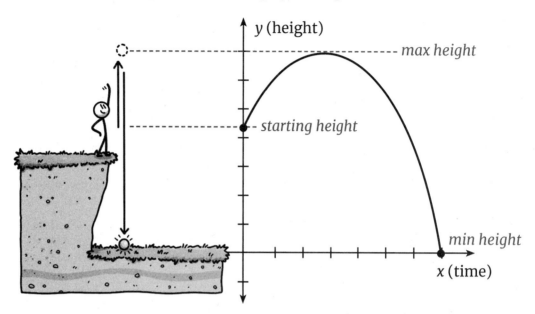

You can use models to find interesting info

There are a few *particularly* interesting things about a quadratic model that the test is likely to focus on. Let's consider each in the context of the models shown.

- **The y-intercept:** If we set x to zero, in the examples above, we find the *starting height* of the ball when thrown. When in doubt, try plugging zero in for your input variable and see what you learn!

- **The x-intercepts:** If we set y to zero, the model will tell us when the ball hits the ground (where the height is zero). With a quadratic curve, this will give you <u>two</u> answers—use common sense to determine which answer makes the most sense in context.

- **Maximums and minimums:** The highest and lowest points on a curve, which is the vertex of the parabola. Pay careful attention to whether they are asking for the input or the output on this kind of question.

- **A particular point on the curve:** You may be asked to find a specific piece of information by plugging in an input and finding the corresponding output. In this case, you simply treat the model like a function with inputs and outputs.

PORTAL

For a review of quadratic equations and their graphs, turn to Quadratic Functions in *All About Graphs* on page 422.

Interpreting and using a quadratic model

Some quadratic modeling problems will ask you to *interpret* a model that you are given. To do this you have to combine what you know about the different forms of the quadratic equation which we discussed in the All About Graphs chapter with the context of the problem. Let's look at an example:

EXAMPLE 1

Amelia tosses a penny from her apartment's balcony and determines that its height above the ground can be modeled by the equation $h = -16t^2 + 6t + 42$ where h is the penny's height in feet and t is the number of seconds since she released it. Which of the following is the best interpretation of the number 42 in this equation?

A) The maximum height the penny will reach
B) The height that Amelia tosses the penny from
C) The amount of time before the penny hits the ground
D) The speed the penny will be traveling at when it hits the ground

SOLUTION

The equation we are given is in the standard form:

$$y = ax^2 + bx + c$$
$$h = -16t^2 + 6t + 42$$

We can see the 42 matches up with c. If you remember your standard form, you know that c tells you the **y-intercept** of the graph. You can check this by plugging in 0 for t; when no time has passed ($t = 0$), the height (h) is equal to 42.

In other words, the **initial height** of the penny is 42 feet.

B

TIP

You could solve this problem algebraically if you really wanted to. To do so, you would set $y = 0$, solve for t, and then use the symmetry of a parabola to determine that the t coordinate of the vertex is halfway between the zeros, and then plug that halfway point in to solve for the height. Using your calculator and just graphing the equation can save you a lot of time here!

TIP

You may need to adjust the window to see the maximum height clearly.

Some modeling questions assume you understand how to interpret the equation and ask you to compute a specific piece of information.

EXAMPLE 2

Liam kicks a soccer ball and determines that the height of its path can be modeled by the quadratic equation $y = -4.9x^2 + 17.6x$, where x is the number of seconds after he kicks the ball and y is the height of the ball in meters. What is the maximum height the ball reaches, to the nearest tenth of a meter?

SOLUTION

We are given a quadratic model, $y = -4.9x^2 + 17.6x$, and asked to find the **maximum height**. Height is the *output* of the model, which means we are looking for the y-coordinate of the highest point (the vertex) of the parabola. We could put this equation into **vertex form** to more easily see the vertex coordinates. But the easiest way to solve this problem is to use Desmos to graph it!

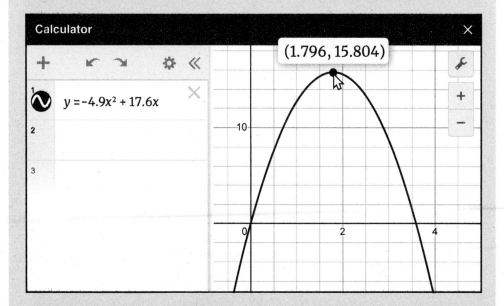

From this graph we see that when $x = 1.796$ seconds, the ball is at a height of 15.804 meters. The question asks us to round the height to one tenth of a meter, so the answer is 15.8.

PORTAL

This problem is a good example how the the skills you learned in *Zeros, Solutions, and Roots* can be applied in a broader context. To review, turn back to page 377.

TIP

You could also use Desmos to find the zeros for this problem!

EXAMPLE 3

$$h = -4.9t^2 + 80t$$

Michael is setting up for a fireworks show and needs to determine how far from his launch site the spent fireworks can safely land. He knows that t seconds after launch, the height of a particular firework is given by the above equation. He also knows that, while it is in the air, the firework travels at a rate of 13.6 m/s horizontally from the launch site. About how many meters away from the launch site will the firework remains land?

A) 13.6
B) 16.3
C) 222
D) 327

SOLUTION

We're asked to find the **distance** between where the firework was launched and where it will land. Let's draw a picture to help us:

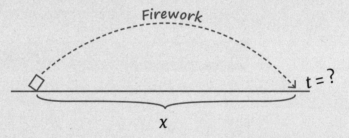

We know it travels left to right at a rate of 13.6 m/s. For this to be helpful, we need to know how long it is in the air. That's where the equation comes in! The equation has two variables: time and height. If we know one, we can find the other.

So... what is the height of the firework when it lands? That would be zero! That means if we find the zeroes of the equation we can figure out how long it was in the air:

① *set equal to zero* $-4.9t^2 + 80t = 0$

② *factor* $t(-4.9t + 80) = 0$

Now we need to solve for t.

continue →

③ *find values of t* $\qquad$ $t(-4.9t + 80) = 0$

$$t_1 = 0$$

$$t_2 = \frac{80}{4.9} \approx 16.3$$

So there are two values of t that would make the height zero. That makes sense! The height is zero at two times: when it launches and when it lands. The launch happens at $t = 0$, so the landing must happen at $t \approx 16.3$ seconds.

To find the distance the firework traveled during that time, we multiply 16.3 seconds by the rate it travels:

TIP

Remember, distance is equal to rate times time. The total distance you drive (100 miles) is your speed (50 mph) times how long you drove (2 hours).

④ *multiply by the rate* $\qquad$ *distance* = (*rate*)(*time*)

distance = (13.6 m/s)(16.3 s)

distance = 221.68 meters

The question asked about how many meters away it lands, so we can round this to get 222, choice C.

Boom, problem solved! **C**

Picking the best model for the occasion

Some questions will give you a scenario and data and ask you to pick an equation or graph that best models the situation. For these problems you can work out the equation yourself and then match it to the answer choices if you want to, but most of the time it is going to be much faster to **work backwards**. Check the proposed models against the information/data you are given and see which one makes sense. This is notably easier than the toughest type of modeling question...

Creating your own model

The hardest quadratic modeling problems will give you a situation, tell you that you need a quadratic model, and then expect you to both create *and* apply the model. For these problems you will be given one or more points, and your job is to use the different forms of quadratic equations:

> Use **standard** form, $y = ax^2 + bx + c$, if given coordinate points.
>
> Use **vertex** form, $y = a(x - h)^2 + k$, if given the vertex.
>
> Use **intercept** form, $y = a(x - u)(x - v)$ if given the x-intercepts.

EXAMPLE 4

Velocity (m/s)	Kinetic Energy (J)
0	0
5	145
10	580

The kinetic energy, in Joules, of an object is related to its velocity, in meters per second, by a quadratic model. The kinetic energy of a particular object at three different velocities is given in the table above. What would the kinetic energy be in Joules when the velocity of this object is 20 m/s?

SOLUTION

Our eventual goal is to find the kinetic energy given a particular value for the velocity. This means we need an equation. The question tells us that we want a **quadratic** model, and we are given three coordinates in the table.

Let's **try to make an equation** in the form of $y = ax^2 + bx + c$, where our input (x) is velocity and our output (y) is kinetic energy. Let's then plug in the first point and see what we learn.

① *write the equation form* $\qquad$ $y = ax^2 + bx + c$

② *plug in first point (0,0)* $\qquad$ $0 = a(0)^2 + b(0) + c$

$\qquad\qquad\qquad\qquad\qquad\qquad 0 = c$

Great! We've got one of the constants figured out. Now let's plug in the other two points:

③ *plug in second point (5, 145)* $\qquad$ $y = ax^2 + bx$

$\qquad\qquad\qquad\qquad\qquad 145 = a(5)^2 + b(5)$

$\qquad\qquad\qquad\qquad\qquad 145 = 25a + 5b$ ✓

④ *plug in third point (10, 580)* $\qquad$ $580 = a(10)^2 + b(10)$

$\qquad\qquad\qquad\qquad\qquad 580 = 100a + 10b$ ✓

Now we have a **system of equations** with two unknowns, so you can use your favorite method for solving systems. We'll try multiplying the first equation by two, then subtracting:

⑤ *multiply 1st equation by 2* $\qquad$ $2(145) = 2(25a + 5b)$

$\qquad\qquad\qquad\qquad\qquad 290 = 50a + 10b$

⑤ *stack n' smash (subtract)* $\qquad$ $290 = 50a + 10b$

$\qquad\qquad\qquad\qquad - \quad 580 = 100a + 10b$

$\qquad\qquad\qquad\qquad\overline{\qquad -290 = -50a}$

$\qquad\qquad\qquad\qquad\qquad 5.8 = a$

Whew! Finding a was some work, but now we can easily find b by plugging in 5.8 for a in either equation...

TIP

If you are given a point where $x = 0$, that's always going to be the best place to start plugging in: it will simplify the equation and reveal helpful information.

PORTAL

If you got stuck on solving this system of equations, review *Linear Systems* on page 448.

Continued on next page →

TIP

In this case, the vertex of the parabola was at the origin. Had we known that for sure, we could have skipped a number of steps; however, this will not always be the case!

(6) *plug in 5.8 for a to find b* $580 = 100a + 10b$

$580 = 100(5.8) + 10b$

$580 = 580 + 10b$

$0 = b$

Aha! Now we know that $a = 5.8$, $b = 0$, and $c = 0$. Let's plug that into our model. Then, to find the kinetic energy (y) where the velocity (x) is 20, we simply plug in 20 for x:

(7) *write the final model* $y = 5.8x^2$

(8) *plug in 20 for x and solve* $y = 5.8(20)^2$

$y = 5.8(400)$

$y = 2{,}320 \, J$

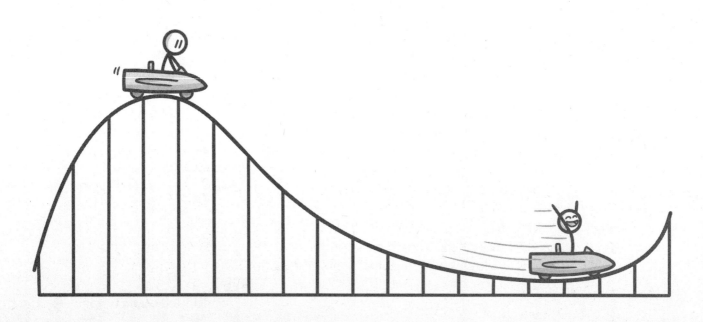

Practice Problems

Use your new skills to answer each question.

1

$$f(x) = -0.5(x - 1.9)^2 + 1.805$$

A particular garden has an arched bridge that spans a small stream. The bridge's elevation, in meters, above the rest of the path can be modeled by the function above, where x is the horizontal distance, in meters, from the bridge entrance. The graph of $y = f(x)$ is shown in the xy-plane below.

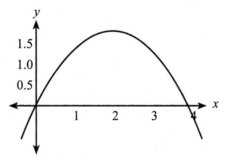

The gardener is considering replacing this arched bridge with a flat bridge. How long would the flat bridge need to be?

A) 1.805 meters
B) 1.9 meters
C) 3.61 meters
D) 3.8 meters

2

$$t(x) = -0.16x^2 + 3.84x + 56$$

A scientist uses a quadratic model to model the temperature changes over the course of a particular spring day. The equation above gives the temperature, in degrees Fahrenheit, x hours after sunrise. What is the meaning of $(8, t(8))$ in this context?

A) The temperature is 8 degrees $t(8)$ hours after sunrise.
B) The temperature is $t(8)$ degrees at 8 am.
C) The temperature is $t(8)$ degrees 8 hours after sunrise.
D) The temperature increases by $t(8)$ degrees every 8 hours.

t	f(t)
−5	0
−3	−4
−1	0
0	5

A particle is moving a long a line and its position, $f(t)$, at several times, t, is given in the table above. Which of the following functions best models the particle's motion?

A)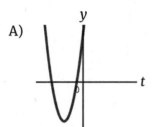

B)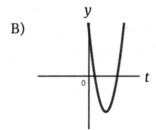

C)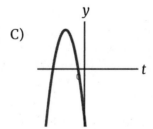

D)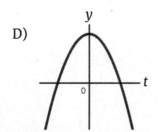

4

$$p(d) = -50d^2 + 1250d - 6000$$

A company has discovered that its profit can be modeled by the above equation where d is the price, in dollars, at which it sells its devices. Based on this model, what is the company's expected profit in dollars if it sells its devices for $10 each?

5

A toy rocket is launched from the ground. It reaches a maximum height of 144.6 feet after 3.2 seconds and lands after 6.4 seconds. Which equation represents the height above the ground h, in feet, of the rocket t seconds after it is launched?

A) $-16(t - 3.2)^2 + 144.6$
B) $-16(t - 6.4)^2 + 144.6$
C) $-t^2 + 144.6$
D) $-t^2 + 6.4$

6

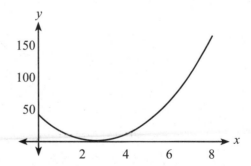

A toy car initially traveling East experiences constant acceleration as it slows down and then continues back to the West. The graph shows the quadratic function K that models the kinetic energy, in joules, of the car as a function of the time t in seconds since the car began accelerating. Which of the following equations could define K?

A) $K(t) = 5.76(t - 2.7)^2$
B) $K(t) = 5.76(t - 2.7)^2 + 42.3$
C) $K(t) = 5.76(t + 2.7)^2 + 42.3$
D) $K(t) = 5.67(t - 42.3)^2 + 2.7$

7

A rock is thrown from a 6 meter high platform. A quadratic model estimates that the rock reaches a maximum height of 15.3 meters above the ground after 2.7 seconds. How many seconds after the launch does the model estimate that the rock will return to 6 meters above the ground?

A) 2.7
B) 5.4
C) 6.0
D) 7.3

8

$$h(t) = -16t^2 + 48t + 160$$

A stick is dropped from a bridge into the river below. The equation above models the height, in feet, of the stick above the water t seconds after the stick was released. After how many seconds does the stick hit the water?

9

$$r(d) = 516d - 43d^2$$

The drama club is preparing for the upcoming school musical and deciding how much it should charge per ticket. By looking at ticket sales from previous years, they estimate that the amount of revenue brought in can be modeled by the equation above, where d is the price of the ticket in dollars. Which of the following is the best interpretation of the vertex of the graph of $y = r(x)$ in the xy-plane?

A) The drama club will make at least 516 dollars regardless of the ticket price
B) The maximum revenue the drama club can earn is 1,548 dollars
C) The drama club will earn the maximum possible revenue if they charge 12 dollars per ticket
D) The drama club will earn the maximum possible revenue if they charge 43 dollars per ticket

10

An object moving in a circle has a centripetal acceleration equal to the square of the object's speed divided by the radius of the circle. If an object with a centripetal acceleration of 4 meters per second squared is moving around a circle with a radius of 9 meters, what is the speed, in meters per second, of the object?

11

The distance in meters an object in free fall remains from the ground can be modeled by a quadratic function that is defined in terms of t, where t is the time in seconds since the object was released. An object is dropped from 4,250 meters above the ground. After 10 seconds, it is 3,750 meters above the ground; after 20 seconds, it is 2,250 meters above the ground. How many meters above the ground will it be after 25 seconds?

12

$$y = -4.9t^2 + 5t + 3$$

Maureen dives into a pool from a springboard mounted 3 meters above the water. The function $f(t)$ gives her height above the water t seconds from when she jumps. After about how many seconds does she hit the water?

A) −1
B) 0
C) 1
D) 4

Exponential Modeling

Tags: Advanced Math • Exponential Functions • Nonlinear Models

When we need to model a situation where one variable grows or shrinks by a *constant amount* for every unit change in a second variable, we use a **linear model**. For example, every ticket sold adds exactly $3 to the total amount raised. The *hundredth* ticket sold earns just as much as did the *first* ticket sold: three dollars.

In this chapter, we will look at a different kind of growth. For example, a population of rabbits that is *doubling* each year or a savings account that gains interest based on a *percentage* of the current balance. In these situations where something is being multiplied (or divided) by a constant factor, we need a model that shows **exponential** growth.

Identify whether each situation is linear or exponential.

Situation		Linear or Exponential?
1.	The population of mosquitos at a lake doubles every week.	
2.	Jace earns $8 per hour for babysitting.	
3.	A savings account earns 0.05% interest.	
4.	A swimming pool is being filled by a hose at a rate of 6 gallons per minute.	
5.	A treatment wipes out one-third of the remaining bacteria with every dose.	
6.	The population of a town has been increasing by factor of 4 every 5 years.	
7.	A 7% sales tax is added to all purchases.	

Answers: *See next page*

EXAMPLE 1

A mad scientist has figured out how to program his robots so that they can build and program *more* robots. It takes each robot one day to make and program a new robot. The mad scientist builds three robots before turning them loose to construct an army. Since each robot makes a new robot each day, the number of robots will double each day. The following table summarizes the number of robots he has at the end of each day:

Time (days)	# of Robots	Written with Multiples	Written with Exponents
0	3	3	3
1	6	3 × 2	3×2^1
2	12	3 × 2 × 2	3×2^2
3	24	3 × 2 × 2 × 2	3×2^3
4	48	3 × 2 × 2 × 2 × 2	3×2^4

Q1) Write an equation to model the number of robots after t days.

SOLUTION

We were told that the number of robots **doubles** each day. So we can see from the table that we get the next day's number of robots by **multiplying** by 2. This means we are dealing with *exponential growth*.

Exponents are just a shorthand for repeated multiplication. In the table, we can see how to write the number of robots using exponents. If, for example, we wanted to know how many robots he would have after **1 day**, it would be **3 × 2^1 = 6** robots. To see how many robots he'd have after 2 days, it would be **3 × 2^2 = 12,** and so on. So to model this growth, the number of robots after t days would be:

$$f(t) = 3(2)^t$$

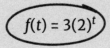

Answers: 1. *Exponential* 2. *Linear* 3. *Exponential* 4. *Linear*
5. *Exponential* 6. *Exponential* 7. *Linear*

523

PORTAL

Sometimes it is helpful to think of exponential growth as <u>repeated percent change</u>. When you do, you might write:

$$1 + \frac{c}{100}$$

instead of r, where c is the percent the quantity is being increased or decreased by. For more practice with percent change, go to page 550.

In the previous example, our model follows the standard equation for exponential growth:

$$\textit{Exponential Growth:} \quad f(t) = P(r)^t$$

Where P is the **starting amount**, r is the **rate** at which it is growing (or decaying), and t is the length of time it's been growing.

When it's Tougher

The majority of the time the basic exponential growth function above will be all you need to know. Occasionally, the SAT gives problems with more complicated time intervals that require you to tweak the basic equation. Suppose our mad scientist wanted to know how many robots he has in terms of *hours* instead of days. Then, the number doesn't double when $t = 1$, it doubles when $t = 24$ (robots don't need sleep). So how could we rewrite the equation to show this?

$$f(t) = 3(2)^{\frac{t}{24}}$$ # of robots doubles at $t = 24$

This way, the exponent doesn't become 1 until $t = 24$. Now, suppose he optimizes the programming so that the robots can make a new robot every **8 hours**. This means that the first doubling occurs at $t = 8$, so the exponent needs to be 1 when $t = 8$.

$$f(t) = 3(2)^{\frac{t}{8}}$$ # of robots doubles at $t = 8$

INTERACTIVE EXAMPLE 2

Kaja opened a new savings account. She determines that if she doesn't deposit or withdraw any money, the amount of money (in dollars) in the account after t years will be modeled by the equation:

$$f(t) = 8{,}000(1.03)^t$$

Q1) What was Kaja's initial deposit?

SOLUTION

The variable, t, is in the exponent, so we know we are dealing with an exponential model. The standard form of an exponential model is:

$$f(t) = P(r)^t$$

In the standard form, the starting amount is **P**. If we compare Kaja's model to the standard model, we can see that **P = $8,000**.

$$f(t) = P(r)^t$$

$$f(t) = 8{,}000(1.03)^t$$

TIP

In the financial world, the starting amount is often refered to as the *principal*. This is why we use the letter P in the general model for exponential growth.

TIP

In general, for interest problems, you can think of the rate as

$$r = 1 + \frac{I}{100}$$

where I is the interest rate.

Q2) What is the **interest rate** on the account?

A) 1.03%
B) 0.03%
C) 3.00%
D) 8,000%

SOLUTION

This one's a bit trickier! We want to know about the *interest* **rate**, so we want to look at **r = 1.03**. This tells us that the amount in the account at the end of one year, or $f(1)$, will be **1.03 times** the amount at the beginning of the year.

But we have to be careful. The interest is the **new money** added each year. If we were just multiplying by 1, then the money would never change. If we multiplied by 2, then the amount would double every year. So what does mutiplying by 1.03 mean? It means we're **increasing** the current balance by **3%** year.

C

PORTAL

For more on exponential graphs, turn to the *All About Graphs* chapter on page 422.

Q3) Which of the following graphs shows the growth of the money in Kaja's account?

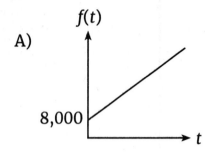

A)

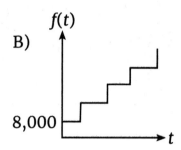

B)

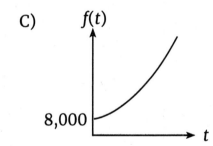

C)

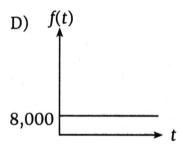

D)

TIP

Since you were given the model in this problem you can just graph it in Desmos to check which answer matches. However, you should be able to recognize the basic shape of an exponential function, as the test may not always give you the model.

SOLUTION

Let's look at each answer choice:

Choice A shows **linear** growth, where the growth rate (slope) is constant. We are dealing with **exponential** growth, where the amount earned increases each year. This one's out.

Choice B shows a step function. This is what the graph might look like if Kaja were regularly depositing money into her account in chunks. That isn't the situation though, so we can eliminate B.

Choice C looks good - it starts at 8,000 and then grows at an increasing rate, earning more and more each year. This kind of curve looks like exponential growth. C is probably the right answer.

Choice D shows Kaja's money remaining constant – she never has more than $8,000. This is what the graph might look like if Kaja just put the money under her mattress and forgot about it.

Thus, the answer is C!

C

INTERACTIVE EXAMPLE 3

Arturo is a chemist and discovers that the rate of a particular chemical reaction is dependent on the concentration of one of the reactants. The integrated rate law states that the concentration of this reactant decreases exponentially. Arturo runs experiments and finds that 10% of the remaining reactant is converted to products each minute. He starts an experiment with 350 grams of the reactant.

Q1) Which of the following equations could Arturo use to determine the amount of reactant remaining after t minutes?

A) $f(t) = 0.9(350)^t$
B) $f(t) = 350(0.1)^t$
C) $f(t) = 350(1.1)^t$
D) $f(t) = 350(0.9)^t$

TIP

If you don't remember how to construct an exponential function on the test (or otherwise encounter a function you aren't comfortable with), you can always try using Desmos to plug in values and see which answer choices give you results that make sense in context.

SOLUTION

The general form of an exponential equation, as we know, is

$$f(t) = P(r)^t$$

P is the starting amount, which here is **350**. This means we can immediately eliminate choice A.

r is the rate, the fraction of the initial amount that will be present when $t = 1$. Here, we know that it is **decreasing by 10%**. This means that r will be $1 - 0.10 = 0.9$. Alternately, you know that if it is decreasing by 10% there will be 90% left, so **r = 0.9**. So our formula would be:

$$f(t) = 350(0.9)^t$$

This matches answer choice D.

D

Q2) Rounding to the nearest gram, how much of the reactant has been converted after 10 minutes?

A) 0
B) 122
C) 228
D) 350

TRAP

Always double-check what the question is asking for before you decide you are done!

SOLUTION

In the previous problem, we found the formula for the amount of reactant remaining after t minutes. Let's plug in 10 for t:

$$f(t) = 350(0.9)^t$$

$$f(t) = 350(0.9)^{10} = 122$$

But be careful! Rereading the question, we notice that it doesn't ask how much is **left**, it asks how much has been *converted*. Since we started with 350 and have 122 left, we can subtract to find that $350 - 122 = $ **228 grams** have been converted. Tricky!

So the answer is **C**.

C

Practice Problems

Use your new skills to answer each question.

1

The number of bacteria in a sample doubles every hour. There are 25,000 bacteria in the sample at the start of an observation. Which of the following represents the number of bacteria, y, in the sample t hours after the start of the observation?

A) $y = \frac{1}{2}(25{,}000)^t$

B) $y = 2(25{,}000)^t$

C) $y = 25{,}000(\frac{1}{2})^t$

D) $y = 25{,}000(2)^t$

2

The population of birds in a state forest is estimated over the course of twelve years, as shown in the table below.

Year	Population
1994	200
1997	400
2000	800
2003	1,600
2006	3,200

Which of the following best describes the relationship between the year and the estimated bird population over the 12 year time period?

A) The estimated population of birds has increased linearly.
B) The estimated population of birds has decreased linearly.
C) The estimated population of birds has experienced exponential growth.
D) The estimated population of birds has experienced exponential decay.

3

Company XYZ had a poor earnings report, which resulted in its stock price of $142 dropping by 3% each day for five days after the report was released. Which of the following functions f models the company's stock price, in dollars, x days after the earnings report, where $x \leq 5$?

A) $f(x) = 142(0.97)^x$
B) $f(x) = 142(0.03)^x$
C) $f(x) = 0.97(142)^x$
D) $f(x) = 0.03(142)^x$

4

Which of the following scatterplots shows a relationship that is appropriately modeled by the equation $y = ax^b$, where both a and b are positive and $b > 1$?

A)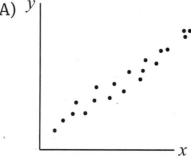

B)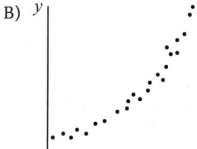

C)

D)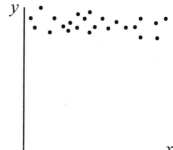

5

The population of lizards in a particular forest has increased every year since the start of a new wildfire preservation initiative. Scientists have determined that the population of lizards can be modeled by the function $f(t) = 2{,}000(1.08)^t$ where $f(t)$ is the number of lizards in the forest t years after the start of the initiative. Which of the following is the best interpretation of the y-intercept of the graph in this context?

A) The estimated lizard population the year the initiative was started was 2,000.

B) The estimated lizard population the year the initiative was started was 2,160.

C) The maximum lizard population since the start of the initiative was 2,000.

D) The maximum lizard population since the start of the initiative was 2,160.

6

The number of bacteria in a population t minutes after an initial observation can be modeled by the function:

$$f(t) = 45{,}000(2)^{\frac{t}{320}}$$

How much time, in minutes, does it take for the population to double?

7

A village located in a region that is in a severe drought has not been able to supply enough crops to its citizens. This has resulted in the population of the village decreasing by 6% every 2 years. If the current population of the village is 15,000, which of the following expressions shows the village's population t years from now?

A) $f(t) = 15,000(0.94)^{\frac{t}{2}}$

B) $f(t) = 15,000(0.94)^{2t}$

C) $f(t) = 15,000(0.06)^{\frac{t}{2}}$

D) $f(t) = 15,000(0.06)^{2t}$

8

The people in a town in Paraguay are currently trying to control the piranha population of a lake. The plan they will implement is predicted to decrease the number of piranhas by 22% every 3 years. The current population of piranhas is 2,000. This situation can be modeled by an exponential function of the form $P = C(.88)^{rt}$ where r and C are constants and P is the predicted population of the piranhas in the lake t years after the program is implemented. What is the value of r?

A) $\dfrac{1}{2000}$

B) $\dfrac{1}{3}$

C) 3

D) 2000

9

A 525-gram sample of an unknown substance is observed in a laboratory. Once the substance is put in a graduated cylinder filled with salt water, the substance starts to dissolve at an hourly rate of 4 percent. Which of the following functions f models the amount of dissolved substance, in grams, x hours later?

A) $f(x) = 525(0.96)^x$
B) $f(x) = 525(0.04)^x$
C) $f(x) = 525 - 525(0.96)^x$
D) $f(x) = 525 - 525(0.04)^x$

10

The mayor of a city in Kansas decided to increase the city's population by giving anyone who moved to the city a free t-shirt. This initiative caused a population boom where the number of residents increased by 8% every four months. If the initial population of the city was 5,000, which of the following expressions shows the city's population y years from now?

A) $f(y) = 5,000(1.08)^{4y}$

B) $f(y) = 5,000(1.08)^{3y}$

C) $f(y) = 5,000(0.92)^{4y}$

D) $f(y) = 5,000(0.92)^{3y}$

Applied Algebra

Tag: Advanced Math • Rational Expressions • Nonlinear Models

PORTAL

We first learned to solve for one variable in terms of others in *Basic Algebra*. Turn to 270 to review.

Alphabet Soup

The modeling problems in the last couple of chapters ask you to read or create a model, then use it to solve a problem. This chapter looks at problems that give you complicated looking models for involved situations. Luckily, you don't really need to understand what these models mean. Instead, your main task on these problems is to rearrange the complicated formula to solve for a specific variable.

As a warm-up, let's practice solving for different variables. The algebra rules you have practiced work just as well with a bunch of variables as they did when there were just one or two!

Fill in the blanks to complete the solution below.

If $s = 654 + 5.7t$, then $t = ?$	
1. *Rewrite equation*	
2. *Subtract to isolate t*	$s - (\quad) = 654 - (\quad) + 5.7t$
3. *Write the result*	$= 5.7t$
4. *Divide*	$=$
5. *Write the result*	$= t$

Answers: 1. $s = 654 + 5.7t$ 2. $654, 654$ 3. $s - 654$
4. $(s - 654) \div 5.7 = 5.7t \div 5.7$ 5. $(s - 654) \div 5.7 = t$

EXAMPLE 1

$$PV = nRT$$

For an ideal gas, the pressure P, volume V, number of moles n, and temperature T are related by the above equation through the proportionality constant R. Which of the following equations lets you solve for the temperature if you know the other variables?

A) $T = \dfrac{nR}{PV}$

B) $T = PVnR$

C) $T = \dfrac{1}{PVnR}$

D) $T = \dfrac{PV}{nR}$

Chemiwhat?

This equation comes from Chemistry, but (mercifully) you don't need to know a *thing* about Chemistry to solve these problems. They are just basic algebra problems in disguise.

DISCLAIMER:
We are in no way knocking Chemistry – it's actually pretty awesome when you get into it.

TIP

Variables won't always be the first letter of the word they represent, so it's always smart to check the paragraph!

Checking the answer choices is an easy way to see what variable you are solving for.

SOLUTION

First, **identify what you're solving for**: temperature.

Next, scan the paragraph (or just glance at the answer choices) to **find the variable** that represents temperature: T. So really, the problem is as simple as "solve the equation for T." We might not fully comprehend what happens to gassy moles under pressure, but we can *definitely* solve for T:

our focus!

① *rewrite the equation* $PV = nRT$

② *isolate T* $(\frac{1}{nR})PV = nRT(\frac{1}{nR})$

③ *celebrate. ya done.* $\dfrac{PV}{nR} = T$

D

(Gassy mole)

EXAMPLE 2

$$P = \frac{S-E}{S}$$

A company uses the above equation to determine what profit ratio P they get when they make S dollars worth of sales and have E dollars in expenses. Which of the following equations would allow the company to determine how much it needs to make in sales to reach a target profit ratio if expenses are fixed ?

A) $S = \dfrac{E}{1-P}$

B) $S = \dfrac{P-1}{E}$

C) $S = \dfrac{1-P}{E}$

D) $S = \dfrac{P-E}{P}$

SOLUTION

The first step is always to **determine what you are solving for**. In this case, we are asked for **sales**, which is represented by **S**.

  GOAL: solve for S $P = \dfrac{S-E}{S}$

Unfortunately, our target variable (**S**) is in both the top *and bottom* of the fraction. That's trouble. So let's multiply both sides by S to **get rid of that fraction** and go from there:

①	*clear denominator*	$(S)\,P = \dfrac{S-E}{S}(S)$
		$SP = S - E$
②	*gather the S's*	$SP - (S) = S - (S) - E$
		$SP - S = -E$
③	*factor out an S*	$S(P-1) = -E$
④	*solve for S*	$S = \dfrac{-E}{P-1}$ or $\boxed{\dfrac{E}{1-P}}$ **A**

EXAMPLE 3

$$E = \tfrac{1}{2}mv^2 + mgh$$

Conservation of energy tells us that the total energy E of a pendulum of mass m is constant at every point in its swing. The above equation shows how that energy is split between kinetic and potential energy at any given point, in terms of the pendulum's velocity v, its height h above the lowest point in its swing, and the gravitational constant g. Which of the following equations gives the height of the pendulum in terms of the other variables?

A) $h = \dfrac{E - \tfrac{1}{2}v^2}{g}$

B) $h = E - \tfrac{1}{2}mv^2 - mg$

C) $h = \dfrac{E}{mg} - \dfrac{v^2}{2g}$

D) $h = \dfrac{E - v^2}{mg}$

SOLUTION

The first thing we need to do is **formulate the first law of thermodynamics** for a compressible, closed system:

 (!) *just kidding*   *we = jk*

We defintely don't have to do that. While that *is* an impressive paragraph of physics goodness up there, we're just here to rearrange some formulas and go home. Our goal is to make balanced changes until height, **h**, is alone on one side:

(1) *rewrite equation* $E = \tfrac{1}{2}mv^2 + mgh$

(2) *subtract* $E - \tfrac{1}{2}mv^2 = mgh$

(3) *divide* $\dfrac{E - \tfrac{1}{2}mv^2}{mg} = h$

Hmm... we got **h** alone on one side but the equation doesn't match any of the answer choices! Our work is good so far, though, so there **must** be a way to simplify our equation...

Work with confidence!

If you carefully write out each step of your work, you can quickly check to see that you're on the right track when you hit a slight roadblock. That way, you can focus on finding a way **forward**.

Continued on next page →

So, now we have a new goal:

GOAL: simplify $\qquad h = \dfrac{E - \frac{1}{2}mv^2}{mg}$

What could we do to simplify? Well, one idea is to try **splitting the fraction**... so why not, let's try it:

(4) *split the fraction* $\qquad h = \dfrac{E}{mg} - \dfrac{\frac{1}{2}mv^2}{mg}$

(5) *cancel the m's* $\qquad h = \dfrac{E}{mg} - \dfrac{\frac{1}{2}\cancel{m}v^2}{\cancel{m}g}$

$$h = \dfrac{E}{mg} - \dfrac{\frac{1}{2}v^2}{g}$$

This looks familiar! Our equation is looking a lot like choice C:

C) $\quad h = \dfrac{E}{mg} - \dfrac{v^2}{2g} \qquad \longleftrightarrow \qquad h = \dfrac{E}{mg} - \dfrac{\frac{1}{2}v^2}{g}$

The only difference is a **2** in the denominator instead of a **1/2** in the numerator... and that's the same thing!

Think about it: we could write **1/2** as **2⁻¹**... and then drop the 2 to the denominator. Which means... *C is the correct answer!*

C

TIP

You can split a fraction when there are things being added or subtracted in the **numerator**.

If the addition was in the denominator we would have to find something else to try.

Practice Problems

Select the best answer choice for each question.

1

$$\frac{1}{T} = \frac{1}{R} + \frac{1}{S}$$

When two resistors are in parallel in a circuit, their combined resistance T is the reciprocal of the sum of the reciprocals of the resistance of the two individual resistors R and S as shown in the equation above. Which of the following equations gives the resistance S needs to have if we know the resistance of R and the desired combined resistance?

A) $S = \frac{T(R)}{R - T}$

B) $S = \frac{T(R)}{T - R}$

C) $S = R + T$

D) $S = \frac{T - R}{R(T)}$

2

$$V = IR$$
$$P = IV$$

When we are looking at an ideal circuit, the above equation explains the relationship between the voltage V, current I, resistance R, and power P. Which of the following equations gives an expression for the resistance of the circuit in terms of the voltage and power?

A) $R = \frac{V}{P}$

B) $R = \frac{V^2}{P}$

C) $R = \frac{P}{V^2}$

D) $R = \frac{P}{V}$

3

$$F = \frac{G(m_1 \cdot m_2)}{r^2}$$

The gravitational force F between two objects a distance r apart with masses m_1 and m_2 respectively is shown in the equation above. G is a gravitational constant. Which of the following expressions gives the mass of the first object in terms of the other values?

A) $m_1 = \frac{FGm_2}{r^2}$

B) $m_1 = -\frac{FGm_2}{r^2}$

C) $m_1 = \frac{Fr^2}{G} - m_2$

D) $m_1 = \frac{Fr^2}{Gm_2}$

4

$$\delta = \frac{1}{\sqrt{1 - (\frac{v}{c})^2}}$$

The Lorentz factor δ is important for a number of calculations in relativistic mechanics. In the above equation, v is the relative velocity of the object and c is the speed of light. Which of the following equations would let us find the relative velocity of the object if we knew the Lorentz factor?

A) $v = c\sqrt{1 - \frac{1}{\delta^2}}$

B) $v = c - \frac{c}{\delta}$

C) $v = c^2 - \frac{c^2}{\delta^2}$

D) $v = c\sqrt{\delta^2 - 1}$

5

$$n_1\sin(\Theta_1) = n_2\sin(\Theta_2)$$

When a ray of light passes between materials, it refracts. Snell's law, given above, describes the relationship between the angle of incidence Θ_1 in a material with index of refraction n_1 and the angle of refraction Θ_2 in a material with index of refraction n_2. A scientist knows the angle of incidence and index of refraction of the first material. If they want to find the necessary index of refraction to attain a specific angle of refraction in the second material, which of the following equations should they use?

A) $n_2 = n_1\sin(\Theta_1) - \sin(\Theta_2)$

B) $n_2 = \dfrac{\sin(\Theta_1)}{n_1\sin(\Theta_2)}$

C) $n_2 = \dfrac{n_1\sin(\Theta_1)}{\sin(\Theta_2)}$

D) $n_2 = \dfrac{n_1\Theta_1}{\Theta_2}$

6

$$v^2 = v_0^2 + 2a(x - k)$$

The above equation gives the square of the velocity v of a car given its initial velocity v_0, constant acceleration a, current position x and starting position k. Which of the following equations would allow you to solve for the starting position of the car if you knew its current position, acceleration, and current velocity?

A) $k = \dfrac{v_0^2 - v^2 - x}{2a}$

B) $k = v^2 - v_0^2 - 2ax$

C) $k = \dfrac{v^2 - v_0^2}{2ax}$

D) $k = x - \dfrac{v^2 - v_0^2}{2a}$

7

The real cash flow, R, in dollars, from a bank deposit after one year is given by $R = \frac{N}{1+I}$, where R is the real cash flow in dollars, N is the nominal cash flow in dollars, and I is the rate of inflation. Which of the following equations gives the rate of inflation in terms of real and nominal cash flow?

A) $I = \frac{N}{R} - 1$

B) $I = \frac{R-1}{N}$

C) $I = \frac{N}{R+1}$

D) $I = \frac{R}{N} + 1$

8

$$t = \sqrt{\frac{2h}{9.81}}$$

The time t it takes, in seconds, for an object to hit the ground after getting dropped from rest at a height h, in meters, is given by the equation above. Which of the following equations gives the height from which the object was dropped in terms of the time it took for the object to hit the ground?

A) $h = \sqrt{\frac{9.81t}{2}}$

B) $h = \frac{2t^2}{9.81}$

C) $h = \frac{9.81t^2}{2}$

D) $h = (9.81)(2)t^2$

9

$$\$2{,}750 + \$37E = B$$

The total operating budget for a certain manager each year is given by the equation above, where E represents the number of employees the manager oversees and B represents the total operating budget in dollars. Which of the following expressions gives the number of employees in terms of the total operating budget?

A) $E = \dfrac{2750 - B}{37}$

B) $E = \dfrac{2750 + B}{37}$

C) $E = \dfrac{B - 2750}{37}$

D) $E = \dfrac{B + 2750}{37}$

UNIT | Problem Solving and Data Analysis: Part 1

Chapters

Overview

Problem Solving and Data Analysis is a relatively broad category of questions on the SAT. There are a lot of different topics that fall into this basket, and they won't all show up on every test.

We'll start with this first unit, where we will learn the basics of working with **percentages**, doing **unit conversions**, and thinking about **probability and proportions**.

Percentages

Tags: Problem Solving & Data Analysis • Percentages

NOTE

Dividing by 100 is the same as moving the decimal point of the numerator two points to the left:

$$23\% = \frac{23}{100} = 0.23$$

You can use whichever form makes the most sense to you. Just know the test could use either one!

Percentages

The word percent tells us that we are looking at how many we get for every (**per–**) one hundred (**–cent**). This gives us the following equation for finding a percentage:

$$\frac{\%}{100} = \frac{piece}{whole}$$

Percentage questions focus on three components: the size of a piece, the size of the whole, and the percentage that represents that relationship. You'll be given two of these components and asked to find the third.

EXAMPLE 1

What is 15% of 60?

A) 4
B) 9
C) 15
D) 90

SOLUTION

Our first step with a word problem is to **translate into math**.

 Translate

~~What~~	is	15%	of	60?
?	=	.15	×	60

 Calculate

$$(.15)(60) = ?$$

$$(.15)(60) = \boxed{9}$$

Continued on next page →

TIP

Focus on which numbers are attached to "is" and "of".

(4 is) what percent (of 5)?

You can set up your work using the formula below:

$$\frac{is}{of} = \frac{\%}{100}$$

$$\frac{4}{5} = \frac{x}{100}$$

Then cross-multiply and solve for x!

Let's set up the same problem using a piece-over-whole fraction:

① *write percent formula* $\dfrac{\%}{100} = \dfrac{piece}{whole}$

② *fill in what we know* $\dfrac{15}{100} = \dfrac{x}{60}$

③ *solve for x* $60\left(\dfrac{15}{100}\right) = x$

                $\dfrac{90}{10} = x$

                ⑨ $= x$

B

Translate and solve the word problems below.

Problem	Solution
1. What is 60% of 15?	
2. 32 is 20% of what number?	
3. What percent of 70 is 14?	
4. 5% of 200 is two–fifths of what number?	
5. What is ⅓% of 170?	

Scratch Work

Answers: 1. $x = 0.60(15)$ 1. $32 = 0.20x$ 2. $\left(\frac{x}{100}\right)70 = 14$ 3. $0.05(200) = \frac{2}{5}x$ 4. $x = \frac{1/3}{100}(170)$

              $x = 9$ $x = 160$ $x = 20$ $x = 25$ $x = \frac{17}{30}$

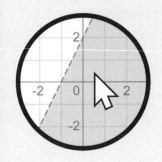

Desmos: Working with Percentages

Understanding how to translate percentages into math is important, especially for setting up more involved problems. However, for one step problems, Desmos can do some of the translation for you!

If you type "%" in Desmos, it will display as "% of", so if you need to find 35% of 80, you can input that directly:

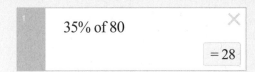

If you are asked "What percent of 80 is 28?", you can translate the "what" to x and "is" to = and input that. If you zoom out far enough, Desmos will give you the answer by graphing a vertical line at the correct value of x:

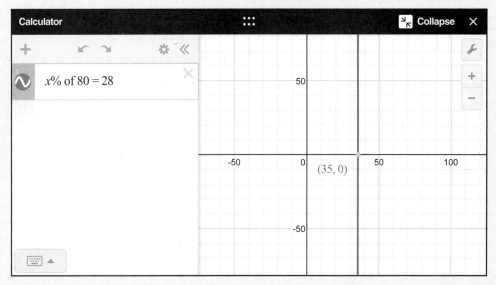

Similarly, if you were asked "28 is 35% of what number?" you can partially translate and get your answer from the graph.

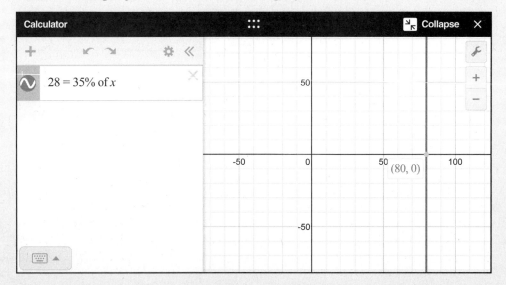

TIP

If you have a keyboard you can just use the % key. In Desmos's built in inputs, you can find it by tapping

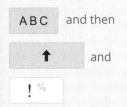

ABC and then

↑ and

! %

EXAMPLE 2

Pooja just returned from a backpacking trip and is going through the pictures she took. Of the 375 pictures, she finds that 28% contain at least one animal. How many of her pictures do not contain an animal?

A) 18
B) 72
C) 105
D) 270

TIP

Note that 28/100 is equivalent to 0.28. Once you get comfortable with percentages, you might be able to translate directly from "28% of 375 pictures" to **0.28(375)**.

It's a Trap!

Beware the traps the SAT lays in the wrong answers! If you aren't reading carefully, it would be easy to take 28% of 375 and think you are done. This gives 105, which is choice C!

SOLUTION

We know that **28%** of the pictures contain an animal, and there are a total of **375 pictures**. We can use the percentage to find out exactly how many of the 375 pictures contain an animal. If **a** is the number of pictures **with** animals, then:

1) *write percent formula* $\dfrac{\%}{100} = \dfrac{piece}{whole}$

2) *fill in what we know* $\dfrac{28}{100} = \dfrac{a}{375}$

3) *solve for a* $0.28(375) = a$

$$105 = a$$

Careful – we're not done yet! We are asked for the number of pictures **without** animals, which means we need to subtract 105 from our total:

4) *subtract 105 from total* $375 - 105 = \boxed{270}$

Bonus Solution
We could have easily skipped a step here. They told us that 28% of the pictures DO contain an animal, but asked for the number that do NOT contain an animal... which means that 28% isn't *really* our percentage. 100% – 28% = **72%**. *That's* the percentage of the whole without animals in them. This makes it simple:

5) *multiply whole by percent* $(0.72)(375) = \boxed{270}$ D

Percent change with decimals

Say you learn that the price of a pair of pants (x) has **increased by 20%**. Let's write that in words and then translate to math:

"the new price	is equal to	the price	plus	20% of the price."
new price	=	$(100\%)x$	+	$(20\%)x$

$$\textit{new price} = (120\%)x \ \text{ or } \ \boxed{1.2x}$$

Notice that, to show a 20% increase, we end up just **multiplying by 1.2**. This is an extremely helpful shortcut, and it works for decreases too. If you see a "20% decrease", you can write that as:

$$100\%x - 20\%x = 80\%x$$
$$1.0x - 0.2x = 0.8x$$

Write each percent increase or decrease **as a decimal**.

% Change	↑ 20%	↑ 18%	↓ 92%	↑ 8%	↓ 2.3%	↑ 120%
Decimal	1.2					

Answers: *bottom of next page*

EXAMPLE 3

Kendrick challenged his friend Sherane to a sit-ups competition. They each took 1 minute to complete as many sit-ups as possible. Kendrick told Sherane how many he did and she responded that she did 15% more. If Sherane did 46 situps, how many did Kendrick do?

A) 7
B) 39
C) 40
D) 54

TIP

We could work backwards here! Since we know that Kendrick did fewer sit-ups than Sherane, we know that choice D can't be right.

We can then calculate 115% of A, B, and C to see which one works out to 46.

SOLUTION

We should always start off word problems like this by translating into math. We know that Sherane did **15% more** than Kendrick. Fifteen percent MORE means 100% of Kendrick's amount **plus** another 15% of Kendrick's amount. Let's translate that:

(1) *Translate:* $S = 100\%K + 15\%K$

"S did 15% more than K" $S = 1K + .15K$

$S = 1.15K$

We're also told that Sherane did 46 situps. Let's plug that in for S:

(2) *substitute 46 for S* $46 = 1.15K$

(3) *solve for K* $\frac{46}{1.15} = K$

$\boxed{40} = K$

C

Compound Percentages

Imagine that you're out shopping and see a pair of pants on a mannequin marked "$100." Next to the mannequin is a sign that says **"50% off!"**, and, upon further inspection, you discover *another* sign that says *"take an additional 50% off!"* Now, odds are you wouldn't think:

"Sweet! Free pants!"

...and skip out of the store with the stolen goods. You'd understand intuitively that the first sign marked the pants down to about $50, and the second knocked it down to something like 20 or 30 bucks. In the "real world", this seems obvious. However, this is a common mistake students make when working with percentages on the test. Remember, you have to take each percent change one at a time:

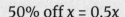

50% off $x = 0.5x$

50% off the 50% sale price $= 0.5(0.5x) = 0.25x$

PORTAL

How do you get to the top of Mount Everest?

One step at a time.

Word problems might sound complicated when you first read them, but each individual step is one you already know how to do! Turn to page 482 for practice with modeling word problems.

EXAMPLE 4

Eloise bought dinner at her favorite restaurant. She brought a coupon for 15% off the total cost of the meal. A 7% sales tax was added to the discounted price and Eloise added a 20% tip on the original price of the meal. In terms of the original price p, how much did Eloise pay?

A) $1.12p$
B) $(1.07)(0.85)(1.2)p$
C) $(1.07)(0.85) + (1.2)p$
D) $(1.07)(0.85)p + (0.20)p$

TIP

If you don't immediately see your answer in the choices, don't panic! See if you can simplify or rearrange your answer to get one of the choices. For example, here, a correct choice could even have looked like:

[(1.07)(0.85) + 0.2]p

There's a lot going on here, so let's work through one bit at a time. First, we're told she has a 15% coupon. This means **15% less**, which we can represent as **0.85p**.

$$\text{Discount price after coupon} = (1 - 0.15)p = \mathbf{0.85}p$$

Next, there is a **7%** sales tax **added** to this discounted price. To increase by 7%, we can **multiply the discount price by 1.07**.

$$\text{Discount Price + Sales Tax} = 1(0.85p) + 0.07(0.85p) = \mathbf{(1.07)(0.85}p\mathbf{)}$$

Then we just need to **add** the tip. We have to be careful here: it says the tip is **20% of the *original* price**, which we can represent as (0.20)p.

$$\text{Taxed Discount + Tip} = \boxed{(1.07)(0.85p) + (0.20)p}$$

D

Calculating Percent Change

Occasionally, you'll be asked to calculate a percent change by comparing a new and old value. For example, in keeping with our stolen pants example, you might be told that the pants were originally $52 and were marked down to $13. That's a great deal! But *how* great is it? To find the **percent change** between those prices, you can use this simple formula:

$$\% \text{ Change} = \frac{|new - old|}{old} \times 100$$

$$\% \text{ Change} = \frac{|13 - 52|}{52} \times 100 = \frac{39}{52}(100) = \boxed{75\% \text{ change}}$$

One thing to watch out for when working with percent change: this does NOT mean that the new price is 75% of the original price. Since we **decreased** by 75%, that means the new price is 100% – 75% = **25%** of the original price. Remember your piece-over-whole relationships and work out each step carefully!

Use the percent change formula to complete the table below.

#	Old Price	New Price	% Change
1	$200	$80	
2	$65	$39	
3	$1,000	$1,120	
4	$16	$1	
5	$11,235	$6,516.30	
6	$81,321	$47,166.18	

Answers: 3. 60%   1. 40%   2. 12%   3. 93.75%   4. 42%   5. 42%

Practice Problems

Use your new skills to answer each question.

1

What is 20% of 450?

A) 25
B) 45
C) 90
D) 430

2

Of 60,000 bottles produced in a factory, 9,000 are selected for inspection. What percentages of the bottles are selected for inspection?

A) 15%
B) 51%
C) 66%
D) 85%

3

On Friday, an ice cream shop sold 300 scoops of ice cream. On Saturday it sold 126% of the number of scoops it sold on Friday. How many scoops did it sell on Saturday?

4

36% of the seniors at Washington High School take AP Calculus. If there are 575 seniors, how many are taking AP Calculus?

A) 16
B) 36
C) 207
D) 517

5

The length of a certain rectangle is 74% of the height of the rectangle. Which expression represents the length of the rectangle where h is the height of the rectangle?

A) $0.074h$

B) $0.74h$

C) $7.4h$

D) $74h$

6

	robins	cardinals	chickadees	blue jays
Saturday	3	7	5	7
Sunday	4	9	7	8

Loretta went bird watching one weekend and recorded the number of the four most common birds she saw in the table above. If 24% of the birds she saw were her favorite type of bird, which bird is her favorite?

A) robin

B) cardinal

C) chickadee

D) blue jay

7

	Likes Spam	Does NOT Like Spam
Male	92	158
Female	8	242
Total	100	400

The owner of a local deli is considering the idea of selling spam. In order to decide if this is a good idea or not, the owner takes a survey of 500 of his customers. The results of his survey are shown in the table above. What percentage of his female customers like spam?

A) 16%

B) 8%

C) 3.2%

D) 1.6%

8

A shirt that originally costs $30 is on sale for 15% off. What is the sale price of the shirt?

A) $4.50
B) $15.00
C) $25.50
D) $34.50

9

The population in a town increased by 15% from 2015 to 2020. If the population of the town was x in 2020, which expression gives the population of the town in 2015?

A) $0.15x$

B) $1.15x$

C) $0.85x$

D) $\frac{x}{1.15}$

10

Bryant is looking at his power bill. He sees that in May when the weather was mild it was $48, and in July when he ran the AC a lot it was $178. Which of the following is the best estimate of the percent increase from May to July?

A) 2.7%
B) 3.7%
C) 270%
D) 370%

11

Liana went shopping and her bill came to $137.53 after an 8% sales tax was added. What was her total before the tax was added?

A) $126.52
B) $127.34
C) $129.83
D) $148.53

12

A triangle's base was increased by 15%. If its area is increased by 38%, what percent was the height of the triangle increased by?

Ratios & Proportions

Tags: Problem Solving & Data Analysis • Rates and Proportions • Ratios • Units

TIP

Percentages are an easy way to show how a piece relates to a whole. Ratios and proportions show how different pieces relate to each other.

Ratios show the relative size of different pieces

Say Zeke is purchasing materials to build a city of *identical block towers*, each of which is made out of 4 cubes, 3 cylinders, and 1 pyramid. That means for every 4 cubes that he buys, he needs to buy 3 cylinders and 1 pyramid. In math, we write that ratio using colons; the ratio of *cubes to cylinders to pyramids* is 4 to 3 to 1.

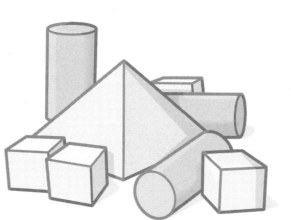 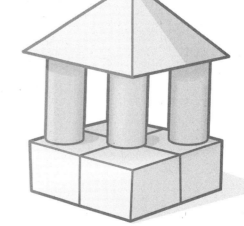

Scale a ratio by multiplying by a common factor

This ratio helps us figure out how many blocks of each type we need to build *more towers*. If we want to build 10 towers, we multiply each piece of the ratio by 10.

1 tower	4 cubes	:	3 cylinders	:	1 pyramid
	↓ (× 10)		↓ (× 10)		↓ (× 10)
10 towers	40 cubes	:	30 cylinders	:	10 pyramids

So we need 40 cubes, 30 cylinders, and 10 pyramids to make 10 towers.

Simplify ratios like you do fractions

The ratio doesn't *change* when we scale up to 10 towers, because ratios simplify just like fractions. We can cancel out any common factor:

$$\frac{40}{30} = \frac{4}{3}$$

$$40{:}30{:}10 = 4{:}3{:}1$$

The relationship of 40 to 30 is the same as the relationship of 4 to 3. In other words, the quantities are in the same **proportion**. We use this idea of proportions when we solve ratio problems.

You can think about ratios in different ways

A ratios problem will give you a ratio, tell you about one piece, and ask for information about another. Let's think through an example. Solve it if you can, then see *how* you thought about the solution.

NOTE

Continue using the same cubes to cylinders to pyramids ratio of 4:3:1.

THINK IT THROUGH

If Zeke used 12 cubes to build his towers, how many cylinders did he use?

SOLUTION

One way to think of this is as a **system of equations.** We can use what we know to figure out how many towers Zeke built, then scale up the 4:3:1 ratio to find the answer.

① *If there are 4 cubes per tower, how many towers require 12 cubes?*

$4x = 12$

$x = 3$ towers

② *If there are 3 cylinders per tower, how many are in 3 towers?*

$3x = ?$

$3(3) =$ **9 cylinders**

That works! But we can also think in terms of **proportions**...

Continued on next page →

TIP

Neither approach to this problem is "better" than the other. Depending on the way a test question is worded, one path may be clearer than the other.

We know the ratio is 4 cubes : 3 cylinders. That should be the case no matter how many towers we make. We need to find the number of cylinders that keeps this relationship when we have 12 cubes.

$$\frac{cubes}{cylinders} = \frac{4}{3} = \frac{12}{x} \rightarrow 4x = 36 \rightarrow x = 9$$

If we have 12 cubes, we need 9 cylinders to keep the proportion/ratio of 4:3.

TIP

If you write the ratio as a sum over its total, you can see the fraction represented by each piece.

$\frac{4+3+1}{8}$ cubes

$\frac{4+3+1}{8}$ cylinders

$\frac{4+3+1}{8}$ pyramids

You can use ratios to find fractions of the whole

If we know that Zeke only uses 3 types of blocks and that he uses cubes, cylinders, and pyramids in a ratio of 4:3:1, we can easily determine what fraction of the blocks are cubes:

$$\frac{piece}{whole} = \frac{4 \text{ cubes}}{4 \text{ cubes} + 3 \text{ cylinders} + 1 \text{ pyramid}} = \frac{4 \text{ cubes}}{8 \text{ blocks}}$$

Notice that the denominator of the fraction is found by taking the sum of each item in the ratio. The numerator is whatever piece you're focusing on. Let's practice working with ratios using a few examples.

EXAMPLE 1

Jasmine cuts a 72 inch rope into 3 pieces. The lengths of the pieces are in a ratio of 2 to 3 to 4. What is the length of the *shortest* piece, in inches?

A) 2
B) 8
C) 16
D) 24

TIP

The actual lengths of the pieces are <u>not</u> 2 inches, 3 inches, and 4 inches. That wouldn't add up to 72!

REFLECT

How did you think of the solution originally? Looking back, which solution looks better or easier to you?

SOLUTION

We are given three key pieces of information. First, the total length is **72 inches**. Next, there are **three pieces**. Finally, the **ratio** is **2:3:4**. We can solve this in a couple of ways.

Option 1: Set up an equation
The lengths are in a *ratio* that simplifies to 2:3:4. Multiplying by some common factor would give us lengths of $2x$, $3x$, and $4x$ that add up to 72. Let's use that information to find x, then find the shortest length.

   (1) *write what you know* $2x + 3x + 4x = 72$

   (2) *simplify* $9x = 72$

   (3) *find x* $x = 8$

Now we know what to multiply each piece of the ratio by to find the actual lengths of any piece. We are asked for the shortest:

   (4) *find the shortest length* $2x = 2(8) = \boxed{16}$

Option 2: Set up a fraction
Since we have the ratio of all 3 lengths, we can determine what fraction of the whole the shortest length is:

   (1) *what fraction is the shortest length?* $\dfrac{2}{2 + 3 + 4} = \dfrac{2}{9}$

   (2) *find that fraction of the total* $\dfrac{2}{9}(72) = \boxed{16}$

C

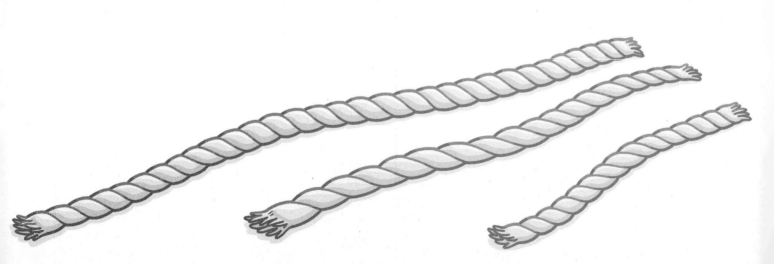

EXAMPLE 2

Karen's brownie recipe yields 16 brownies using 2 eggs and 5 tablespoons of cocoa powder. She wants to modify the recipe to make 24 brownies. If she increases all of the ingredients proportionally, how much cocoa powder will she need, in tablespoons?

A. 3

B. $6\frac{1}{3}$

C. $7\frac{1}{2}$

D. $9\frac{1}{3}$

SOLUTION

REFLECT

How did you think of the solution originally? Looking back, which solution looks better or easier to you?

This question may not immediately scream "RATIOS!" to you, but the word "proportionally" is your signal think in terms of ratios or rates:

$$\underset{eggs}{2} \underset{to}{to} \quad \underset{cocoa}{5} \quad \underset{to}{to} \quad \underset{brownies}{16}$$

Option 1: Set up an equation
Multiplying by the factor that takes us from 16 to 24 brownies will take us from 5 tablespoons of cocoa powder to the answer we need. So let's set up an equation to find that value:

(1) *write equation* $16x = 24$

(2) *find x* $x = \frac{24}{16}$ or $\frac{3}{2}$

Now we can scale up our cocoa powder by the same factor:

(3) *scale up 5 tablespoons* $5x = 5(\frac{3}{2}) = \frac{15}{2} = \boxed{7\frac{1}{2}}$

Option 2: Set up a fraction
We can see that the ratio is 5 *cocoa* : 16 *brownies*. That should be the case no matter how many brownies Karen makes. We need to find the number of tablespoons of cocoa powder that keeps this relationship when we have 24 brownies. Let's set up a fraction:

$$\frac{cocoa}{brownies} = \frac{5}{16} = \frac{x}{24} \rightarrow 16x = 120 \rightarrow x = \boxed{7\frac{1}{2}}$$

C

VOCAB: Directly and Inversely Proportional

If two quantities x and y are related proportionally, that means that one quantity grows (or shrinks) as the other quantity grows (or shrinks). The number of cube blocks was proportional to the number of towers, and the amount of cocoa was proportional to the number of brownies. You can always think of proportional quantities in terms of ratios, but you should know some vocab the test may throw at you.

- y is **directly proportional** to x if y *grows* when x grows.

$$\text{Directly Proportional: } y = kx$$

- y is **inversely proportional** to x if y *shrinks* when x grows.

$$\text{Inversely Proportional: } y = \frac{k}{x}$$

In these equations, k is called the **proportionality constant**. This is what determines *how much* y grows or shrinks for every change in x.

Let's solve the previous example about brownies in these terms.

Option 3: Set up a proportion
The number of brownies (b) is **directly proportional** to the amount of cocoa powder used (c). We know that 5 tablespoons of cocoa makes 16 brownies, so we can use that to find k:

(1) *set up proportion* $\qquad\qquad\qquad$ $b = kc$

(2) *plug in what you know* $\qquad\qquad$ $16 = k5$

(3) *find k* $\qquad\qquad\qquad\qquad\qquad$ $k = \frac{16}{5}$

Now that we have k, we can figure out the amount of cocoa we would need to bake ANY number of brownies! Let's solve for 24:

(4) *plug in 24 for b and $\frac{16}{5}$ for k* $\qquad$ $24 = \frac{16}{5}c$

(5) *solve for c* $\qquad\qquad\qquad\qquad$ $24(\frac{5}{16}) = c$

$\qquad\qquad\qquad\qquad\qquad\qquad$ $\boxed{7.5} = c$

$\qquad\qquad\qquad\qquad\qquad\qquad\qquad\qquad$ C

Unit Conversion

Unit conversion is really just working with ratios. When we say there are 100 centimeters in a meter, that is the same as saying that the ratio of centimeters to meters is 100 to 1. Most of the time, the SAT will provide the ratio for you on unit conversion problems, but they may expect you to know some common ones:

Common Unit Conversions	
1 yard = 3 feet	24 hours = 1 day
12 inches = 1 foot	7 days = 1 week
12 = 1 dozen	12 months = 1 year
100 centimeters = 1 meter	60 seconds = 1 minute
1000 meters = 1 kilometer	60 minutes = 1 hour

EXAMPLE 3

The density of gold is 19.3 grams (g) per cubic centimeter (cm³). A solid gold necklace is crafted from 4.6 cubic centimeters of gold. About how many <u>ounces</u> does the necklace weigh? (1 ounce = 28.35 grams)

A) 3.13
B) 6.75
C) 118.95
D) 2516.91

SOLUTION

Our goal here is to find the number of ounces the necklace weighs. The note that (1 ounce = 28.35 grams) means that we should probably start by finding how many <u>grams</u> the necklace weighs.

You might be completely comfortable working with density from your science classes, but if you aren't don't let this problem scare you! You can work with density just as you work with any other rate or ratio. A density of 19.3 grams per cubic centimeter means that for every 1 cubic centimeter you get 19.3 grams.

Continued on next page →

Option 1:

Set it up as a ratio: 19.3 grams to 1 cubic centimeter.

And we want to find x grams to 4.6 cubic centimeters, so we need to scale our ratio up by 4.6. Multiplying both parts by 4.6 gives us 88.78 grams to 4.6 cubic centimeters, so the necklace weighs 88.78 grams.

Then we have the ratio 1 ounce = 28.35 grams and need to scale it to y ounces = 88.78 grams. So we are scaling the ratio here by y, our unknown number of ounces. This tells us that $28.35 \cdot y = 88.78$, so y is about 3.13.

Option 2:

Let's think in terms of fractions and unit labels. Our necklace is 4.6 cm³ and we can write the density as $\frac{19.3\,\text{g}}{1\,\text{cm}^3}$. Then if we multiply these together we can "cancel" the cm³ and will be left with grams:

$$4.6\,\cancel{\text{cm}^3} \cdot \frac{19.3\,\text{g}}{1\,\cancel{\text{cm}^3}} = 88.78\,\text{g}$$

Then we can can write our unit conversion ratio from ounces to grams as $\frac{1\,\text{ounce}}{28.35\,\text{g}}$ so that we can multiply again to cancel out the grams and get to the ounces we need:

$$88.78\,\cancel{\text{g}} \cdot \frac{1\,\text{ounce}}{28.35\,\cancel{\text{g}}} = \frac{88.78}{28.35}\,\text{ounce} \approx 3.13\,\text{ounce}.$$

A

EXAMPLE 4

The average flight speed of a particular gryphon is 78 km/hr. At this rate, which of the following is closest to the distance, in kilometers, the gryphon can travel in 13 <u>minutes</u>?

A) 6
B) 17
C) 360
D) 1,014

SOLUTION

You might see this problem and recall that:

$$distance = rate \times time$$

The only problem is that the time unit in the given rate (km/hr) is not the same as the unit we are asked about (minutes)! Since the rate is already in hours, let's just convert 13 minutes into hours. There are 60 minutes in an hour, so:

TIP

You could also convert speed into km/min, and then multiply by 13.

$$13 \ \cancel{minutes} \times \frac{1 \ hour}{60 \ \cancel{minutes}} = \frac{13}{60} \ hr$$

So we know that the gryphon flies 78km per hour, and we want to know how far it would get in $\frac{13}{60}$ of an hour:

$$\frac{13}{60} \ \cancel{hr} \times \frac{78km}{1 \ \cancel{hr}} = \boxed{16.9 \ km}$$

BONUS: Estimation

In the midst of all this hardcore math genius that we've got going on, it can be easy to forget that sometimes "just sorta estimating" can often work wonders. Take this problem for example...

13 minutes is a little under a quarter of an hour. Which means the gryphon will fly *about* a quarter of the distance it would fly in an hour. We know it flies 78km in an hour, so...

$$78 \div 4 = 19.5$$

The only answer that's close to that number is **Choice B**, 17 km. Behold, the power of estimating!

B

How many square feet in 6 square yards?

Watch out if your brain immediately said *"18!"* You can't use the same ratio for *area* that you use for *length*. To see why, let's convert a 2 yards by 3 yards rectangle from **square yards** to **square feet**.

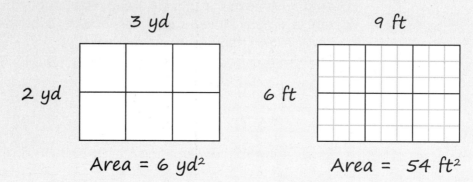

The ratio of their **lengths** is 1 to 3, but the ratio of their **areas** is 1 to 9. Square feet and feet are not the same unit - the first measures area and the second measures length! When unit conversions show up in problems with area or volume, it is often easiest to convert any lengths you are given before computing areas and volumes. If you do need to convert areas or volumes directly, be extra careful to use the correct ratio!

Practice Problems

Use your new skills to answer each question.

1

A machine produces widgets at a constant rate of 35 widgets per minute. At what rate, in widgets per <u>hour</u>, does the machine produce the widgets?

2

A marathon is a race with a course that is about 26.2 miles long. The average time to complete the marathon in a particular race was 4 hours and 35 minutes. Which of the following is the the best approximation of the average speed, in <u>minutes per mile</u>, of the contestants in this race?

A) 0.1
B) 5.7
C) 10.5
D) 16.7

3

In a bag of marbles, the ratio of green marbles to yellow marbles is 3 to 5. There are 30 green marbles in the bag. How many yellow marbles are in the bag?

A) 11
B) 18
C) 30
D) 50

4

x	y
2	6
4	12
8	24
a	105

In the table above, the ratio of y to x for each ordered pair is constant. What is the value of a?

A) 16
B) 35
C) 101
D) 315

5

A trail is 3,700 meters long. To the nearest tenth of a mile, how many <u>miles</u> long is the trail? (1 mile =1609 meters)

6

Virginia is laying out a path using 10 inch square paving tiles. If the path is 15 feet long, how many tiles will she need to complete it? (12 inches = 1 foot)

A) $\frac{3}{2}$

B) 8

C) 18

D) 180

7

As lava flows and cools, the radius of a particular volcanic island is growing at an average rate of 0.75 inches per hour. Given that there are 12 inches per foot, about how many days will it take for the island's radius to grow by 3.5 feet?

A) 2.33
B) 4.67
C) 31.75
D) 42

8

In a chemistry lab, two identical beakers each contain 150 milliliters of liquid. The liquid in the first beaker has a density of 2.5 grams per milliliter. The liquid in the second beaker has a density of 1.3 grams per milliliter. What is the difference, in <u>grams</u>, of the weights of the two beakers and their liquids?

A) 1.2
B) 55
C) 180
D) 195

9

Rectangle R has a length of 25 and a width of w. Rectangle S has a length of 30 and the same length to width ratio as rectangle R. What is the width of rectangle S in terms of w?

A) $\frac{5}{6}w$

B) $\frac{6}{5}w$

C) $w + 5$

D) $w - 5$

10

A large park has an area of 1.46 square miles. What is the area, in <u>square yards</u>, of this park? (1 mile = 1,760 yards)

A) 1,205
B) 2,570
C) 2,121,644
D) 4,522,496

11

Eduardo is going to convert 279 Euros to US dollars. The currency exchange service has posted that the current exchange rate is 1 US dollar = 0.93 Euros and it will charge a 1.5% fee on the converted amount. How many US dollars will Eduardo receive after the fee is applied?

A) $255.58
B) $259.47
C) $295.50
D) $305.50

Probability

Tags: Problem Solving & Data Analysis • Probability

Probability is a tool for measuring the likelihood that something will happen on a scale of 0 (not gonna happen) to 1 (definitely happening).

0	0.5	1
not gonna happen	*a coin flip*	*definitely happening*

If you are computing a probability based on data given, there are two things you need to determine:

- **Event**: the set of possible outcomes that meet some requirement
- **Sample space:** The set of all possible outcomes

Once you know these numbers, you can calculate the probability:

$$\text{Probability of an event} = \frac{\# \text{ of outcomes in event}}{\# \text{ of outcomes in sample space}}$$

A roll of a 6-sided die has a sample size of 6

If we roll a standard 6-sided die, there are **six possible outcomes**.

$$\# \text{ of possible outcomes } \{1, 2, 3, 4, 5, 6\} = 6$$

TIP

To convert a **percent chance** into a probability, just divide by 100.

For example, if something has a 20% chance of happening, then the probability it occurs is 0.20.

TIP

Probability has some fancy vocabulary that it is good to be aware of, but you can also think about the **event** as the **piece** you care about and the **sample space** as the **whole** so that this is just another version of piece over whole!

572

What's the probability of rolling a 1?

How many outcomes in our sample space meet this requirement?

# of outcomes in event = 1

$$Probability\ of\ rolling\ a\ 1 = \frac{\{1\}}{\{1, 2, 3, 4, 5, 6\}} = \frac{1}{6} \approx 0.167$$

TIP

We can write probability as a function P. If we call the event of rolling a 1 **event A**, we can say:

$$P(A) \approx 0.167$$

What's the probability of rolling an even number?

How many outcomes in our sample space meet this requirement?

# of outcomes in event = 3

$$Probability\ of\ rolling\ an\ even\ number = \frac{\{2, 4, 6\}}{\{1, 2, 3, 4, 5, 6\}} = \frac{3}{6} = 0.50$$

What's the probability of rolling at least a 3?

How many outcomes in our sample space meet this requirement?

# of outcomes in event = 4

$$Probability\ of\ rolling\ at\ least\ a\ 3 = \frac{\{3, 4, 5, 6\}}{\{1, 2, 3, 4, 5, 6\}} = \frac{4}{6} \approx 0.67$$

TIP

Probability can be shown as either a fraction or a decimal. To convert a fraction to a decimal, just divide the numerator by the denominator.

EXAMPLE 1

Grade Level	Number of Students
9th	6
10th	3
11th	4
12th	5

The student council at Forest View High School will randomly choose 1 student representative from the council. The number of student council members in each grade level is given in the table above. Which of the following is equivalent to the probability that the randomly chosen student is <u>not</u> a 9th grader?

A. $\frac{1}{3}$

B. $\frac{2}{3}$

C. $\frac{1}{2}$

D. $\frac{1}{6}$

SOLUTION

Option 1: Calculate directly

The problem is asking for a probability and gives us data, so we need to identify the sample space, the event, and the size of each:

sample space: to find the council size, we can add up the numbers in the right column: 6 + 3 + 4 + 5 = **18 students**.

event size: the number of students who are NOT a 9th grader is 3 + 4 + 5 = **12 students**.

Now we can find the probability using our equation:

$$P(\text{not in 9th grade}) = \frac{12}{18} = \left(\frac{2}{3}\right)$$

Continued on next page →

VOCAB

Two events are **complements** if every possible outcome is in exactly one of the events. Since the result MUST be one of the two events, then the **sum of their probabilities is 1**.

Option 2: Complementary events

We are interested in the event "not in 9th grade" but we could start by looking at the event "in 9th grade." The table tells us there are 6 students in the 9th grade, so

$$P(in\ 9th\ grade) = \frac{6}{18} = \frac{1}{3}$$

Once we know the probability of the student being in 9th grade, we can find the probability of the student NOT being in 9th grade by subtracting from 1:

$$P(in\ 9th\ grade) + P(NOT\ in\ 9th\ grade) = 1$$

$$P(NOT\ in\ 9th\ grade) = 1 - P(in\ 9th\ grade)$$

$$P(NOT\ in\ 9th\ grade) = 1 - \frac{1}{3} = \boxed{\frac{2}{3}}$$

B

EXAMPLE 2

	Shady Grove	Johnson Park
Swallowtails	12	6
Monarchs	18	10
Other	7	5

Kai is studying butterfly populations at two local parks. He spent an afternoon at each park catching, classifying, and releasing butterflies. The table above shows a record of all butterflies caught during the afternoon. Assuming that Kai's sample is representative of the butterfly populations in each park, what is the probability that a random butterfly caught in Shady Grove will be a swallowtail?

A) $\frac{3}{17}$

B) $\frac{7}{17}$

C) $\frac{12}{37}$

D) $\frac{28}{37}$

PORTAL

For this question, you don't need to worry about what a "representative sample" is.

However, if you're curious, check out the *Study Design* chapter on page 623 to see how the SAT will test this idea directly.

SOLUTION

We are asked for the probability that a butterfly caught in Shady Grove will be a swallowtail. That means our proportion will be:

$$\text{probability} = \frac{piece}{whole} = \frac{\#\ of\ swallowtails\ in\ Shady\ Grove}{total\ \#\ of\ butterflies\ in\ Shady\ Grove}$$

Our job then is to find the values for the numerator and the denominator using the table. First, let's grab the numerator. The # of swallowtails in Shady Grove can be found in the first row of the Shady Grove column: **12 swallowtails.** Let's fill that in:

$$\text{probability} = \frac{piece}{whole} = \frac{12\ swallowtails}{total\ \#\ of\ butterflies\ in\ Shady\ Grove}$$

Now to find our denominator. The table doesn't tell us any totals, so we'll need to add up the Shady Grove column ourselves...

$$\text{Shady Grove total} = 12 + 18 + 7 = 37$$

Adding up the Shady Grove column, we get **37** for our "whole" population. That's our denominator, and it gives us an answer!

$$\text{probability} = \frac{12\ swallowtails}{37\ butterflies\ in\ Shady\ Grove} = \boxed{\frac{12}{37}}$$

There we have it! The probability of catching a swallowtail butterfly in Shady Grove is 12 over 37. Our answer is **C**!

C

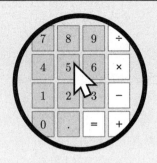

Desmos Reminder

As we talked about earlier, probabilities are all numbers between zero and one. Answer choices will sometimes give them as fractions and sometimes as decimal values. If you have one and need the other, Desmos is your friend. Any time you type a fraction or decimal into the entry box you will get the ⊕ symbol. Remember that clicking it will switch the answer between fraction and decimal mode!

EXAMPLE 3

	< 70%	70-90%	91-100%	Total
Teacher A	3	15	7	25
Teacher B	5	10	12	27
Total	8	25	19	52

The data in the table summarize the results of a Calculus test. There are two sections of the class, each taught by a different teacher. The number of students in each class whose score fell within a given range is recorded above. If a student is chosen at random from among those who scored a 70 or above, what is the probability that student is from Teacher A's section?

A) 0.25
B) 0.48
C) 0.50
D) 0.52

We need to determine the total **population** we are choosing the student from, and the **trait** that we're interested in.

The question says "If student is chosen at random from among those who scored a 70% or above..." so our population is **all students who scored 70 or above**. This means we need to add up all students in the "70-90%" and "91-100%" columns. Luckily, we have a "total" row that we can use.

	< 70%	70-90%	91-100%	Total
Teacher A	3	15	7	25
Teacher B	5	10	12	27
Total	8	**25**	**19**	52

$$25 + 19 = 44$$

So our population of students who scored 70% or above is **44**.

We want to find the probability that a student in this population is in Teacher A's section. To do that, we should focus on just the first row for those same two columns:

	< 70%	70-90%	91-100%	Total
Teacher A	3	**15**	**7**	25
Teacher B	5	10	12	27
Total	8	**0**	**19**	52

$$15 + 7 = 22$$

There are 22 students who scored a 70% or above in Teacher A's section. That's the "piece" with the trait we want! Now we can set up our proportion. Looking at the answer choices, we can see that we need to divide our fraction to get a decimal:

$$probability = \frac{\#\ with\ trait}{population} = \frac{22}{44} = \frac{1}{2} = \boxed{0.50}$$

C

Practice Problems

Use your new skills to answer each question.

1

Color	Number
Black	12
Brown	8
White	20
Total	40

The table shows the number of different colors of socks in a drawer. If a sock is chosen at random from the drawer, what is the probability that it will be brown?

2

Of the 20 candies in a bowl, 5 contain nuts. If someone chooses a candy randomly, what is the probability that the chosen candy contains nuts?

A) $\frac{1}{20}$

B) $\frac{1}{4}$

C) $\frac{1}{5}$

D) 4

3

Each face of a fair 12-sided die is labeled with a number from 1–12, with a different number appearing on each face. If the die is rolled one time, what is the probability of rolling a 5?

A) $\frac{1}{12}$

B) $\frac{5}{12}$

C) $\frac{7}{12}$

D) $\frac{11}{12}$

4

	Math	Reading	Writing	Total
Baseball	15	39	50	104
Basketball	7	32	11	50
Soccer	20	19	7	46
Total	42	90	68	200

The graph above shows the distribution of preferred subject in school and preferred sport to play for 200 students at a local high school. If a student is chosen at random, what is the probability that the student will be a soccer player whose favorite subject in school is writing?

A) 0.035
B) 0.103
C) 0.152
D) 0.255

5

A bag contains a total of 80 tiles that are identical except for color. A tile will be randomly selected from the bag. If the probability that a randomly selected tile is green is 0.15, how many tiles in the bag are green?

6

A flower garden has n plants with white flowers and 8 plants with yellow flowers. There are no other plants in the garden. If a plant is selected at random, what is the probability of selecting a plant with yellow flowers in terms of n?

A) $\dfrac{n}{8}$

B) $\dfrac{n}{n+8}$

C) $\dfrac{8}{n}$

D) $\dfrac{8}{n+8}$

7

Results of a Math Test					
	100-90	89-80	79-70	69-60	≤ 59
Attended review sessions	15	10	2	1	0
Did NOT attend review sessions	8	8	6	6	4

The table above summarizes the results of 60 high school students who took the same math test. If one of the high school students who made an 80 or higher was chosen at random, what is the probability that the student attended the review sessions?

A) $\dfrac{15}{26}$

B) $\dfrac{7}{18}$

C) $\dfrac{15}{41}$

D) $\dfrac{25}{41}$

8

Height (inches)	Number
at most 48	2
49 - 54	6
55 - 60	12
61 - 66	10
67 - 72	4
over 72	1

Students in a statistics class recorded their heights in the table above. Of those students who are at least 55 inches tall, what fraction are at most 66 inches tall?

A) $\frac{22}{35}$

B) $\frac{22}{27}$

C) $\frac{27}{35}$

D) $\frac{5}{27}$

9

There are 25 dogs playing at a dog park. Each dog can be classified as large, medium or small. If one dog is selected at random, the probability of selecting a large dog is 0.24 and the probability of selecting a small dog is 0.32. How many of the dogs are classified as medium?

10

In a bag there are 8 solid colored marbles, 15 marbles with stripes, 12 marbles with a swirly pattern, and 6 cat's eye marbles. If one of the marbles is chosen at random, what is the probability that it is neither striped nor swirly?

UNIT

Problem Solving and Data Analysis: Part 2

Chapters

Overview

Problem Solving and Data Analysis is a relatively broad category of questions on the SAT. There are a lot of different topics that fall into this basket, and they won't all show up on every test.

We'll start this unit by learning the basics of **descriptive statistics** like mean, median, mode, range, and standard deviation. We'll then learn to model and interpret **data in two variables**. Finally, we'll learn how to draw appropriate conclusions from data with proper **study design**.

Basic Statistics

Tags: Problem Solving & Data Analysis • Descriptive Statistics • One Variable Data

The average is the sum divided by the count

The most straightforward statistics problems ask for the average (or mean) of a list of numbers. To find the average, find the **sum** of the numbers and divide by the **count**. If you wanted to find the average of the *first five integers*, you'd calculate:

$$\text{Average} = \frac{SUM}{COUNT} = \frac{1 + 2 + 3 + 4 + 5}{5} = \frac{15}{5} = ③$$

VOCAB

The sum of a data set is what you get if you add each item.

The count is the number of items in a data set.

NOTE

Some problems, like this one, will give you the individual values. Other problems may just give you a sum, average, or count.

EXAMPLE 1

Morgan went out to lunch for 5 consecutive days and spent the following amounts: $6.50, $11.78, $15.32, $9.21, and $9.17. To the nearest cent, what was the **average** cost of Morgan's lunches?

A) $5.52
B) $8.67
C) $10.00
D) $10.40

Just some average Count.

584

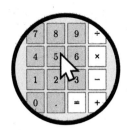

TIP

For the most basic questions involving means, you can use Desmos. For the data set here, you can type:

mean(6.5, 11.78, 15.32, 9.21, 9.17)

and Desmos will tell you that the mean is 10.396.

SOLUTION

To find the average, we need the sum and count. To find the sum, we just add up the prices we're given. Since we have 5 prices, the count is 5. Let's roll:

$$Average = \frac{SUM}{COUNT} = \frac{6.5 + 11.78 + 15.32 + 9.21 + 9.17}{5} = \frac{51.98}{5} = \boxed{10.396}$$

If we round that average to the nearest cent, we get **$10.40**.

D

Use what you're given to find what you need

The average formula is made up of three components: average, sum, and count. Often, the SAT will give you two of these and ask you for the third. Just **plug in what you know** and **solve for what you need**.

EXAMPLE 2

The mean of Jerome's scores on his first 3 calculus tests is 87. There are two tests remaining and he wants his final test average to be at least 90. What is the minimum mean he can get on his final two tests to achieve his goal?

A) 90
B) 91.5
C) 93
D) 94.5

TIP

Tackle multistep problems one bit at a time. If you can't see the path to the answer right away, follow this strategy:

1. Write what you know

2. Find out what you can

When you find new information, ask "how can I use this?" This will lead you through the problem.

SOLUTION

This is a multistep problem, but each step is just using the average formula to solve for a missing piece. Even if you can't see the path to the answer, just **find what you can** with what you're given.

(1) *write what you know* $87 = \dfrac{\text{sum of first 3 tests}}{3}$

(2) *find what you can* $261 = \text{sum of first 3 tests}$

This is a good start! We used the average formula, plugged in what we were given, and found new information. Let's keep going.

Continued on next page →

TIP

This problem is a great opportunity to try working backwards!

Let's write out Jerome's goal, using this new information. Over 5 tests, Jerome wants an average of 90. The only piece we don't know is the sum of the last 2 tests:

③ *write Jerome's goal* $$90 = \frac{261 + sum\ of\ last\ 2\ tests}{5}$$

④ *find what you can* $$450 = 261 + sum\ of\ last\ 2\ tests$$

$$189 = sum\ of\ last\ 2\ tests$$

Now we know the sum and count for the last 2 tests. We're set up to find the average:

⑤ *find average of last 2 tests* $$x = \frac{sum}{count}$$

$$x = \frac{189}{2}$$

$$x = \boxed{94.5}$$

D

TIP

If we had an even number of students, then nobody would be standing directly in the middle. In that case, the median is the **average of the two students in the middle.**

The median is the middle number

Average is only one way to describe a data set. The SAT will also ask about the **median** of a data set. For example, let's look at the heights of a college basketball starting lineup:

Height (in inches)				
77	75	73	77	79

When the data is arranged *in numerical order*, the **median** is the number smack-dab in the center. Since the heights above are not in numerical order, we need to rearrange to find the median:

73, 75, ⑦⑦, 77, 79

median

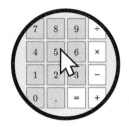

TIP

For the most basic questions involving medians, you can use Desmos. For the data set here, you can type:

median(69, 65, 22, 20, 31, 24, 28, 24, 21, 21, 21, 7)

and Desmos will tell you that the median is 23.

EXAMPLE 3

69, 65, 22, 20, 31, 24, 28, 24, 21, 21, 21, 7

The values listed above show the number of points scored by the Green Valley high school football team in the first 12 games of the season. What was the median number of points?

A) 21
B) 22
C) 23
D) 24

SOLUTION

Any time you are looking for the median, the first step is to rewrite the numbers in numerical order:

7, 20, 21, 21, 21, 22, 24, 24, 28, 31, 65, 69

Now we need to find the middle number. One way to do this is to cross of pairs of of highest/lowest numbers until only 1 or 2 numbers remain.

7, 20, 21, 21, 21, 22, 24, 24, 28, 31, 65, 69

We have 2 numbers left, so our median will be their *average*:

$$median = \frac{22 + 24}{2} = \boxed{23}$$

C

mode (n.)

The word *mode* can mean "a fashion or style in clothes, art, literature, etc."

In fact, "mode" is the French word for "fashion."

When something is in fashion, you tend to see it everywhere—just like the mode in a data set!

The mode is the number that occurs most often

In our data set, the number 77 occurs *twice*, while every other number occurs only once. That means our **mode** is 77.

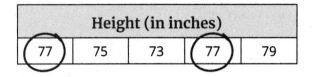

Height (in inches)				
77	75	73	77	79

The range is a measure of data's spread

Measures of spread describe how similar or varied the set of observed values are. The **range** of a set of data is the difference between the largest and smallest values. A large range suggests that the data set is spread out, while a small range suggests that it is highly concentrated. In our data set, the shortest person has a height of 73 inches and the tallest has a height of 79 inches, so the range is:

$$\text{Range} = 79 - 73 = 6 \text{ inches}$$

Fill in the statistics for each data set below.

Set A 4, 4, 7, 10, 1, 6, 3, 3, 4, 4	1. *mean* =
	2. *median* =
	3. *mode* =
	4. *range* =

Set B 17, 18, 16, 20, 20, 20, 36, 39, 39, 38	5. *mean* =
	6. *median* =
	7. *mode* =
	8. *range* =

Set C 12, 12, 12, 11, 12, 13, 14, 12, 11	9. *mean* =
	10. *median* =
	11. *mode* =
	12. *range* =

Answers: 1. 4.6   2. 4   3. 4   4. 9   5. 26.3   6. 20

7. 20   8. 23   9. 12.1$\bar{1}$ 10. 12   11. 12   12. 3

deviate (v.)

The verb "to deviate" means to stray or swerve from a primary path.

So it makes sense that small "deviations" mean the data is tightly clustered, while large deviations mean it's all over the place.

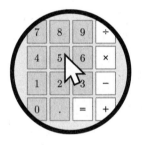

TIP

You should never have to actually calculate the standard deviation, but if you have a data set and want to, Desmos can help. For Data Set A here you can type:

stdev(4, 4, 7, 10, 1, 6, 3, 3, 4, 4)

and Desmos will tell you that the standard deviation is about 2.5.

Standard Deviation

The **standard deviation** is a measure of the average distance between any given data point and the mean. In our data set, it would tell us whether there were a lot of different heights in the lineup, or if players were mostly similar in height. Luckily, the SAT doesn't require you to compute the standard deviation. Instead, you may need to estimate which of 2 sets likely has the larger or smaller standard deviations.

Tools for estimating standard deviation:

- The minimum possible standard deviation is 0 and occurs when every number in a set is identical.

- Larger range tends to lead to larger standard deviations.

- Data points far from the mean increase standard deviation.

TRY IT OUT

Order Sets A, B, and C from the exercise on the previous page from smallest standard deviation to largest.

SOLUTION

In Set C, the numbers are tightly clustered around the mean (12). Its range (3) is the smallest of the sets. This set probably has the smallest standard deviation.

Set A is more spread out than Set C, but there are still many points clustered around the mean (4.6). The range (9) is larger than Set C's, but not as large as Set B's.

Set B has the largest range (23). Notice that the mean is 26.3 but the closest point to the mean (20) is a whole 6.3 away! These two factors mean Set B likely has the largest standard deviation.

Standard Deviations: Set C < Set A < Set B

Boxplots

A boxplot is a way to visualize five different statistics in a given data set, including: ① the minimum value, ② the 25th percentile, ③ the median, ④ the 75th percentile, and ⑤ the maximum value.

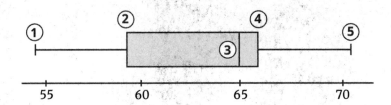

This boxplot tells us that the minimum value is just below 55, the 25th percentile is just below 60, the median is right at 65, the 75th percentile is about 66, and the maximum value is just above 70.

INTERACTIVE EXAMPLE

Number of cars washed								
Time	9–10	10–11	11–12	12–1	1–2	2–3	3–4	4–5
Saturday	3	5	7	8	6	4	6	5
Sunday	2	3	2	10	5	5	3	5

To raise funds for their high school e-sports team, a number of students held a weekend carwash. They washed cars each day, starting at 9 a.m. and going until 5 p.m. The above table lists the number of cars that were washed during each hour. Use the data in the table to answer the questions below.

Q1) Finish the following histogram to accurately represent the data.

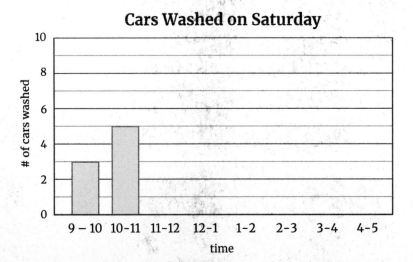

Cars Washed on Saturday

TIP

The *x*-axis on this dot plot lists the possible # of cars washed each hour. The number of dots above each possibility is just a count of the number of times that # shows up in the table.

Here, we see no 0's or 1's in the table for Sunday, so there are **no dots** above them. We see "2" twice, so there are **two dots**, etc.

Q2) Finish the following dot plot to accurately represent the data:

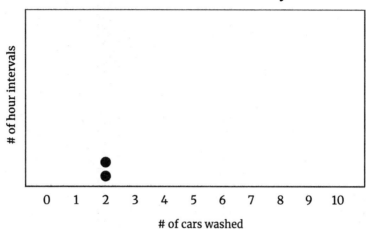

Cars Washed on Sunday

Stack dots to show the # of times each number shows up in the "Sunday" row

Q3) What was the median number of cars washed per hour on Saturday?

S1) Since we are looking for the **median**, we need to put the data for Saturday in numerical order. Fill in the blanks below, starting with the smallest number and ending with the largest:

_____ , _____ , _____ , _____ , _____ , _____ , _____ , _____

How many data points are there? _____

Since there are an **even** number of data points, we need to average the two middle terms to find our median. In other words, we need a number that is directly between the two numbers in the middle of the list. If they are the same number, then it's just that number!

Median: _____

Answers: 3. List = 3, 4, 5, 5, 6, 6, 7, 8   Data points = 8   Median = 5.5

Q4) What was the **mean** number of cars washed per hour on Sunday?

Q5) Which day had the wider **range** of cars washed per hour?

Q6) Which day do you think has the larger **standard deviation**?

SOLUTION

To find the **mean** number of cars washed on **Sunday**, we take the data from the appropriate row of the table (or from the dot plot we made earlier), find the sum, and then divide by the total number of data points. **Fill in the blanks** below to find the mean:

$$\textbf{Mean} = \frac{sum\ of\ terms}{\#\ of\ terms} = \underline{\hspace{3cm}} = \underline{\hspace{3cm}}$$

The **range** is the largest value minus the smallest value. Fill in the blanks below to find the range for each day:

$$Range = Largest - Smallest$$

$$Saturday = \underline{\hspace{1.5cm}} - \underline{\hspace{1.5cm}} = \underline{\hspace{1.5cm}}$$

$$Sunday = \underline{\hspace{1.5cm}} - \underline{\hspace{1.5cm}} = \underline{\hspace{1.5cm}}$$

So the wider range is on which day? _____

The **standard deviation** is a measure of the spread of the data set. So we need to determine which day's data are **more spread out**. On both days, the data is fairly clustered EXCEPT for the hour where they washed **10 cars on Sunday**. This data point will significantly increase the standard deviation on Sunday.

Answers:

4. MEAN = $\frac{35}{8}$ = 4.375

5. Saturday = 8 − 3 = 5   Sunday = 10 − 2 = 8   Wider range = Sunday

6. The largest standard deviation is probably Sunday.

Some questions test your ability to think logically

Some questions ask for statistics without giving you the raw data set. In these cases, you can use logic or picking numbers to find the answer.

TIP

"Consecutive" numbers follow each other in order, without any gaps. So "consecutive even" numbers would be numbers you get by counting by 2.

EXAMPLE 4

A data set contains 10 consecutive even numbers. What is the difference between the mean and the median for this set?

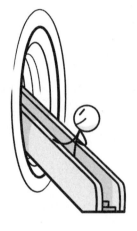

PORTAL

We can also pick numbers to solve this problem, though that can be more time-consuming. For practice with *Picking Numbers*, turn to page 262.

SOLUTION

One way to think about the mean of a data set is what you get if you evened out the distribution: borrowing from the bigger numbers and giving to the smaller ones. To help see this, imagine a row of **baskets of apples**, each with 2 more apples in than the one before. We have an even number of baskets (10), so the **median** falls between the two middle baskets. One basket has 1 fewer apples than the median, and the next has 1 more than the median. Imagine you move 1 apple from the larger basket to the smaller one; now, you've *averaged* the two middle baskets, leaving the median number of apples for the row in each basket.

Next, picture the baskets on either side of the middle two: the smaller one has 3 fewer apples than the median, while the larger has 3 more. Again, we can average these two to the median amount by moving 3 apples from the larger basket to the smaller.

We can repeat this process for each subsequent pair of baskets, and they'd always average out to the same number of apples as the median baskets. That shows us that if you have 10 consecutive, even numbers, the difference between their mean and median would always be <u>zero</u>.

Continued on next page →

EXAMPLE 5

Data set B is formed from data set A by adding 5 to every element of set A. Which of the following statements must be true?

I.   The mean of set A is 5 more than the mean of set B.
II. Set A and Set B have the same range.
III. The median of set B is 5 more than the median of set A.

A) I only
B) II only
C) II and III only
D) I, II and III

TIP

To pick numbers, just create set A then add 5 to each number for set B:

A: {4, 5, 16, 29, 40}

B: {9, 10, 21, 34, 45}

From here, you can calculate the mean, median, and range for each set and check the given statements.

SOLUTION

We could pick numbers to create our own data set, but it is safer and faster if we can think through each statement logically.

I. **The mean of set A is 5 more than the mean of set B.**

If each number in the set is larger, the average will be larger. Set B was formed by adding 5 to each term in set A. This means that the mean of set B should be *bigger* than the mean of set A, not the other way around, so this statement is FALSE.

Continued on next page ➡

II. Set A and Set B have the same range.

The range is the difference between the biggest and smallest numbers in the set, or how far apart they are on the number line. Since we added the same number (5) to each number, we simply shifted the biggest and smallest numbers the same distance up the number line, keeping the range the same. This statement must be TRUE.

III. The median of set B is 5 more than the median of set A.

If we add 5 to every number in set A, we do not change the order of the elements: we just shift them up the number line. This means that the median is also just shifted up by the same amount, so this statement is TRUE.

Since II and III are true and I is false, the answer is **C**.

C

EXAMPLE 6

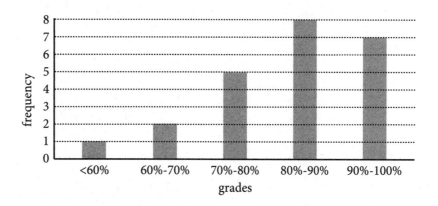

Mr. Evans created the histogram above to summarize the scores his students got on a recent test. Which of the following could be the median score for the class on this test?

A) 65 %
B) 72 %
C) 83 %
D) 96 %

SOLUTION

Note that we don't actually have all of the data we would need to calculate the median. However, this question doesn't ask us to determine what the median definitely <u>is</u>, it just asks us to use the information we are given to determine whether the numbers we are given *could* be the median.

While we can't determine the median exactly, we can determine **which of the histogram bars contains the median**. By counting up the number of students represented by each bar, we can determine that there are 1 + 2 + 5 + 8 + 7 = **23 students** in the class. That means there should be 12 students below the student with the median score and 12 students above the student with the median score. If we start counting up 12 students from the left...

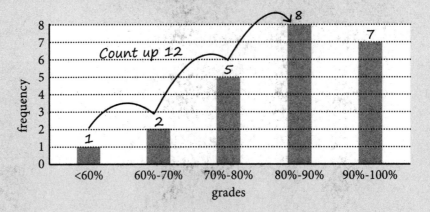

...we need to dip into the 80%-90% group to reach 12 students. That means the median *must* be between 80% and 90%, making **choice C** the only answer.

C

Practice Problems

Use your new skills to answer each question.

1

A list of 8 data values is shown.

$$15, 20, 45, 24, 16, 4, 37, 15$$

What is the mean of these data?

2

Number	Frequency
3	4
5	3
6	2

Which list of data is correctly represented by the frequency table above?

A) 3, 3, 3, 3, 5, 5, 5, 6, 6
B) 4, 4, 4, 3, 3, 3, 3, 3, 2, 2, 2, 2, 2, 2
C) 2, 3, 3, 4, 5, 8
D) 12, 12, 15

3

Over the course of 10 days, a certain town had 4.7 inches of rainfall. Which of the following can be calculated from this information?

A) The number of days it rained
B) The average number of inches of rain that fell per day
C) The median number of inches of rain that fell per day
D) The greatest number of inches of rain that fell on a single day

4

Tornadoes in Six Counties from 2004 to 2005

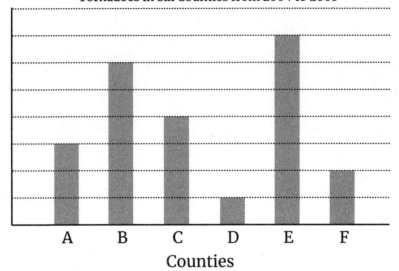

Counties

The number of tornadoes in 6 counties from 2004 to 2005 is shown in the graph above. If the total number of tornadoes from 2004 to 2005 is 2,300, how many tornadoes did County E have in that time period?

A) 7
B) 70
C) 700
D) 7,000

5

Set A contains 10 integers and has a mean of 23. Set B contains 20 integers and has a mean of 32. Suppose Set C is formed by combining sets A and B. What is the mean of Set C?

A) 15.8
B) 27.5
C) 29
D) 30

6

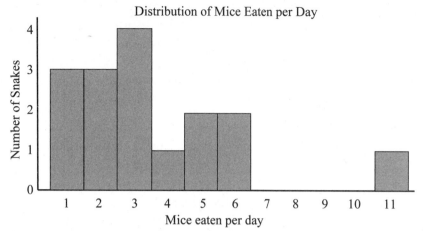

The bar graph above shows the number of mice eaten per day by snakes of the viperidae family observed in the jungle. The outlier snake that ate 11 mice was found to be of the colubris family, not of the viperid family. Which will change the most if the outlier is removed from the data?

A) Mode
B) Mean
C) Median
D) They will all change by the same amount.

7

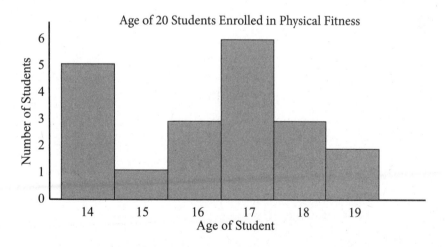

Based on the histogram above, of the following, what is the closest to the average (arithmetic mean) age of the students in the Physical Fitness class?

A) 14
B) 15
C) 16
D) 17

8

An accountant of a Fortune 500 company found that the mean salary of an employee in the company was $84,302 and the median salary of an employee in the company was $55,000. Which of the following situations could explain the difference between the mean and the median salaries of employees in the company?

A) The salaries of employees are all very similar.
B) Most salaries of employees in the company are between $55,000 and $84,302.
C) There are a few employee salaries that are much higher than the rest.
D) There are a few employee salaries that are much lower than the rest.

9

$$12, 5, 17, 21, 9$$

What is the absolute value of the difference between the mean and median of the list of numbers above?

10

The median of a set of consecutive integers is s and the range of the same set is r. In terms of r and s, what is the minimum number in the set?

A) $s - \frac{r}{2}$

B) $\frac{s-r}{2}$

C) $r - s$

D) $s - r$

11

Team A		Team B		Team C		Team D	
Player 1	20	Player 1	5	Player 1	25	Player 1	5
Player 2	20	Player 2	10	Player 2	30	Player 2	5
Player 3	25	Player 3	15	Player 3	35	Player 3	25
Player 4	30	Player 4	20	Player 4	35	Player 4	35
Player 5	30	Player 5	25	Player 5	45	Player 5	45

The table above shows the average number of points scored per game by the players of four teams. Based on this data, which team has the largest standard deviation in number of points per player per game?

A) Team A
B) Team B
C) Team C
D) Team D

12

Top 10 Home Run Hitters as of 2015			
Baseball Player	Number of Home Runs	Baseball Players	Number of Home Runs
1. Barry Bonds	762	6. Ken Griffey	630
2. Hank Aaron	755	7. Jim Thome	612
3. Babe Ruth	714	8. Sammy Sosa	609
4. Alex Rodriguez	687	9. Frank Robinson	586
5. Willie Mays	660	10. Mark McGwire	583

The table above lists the lifetime number of homeruns hit by the top ten home run hitters as of 2015. According to the table, what was the mean number of home runs of the baseball players listed above? (Round your answer to the nearest home run.)

13

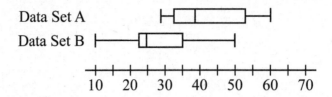

Data set A and data set B are represented by the box plots above. Which of the following statements must be true?

I. The median of data set A is greater than the median of data set B.
II. The range of data set A is greater than the range of data set B

A) I only
B) II only
C) I and II
D) neither I nor II

14

A data set of 15 different numbers has a mean of 54 and a median of 45. The three numbers 25, 43 and 105 are added to the set. Which of the following statements is true about the mean and median of this new set?

A) Both the mean and median are larger
B) Both the mean and median are smaller
C) The mean is larger but the median is smaller
D) The mean is smaller but the median is larger.

Two Variable Statistics

Tags: Problem Solving & Data Analysis • Two Variable Data • Sample Statistics

In this section we are going to be looking at how to work with two-variable data. This means we aren't just interested in questions like "What is the current temperature?" or "What time is it?" but "What was the temperature at several different times?" This data will often be displayed in a scatter plot or line graph. Our job is to model and interpret the data.

INTERACTIVE EXAMPLE

The graph below shows the elevation of a loop trail, with trail distances measured clockwise from the trail head.

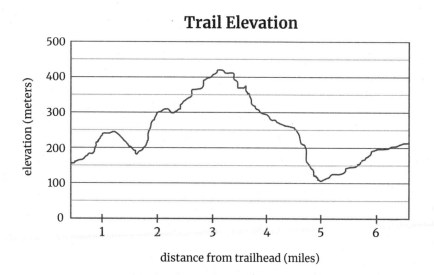

Q1) How many miles along the trail does a hiker reach the maximum elevation?

A) 1.2
B) 3.1
C) 5
D) 430

S1) Since the y-axis is elevation, we need to find the tallest point on the graph. The question asks us to report "how many miles along the trail" this peak happens, so we need to find the x-coordinate.

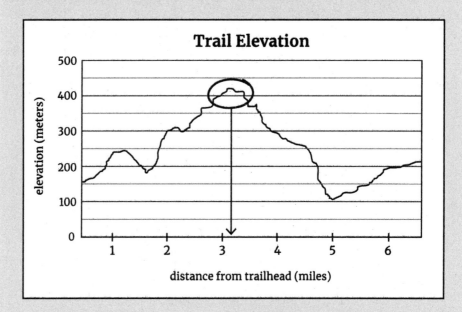

The peak happens a little past **3 miles**, so the answer is B!

B

Q2) What is the significance of the y-intercept in this graph?

    A) The trail starts at an elevation of 0 meters.
    B) The trail never crosses the x-axis, so it never gets to sea level.
    C) The trail's lowest point has an elevation of about 155 meters.
    D) The trailhead has an elevation of about 155 meters.

S2) Let's look at the y-intercept and see what we learn:

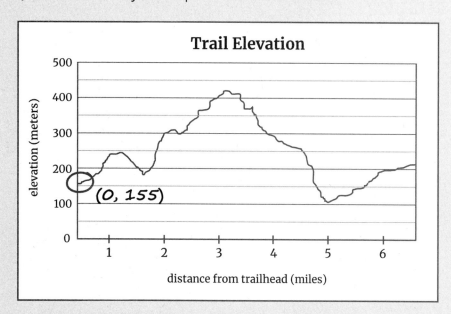

The coordinates of the point are somewhere around:

$$y\text{-}intercept = (0, 155)$$

Now we just need to interpret this in context using the axis labels.
Let's **write in the labels** for the x and y coordinate:

$$y\text{-}intercept = (0 \text{ miles from trailhead}, 155 \text{ meters elevation})$$

Aha! Just labeling x and y does most of the interpretation for us! The y-intercept tells us that if you're standing at the trailhead, you are at 155 meters elevation. That's exactly what **choice D** says!

D

Q3) What is the elevation difference between the highest and lowest points on the trail?

A) 110
B) 280
C) 330
D) 430

S3) To find the elevation difference, we first need to find the min and max elevations on the graph.

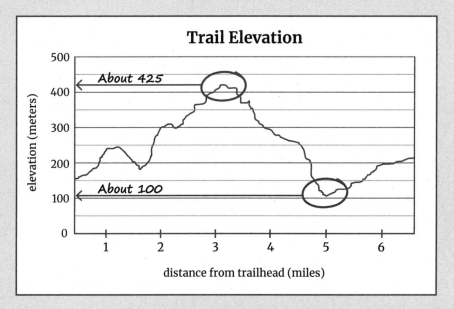

So the max elevation is around 425 meters, and the min elevation is around 100 meters. Now we just need to find the difference:

$$425 - 100 = 325 \text{ } meters$$

The choice that is closest to our estimate is **choice C**.

C

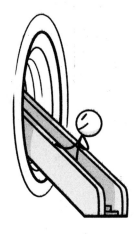

PORTAL

For more on finding the slope of a line, turn to the *Linear Equations* chapter on page 320.

TIP

You might have noticed here that our calculation for the average rate of change ignored that big dip in the trail between mile 1 and mile 2. Average rate of change doesn't care about *how* you get between the two points, it only cares about where you started and where you ended and what the rate *would* have been if you had taken a straight line path.

Q4) Which of the following is the best estimate for the average rate of change in elevation from mile marker 1 to mile marker 2?

A) −60 meters per mile

B) $\frac{1}{60}$ meters per mile

C) 60 meters per mile

D) 120 meters per mile

S4) The words "average rate of change" may look new, but the concept isn't - this question is just asking you to find two points, pretend there is a straight line connecting them, and find the slope of that line!

Our first step is to find the elevations at mile 1 and mile 2:

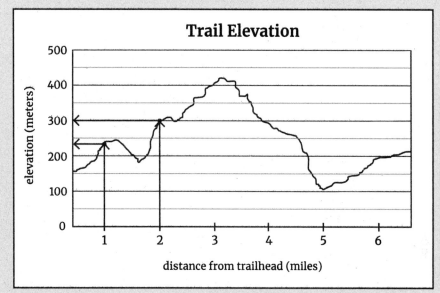

So we see that at mile 1 the elevation is about 240 meters and at mile 2 the elevation is about 300 meters. You can think of this data as a pair of points: (1,240) and (2,300). To get the average rate of change, we just need to pretend we got these two points from a straight line and find the slope!

$$\frac{y_2 - y_1}{x_2 - x_1} = \frac{300 - 240}{2 - 1} = 60$$

Since the numbers in the numerator are measured in meters and the numbers in the denominator are measured in miles, the units on this rate are meters per mile (as the answer choices indicated!). The choice that matches our answer here is **C**!

Notice that the other answer choices are very different from the correct choice. This graph is hard to read exactly and the test writers took this into account. You could have read the elevation at mile 1 as 135 or 145 and **choice C** would still have been by far the closest answer.

C

EXAMPLE 2

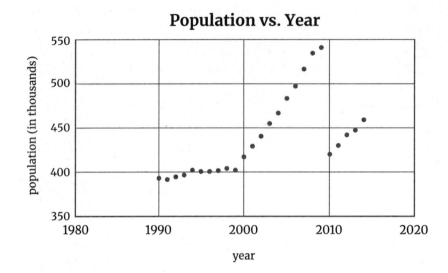

Population vs. Year

The graph above shows the population of Atlanta, GA each year from 1990 to 2014. Based on the graph, which of the following best describes the general trend of the population over this time period?

A) The population generally increased each year since 1990.
B) The population was relatively steady until 2000, after which it steadily increased.
C) The population changed unpredictably, so there is no general trend.
D) The population stayed fairly steady between 1990 and 2000, when it started growing quickly. It fell sharply in 2010 before starting to grow again.

SOLUTION

Let's test each answer choice with the graph. Only the correct choice will accurately describe the trends we see.

A) There was a a huge drop in 2010, so it's not true that the population generally increased.

B) The statement here is only true up until 2010, not 1990-2014.

C) There were two points where the behavior changed, but there are clear trends in each decade.

D) **Yes!** This answer identifies the three different regions of the graph and appropriately describes each of them.

D

Slope & Relationships

The great thing about graphs and other visualizations is that they allow us to see **relationships** between variables. In the previous example, the graph showed us the relationship between time and the population of Atlanta. When we described the trends in that graph, we were describing the **direction** and **strength** of that relationship.

Let's say we were curious whether adding a new "miracle" fertilizer will correlate ('have a relationship') with the size of a plant. If adding more fertilizer made the plant grow, we'd say there was a **positive** relationship. If adding more fertilizer made the plant shrink, then we'd say there was a **negative** relationship. If adding more and more fertilizer did zilch for the plant, then we'd say there was **no relationship**.

Positive   Negative   None

Finally, we use the words **strong** and **weak** to describe how tight the connection is between the two variables. If every application of the fertilizer caused a proportional growth spurt (or shrinkage), we'd say there was a strong relationship. If instead the growth spurts were less predictable, we'd say there was a weak relationship. Now that we know the connection between slope and relationships, let's look at examples of what different correlations look like **graphically**.

Digging Deeper

Notice that we use the exact same words (*positive* & *negative*) to describe **relationships** as we do to describe **slope**. That's because slope, relationships, and rates are all getting at the same idea: how much does changing *one* variable (*x*) affect a different variable (*y*) ?

When you have an equation with a large, positive slope, like:

$$y = 50x + 2$$

..then changing *x* even from 1 to 2 has a **positive** impact on *y*. Another way to phrase that is to say "*x* and *y* have a **positive** relationship."

PORTAL

Here we are looking at **linear** relationships, but sometimes data has a **non-linear** relationship. On the SAT it might look exponential or like a parabola. For more on modeling with these other functions, check out *Quadratic Modeling* on page 508.

Positive Relationships

When variables have a **positive** relationship, they increase together.

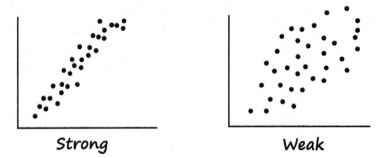

Negative Relationships

In a **negative** relationship, one variable decreases when the other increases.

No Relationship

When there is no relationship between the variables, you'll see a straight horizontal or vertical line, or a seemingly random spread of data points.

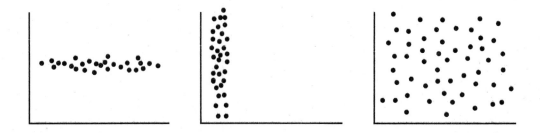

Notice that when you look at a scatterplot with a strong relationship, your brain automatically notices a line-like pattern in the data:

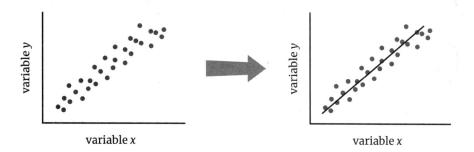

TIP

The SAT won't expect you to work out the exact slope of the line of best fit from a set of data, but they might give you a scatter plot and ask you to pick the an "appropriate linear model" from the answer choices. If they do, determining whether the slope should be positive or negative and roughly what the y-intercept should be will get you to the correct answer!

The data points **look** like they are clustered around a line. We call this invisible (but super important) line the **line of best fit** for the data. And like all lines, the line of best fit has an equation and a slope that we can use to find out interesting stuff! Most of the time, you will be given a line of best fit and asked to use your knowledge of slope and the equation of a line to make **estimates** about the data.

Estimation Tool

A line of best fit is an extremely useful estimation tool. If we plug an x into the equation of the line of best fit, it will spit out a y-value that is **most likely** to correspond with that input. People use this statistical tool all the time. A business might use it to predict future sales based on past years' sales, or an airport might use it to predict how many travelers to expect during the summer.

The math behind all of this is simple equation-of-a-line stuff. As we've done before, we'll be working with $y = mx + b$, plugging in points, and focusing on slopes. Let's get some practice!

INTERACTIVE EXAMPLE

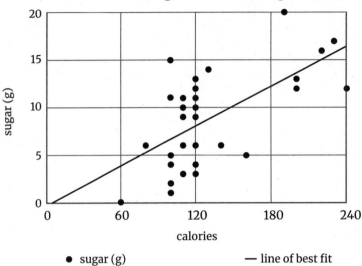

Calories vs. Sugar in a Serving of Cereal

● sugar (g)   — line of best fit

The above graph shows the number of calories and grams of sugar in a suggested serving of 30 different breakfast cereals. The line of best fit is also shown, and has the equation $y = 0.0697x - 0.335$.

Q1) According to the line of best fit, how much sugar would you expect a cereal with 180 calories per serving to have?

A) about 5 grams
B) about 8 grams
C) about 10 grams
D) about 12 grams

NOTE

Notice that even though we don't have a data point at 180 calories, we can **estimate** it using the line of best fit!

S1) This question asks us to use the line of best fit to estimate the amount of sugar per serving for a cereal with 180 calories per serving. Sugar is on the y-axis, so we want the y-value on the line of best fit at 180 calories. If we slide our finger up from 180 on the x-axis until we hit the line of best fit, we see that the line crosses somewhere between 10 and 15 on the y-axis. Only **choice D** falls in that range, so it must be our answer!

D

Q2) One cereal in the study had 0 grams of sugar per serving, as shown on the graph. For that cereal, about how much less sugar does it have than the line of best fit would predict?

A) 0
B) 2
C) 4
D) 6

S2) Step 1 is to find the data point that represents the cereal with 0 grams of sugar. Since sugar is on the y-axis, we are looking for a data point on the x-axis, where the y-coordinate is zero. That data point is at 60 calories:

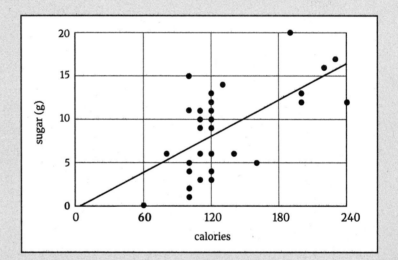

Next we need to know how much sugar the **line of best fit** predicts at $x = 60$. If we slide up to the line and check the y-value at that point, we see that it predicts about **4 grams** of sugar for 60 calories. To find how much less it has than was predicted, we need to subtract:

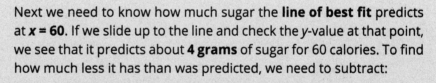

$$predicted - actual = 4 - 0 = \boxed{4}$$

Choice C is the best answer.

C

PLUG IN!

Remember, we can always find a point on a line if we're given the equation and a coordinate.

$$0.0697x - .335 = y$$
$$0.0697(60) - .335 = 3.8$$

Which is about 4!

Q3) Which of the following best explains how the number 0.0697 in the equation of the line of best fit relates to the scatterplot?

    A) Every cereal will have at least 0.0697 grams of sugar per serving.

    B) On average, we estimate that the amount of sugar per serving will increase by 0.0697 grams for every additional calorie per serving.

    C) A gram of sugar has 0.0697 calories.

    D) There are exactly 0.0697 grams of sugar per calorie of cereal.

S3) Let's compare the equation of the line of best fit to the standard equation of a line:

$$y = mx + b$$

$$y = 0.0697x - .335$$

This shows us that 0.0697 is the slope of the line of best fit. Slope is rise over run, or how much the *y*-axis changes for each change in the *x*-axis. In this case, that's the amount of **sugar per calorie**. Choices B and D get this idea right. However, line of best fit gives us *estimates*, NOT exact absolutes. So the answer must be choice B.

B

Use the previous graph to answer each question.

Question	Prediction
One serving of *Sweet Cuppin' Cakes* cereal has 15 grams of sugar. About how many calories does the line of best fit predict it will have?	
If *Chunky Tree Bark* cereal contains 140 calories per serving, about how many grams of sugar does the line of best fit predict it will have?	
If a single serving of *Chocolate Frosted Sugar Bombs* has 300 calories, how many grams of sugar does the line of best fit predict it to have?	

Answers:

1. Sweet Cuppin' Cakes: ~220 calories

2. Chunky Tree Bark: ~9g sugar

614

3. Chocolate Frosted Sugar Bombs: ~20g sugar

Practice Problems

Use your new skills to answer each question.

1

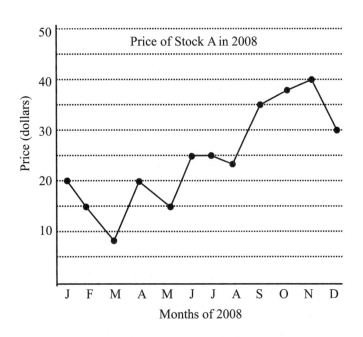

The price of a stock was recorded on the first day of every month of 2008. Based on the graph, which of the following gives a two month interval in which the price of the stock increased and then decreased?

A)   February to April
B)   June to August
C)   September to November
D)   October to December

2

Phoebe is a professional photographer who hiked to a waterfall in order to take some pictures for her next art show. The graph below shows the speed at which she hiked during her trip to and from the waterfall. During which interval did Phoebe stop to take pictures of the waterfall?

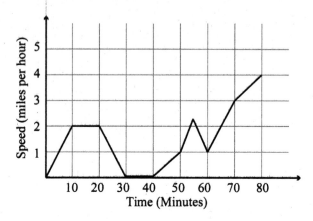

A) Between 10 and 20 minutes
B) Between 30 and 40 minutes
C) Between 50 and 60 minutes
D) Between 60 and 70 minutes

3

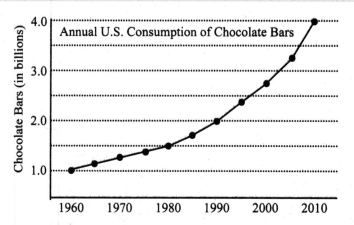

The graph above shows the total number of chocolate bars consumed each year in the United States. Based on the graph, which of the following best describes the relationship between the chocolate bar consumption growth from 1960 to 1980 and the growth from 1990 to 2010?

A) From 1960 to 1980, consumption growth was linear, whereas from 1990 to 2010, the growth was exponential.
B) From 1960 to 1980, consumption growth was exponential, whereas from 1990 to 2010, the growth was linear.
C) Consumption growth was exponential for both time periods.
D) Consumption growth was linear for both time periods.

4

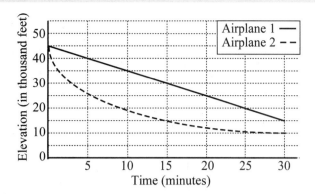

The graph above shows the elevation of two airplanes. Which of the following statements correctly compares the average rate at which the elevation of the two airplanes changed?

A) From 0 to 15 minutes, the rate of change in elevation of Airplane 1 is greater than that of Airplane 2, whereas from 20 to 30 minutes, the rate of change in elevation of Airplane 2 is greater than that of Airplane 1.

B) From 0 to 15 minutes, the rate of change in elevation of Airplane 1 is less than that of Airplane 2, whereas from 20 to 30 minutes, the rate of change in elevation of Airplane 2 is less than that of Airplane 1.

C) In every 5-minute interval, the rate of change in elevation of Airplane 1 is greater than that of Airplane 2.

D) In every 5-minute interval, the rate of change in elevation of Airplane 1 is less than that of Airplane 2.

5

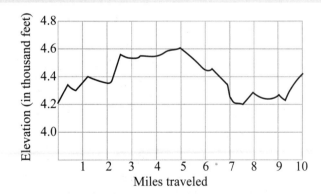

Kari went on a hiking trip, and the graph above shows Kari's elevation while hiking on the trail. Over which interval did Kari experience the largest change in elevation?

A) From mile 1 to mile 3
B) From mile 2 to mile 4
C) From mile 5 to mile 7
D) From mile 7 to mile 10

Which of the following graphs best shows a strong positive association between x and y?

A)

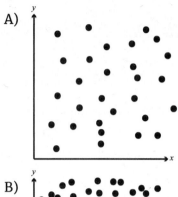

B)

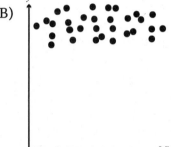

C)

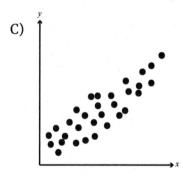

D)

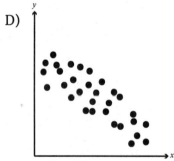

7

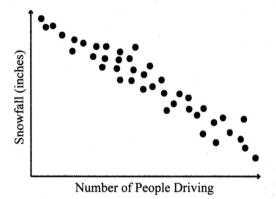

Number of People Driving

The graph above gives the number of people in Telluride, Colorado who drove each day it snowed in the city in relation to the number of inches of snowfall on that respective day. Which of the following correctly describes the correlation of the graph above?

A) Strong positive correlation
B) Strong negative correlation
C) Weak positive correlation
D) Weak negative correlation

8

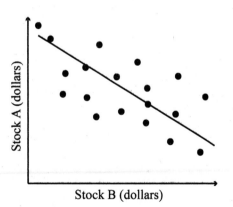

Stock B (dollars)

Nick has been tracking the prices, in dollars, of two stocks and recording their values in relation to one another in the graph above. If the price of Stock A drops, what will Nick's line of best fit predict Stock B will do?

A) Stock B will decrease in value.
B) Stock B will increase in value.
C) Stock B will remain at the same price.
D) A prediction cannot be determined.

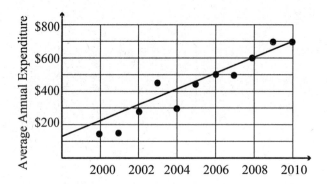

According to the line of best fit in the scatterplot above, which of the following best approximates the year in which the average annual expenditure on cellular phone services was estimated to be $300?

A) 2002
B) 2003
C) 2004
D) 2005

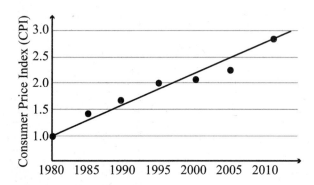

The Consumer Price Index (CPI) of the U.S. in the graph above is defined to be the ratio of the current average price of goods to the average price of goods in 1980. Which of the following conclusions is supported by the graph?

A) The initial CPI of 1980 was 1.
B) The initial CPI of 1980 was $1.
C) The CPI in 1981 was 100 percent greater than the CPI in 1980.
D) The CPI has grown by about 100% since 1980.

11

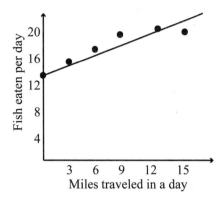

The scatterplot above gives the number of fish a grizzly bear eats in one day in relation to the number of miles the grizzly bear traveled that day. The line of best fit is also shown and has the equation $y = 0.5x + 13$. Using the line of best fit, what would be the best approximation for how many fish a bear would eat in one day if it traveled 22 miles that day?

A) 11 fish
B) 22 fish
C) 24 fish
D) 35 fish

12

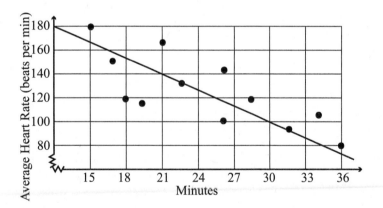

The runners of a 5K race all wore heart rate monitors. The data from each runner's heart rate monitor was then plotted against the number of minutes it took them to finish the 5K. The runner with an average heart rate of 80 beats per minute ran the 5K in how many more minutes than the time predicted by the line of best fit?

A)   1.5 minutes
B)   8.0 minutes
C) 10.0 minutes
D) 36.0 minutes

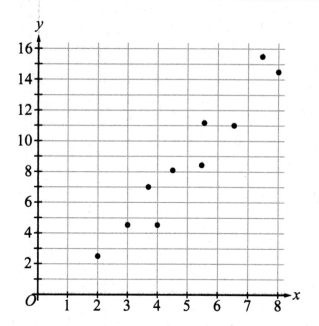

Which of the following is the most appropriate linear model for the data shown in the scatterplot?

A) $y = -1.4x + 2$

B) $y = 1.4x + 2$

C) $y = -2x - 1.4$

D) $y = 2x - 1.4$

Study Design

Tags: Problem Solving & Data Analysis • Sample Statistics • Statistical Inference • Evaluating Statistical Claims

....

Study Vocabulary

Let's start with a review of some basic vocabulary. All studies begin with a basic question that the scientists are seeking to answer. For example, let's say we want to design a study to answer the question:

> **Question:** Do 10th graders feel prepared for the SAT?

WHY SAMPLE?

Most of the time, it isn't practical (or possible) to survey every single member of a population (things cost money).

Luckily, we don't need to! If we are smart about it, we can study a small piece of that bigger population and still answer our question. That small piece is called a **sample**.

A **population** is the *entire* group we want to learn something about. Depending on what we're interested in, this could be "all girls in third period calculus" or "all teenagers in the United States." In our case, the population would be "all 10th graders."

A **sample** is a smaller piece of the larger population. The difference between a good sample and a bad sample rests on whether the sample is *representative* of the population. Scientists have to be very careful about how they choose their sample – if they mess this part up, then they can't really claim that their findings answer the question at hand!

population

sample

What is a bad sample?

A bad sample is one that is *not* representative of the larger population. In our study, if we only surveyed 10th graders who have a copy of *Applerouth's Guide to the SAT*, then we would have picked a *bad* (not representative) sample. Can you see why?

Because... those students probably feel **more** prepared than students who do NOT have a study guide. That would cause us to overestimate how prepared ALL 10th graders feel for the SAT.

What is a good sample?

PROPORTIONS

If 5% of all 10th graders own this book, then 5% of our sample should too. Similarly, if only 15% of 10th graders in the country go to private school, then we should make sure only 15% of our sample goes to private school.

A good sample is one that *is* representative of the larger population. When it comes down to it, it's really all about **proportions**. It's okay if SOME proportion of the students we survey own a copy of *Applerouth's Guide to the SAT,* so long as it's the same proportion as in the population of all 10th graders.

If a sample is chosen **randomly** from the entire population, we usually assume it is representative. That's because, when a sample is chosen from the population at random, every individual has an equal chance of being chosen. Let's look at a couple of examples of good and bad sampling. For each example, ask yourself "Why might the bad sample affect our conclusion?"

> **Question:** Do students at Emory University like coffee?
>
> **Population**: all students at Emory University
> **Good Sample:** random selection of all Emory students
> **Bad sample:** all students in an 8:00 am History class.

> **Question:** Are female students at your high school interested in adding a competitive math team?
>
> **Population**: female students at your high school
> **Good Sample:** random selection of girls in your high school
> **Bad sample:** random selection of all U.S. high school students

EXAMPLE 1

When applying for funding, zoologists want to discuss the public interest in their research. They take a random sample of 500 people in their nation to contact with a survey. They fail to reach 17 of the people but receive responses from the other 483. One of the questions on their survey asks "In your opinion, how important is it to you to have access to a zoo ?" Options include "Not important," "Somewhat important," "Very important," and "No opinion." When zoologists analyze the data, they find that 73% of all respondents either said "Somewhat important" or "Very important."

For which of the following regions is it reasonable to assume that the survey is a representative sample?

I.   The city in which the scientists live

II. The nation in which the scientists conducted the study

III. Countries neighboring the nation in which the scientists conducted the study

    A) II only
    B) I and II only
    C) II and III only
    D) None

SOLUTION

Any time you get a problem that asks you to determine which of three statements is valid, you need to go through each statement and determine whether it is correct.

Statement I: The random sample was taken from the nation as a whole. It's very possible that different cities within the country have different opinions about zoos; maybe the city where the scientists live is particularly Pro-Zoo! We can't assume data for the whole country applies to one city, so we can eliminate I.

Statement II: The survey was given to a random sample chosen from the whole nation, so it is indeed reasonable to assume that it is a representative sample! This one's good.

Statement III: The passage indicates that only the one nation was included in the sample. Neighboring countries are a separate population, so we can't use this sample to talk about them.

Since only statement II checks out, our answer is A.

A

Let's think about margin of error (then candy)

Taking a smart sample lets us estimate properties of the entire population, **but it is still an estimate**. A sample's *margin of error* is the measure of how far above or below an estimate based on that sample is likely to be, just due to the random nature of sampling.

The basic math of margin of error works like this: if you are told that a random sample of a population shows 15% with a specific trait, but are told there is a **margin of error** of 10%, that means that the actual fraction of the total population with that trait is most likely between 5% and 25%. If that's still a little unclear, then let's think about candy.

Okay NOW let's think about candy

Imagine you have a **bucket of 1000 assorted candy pieces** and you want to know what percent of the candies are Sour Tarts (your fave).

our favorite

You *could* carefully sort and count all 1000 of the candies, but most people don't consider that a fun use of time. Instead we can estimate by taking out smaller **samples**. Let's grab a handful of candy and see how many are our favorite:

Sample size: 10
# of favorite: 4 (40%)
Margin of Error: 30%

In this handful, <u>4 out of 10</u> (40%) of the candies are your favorite type. Not bad! But, does that mean we can say for sure that 40% of the *entire* bucket is your favorite? Nope! Do you see why not?

What if we pulled out different samples?

Maybe you got lucky and happened to grab a good handful, or maybe there's actually a lot more of your favorite hiding in there. We could **repeat this test** and see different results:

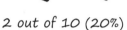

2 out of 10 (20%)   4 out of 10 (40%)   5 out of 10 (50%)

Each of the new piles is a random sample of the candies in the bowl, so it is reasonable to use <u>any</u> of them to estimate the percent of the candies that are your favorite. However, random chance means that the exact make up of the samples vary. The **margin of error** is a reminder that even though sampling is useful, it is not exact.

So far, drawing 10 pieces at a time, we're seeing a 30% margin of error. That is pretty large - knowing that the percentage is somewhere between 10% and 70% isn't very useful. If you want a more precise estimate, you could take a **larger sample** of 50 candies:

Sample size: 50
# of favorite: 17 (34%)
Margin of Error: 13%

Counting a pile of 50 is still a lot less work than counting 1000, and by taking a larger sample we **decrease the margin of error**. Instead of 30%, the margin of error here is about 13%. Since 34% of this sample were your favorite, this tells us that the true percentage of the candies in the bowl that are your favorite is likely somewhere between 21% and 47%:

34 − 13 = 21%
34 + 13 = 47%

EXAMPLE 2

A high school with 3000 students is considering making a change to the dress code. A member of the student council randomly surveys 300 students to see whether they support the change. After analyzing the survey she reports back to the student council that the 68% of the students approved of the change, with a margin of error of 3%. Which of the following statements is a plausible conclusion based on her results?

A) Exactly 68% of the students in the school approve of the proposed new dress code.

B) There are 2040 students in the school who approve of the proposed new dress code.

C) About 3% of the students were not surveyed.

D) It is likely that somewhere between 65% and 71% of the students in the school approve of the proposed new dress code.

SOLUTION

This is a straightforward test of your understanding of margins of error. The survey gives 68% as an estimate of the proportion of the students who approve of the dress code, but it doesn't tell us that exactly 68% actually do...

There could be some error due to the nature of randomness in sampling, so choice A is wrong.

Choice B computes 68% of 3000 and asserts that this is the <u>exact</u> number of students who support the dress code. Again, we don't know that it is exactly this value, so it is wrong.

Choice C gives a misconception of the meaning of margin of error. The Margin of Error measures how far off our estimate is based just on randomness - it doesn't take potential problems with the survey method into account.

Choice D is correct. It gives a range for the population percentage by taking the estimate and adding and subtracting the given margin of error: 68 − 3 = 65% and 68 + 3 = 71%.

D

Study Types

There are three main types of studies that the SAT looks at. In an **observational study**, scientists simply observe how a sample acts in its natural environment, recording what they see. In a **sample survey**, scientists recruit a sample, ask questions, and record the responses. In a **controlled experiment**, scientists carefully create a controlled environment, recruit a sample, divide it into two groups, then compare the outcomes for the two groups.

The benefit of controlled experiments over other types of studies is they allow scientists to show a *causal relationship* between variables. If you're just observing that happier people go on more walks, for example, you can't say whether being happy causes people to walk more, or vice-versa, or whether some third factor is causing both!

Must, Likely, Could, Can't

Throughout the SAT, the test will sometimes ask you to evaluate the **validity** of statements by using qualifiers like "must be true" or "could be true." This is particularly common on statistics questions. When these come up, it is important to pay careful attention to how they qualify what they are asking. Think about what it means when you say the following things about a statement:

- **Must be true**: Given the information you have, you *know* that the statement *absolutely* has to be true in <u>all</u> cases, not just one. If they've given you the data for a sample and you can calculate the sample mean, you know the mean exactly.

- **Likely true**: The evidence you have supports the statement you've been asked to evaluate, but you don't have enough evidence to say that it is 100% definitely true. A statement that is likely to be true is a reasonable (or plausible) conclusion to draw.

- **Could be true**: The statement you've been asked to evaluate and the other information you are given in the problem are *compatible*. You don't know for sure if the statement is true, but you also don't know for sure that it is false.

- **Can't be true**: The statement you've been asked to evaluate <u>contradicts</u> information you were given in the problem. For example, you are given incomplete data and can tell that the median *must* be somewhere between 5 and 10. It **can't** be 4.

TIP

Be extra careful with "must be true" statements, especially if you solved a problem by picking numbers. It's possible to get an outcome with one set of data that is not true for ALL possible sets.

TIP

Note that anything that is likely to be true could be true, but not the other way around. There are some unlikely scenarios that might not directly contradict the information you've been given.

Use the survey results below to evaluate the 10 statements that follow by checking the column for each to indicate whether it must, could, or can't be true.

A researcher wants to study how much time local high school students are spending on homework each day. They give a survey to a random sample of 300 students at the local high school. The results of the survey are shown in the table below. The researcher reports that 37% of the local students are spending between 2 and 4 hours on homework per day (margin of error: 5%)

	< 2hrs / day	2–4hrs / day	4+hrs / day
# of Students	145	111	44

#	Statement	Must be true	Likely true	Could be true	Can't be true
1	37% of the students in the sample spend 2-4 hours per day on homework.				
2	37% of the students at the high school spend 2-4 hours per day on homework.				
3	40% of the students in the high school spend between 2 and 4 hours a day on homework.				
4	45% of the students in the high school spend between 2 and 4 hours a day on homework.				
5	If the researcher took another sample, exactly 37% of the students in that sample would spend 2-4 hours per day on homework.				
6	All students spend at least 1 hour a day on homework.				
7	Between 32 and 42% of the students at the high school spend between 2 and 4 hours per day on homework.				
8	37% of the students in the sample spend at least two hours a day on homework				
9	More than half of the students in the sample spent at least 2 hours a day on homework.				
10	The median number of hours per day that students in the sample spend on homework is less than 2.				

Answers: *Bottom of the next page.*

Practice Problems

Use your new skills to answer each question.

1

In order to determine if Migraine Medication A is more effective than Migraine Medication B, a research study was conducted. From a large population of people who have recurring migraines, 600 participants were selected at random. 200 of those participating were given a placebo, 200 of those participating were given Migraine Medication A, and the last 200 participants were given Migraine Medication B. The resulting data show that participants who received Medication A experienced more relief than those who received Medication B, and that both Medications A and B worked substantially better than the placebo. Based on the results of the study, which of the following is an appropriate conclusion?

A) Migraine Medication A is the most effective migraine medication on the market.
B) People with acute migraines need only take the placebo.
C) Migraine Medication A will work for anyone who takes it.
D) Migraine Medication A is likely to give more migraine relief than Migraine Medication B.

2

Samuel owns a chain of restaurants called Sam's Salads that offer a strictly vegetarian cuisine. Samuel wants to open up a Sam's Salads in a new city, so he decides to survey 250 people who entered a local burger place in the city. Of the 250 people surveyed, 7 were vegetarians, 8 did not answer the survey, and the rest were not vegetarians. Which of the following makes it least likely that a reliable conclusion can be drawn about the percentage of vegetarians in the city?

A) The number of people who refused to respond
B) Where the survey was conducted
C) The sample size
D) The population size

Exercise Answers:

1. Must	2. Likely	3. Likely	4. Could	5. Could
6. Could	7. Likely	8. Can't	9. Must	10. Can't

631

3

A mad scientist is doing quality control on the automated production of his robot army. He inspects a random sample and determines that 87% of the robots are error free with a margin of error of 4%. Which of the following is most likely to be the true percentage of robots that are error free?

A) 4%
B) 85%
C) 92%
D) 99%

4

Teresa wants to gauge interest among the senior class in having a class t-shirt, but it isn't practical for her to poll all of the seniors. Which of the following sampling methods would be best?

A) Hand out a survey in her math class
B) Set up a table in the cafeteria where students can choose to stop and fill out a survey
C) Have the counselor give her a random list of seniors to contact
D) Ask everyone on the bus she rides home

5

Cuifu is a biologist studying the panda population of China. His team has been monitoring and tagging the pandas in the Minshan Mountains in Sichuan. When he tells his family about his work, his aunt wants to know how many pandas there are in all of China. She takes the population density he has found and multiplies it by the land area of China. Will this method accurately predict the total panda population?

A) Yes, because you can use a sample to estimate the population.
B) Yes, because Cuifu's team has been studying the entire population in the Minshan Mountains.
C) No, because the sample was not taken randomly.
D) No, because we can't assume that the population in the Minshan Mountains is representative of the population across all of China.

6

A marine biologist selected a random sample of 40 Pacific herring from a school and found that the mean length of the herring in the sample was 25.0 centimeters (cm) with an associated margin of error of 6.1 cm. Which of the following is the best interpretation of the marine biologist's findings?

A) All herring in the sample have a length between 18.9 cm and 31.1 cm.

B) Most herring in the school have a length between 18.9 cm and 31.1 cm.

C) Any length between 18.9 cm and 31.1 cm is a plausible value for the mean length of the herring in the school.

D) Any length between 18.9 cm and 31.1 cm is a plausible value for the mean length of the herring in the sample.

7

A large company provided all of its employees with wearable step-tracking devices. After 6 months, they surveyed a random sample of their employees to find out whether the employees felt that having the step tracker encouraged them to be more active. Using that sample data, the company estimated that 56% of their employees felt that the device encourages them to be more active. The margin of error for this estimation is 4%. Which of the following is the most appropriate conclusion about the employees at the company, based on the given estimate and margin of error?

A) It is likely that at least 56% of the employees feel the device encourages them to be more active.

B) It is plausible that the percentage of employees who feel that the device encourages them to be more active is between 52% and 60%.

C) The percentage of employees who feel that the device encourages them to be more active is between 54% and 58%.

D) The company is between 52% and 60% sure that their employees feel the device encourages them to be more active.

8

The quality control team in a factory selected a random sample of widgets and measured the weight of each widget. After analyzing the results, the report estimated that the widgets produced in the factory have a mean weight of 2.58 grams, with a reported margin of error of 0.16 grams. Which of the following is the best conclusion based on this analysis?

A) It is likely that most widgets produced by this factory weigh exactly 2.58 grams.
B) All widgets produced by this factory weigh at least 2.42 grams.
C) It is likely that all widgets produced by this factory weigh between 2.42 grams and 2.74 grams.
D) The mean weight of all widgets produced in this factory is probably between 2.42 and 2.74 grams.

9

A random sample of 70 people from a town with a population of 15,365 were asked whether they have any pets. If 53 people in the sample said they have at least one pet, about how many people in the town would be expected to have at least one pet?

A) 3710
B) 3731
C) 11,634
D) 11,755

UNIT | Geometry

Chapters

Overview

The SAT tests a wide range of Geometry topics. The reference formulas below will give you a good idea of the types of calculations you may need to do on test day. Remember you can access these formulas at anytime on the Bluebook app!

REFERENCE

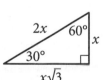

$A = \pi r^2$
$C = 2\pi r$

$A = \ell w$

$A = \frac{1}{2}bh$

$c^2 = a^2 + b^2$

Special Right Triangles

$V = \ell wh$

$V = \pi r^2 h$

$V = \frac{4}{3}\pi r^3$

$V = \frac{1}{3}\pi r^2 h$

$V = \frac{1}{3}\ell wh$

The number of degrees of arc in a circle is 360.

The number of radians of arc in a circle is 2π

The sum of the measures in degrees of the angles of a triangle is 180.

Angles & Triangles

Tags: Geometry & Trigonometry • Lines and Angles • Triangles

How to name an angle

When you name an angle in terms of points, you need to list **three** points. The middle point is the vertex of the angle and the other two points determine the legs of the angle.

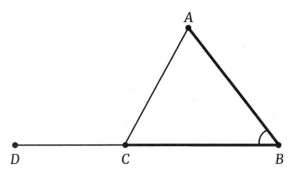

In the figure above, $\angle ABC$ is marked. You could also name it $\angle CBA$, but **not** $\angle BAC$. In this case, where it's clear, we can simply say $\angle B$.

Obtuse, right, and acute angles

We can't measure angles in terms of inches or centimeters; instead, we use **degrees**. When a question asks you for the measure of an angle, your job is to use the information in the problem to work it out. The figures below show what obtuse, right, and acute angles look like, but be cautious relying on how they *look* when the figure is not to scale (which is most of the time on the SAT).

TIP

When two lines meet at right angles, they are called **perpendicular**, the angle measures 90°, and you'll usually see a little right angle box.

Obtuse Angles
(greater than 90°)

Right Angle
(exactly 90°)

Acute Angles
(less than 90°)

There are 180° in a straight line

This is true for ANY straight line, no matter how many tiny angles that 180° is divided into:

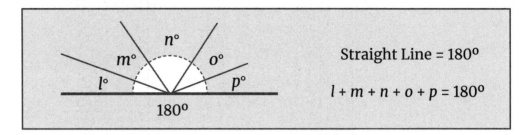

Straight Line = 180°

$l + m + n + o + p = 180°$

Vertical angles are equal

If two lines intersect, we call the angles that are opposite each other **vertical** angles. Vertical angles always have the **same angle measure**.

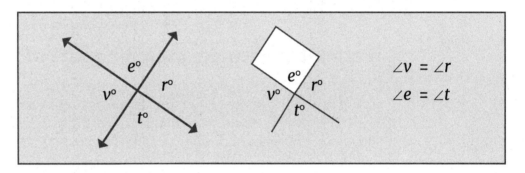

$\angle v = \angle r$

$\angle e = \angle t$

EXAMPLE 1

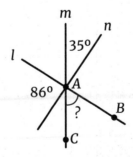

In the figure above, A is at the intersection of lines l, m, and n and two angle measures are given. What is the measure of $\angle BAC$?

A) 35°
B) 51°
C) 59°
D) 86°

637

SOLUTION

On any angle problem, it's a good bet to start filling in any angles you can figure out... even if they don't seem immediately useful.

In this case, both of the given angles are part of **vertical angles**. Since vertical angles are equal, we can fill those in.

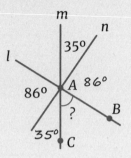

We also know that if a **straight line** is divided into multiple angles, those angles **add to 180°**. If we look at any of the three lines on their own, we see the same thing:

$$35° + 86° + \angle BAC = 180°$$

$$\angle BAC = \boxed{59°}$$

C

Parallel lines make matching sets of angles

A line that crosses a pair of parallel lines (called a transversal) creates a set of **matching angles**. Four angles will have the same BIG measure and four will have the same small measure. This is a rule we can use to find angles in a number of problems, so let's look at it in a diagram:

transversal

(noun) – a line that crosses a pair of parallel lines, creating sets of corresponding angles.

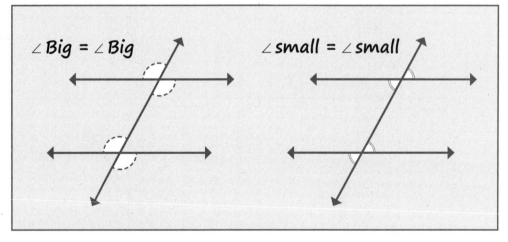

Notice here that the Big angles and small angles together make up a line, so for any transversal Big + small = 180.

EXAMPLE 2

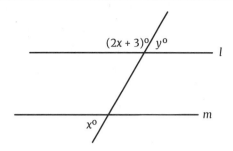

In the figure above, $l \parallel m$. What is the value of y?

A. 40
B. 59
C. 72
D. 177

$l \parallel m$

We use the || symbol to show that two lines are parallel.

SOLUTION

We have a transversal crossing two parallel lines, so we can start filling in equivalent angles. In geometry problems, our first step is always to **fill in what you know**:

Fill in what you know!

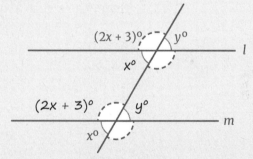

So what can we learn from here? Two things jump out. First, we can tell that $x = y$ because they are **vertical angles**. We can also see that a **straight line** is formed by x and $(2x + 3)$. Let's use that:

$$(2x + 3) + x = 180$$
$$3x + 3 = 180$$
$$3x = 177$$
$$x = 59$$

Now that we know x, we know $y = 59°$ as well!

B

TIP

In this triangle, angles a, b, and c are inside, so we call them interior angles. Angle d was formed by extending one side of the triangle and then looking at the angle outside of the triangle, so it is called an exterior angle. Notice that $(a + b) + c = 180$ and $d + c = 180$, so $a + b = d$!

There are exactly 180° inside every triangle

No matter how skinny, wide, tall, or short the triangle, it always contains exactly 180° inside its Triangly Shell™. Remember: that's the same angle measurement as in a straight line.

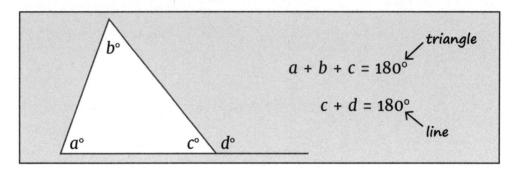

$$a + b + c = 180°$$
$$c + d = 180°$$

EXAMPLE 3

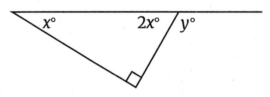

Given the figure above, which of the following is equivalent to y?

A) 30
B) 60
C) 120
D) 150

 SOLUTION

We know two things for sure in this world: triangles and lines both contain 180°. With that knowledge, we can figure out y:

1. triangles have 180° so... $90 + x + 2x = 180$
2. subtract 90 $3x = 90$
3. divide by 3 $x = 30$
4. straight lines have 180° so... $2x + y = 180$
5. substitute 30 for x $2(30) + y = 180$
6. solve for y $y = \boxed{120}$

C

There are exactly 360° inside every quadrilateral

This is true for every four-sided shape: of which there are many!

Rectangle: All angles are 90° and opposite sides have the same length. A *square* is a rectangle with four equal sides.

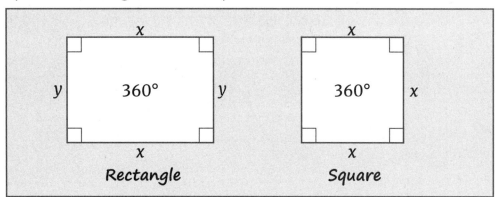

Parallelogram: The two pairs of opposite sides are both parallel. The opposite sides have the same length and opposite angles have the same measure. A *rhombus* is a parallelogram with four equal sides.

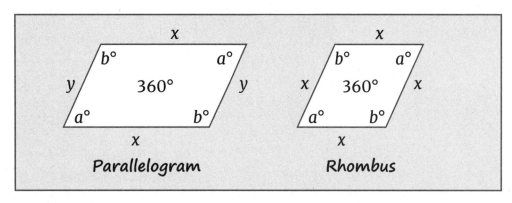

Trapezoid: One pair of sides is parallel and one pair of sides is not. A trapezoid is *isosceles* if its non-parallel sides are the same length.

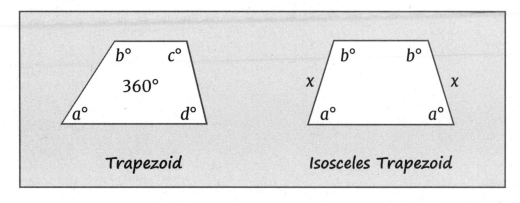

We name triangles based on the # of equal sides

All triangles fall into one of three categories—equilateral, isosceles, or scalene—based on how many equal sides and angles they have.

- **Equilateral** triangles have **three** equal sides and angles. Since there are 180° in a triangle, that means each angle is 60°.

- **Isosceles** triangles have **two** equal sides and the angles opposite those sides are also equal.

NOTE

An equilateral triangle is just a **regular** three sided polygon ("3-gon")!

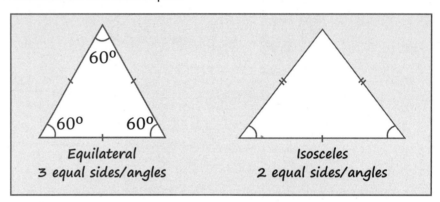

- **Scalene** triangles have **zero** equal sides and angles. Every side is a distinct length and every angle is a distinct angle.

NOTE

"Distinct" is a fancy math word that just means "different."

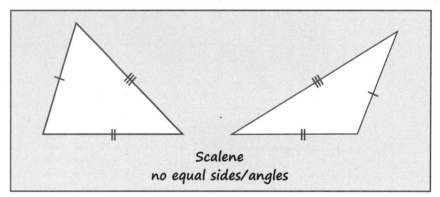

Angles and opposite sides are proportional

If you try to make one side of a triangle bigger, the angle *opposite* that side gets bigger too. For this reason, the longest side is always opposite the largest angle and the shortest side is always opposite the smallest angle.

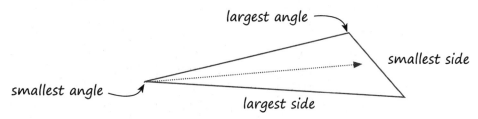

The sum of any two sides is longer than the third

This is easy to understand if you imagine "pushing down" on any corner to flatten out the sides of a triangle. These two sides **must** be longer than third, or they wouldn't reach to form a triangle in the first place!

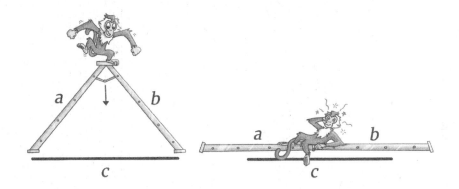

EXAMPLE 4

TIP

Remember, the interior angles of a triangle all add up to 180.

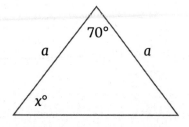

What is the value of *x* in the triangle above?

SOLUTION

First step is to fill in what we know using what we're given. What should immediately jump out is that this is an **isosceles** triangle. Two sides of the triangle are the same length: *a*. That means the angles opposite those sides must BOTH measure *x*°.

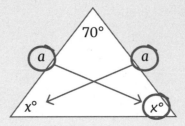

Now we can find *x* using that fact that every triangle's interior angles add up to 180°.

$$2x + 70 = 180$$

$$2x = 110$$

$$x = \boxed{55}$$

The biggest angle names the triangle

In addition to the three categories already mentioned, all triangles also fall into one of the following three categories:

- **Acute** - Every angle of the triangle is **less than 90°.**

- **Obtuse** - One angle is **more than 90°.**

- **Right** - One angle is **exactly 90°.**

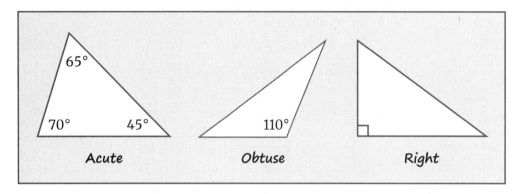

When you see right triangles, think Pythagoras

For a right triangle, the two sides that form the right angle are known as the **legs** of the triangle and the side opposite the right angle is the hypotenuse. The **Pythagorean Theorem** tells us the relationship between the length of the legs and the length of the hypotenuse:

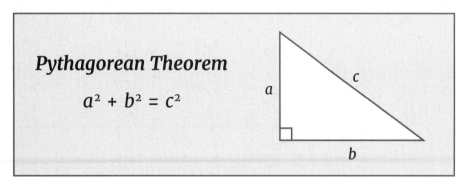

Pythagorean Theorem

$$a^2 + b^2 = c^2$$

Some right triangles are special and show up a lot

The SAT really likes right triangles and there are a few that show up often enough that it is helpful to recognize them.

- **3, 4, 5 Triangles** and its multiples.

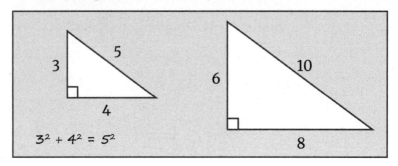

- **5, 12, 13 Triangles** and its multiples.

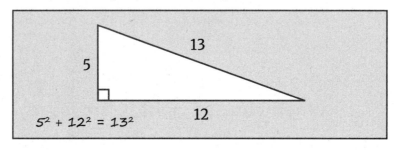

- **45°, 45°, 90° Triangles** have x, x, $x\sqrt{2}$ sides

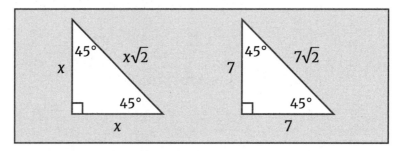

- **30°, 60°, 90° Triangles** have x, $x\sqrt{3}$, $2x$ sides

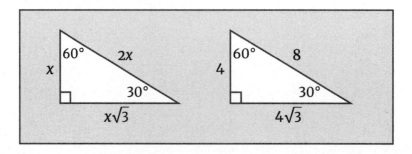

Determine as many angles and sides as possible for each triangle using the information provided.

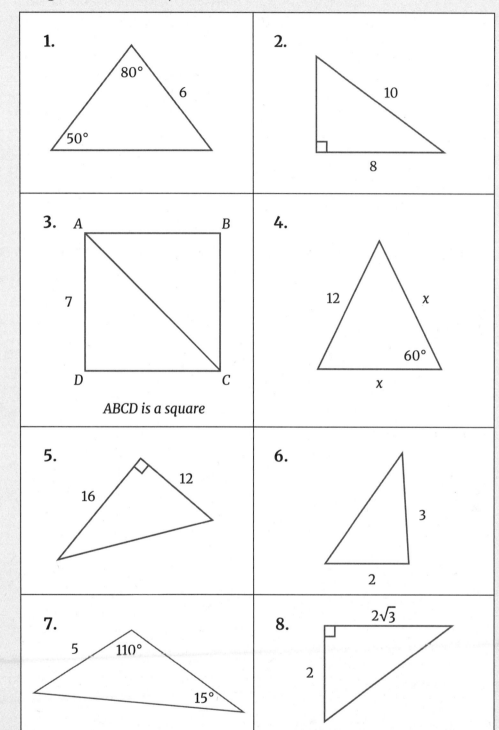

1.

80°

6

50°

2.

10

8

3. A ⎯⎯⎯ B

7

D ⎯⎯⎯ C

ABCD is a square

4.

12   x

60°

x

5.

16   12

6.

3

2

7.

5   110°

15°

8.

2√3

2

PORTAL

You can work out even more information using *Trigonometry*, which we cover on page 671.

Answers: *Completed triangles at the bottom of page 648.*

congruent

Anytime you see the ≅ symbol in geometry, it means the two objects are the same size and shape.

Notice we write the letters "ABC" and "DEF" in that order so the corresponding vertices and angles line up.

e.g., ∠A = ∠D

CONGRUENT triangles are the same size and shape

This means they are **identical**: same side lengths, same angles. Of course, they might not be FACING the same way...

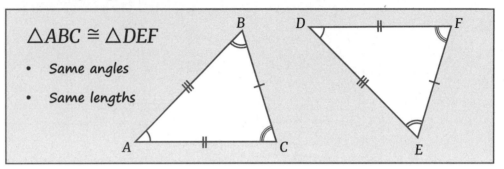

$$\triangle ABC \cong \triangle DEF$$

- Same angles
- Same lengths

SIMILAR triangles only have the same angles

If two triangles have the **same angles** but are **different sizes**, then we say the two triangles are *similar* (aka *proportional*).

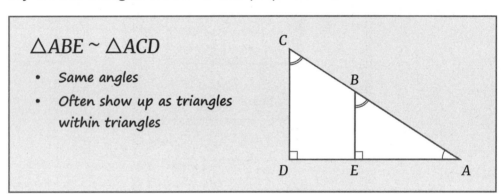

$$\triangle ABE \sim \triangle ACD$$

- Same angles
- Often show up as triangles within triangles

PORTAL

Working with similar shapes is an application of some of the skills covered in *Ratios and Proportions*, starting on page 559.

Answers: *Completed triangles from previous page.*

1.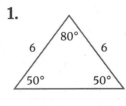

2.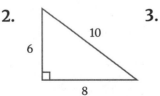

3.

4.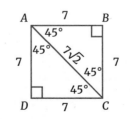

5.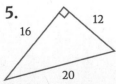

6. *(as is)*

7.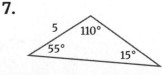

8.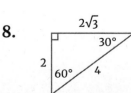

Similar triangles have proportional sides

Because similar triangles have the exact same angles, corresponding sides are in **proportion**. If you can identify corresponding sides in the triangles, you can do some cool stuff:

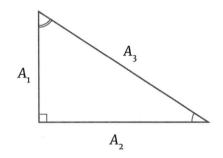 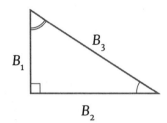

The **internal proportions** will be the same for two similar triangles.

$$\frac{Length}{Height} = \frac{A_2}{A_1} = \frac{B_2}{B_1}$$

The **relationship between triangles** will be the same for each side.

$$\frac{A_1}{B_1} = \frac{A_2}{B_2} = \frac{A_3}{B_3}$$

However you set it up, you can use this proportional relationship to find missing values for either triangle. Remember, if two triangles have the **same angles**, their sides are **proportional**.

NOTE

We are focusing on triangles here, but you can use these ratios for any similar polygons.

Warning: the area of the shapes does not scale at the same ratio

locked ratio

We call the shared internal proportions for similar shapes their **locked ratio**.

side 1 : side 2 : side 3

TIP

Any time you have a shape that is cut by a line that is parallel to one of its sides, there's a good chance that similar shapes are in play!

EXAMPLE 5

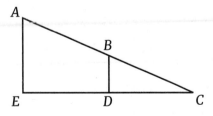

In the triangle above, $\overline{AE} \parallel \overline{BD}$. If $\overline{EC}$ = 40, $\overline{ED}$ = 20 and $\overline{AE}$ = 10. What is the length of $\overline{BD}$?

SOLUTION

We should start out by labeling our figure with what's given. We can also figure out that $\overline{DC}$ is half of $\overline{EC}$.

(1) *label what's given*

$AE = 10, ED = 20, EC = 40$

(2) *figure out what you can*

$DC = 20$

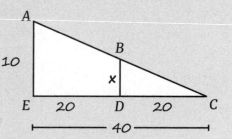

We aren't told that triangles *ACE* and *BCD* are **similar**, but we're given the keys to figure it out. Since $\overline{AE}$ is parallel with $\overline{BD}$, they make identical angles when they cross the same line. That means $\angle AEC = \angle BDC$ and $\angle EAC = \angle DBC$. And they *share* angle C.

Option 1: Find Locked Ratio

Since the triangles are similar, let's use the big triangle to find their **locked ratios**, then apply it to the small triangle to find *x*.

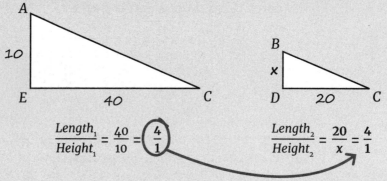

$$\frac{Length_1}{Height_1} = \frac{40}{10} = \frac{4}{1}$$

$$\frac{Length_2}{Height_2} = \frac{20}{x} = \frac{4}{1}$$

(3) *cross multiply* $\frac{20}{x} = \frac{4}{1}$ *to find x*

$$4x = 20$$

$$x = 5$$

Option 2: Find Relationship Between Triangles

Alternatively, we could just compare $\overline{EC}$ (40) to $\overline{DC}$ (20) to determine that $\triangle BCD$ is **half the size** of $\triangle ACE$, and that will be true for every corresponding side! Since *AE* is **10**, *BD* must be **5**.

Similar and Congruent Triangles

Sometimes the SAT will tell you <u>explicitly</u> that you are working with two similar triangles. Sometimes you will have to recognize it <u>yourself</u> as a step in solving a problem. Occasionally, the SAT will ask you what additional information you would need to **prove** that two triangles are similar (or congruent).

Proving Triangle Similarity

There are three good ways on the SAT to prove triangles are similar.

(1) **Two angles match:** If two angles of one triangle are the same as two corresponding angles of another triangle then the two triangles are similar.

(2) **Equal side-ratios:** If <u>all three</u> ratios of corresponding sides are the same, then the two triangles are similar.

(3) **Side-ratio and angle matches:** If you know two corresponding sides have the same ratio in each triangle and the angle between them is the same, then the two triangles are similar.

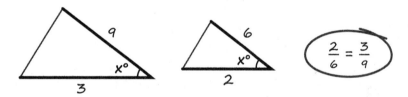

Proving Triangle Congruence

Congruence takes a bit more evidence to prove.

(1) **Three equal sides:** If you know the side lengths of all three sides of both triangles and the corresponding sides are all equal, then the triangles are congruent.

(2) **Two equal angles, one equal side:** If you know two angles and one side are equal to their corresponding parts of the other triangle, then the two triangles are congruent.

(3) **Side-angle-side equal:** If you know two sides and the angle <u>between them</u> are equal to their corresponding parts of the other triangle, then the two triangles are congruent.

Practice Problems

Use your new skills to answer each question.

1

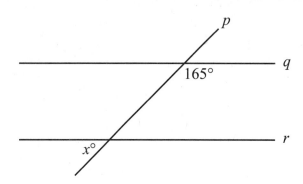

In the figure, line *q* is parallel to line *r*. What is the value of *x*?

A) 15
B) 35
C) 65
D) 165

2

In isosceles triangle *ABC*, *AB* = *BC* and ∠*ABC* has a measure of 44°. What is the measure of ∠*BAC*?

A) 22°
B) 44°
C) 68°
D) 92°

3

Triangles *ABC* and *PQR* are similar where *A* corresponds to *P* and *B* corresponds to *Q*. If the measure of angle *A* is 32° and the measure of angle *Q* is 45°, what is the measure of angle *C*?

A) 23°
B) 45°
C) 58°
D) 103°

4

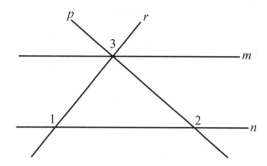

In the figure above, lines *m* and *n* are parallel. If ∠1 is 120°
and ∠2 is 140°, what is the measure of ∠3?

A) 20°
B) 40°
C) 60°
D) 80°

5

In △*RST*, the measure of ∠*R* is 57° and the measure of ∠*S* is
73°. In degrees, what is the measure of ∠*T* ?

6

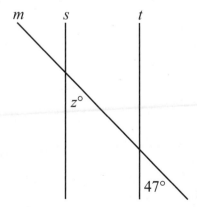

In the figure, line *s* is parallel to line *t*, and line *m* intersects
both lines. What is the value of *z*?

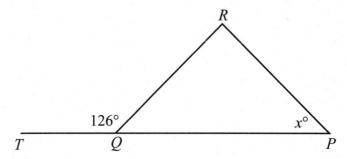

In the given figure $\overline{PQ}$ extends to point T. If the length of $\overline{RP}$ is equal to the length of $\overline{RQ}$, what is the value of x?

A) 54
B) 63
C) 72
D) 126

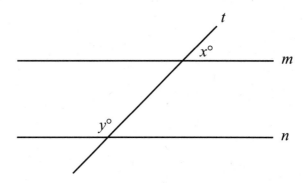

In the figure, line m is parallel to line n, and both lines are intersected by line t. If $y = 3x + 5$, what is the value of x?

9

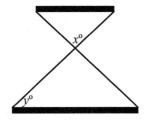

The drawing of an hourglass above consists of two similar isosceles triangles. If x is not equal to y, what is the value of x in terms of y?

A) $x = y$

B) $x = 180 - y$

C) $x = 180 - 2y$

D) $x = \dfrac{180 - y}{2}$

10

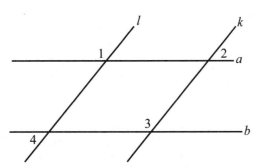

In the figure above, lines a and b are parallel, and lines l and k are parallel. What are two pairs of angles that each add up to 180°?

A) $\angle 2$ and $\angle 4$, $\angle 1$ and $\angle 3$
B) $\angle 2$ and $\angle 1$, $\angle 4$ and $\angle 3$
C) $\angle 1$ and $\angle 2$, $\angle 4$ and $\angle 2$
D) Cannot be determined.

11

Trapezoid ABCD is similar to trapezoid PQRS where A corresponds to P, B corresponds to Q, and C corresponds to R. If AB = 8, BC = 12, and PQ = 6, what is the length of QR?

A) 8
B) 9
C) 10
D) 12

12

A tree and a flag pole are both perpendicular to the ground, which is flat. The flag pole is 20 feet tall and has a shadow that is 15 feet long. At the same time, the tree has a shadow that is 12 feet long. How tall, in feet, is the tree?

13

In right triangle ABC, the measure of $\angle ACB$ is less than 30°. If $\angle ABC$ is a right angle and the measure of $\angle BAC$ is x°, which of the following must be true?

A) $x < 30$
B) $x < 60$
C) $x > 60$
D) $x > 150$

14

In triangle RST, the measure of angle R is 70°. If triangle RST is isosceles, which of the following is NOT a possible measure of angle S?

A) 40°
B) 55°
C) 70°
D) 140°

15

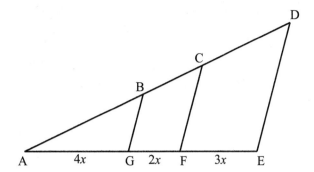

In the figure above, line segments $\overline{BG}$, $\overline{FC}$, and $\overline{DE}$ are all parallel. If the length of $\overline{AD}$ is 108 inches, what is the length, in inches, of $\overline{BC}$?

A) 12
B) 24
C) 36
D) 48

16

Rectangle *ABCD* is similar to rectangle *RSTU* where *A* corresponds to *R*, *B* corresponds to *S*, and *C* corresponds to *T*. *AB* = 30, *BC* = 45, and the length of $\overline{TU}$ is 5 more than the length of $\overline{AB}$. To the nearest tenth, what is the length of $\overline{RU}$?

17

In triangles *ABC* and *PQR*, angles *A* and *P* each have measure 35° and *AB* = *PQ*. Which additional piece of information is sufficient to determine whether triangle *ABC* is congruent to triangle *PQR*?

A) The lengths of sides *BC* and *QR*
B) The measures of angle *B* and angle *R*
C) The lengths of sides *AC* and *QR*
D) No additional information is necessary

Measuring Shapes

Tags: Geometry & Trigonometry • Area and Perimeter • Volume and Surface Area

....

Definitions

- **Perimeter** is the distance around the outside edge of a shape. If a question is asking about fencing for a yard or ribbon to wrap around a craft project, you're dealing with a perimeter problem.

- **Area** is the amount of space inside a shape. If a question is about tiling a floor, painting a wall, or laying carpet, it's an area problem.

- **Congruent** objects are the same shape and size.

- **Similar** objects have the same angles but are different sizes.

- **Volume** is the amount of space contained inside a 3 dimensional shape. If a question is about the amount of liquid a container can hold or the amount of water displaced when an object is placed in a tank, it's a volume problem.

When you are taking the SAT in Bluebook, in the upper right corner there is a Reference button and clicking it will open a box of useful geometry formulas, so you don't need to memorize these unless you want to.

x²

Reference

REFERENCE

    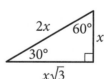

$A = \pi r^2$ $A = \ell w$ $A = \frac{1}{2} bh$ $c^2 = a^2 + b^2$ Special Right Triangles
$C = 2\pi r$

$V = \ell w h$ $V = \pi r^2 h$ $V = \frac{4}{3}\pi r^3$ $V = \frac{1}{3}\pi r^2 h$ $V = \frac{1}{3}\ell w h$

The number of degrees of arc in a circle is 360.
The number of radians of arc in a circle is 2π
The sum of the measures in degrees of the angles of a triangle is 180.

All About Triangles

To find the **perimeter** of a triangle, just add up the three side lengths. That's the easy part; sometimes, you might have to use the Pythagorean Theorem to find a missing side.

To find the **area** of a triangle, find a perpendicular base and height of the triangle, multiply them, and divide by 2.

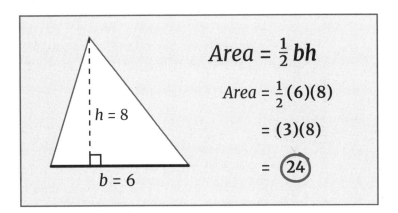

$$Area = \frac{1}{2} bh$$

$$Area = \frac{1}{2}(6)(8)$$

$$= (3)(8)$$

$$= \boxed{24}$$

$h = 8$

$b = 6$

NOTE

If a triangle is **obtuse**, the altitude that gives the height may be **outside** the triangle.

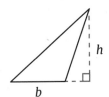

You can find the base and height starting from **any side**. Just pick a convenient side and draw a perpendicular line to the opposite vertex.

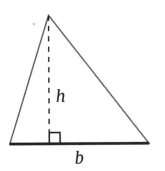
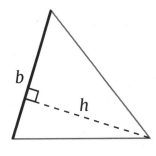
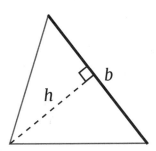

All About Rectangles

The perimeter and area of a rectangle involves its length (l) and width (w). The **perimeter** is just the sum of all four sides ($P = 2l + 2w$). The **area** is the product of the length and width ($A = lw$).

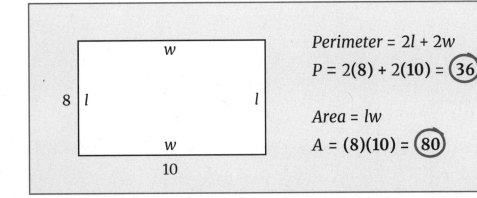

$$Perimeter = 2l + 2w$$

$$P = 2(8) + 2(10) = \boxed{36}$$

$$Area = lw$$

$$A = (8)(10) = \boxed{80}$$

EXAMPLE 1

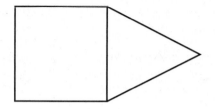

In the figure above, the triangle is equilateral and the area of the square is 25. What is the perimeter of the triangle?

SOLUTION

To find the **perimeter of the triangle**, we need to know a side. Luckily, the square and triangle *share a side*. Let's use what we know about the area of a square to find a side. Since the triangle is equilateral, that'll give us **every** side of the triangle.

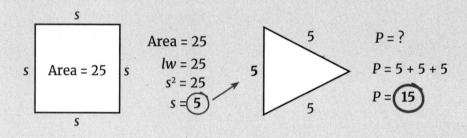

EXAMPLE 2

Square A has side lengths that are 7 times as long as the side lengths of square B. The area of square A is k times the area of square B. What is the value of k?

NOTE

Notice that these two squares are similar shapes. If you have two similar shapes and one has sides n times longer than the other, it's perimeter will be n times as large, its area will be n^2 times as large, and its volume will be n^3 times as large.

TIP

If you don't like working with sides labeled with s, you can just pick a number for the side length of the smaller square!

SOLUTION

Let's start by drawing some pictures:

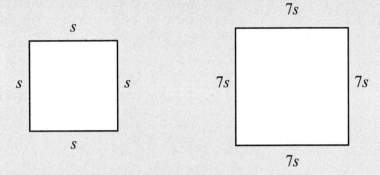

We don't know how long B's sides are, so let's just call them s. Then since the sides of A are 7 times as long, we can label its sides $7s$. Now we can find the area of each of these squares:

$$\text{Area}_B = s \cdot s = s^2$$

$$\text{Area}_A = 7s \cdot 7s = 49s^2$$

Now we can see that the area of square A is 49 times the area of square B, so our answer is 49.

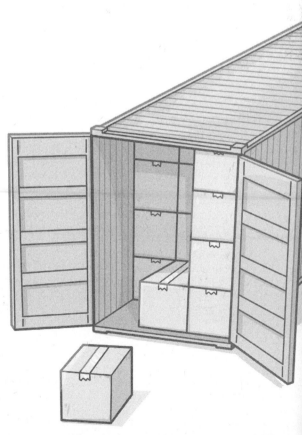

NOTE

If a shape gets wider or narrower along its height (such as with a **cone** or **pyramid**), we'll need to make a small adjustment to this basic formula.

Volume is the amount of space inside an object

Think of volume as the amount of water, confetti, or candy that would fill a given container with parallel and congruent bases. The volume formula looks slightly different depending on the container's shape, but there is a *common pattern* behind each one:

$$Volume = (base\ area) \times (height)$$

Picture stacking 2D shapes to make 3D shapes

We can see WHY this is the volume formula if we think of 3D shapes as "stacks" of 2D shapes. For example, we can think of a **rectangular prism** (box) as a **stack of rectangles**. We get its volume by finding the area of one slice (*length x width*) and multiplying by the number of slices (*height*).

$$Volume\ of\ box = (lw) \times (h)$$

TIP

A **rectangular prism** is made of up six rectangles all meeting at right angles.

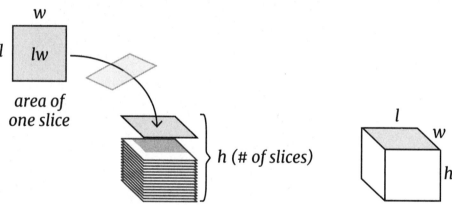

area of one slice   *h (# of slices)*

Check those references!

Remember on test day you can always bring up a cheat sheet of geometry formulas, including the formulas for volume. Just look for that reference button in the top right of the app!

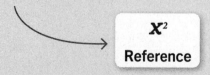

x^2
Reference

EXAMPLE 3

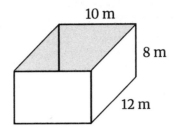

What is the maximum number of cubes with side length 2 meters that will fit into the rectangular box shown above?

SOLUTION

First, identify the goal: we're looking for the **number of cubes** with side 2 that will fit *inside* this box. That means we need to (1) find the **volume** of the box, (2) find the volume of each cube, and (3) divide the box volume by the cube volume.

(1) *find volume of box*

$$V = lwh$$
$$= (8)(10)(12)$$
$$= 960 \text{ m}^3$$

(2) *find volume of cube*

$$V = s^3$$
$$= (2)^3$$
$$= 8 \text{ m}^3$$

(3) *divide box by cube*

$$\# cubes = V_{box} \div V_{cubes}$$
$$= (960 \text{ m}^3) \div (8 \text{ m}^3)$$
$$= \boxed{120}$$

Surface Area is the sum of the area of each face

Think of it as how many square feet of wrapping paper or paint you would need to perfectly cover a box. Really, there's nothing new to learn here! It's just several standard area problems rolled into one.

EXAMPLE 4

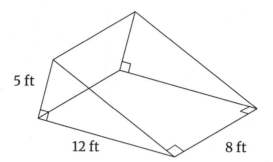

What is the surface area, in square feet, of the solid wedge shown above?

SOLUTION

This shape is made up of two triangles and three rectangles. The only missing measurement is the hypotenuse of the side triangles. We can use the **Pythagorean Theorem** to find that $5^2 + 12^2 = 13^2$, or we could remember that 5-12-13 is a special right triangle! Once we know the side is 13, we can find the area of each piece:

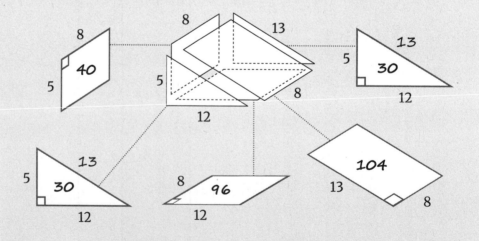

So our surface area is 40 + 30 + 96 + 104 + 30 = $\boxed{300}$

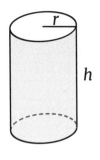

$SA = 2\pi r^2 + 2\pi rh$

$V = \pi r^2 h$

Unwrap cylinders to see their surface area

The curved surface of a cylinder is secretly just a *rectangle* (imagine unrolling the last sheet on a tube of wrapping paper). The area of that rectangle is the **height** of the cylinder times the **circumference** of the circle base:

Surface Area (cylinder) = Area$_{top}$ + Area$_{side}$ + Area$_{bottom}$

Surface Area = $\pi r^2 + 2\pi rh + \pi r^2$

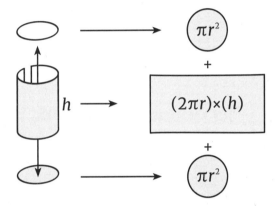

Stack circles to see the volume of a cylinder

Just as a rectangular prism can be thought of as a stack of rectangles, a cylinder can be thought of as a **stack of circles**. The volume of a cylinder is the area of a circle (base) multiplied by the number of circles in the stack (height):

Volume (stack of circles) = Area (πr^2) × Height (h)

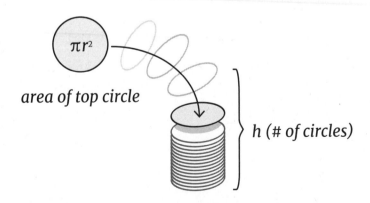

area of top circle

h (# of circles)

Right circular cones have a right triangle inside

The base of a cone is a *circle*. Its **height** (*h*), drawn from tip to base, is perpendicular to the **radius** (*r*). The **slant height** (*s*) is the edge of the cone. Notice the right triangle that these create:

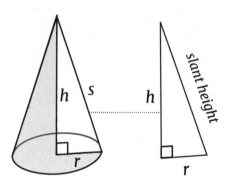

$$\text{Lateral Surface Area} = \pi rs$$

$$\text{Total Surface Area} = \pi rs + \pi r^2$$

$$\text{Volume} = \frac{\pi r^2 h}{3}$$

Rectangular pyramids have a ton of right triangles

The base of the right rectangular pyramid is a *rectangle* and the sides are all *triangles*. Its **height** (*h*), drawn down from the tip, is perpendicular to the base. To find the surface area, you'll need to use the Pythagorean Theorem to find the height of each side triangle. Notice that their **bases** are either *w* or *l*, but the **slant height** is trickier. You need to use a clever right triangle to find those slants:

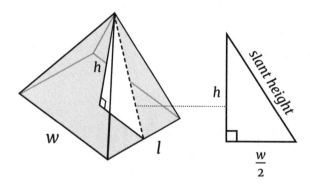

$$SA = \text{side areas} + lw$$

$$\text{Volume} = \frac{lwh}{3}$$

Spheres are all about that radius

A sphere is just a ball. The **radius** of a sphere is the distance from the center to *any* point on the sphere. A **hemisphere** is just half of a sphere.

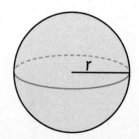

$$\text{Surface Area} = 4\pi r^2$$

$$\text{Volume} = \frac{4}{3}\pi r^3$$

Practice Problems
Use your new skills to answer each question.

1

The side length of a square is 37 centimeters (cm). What is the perimeter, in cm, of the square?

A) 74
B) 148
C) 185
D) 1369

2

The area of a square is 169 square feet. What is the side length, in feet, of this square?

3

What is the area, in square inches, of a rectangle with a length of 65 inches (in) and a width of 48 in?

4

Rectangles $ABCD$ and $PQRS$ are similar rectangles, where $\overline{AB}$ corresponds to $\overline{PQ}$ and $\overline{BC}$ corresponds to $\overline{QR}$. If $PQ = BC = 3AB$ and the perimeter of rectangle $ABCD$ is 40 units, what is the area, in units squared, of rectangle $PQRS$?

A) 75
B) 120
C) 300
D) 675

5

A right circular cone has a radius of 3 centimeters (cm) and a height of 8 cm. What is the volume, in cubic centimeters, of the cone?

A) 8π
B) 24π
C) 64π
D) 72π

6

A right circular cylinder has a volume of 150π. If the radius of the cylinder is 5, what is the height of the cylinder?

7

A cube has volume of 343 cubic inches. What is its surface area, in square inches?

A) 7
B) 49
C) 294
D) 392

8

A particular rectangular packing box is 6 inches long, 8 inches wide, and 2 inches tall. What is the volume of the box in cubic inches?

A) 76
B) 96
C) 152
D) 256

9

A cube has a volume of 54,872 inches cubed. What is the edge length, in inches, of the cube?

10

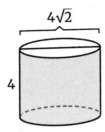

What is the volume, in cubic inches, of the largest rectangular box that will fit inside a right circular cylinder that is 4 inches tall with a diameter that is $4\sqrt{2}$ inches long?

A) 16
B) $16\sqrt{2}$
C) 64
D) $64\sqrt{2}$

11

A cube has a surface area of 96 square meters. What is the volume, in cubic meters, of the cube?

12

Two cylindrical planters each have a height of 30 centimeters (cm). The radius of planter A is 20 cm and the radius of planter B is 30% longer than the radius of container A. What is the volume, in cubic centimeters, of planter B?

A) $5,880\pi$
B) $12,000\pi$
C) $15,600\pi$
D) $20,280\pi$

13

A hexagonal prism has a height of 12 centimeters (cm) and a volume of 312 cm³. What is the area, in cm² of the base of the prism? (The volume of a hexagonal prism is equal to Bh where B is the area of the base and h is the height of the prism.)

14

A rock is placed in an aquarium and then the aquarium is filled with water. The aquarium is shaped like a rectangular prism with a base of 16 in by 48 in. If adding 10,000 cubic inches of water fills it to a depth of 16 inches, what is the volume of the rock in cubic inches?

15

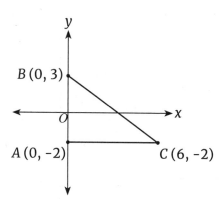

What is the area, in square coordinate units, of $\triangle ABC$ in the figure above?

A) 12
B) 15
C) 24
D) 30

Trigonometry

Tags: Geometry & Trigonometry • Trigonometry

....

SohCahToa

There are three key functions from trig that you need to know: sine, cosine, and tangent. On the SAT, you'll see them labelled as **sin**θ, **cos**θ, and **tan**θ, where θ is the angle of a right triangle. These functions tell us how an *angle* of a right triangle relates to the *sides* of the right triangle. To help us review what we mean by sin, cos, and tan, let's first draw and label a right triangle, focusing on one angle:

Important

If we were focusing on angle *B* instead of angle *A*, the sides would have different labels!

Side *AC* would be "opposite" angle *B*, and side *BC* would be "adjacent." The hypotenuse is always the hypotenuse.

1. *Draw a right triangle*

2. *Focus on angle A*

3. *Label the hypotenuse*

4. *Label legs "adjacent" to A and "opposite" from A*

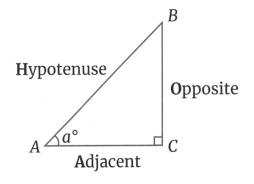

Sine, cosine, and tangent are functions, complete with inputs and outputs. They take an **angle** of a triangle (such as angle *A* above) as an input and spit out a **fraction** which is a ratio of the different sides:

$$\text{Sin } A = \frac{Opposite}{Hypotenuse} \qquad \text{Cos } A = \frac{Adjacent}{Hypotenuse} \qquad \text{Tan } A = \frac{Opposite}{Adjacent}$$

To answer basic trig questions, you'll need to memorize these ratios. Luckily, we have "SohCahToa" to make this a simpler task. "**Soh**" reminds you that Sine is Opposite over Hypotenuse. "**Cah**" reminds you that Cosine is Adjacent over Hypotenuse. And "**Toa**", well, you get the picture!

Use SohCahToa to complete the trig function identities below.

Triangle	SohCahToa
B, 5, 4, A, a°, 3, C	1. Sin A = $\frac{Opposite}{Hypotenuse}$ = $\frac{4}{5}$ 2. Cos A = $\frac{Adjacent}{Hypotenuse}$ = ____ 3. Tan A = $\frac{Opposite}{Adjacent}$ = ____

Now do the same thing, but **focus on angle B.**

Triangle	SohCahToa
B, b°, 15, 12, A, 9, C	4. Sin B = $\frac{Opposite}{Hypotenuse}$ = $\frac{9}{15}$ 5. Cos B = $\frac{Adjacent}{Hypotenuse}$ = ____ 6. Tan B = $\frac{Opposite}{Adjacent}$ = ____

Remember

When we change the angle we're focusing on, the side labels change too!

Familiar

Do these side ratios look familiar? This is one of the "special" right triangles.

Now work backwards! Use SohCahToa to **label the sides of the triangle**.

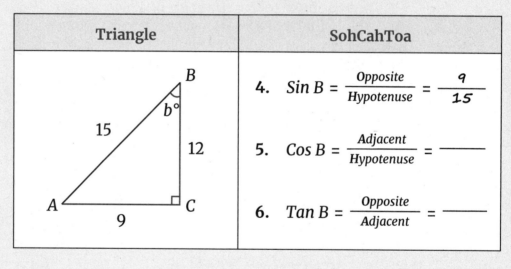

Triangle	SohCahToa
B, b°, A, C	Sin B = $\frac{Opposite}{Hypotenuse}$ = $\frac{13}{26}$ Cos B = $\frac{Adjacent}{Hypotenuse}$ = $\frac{13\sqrt{3}}{26}$ Tan B = $\frac{Opposite}{Adjacent}$ = $\frac{13}{13\sqrt{3}}$

Answers: 1. 4/5 2. 3/5 3. 4/3 4. 9/15 5. 12/15 6. 9/12

Side $\overline{AB}$ = 26   Side $\overline{BC}$ = 13√3   Side $\overline{AC}$ = 13

Even More Drills!

There's no better way to solidify SohCahToa in ya' brain than to use it over and over. Complete the drill below to check your understanding.

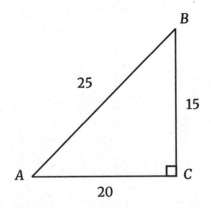

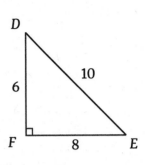

Use SohCahToa and the above triangles to complete the table.

SohCahToa	
1. sin(B) =	7. tan(A) =
2. sin(E) =	8. tan(D) =
3. cos(A) =	9. sin(A) =
4. cos(D) =	10. sin(D) =
5. tan(B) =	11. cos(B) =
6. tan(E) =	12. cos(E) =

Notice

Many of the trig ratios for triangles *ABC* and *DEF* simplify to the same fraction. Why is that?

It's because these triangles are **similar.** Though their side lengths are different, their proportions are the same.

Bonus Notice: they are both special 3-4-5 right triangles!

Answers: 1. 20/25   2. 6/10   3. 20/15   4. 6/10   5. 20/15   6. 6/8

7. 15/20   8. 8/6   9. 15/25   10. 8/10   11. 15/25   12. 8/10

MEMORIZE: Special Trig Identity

There is a special identity that shows up pretty regularly on the SAT, so it's worth memorizing. You don't really need to know WHY it's true, but we'll cover that in a second to help you remember it. Here is essentially the same idea written in three different ways:

$$\sin(\theta) = \cos(90 - \theta)$$
$$\cos(\alpha) = \sin(90 - \alpha)$$

$$\text{if } \sin(x) = \cos(y), \text{ then } x + y = 90$$

One More

Similarly, it can be helpful to remember this handy identity:

$$\sin^2(x) + \cos^2(x) = 1$$

Just memorize that. Stare at it. *Become* it. Burn it into your brain.... Done?

Okay, now let's chat about why this is a thing. Notice that, because what's "adjacent" and what's "opposite" switch depending on which angle you focus on, **sin (A)** is equal to **cos (B)**:

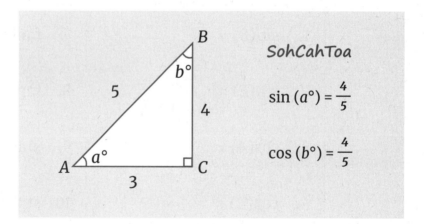

SohCahToa

$$\sin(a°) = \frac{4}{5}$$

$$\cos(b°) = \frac{4}{5}$$

Now, if all angles add up to 180°, and one angle is 90°, then the other two *must* add up to 90°. That means we could write angles A and B in a different way, solving the mystery behind that bulky thing we memorized:

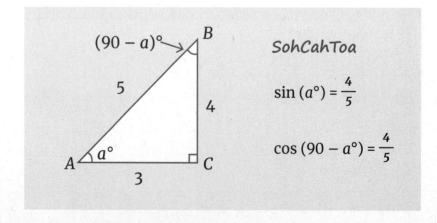

SohCahToa

$$\sin(a°) = \frac{4}{5}$$

$$\cos(90 - a°) = \frac{4}{5}$$

EXAMPLE 1

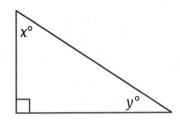

In the triangle above, sine of $x°$ = 0.6. What is cosine of $x°$?

A) 0.36
B) 0.6
C) 0.8
D) 1.66

SOLUTION

At first this problem might seem tough, but we shouldn't worry about that just yet! We see "sine" and "cosine," so we should immediately write SohCahToa:

(1) *write SohCahToa!*   SohCahToa

Step one done! Now, the only weirdness is that the problem uses decimals when we're used to dealing in fractions. But that's no problem, we can change 0.6 to a fraction:

(2) *write 0.6 as a fraction* $\sin(x) = 0.6 = \frac{6}{10}$

Now we're getting somewhere. We know that sine is O/H. So we can use this information to label our triangle.

(3) *label triangle*

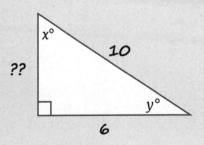

Continued on next page →

Now to find cos(x), we just need that third side. Luckily, we can use the **pythagorean theorem** to find that third side.

④ *use pythag's theorem*

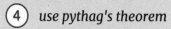

$A^2 + B^2 = C^2$

$6^2 + B^2 = 10^2$

$36 + B^2 = 100$

$B^2 = 64$

$B = 8$

Bingo! Using the information given to us, SohCahToa, and pythagorean's theorem, we know the third side length is 8. Now to find cos(x), we just apply SohCahToa again:

⑤ *find cos(x) with "Cah"*

$\cos(x) = \frac{8}{10} = \boxed{0.8}$

C

PORTAL

Converting between radians and degrees works just like the other unit conversions we practiced in *Ratios and Proportions*! To review, turn to page 559.

Radians

Instead of degrees, we can also measure angles in **radians**. The measure of an angle in radians is the *length of the arc* it would span if it were at the center of a circle with radius 1 (often called the "unit circle"):

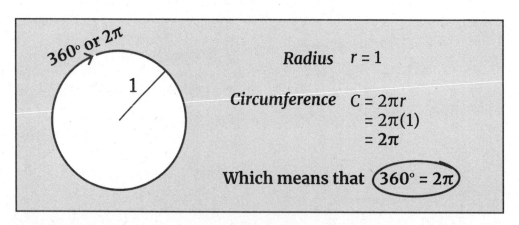

Radius $r = 1$

Circumference $C = 2\pi r$
$= 2\pi(1)$
$= 2\pi$

Which means that $360° = 2\pi$

For most questions involving radians, just remembering that **360° = 2π** will help you convert degrees to radians and vice versa.

Unit Circle

You may remember learning a good bit about the unit circle in school. It looks something like this:

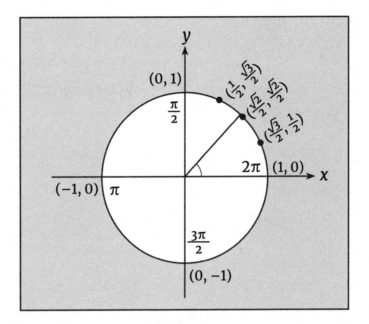

Use Special Right Triangles

Here's some good news: you don't have to memorize this unit circle for the SAT! We can find any point or angle on the unit circle if we draw a right triangle using the information we're given. As we'll see in the practice problems, there are really only two types of special triangles that come up in unit circle problems:

Drawing Triangles

If you're given a radians measurement, you can figure out the right triangle by **converting it to degrees**.

If you're given a point, then the x and y coordinates tell you the **length of the legs** of the triangle.

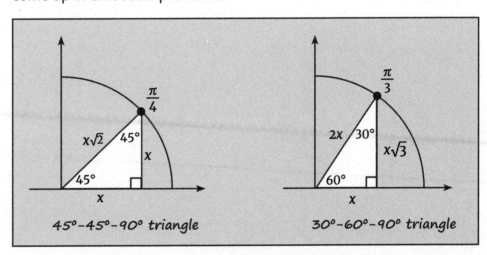

You can use these **special right triangles**, coupled with the knowledge that **360° = 2π**, to answer unit circle questions on the test. And remember, these special right triangles are given to you in the instructions box! So when in doubt, **check the box**.

Practice Problems

Use your new skills to answer each question.

1

In a right triangle, one of the angles measures $x°$ where $\sin(90° - x°) = \frac{3}{5}$. What is $\cos(x°)$?

2

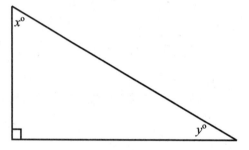

If $\cos(x°) = \frac{1}{2}$, what is the value of $\sin(y°)$?

A) $\frac{1}{2}$

B) $\frac{\sqrt{3}}{2}$

C) $\frac{\sqrt{2}}{2}$

D) $\frac{\sqrt{3}}{3}$

3

In a circle with center O, the central $\angle AOB$ has a measure of $\frac{\pi}{x}$ radians. If the area of the sector formed by angle $\angle AOB$ is one sixth the area of the circle, what is the value of x?

4

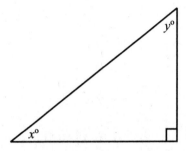

For the right triangle above, which of the following must be true?

I. $\sin(x) = \cos(x)$
II. $\sin(y) = \cos(x)$
III. $\cos(y) = \sin(x)$

A) I only
B) I and II only
C) II and III only
D) I, II, and III

5

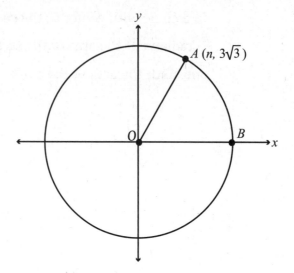

In the *xy*-plane above, points *A* and *B* lie on the circle with center O. The measure of $\angle ACB$ is $\frac{\pi}{3}$ radians. What is the value of *n*?

6

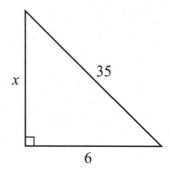

Which equation shows the relationship between the side lengths of the given triangle?

A) $6x = 35$

B) $6 + x = 35$

C) $6^2 + x^2 = 35^2$

D) $6^2 - x^2 = 35^2$

7

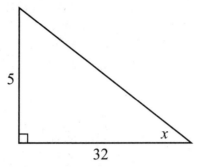

In the triangle shown, what is the value of tan($x°$)?

A) $\frac{5}{32}$

B) $\frac{32}{5}$

C) $\frac{5}{27}$

D) $\frac{27}{5}$

8

An angle has a measure of 156 degrees. What is the measure of the angle in <u>radians</u>?

A) $\frac{11}{12}\pi$

B) $\frac{13}{15}\pi$

C) $\frac{15}{13}\pi$

D) $\frac{13}{30}\pi$

9

The number of radians in a 1,080 degree angle can be written as $a\pi$ where a is a constant. What is the value of a?

The measure of angle S is $\frac{3\pi}{4}$ radians. The measure of angle R is $\frac{2\pi}{3}$ radians greater than the measure of angle S. What is the measure of angle R in degrees?

A) 15

B) 120

C) 255

D) 510

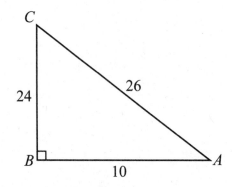

In the figure above, what is the value of $\cos(C)$?

A) $\frac{5}{13}$

B) $\frac{5}{12}$

C) $\frac{12}{5}$

D) $\frac{12}{13}$

Triangle RST is a right triangle and $\sin(R) = \frac{4}{5}$. Side $\overline{RT}$ is the hypotenuse and has a length of 35. What is the length of side $\overline{ST}$?

13

$AB = 64$
$BC = 252$
$AC = 260$

The side lengths of triangle *ABC* are given. Triangle *UVW* is similar to triangle *ABC* where *A* corresponds to *U* and *B* corresponds to *V*. What is the value of tan *W*?

A) $\frac{16}{65}$

B) $\frac{16}{63}$

C) $\frac{63}{65}$

D) $\frac{63}{16}$

NOTE

While fairly common on the SAT, circle questions do not come up on the PSAT.

Circles

Tags: Geometry and Trigonometry • Perimeter and Area • Circles

Circles are all about the radius and proportions

Any line from the center of a circle to its edge is a **radius**. Any line connecting two points of the circle that goes through the center is a **diameter**. A **tangent line** touches the circle at only one point and is perpendicular to the radius at that point.

TIP

If there's a circle involved **find the radius**. Almost everything is related to the radius, so if you find the radius you can usually find whatever is being asked for.

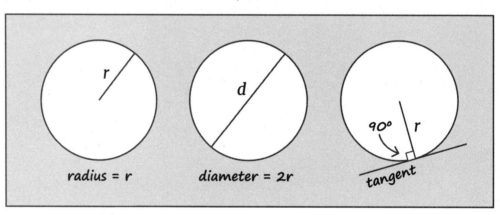

The **circumference** of a circle is equal to $2\pi r$. The **area** is equal to πr^2.

TIP

Circumference is just the word for **perimeter** of a circle.

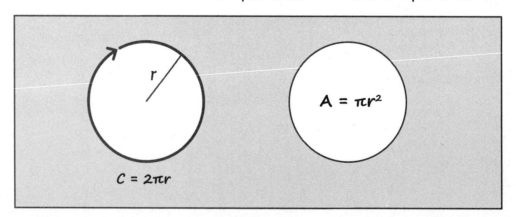

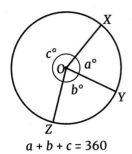

$a + b + c = 360$

Circles can be divided up into sectors

When we talk about angles in a circle, there are clearly no vertices, interior angles, or exterior angles.

If a set of radii are drawn from the center of the circle to its edge, they divide a circle into **sectors**. The measure of the angle between the two radii is called the sector's **arc measure**. The sum of the angles around the center of the circle will always equal 360°. Note that we can say that angle $\angle XOY$ has measure $a°$ and that arc $\overline{XY}$ has measure $a°$. Don't confuse the arc measure with the arc length, which is a fraction of the circumference of the circle.

The **proportion** of a piece (or a wedge) to the whole circle is the same for its angle measurement, arc length, and area.

$$\frac{\text{Piece}}{\text{Whole}} = \frac{\text{Angle measure}}{360°} = \frac{\text{Arc length}}{\text{Circumference}} = \frac{\text{Wedge area}}{\text{Circle area}}$$

$$\frac{\text{PIECE}}{\text{WHOLE}} = \frac{x°}{360°} = \frac{\overset{\frown}{ABC}}{C = 2\pi r} = \frac{}{A = \pi r^2}$$

EXAMPLE 1

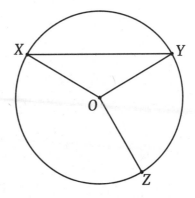

Point O is the center of the circle shown above and the measure of $\angle OXY$ is 20°. If the length of $\overline{OZ}$ is 9, what is the length of arc $\overline{XZY}$?

A) 18π

B) 11π

C) 7π

D) π

Our goal is to find the length of arc $\overline{XZY}$. To do this we will want to set up a piece over whole equation with the angle measure and the circumference.

$\overline{OZ}$ is a radius of the circle, so we know the radius of the circle is 8. From the formula sheet, we have $C = 2\pi r$, so the circumference here is $C = 2\pi(8) = 18\pi$.

Now we need to find the angle. The only angle we are told to start with is that $\angle OXY$ is 20°. If we look at triangle $\triangle XOY$ we see that two sides, $\overline{XO}$ and $\overline{YO}$ are both radiuses of the circle, so they must be the same length. This means that the triangle is isosceles, so $\angle OXY$ and $\angle OYX$ are the same. We can then use the fact that there are 180 degrees in a triangle to find that $\angle XOY$ is 180 – 20 – 20 = 140°. The angle corresponding to arc $\overline{XZY}$ and $\angle OXY$ together form the full circle, so the angle for our arc is 360 – 140 = 220°.

Setting up our piece over whole equation gives us $\frac{220}{360} = \frac{\pi}{18\pi}$.

Solving this gives us 11π, which is **choice B**.

Equation of a Circle

Occasionally, you'll be asked about the equation of a circle. For these problems, you'll need to memorize one more formula:

The standard equation of a circle centered at (h, k) and with radius r is:

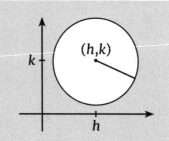

Equation of a Circle

$$(x - h)^2 + (y - k)^2 = r^2$$

Center: (h, k)   Radius: r

Digging Deeper

Ever wonder why the equation of a circle is what it is? No? Well, we'll tell you anyways. A circle is the set of points that are a fixed distance (the radius) from a single point (the center). A circle's equation is actually the same exact thing as using the **Pythagorean theorem** or the **distance formula** to find any point on that circle. We can see this if we draw it out.

Pick a point (x, y) on the circle and draw the radius connecting it to the center (h, k). Now draw a right triangle with that radius as the hypotenuse. With this picture, we can see how the equations are related:

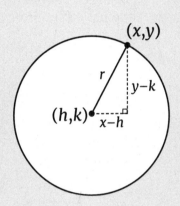

Equation of a Circle

$$(x - h)^2 + (y - k)^2 = r^2$$

Distance Formula

$$(x_1 - x_2)^2 + (y_1 - y_2)^2 = d^2$$

Pythagorean Theorem

$$a^2 + b^2 = c^2$$

EXAMPLE 2

Which of the following is the equation of a circle in the xy-plane with center $(5, -4)$ and a radius with endpoint $(2, 0)$?

A) $(x - 5)^2 + (y + 4)^2 = 25$
B) $(x + 5)^2 + (y - 4)^2 = 25$
C) $(x - 5)^2 + (y + 4)^2 = 5$
D) $(x + 5)^2 + (y - 4)^2 = 5$

SOLUTION

The first step is to plug what we know about our circle into the standard equation of a circle.

① *rewrite circle equation* $(x - h)^2 + (y - k)^2 = r^2$

② *plug in center (5, −4)* $(x - 5)^2 + (y - (-4))^2 = r^2$

                                                            $(x - 5)^2 + (y + 4)^2 = r^2$

After plugging our given center into the equation of a circle, we can see immediately that choices B and D are out. Cross 'em off!

Now we just need to determine the radius of the circle. We aren't told how long the radius is, but we can **solve** for it! We know that point **(2, 0)** is on the circle. Let's plug that into our equation:

③ *plug in point (2, o)* $(2 - 5)^2 + (0 + 4)^2 = r^2$

④ *solve for r^2* $(-3)^2 + (4)^2 = r^2$

                                                            $9 + 16 = r^2$

                                                            $25 = r^2$

Now be careful! It's tempting here to solve for the radius, but the equation of a circle is set equal to r^2, **not r**. Just to be safe, let's rewrite the standard equation one last time:

⑤ *rewrite circle equation* $(x - h)^2 + (y - k)^2 = r^2$

⑥ *plug in what we know* $\boxed{(x - 5)^2 + (y + 4)^2 = 25}$ **A**

TIP

You could also work backwards on this problem by graphing each of the answer choices and seeing which has the required characteristics.

Completing the Square

Occasionally the SAT will give you an equation for a circle that isn't already in the nice form where we can read all of the information off. Sometimes you can get around this by graphing it in Desmos, but sometimes it is more helpful to use algebra to get it into standard form. Our big tool for doing this is **completing the square**.

To understand how to complete the square, lets start by thinking about what it means for a polynomial to be a square:

$$(x + 3)^2 = (x + 3)(x + 3) = x^2 + 3x + 3x + 9 = x^2 + 6x + 9$$

TIP

If you are working with a polynomial equation and not just a polynomial, you could also make a balanced change by adding the squared term to both sides instead of adding zero to one side.

Notice that when we square $(x + 3)$, the coefficient of the x term is 6, twice the 3 in our original binomial. This observation is the key to doing this process backwards.

Now consider the polynomial $x^2 + 8x + 3$. When we say we want to complete the square, our goal is to get the polynomial into the form $(x + h)^2 + k$. Since the coefficient on x^2 is already 1, we can focus on the term $8x$. As we observed with $(x + 3)^2$, the h we are looking for will be half of the coefficient of x, so here $h = 4$. If we multiply out $(x + 4)^2$ we get $x^2 + 8x + 16$. That 16 is missing in our initial polynomial. We can deal with this by adding a clever form of zero: $16 - 16$. This gives us:

$$x^2 + 8x + (16 - 16) + 3 = (x^2 + 8x + 16) - 16 + 3 = (x + 4)^2 - 13$$

EXAMPLE 3

$$x^2 + y^2 - 4x + 6y = 23$$

The above equation represents a circle in the xy-plane. What is the radius of the circle?

A) 2
B) 3
C) 6
D) 36

SOLUTION

Option 1: Completing the Square

Yowza! This is a tough problem, but all we need to know is **(1)** the equation of a circle, and **(2)** how to complete the square.

To figure out the radius of the circle, we'll need to **rearrange** this equation until it's in the standard equation of a circle form. To do this, we're going to need to **complete the square** *twice!* Once for *x*, and once for *y*. First, let's focus on the *x*'s.

TIP

Since the coefficient on the *x* term is –4, our *h* is –2. Since $(-2)^2 = 4$ we add zero in the form of 4 – 4 and then after we factor we move that extra –4 over to the other side of the equation.

① *rewrite equation* $\qquad\qquad x^2 + y^2 - 4x + 6y = 23$

② *gather the variables* $\qquad\qquad x^2 - 4x + y^2 + 6y = 23$

③ *complete the square (x)* $\quad x^2 - 4x + 4 - 4 + y^2 + 6y = 23$

$$(x - 2)^2 - 4 + y^2 + 6y = 23$$

$$(x - 2)^2 + y^2 + 6y = 27$$

④ *complete the square (y)* $\quad (x - 2)^2 + y^2 + 6y + 9 - 9 = 27$

$$(x - 2)^2 + (y + 3)^2 - 9 = 27$$

$$(x - 2)^2 + (y + 3)^2 = 36$$

Aha! Now that the equation is in the proper form, we can read the radius. If $r^2 = 36$, then $r = 6$. Choice C is the right answer!

C

Option 2: Graph with Desmos

Let's try graphing the function in Desmos! Desmos marks several points on the circle including the highest and lowest point with respect to the *xy*-coordinate plane.

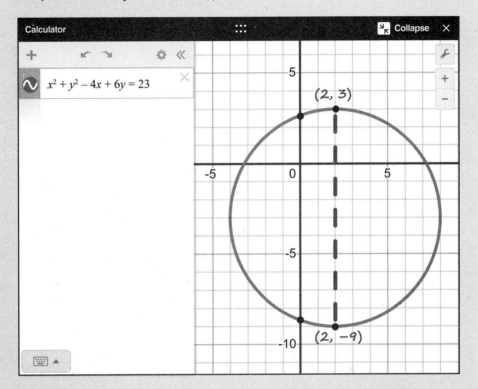

Desmos automatically points out the top and bottom points of the circle. If we add a line to connect them, that would give us a diameter of the circle. Since the two end points of the diameter have the same *x*-coordinate, we can find the length of the diameter by **subtracting the *y*-coordinates:**

$$3 - (-9) = 12$$

This tells us that the <u>diameter</u> of the circle is **12**, so the <u>radius</u> is half of that: **6**.

Practice Problems

Use your new skills to answer each question.

1

A circle has a radius of 3. What is the area of the circle?

A) 3π
B) 6π
C) 9π
D) 12π

2

A circle has a circumference of 87π centimeters. What is the diameter of the circle?

3

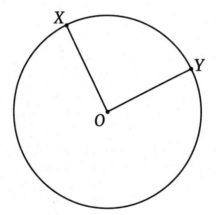

In the circle above with center O, minor arc $\overline{XY}$ has a measure of 37°. What is the measure of $\angle XOY$?

A) 37°
B) 53°
C) 143°
D) 323°

4

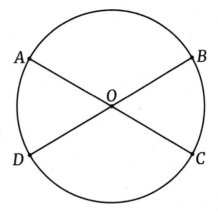

The circle shown has center O and diameters $\overline{AC}$ and $\overline{BD}$. If the length of $\overline{AC}$ is 72 centimeters and the length of arc $\overset{\frown}{AB}$ is three times the length of arc $\overline{AD}$, what is the length of arc $\overline{CD}$ in centimenters?

A) 13.5π
B) 18π
C) 27π
D) 93π

5

A sphere has a volume of $7,776\pi$. What is the radius of the sphere?

6

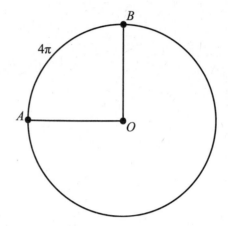

In the circle above, $\angle AOB$ is a right angle and the length of minor arc $\overline{AB}$ is 4π inches. What is the area of the circle, in square inches?

A) 16
B) 16π
C) 64π
D) 128π

7

A circle in the xy-plane has the equation $(x - 3)^2 + (x + 4)^2 = 16$. What is the radius of the circle?

A) 4
B) 8
C) 16
D) 256

8

Which of the following is an equation of a circle in the xy-plane with center $(1, 2)$ and a radius with endpoint $(-5, -6)$?

A) $(x - 1)^2 + (y - 2)^2 = 10$
B) $(x - 1)^2 + (y - 2)^2 = 100$
C) $(x - 1)^2 + (y + 2)^2 = 100$
D) $(x - 1)^2 + (y + 2)^2 = 64$

9

$$x^2 + 4x + y^2 - 6y = 12$$

The equation above represents a circle in the xy-plane. What is the radius of the circle?

A) $2\sqrt{3}$
B) 5
C) 12
D) 25

10

A circle is placed in the xy-coordinate plane so that its center is at $(1, -3)$. Point A is on the circle and located at $(6, -15)$. If $\overline{AB}$ is a diameter of the circle, what are the coordinates of point B?

A) $(6, 12)$
B) $(-6, 15)$
C) $(-4, -15)$
D) $(-4, 9)$

UNIT

Challenge Problems

Chapters

Overview

This unit provides practice and explanations for some of the toughest SAT math problems you are likely to encounter. Anyone can test their mettle against these problems, but only students aiming to get over a 700 on the Math section needs to nail these questions on test day.

Challenge Problem Set 1

These problems represent the toughest SAT math problems you'll see on test day.

1

In the xy-plane, two parabolas intersect at exactly one point, their shared vertex. The first parabola has the equation $y = 2x^2 - 12x + 22$ and the second parabola has the equation $y = -3x^2 - 3bx + c$. What is the value of $b + c$?

2

Triangle ABC is similar to triangle RST where A corresponds to R and B and S are right angles. If $\sin C = \frac{36}{85}$, what is $\tan R$?

3

In triangles *ABC* and *RST*, angles *B* and *S* are both 70°, side *AB* = 5 and side *RS* = 35. Which additional piece of information is sufficient to prove that triangle *ABC* is similar to triangle *RST*?

A)   The measures of angles *A* and *R* are 30° and 40° respectively
B)   *AC* = 7 and *RT* = 49
C)   *BC* = 7 and *ST* = 49
D)   *AC* = 7 and *ST* = 25

4

For groups of 15 or more, a botanical garden charges $20 per person for the first 15 people and then $10 for each additional person. Which function gives the total charge, in dollars, for a group with *n* people where $n \geq 15$?

A) $f(n) = 10n + 300$
B) $f(n) = 20n - 150$
C) $f(n) = 30n - 300$
D) $f(n) = 10n + 150$

5

Data set *A* consists of 6 positive integers. The list shown below gives 5 of the integers from data set *A*:

$$15, 36, 47, 64, 77$$

The mean and median of data set *A* are integers and are equal. What is the missing integer from data set *A*?

Explanations

Answers & explanations for Challenge Problem Set 1

....

1. In the xy-plane, two parabolas intersect at exactly one point, their shared vertex. The first parabola has the equation $y = 2x^2 - 12x + 22$ and the second parabola has the equation $y = -3x^2 - 3bx + c$. What is the value of $b + c$?

SOLUTION

We can **find the vertex** of the first parabola either algebraically or by graphing. To do it algebraically, recall that:

- If a parabola has equation $y = rx^2 + sx + t$, then the x-coordinate of the vertex is $x = \frac{-s}{2r}$.

- Here, that means $x = \frac{(-1)(-12)}{2(2)} = 3$

- We can get the y-coordinate of the vertex by plugging in the x-coordinate: $y = 2(3)^2 - 12(3) + 22 = 4$.

- So our vertex is at $(3, 4)$.

Now we know that we want to find b and c so that the second parabola has the **same vertex**. There are a few ways to approach this. We could follow the same algebraic process again, we could graph it and use sliders, or a clever third option…

Since we know the **vertex** and the **coefficient of the x^2 term**, we have everything we need to get the <u>vertex form</u> of the equation: $y = -3(x - 3)^2 + 4$.

We can expand this out to get the <u>standard form</u> of the equation for the second parabola and compare it to the original equation given in the prompt:

$$y = -3x^2 + 18x - 23$$
$$y = -3x^2 - 3bx + c$$

$b = -6$

$c = -23$

Matching these up, we can now see that $c = -23$ and $b = -6$, so…

$$b + c = -29$$

2. Triangle *ABC* is similar to triangle *RST* where *A* corresponds to *R* and *B* and *S* are right angles. If $\sin C = \frac{36}{85}$, what is $\tan R$?

For geometry and trig problems, it is often helpful to make a sketch of the figure.

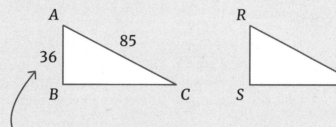

We know that $\sin C = \frac{36}{85}$, so we can write those lengths in.

This doesn't tell us exactly what the side lengths are (since it could be any scaling of this ratio), but since all we care about are the **ratios**, we can take the leg opposite C to be 36 and the hypotenuse to be 85. Then we can use the Pythagorean theorem:

$$BC = \sqrt{85^2 - 36^2} = 77$$

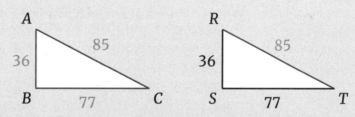

We know that **tan** is **opposite** over **adjacent**, and the leg opposite *A* is the one adjacent to *C*, so...

$$\tan A = \frac{77}{36} = \tan R$$

3. In triangles ABC and RST, angles B and S are both 70°, side $AB = 5$ and side $RS = 35$. Which additional piece of information is sufficient to prove that triangle ABC is similar to triangle RST?

A) The measures of angles A and R are 30° and 40° respectively
B) $AC = 7$ and $RT = 49$
C) $BC = 7$ and $ST = 49$
D) $AC = 7$ and $ST = 25$

SOLUTION

This question is asking us to consider how to prove that two triangles are similar. Ideally, we'll find a choice that makes the triangles have two similar side ratios with a similar angle in between (side-angle-side). Lets look at each answer choice:

A̶) The measures of angles A and R are 30° and 40° respectively

If triangles are similar then they have the same angles. Choice A gives us one **additional** angle in each triangle. This gives us <u>two</u> in each triangle, which is enough to let us work out the third. If the sets of three angles matched this would work, but they don't, so A is not our answer.

B̶) $AC = 7$ and $RT = 49$

We know that angles B and S are the same, so they correspond*. If the two originally given side lengths, AB and RS, correspond, then AC and RT would also correspond, and we see that we have the same ratio (7:1) between the triangles for both. However, this gives us **angle-side ratio-side ratio**, which is not sufficient to prove similarity.

(C)) $BC = 7$ and $ST = 49$

If B corresponds to S and AB corresponds to RS then BC corresponds to ST and both corresponding pairs of sides have the same ratio. Since we have side ratio-angle-side ratio this is sufficient! Let's check choice D just to be sure.

D̶) $AC = 7$ and $ST = 25$

This choice looks like it gives us two pairs of corresponding sides with the same ratio: AC with RS and AB with ST. However, for these pairs to be corresponding, we would also need angles A and S to correspond, and we only have information to let A correspond with R. If the triangles are isosceles they might still be similar, but we don't have enough information to prove it. D won't work either.

*NOTE

Technically, if the triangles were isosceles they might not have to correspond, but in that situation there would be a correspondence where they do, so we can assume they do here. We certainly don't have any other angle information to form other angle correspondences at this point.

4. For groups of 15 or more, a botanical garden charges $20 per person for the first 15 people and then $10 for each additional person. Which function gives the total charge, in dollars, for a group with n people where $n \geq 15$?

A) $f(n) = 10n + 300$
B) $f(n) = 20n - 150$
C) $f(n) = 30n - 300$
D) $f(n) = 10n + 150$

SOLUTION

We know that there are at least 15 people, so the charge will always be at least 20×15. If there are n people in the group, there are $n - 15$ people who are charged at the $10 rate.

Putting this together gives the function $f(n) = 20(15) + 10(n - 15)$. This simplifies to $f(n) = 10n + 150$, which is choice D!

5. Data set A consists of 6 positive integers. The list shown below gives 5 of the integers from data set A:

    15, 36, 47, 64, 77

The mean and median of data set A are integers and are equal. What is the missing integer from data set A?

SOLUTION

To find the median of a set of 6 numbers, we average the two middle numbers. If the missing number is not one of the two middle numbers, then our potential medians for this data set are:

$$\frac{36 + 47}{2} = 41.5 \quad \text{and} \quad \frac{47 + 64}{2} = 55.5$$

Neither are integers, which means they are not the median. That means our missing number, which we'll call x, must be one of the two middle numbers in the set. The median must be the average of 47 and x, and we know this median is equal to the mean of the whole set. Let's set up that equation and solve for x.

$$\frac{47 + x}{2} = \frac{15 + 36 + 47 + x + 64 + 77}{6}$$

Solving this equation for x gives us the answer: $x = 49.$

Challenge Problem Set 2

These problems represent the toughest SAT math problems you'll see on test day.

6

The labor charge at a car repair shop is $255 for the first three hours plus an hourly fee for each additional hour. The total cost for 6 hours of repair is $465. Which function f gives the total cost, in dollars, for x hours of repair, where $x \geq 3$?

A) $f(x) = 85x - 45$
B) $f(x) = 85x + 225$
C) $f(x) = 70x + 45$
D) $f(x) = 70x + 225$

7

$$y = -2x^2 + 4kx + 28k$$

In the given equation, k is a constant and is a negative integer. If the graph of the equation in the xy-plane has two x-intercepts, what is the largest possible value of k?

8

The measure of angle R is $\frac{5\pi}{4}$. The measure of angle S is $\frac{5\pi}{12}$ radians less than the measure of angle R. What is the measure of angle S in degrees?

A) 75
B) 150
C) 225
D) 300

9

A right square pyramid has a height of 5 cm and a volume of C cm³. If the surface area of the pyramid is $\frac{5}{4}C$ cm² , what is the side length, in centimeters, of the square base?

10

	Class A	Class B
≤ 50	0	1
51 – 60	2	4
61 – 70	3	5
71 – 80	7	7
81 – 90	8	4
91 – 100	5	4

Mr. Chen gave the same test to two of his classes and his students' scores are recorded in the frequency table above. Which of the following statements must be true?

A) The range of test scores for Class B is larger than the range of scores for Class A.

B) The average test score for Class A is larger than the average test score for Class B.

C) The median test score for Class A is larger than the median test score for Class B.

D) The highest test score in Class A is larger than the highest test score for Class B.

Explanations

Answers & explanations for Challenge Problem Set 2

....

6. The labor charge at a car repair shop is $255 for the first three hours plus an hourly fee for each additional hour. The total cost for 6 hours of repair is $465. Which function f gives the total cost, in dollars, for x hours of repair, where $x \geq 3$?

   A) $f(x) = 85x - 45$
   B) $f(x) = 85x + 225$
   C) $f(x) = 70x + 45$
   D) $f(x) = 70x + 225$

SOLUTION

We know that $x \geq 3$, so if the hourly rate is c, our function looks like $f(x) = 255 + c(x - 3)$. Plugging in the point we are given, we have $465 = 255 + c(6 - 3)$. Solving this for c we get 70. This gives us the function $f(x) = 255 + 70(x - 3)$ and after distributing and combining terms we get $f(x) = 70x + 45$, or choice C.

7.
$$y = -2x^2 + 4kx + 28k$$

In the given equation, k is a constant and is a negative integer. If the graph of the equation in the xy-plane has two x-intercepts, what is the largest possible value of k?

SOLUTION

If the graph has two x-intercepts, then $0 = -2x^2 + 4kx + 28k$ has two solutions. Using the **discriminant**, we have:

$$0 < b^2 - 4ac = (4k)^2 - 4(-2)(28k)$$

Simplifying this and factoring gives $0 < 16k(k + 14)$. For a product to be greater than zero, either both terms are positive or both are negative. Since we know from the problem statement that k is negative, this means $(k + 14) < 0$, or $k < -14$.

This means the largest possible integer value of k is $\boxed{-15.}$

TIP

The easiest solution to this problem is to graph it with k as a slider. The only tricky bit then is getting a useful range on the slider.

8. The measure of angle R is $\frac{5\pi}{4}$. The measure of angle S is $\frac{5\pi}{12}$ radians less than the measure of angle R. What is the measure of angle S in <u>degrees</u>?

A) 75
B) 150
C) 225
D) 300

SOLUTION

Translating into an equation, we have $S = \frac{5\pi}{4} - \frac{5\pi}{12} = \frac{5\pi}{6}$.

We can convert from radians to degrees by multiplying by $\frac{180}{\pi}$.

That gives us $S = \frac{5\pi}{6} \times \frac{180}{\pi} = \boxed{150°}$

9. A right square pyramid has a height of 5 cm and a volume of C cm³. If the surface area of the pyramid is $\frac{5}{4}C$ cm² , what is the side length, in centimeters, of the square base?

SOLUTION

The volume of a right square pyramid is $\frac{1}{3}x^2 h$ where x is the side of the square base and h is the height. Here, the height is 5, so:

$$V = \tfrac{1}{3}(5)x^2 = C$$

To find the **surface area** we first need to find the area of one of the <u>triangular faces</u>, which means we need the <u>slant height</u> of the pyramid. If we add a vertex in the center of the square base and connect it to the top of the pyramid and the midpoint of one of the sides of the base, we get a right triangle whose legs are h and $x/2$ and whose hypotenuse is the slant height. Using the Pythagorean theorem, slant height is $s = \sqrt{(x/2)^2 + 5^2}$. There are four triangular faces, which each have an area of $(1/2)xs$. Finally we have the square base, which has an area of x^2. Putting this all together, we have:

$$SA = x^2 + 2x\sqrt{(x^2/4) + 25} = \tfrac{5}{4}C$$

$$V = \tfrac{1}{3}(5)x^2 = C$$

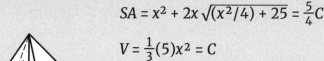

$$(\tfrac{5}{4})(\tfrac{1}{3})(5)x^2 = x^2 + 2x\sqrt{(x^2/4) + 25}$$

Solving this for x gives us $\boxed{x = 24.}$

10.

	Class A	Class B
≤ 50	0	1
51 – 60	2	4
61 – 70	3	5
71 – 80	7	7
81 – 90	8	4
91 – 100	5	4

Mr. Chen gave the same test to two of his classes and his students' scores are recorded in the frequency table above. Which of the following statements must be true?

A) The range of test scores for Class B is larger than the range of scores for Class A.

B) The average test score for Class A is larger than the average test score for Class B.

C) The median test score for Class A is larger than the median test score for Class B.

D) The highest test score in Class A is larger than the highest test score for Class B.

Let's consider each potential answer choice:

A) The range of test scores for Class B is larger than the range of scores for Class A.

We want to know if the range for Class B **must** be larger than the range for Class A. The smallest possible range of Class B occurs if the smallest score is 50 and the largest is 91, for a range of 91 − 50 = 41. The largest possible range of Class A occurs if the smallest score is 51 and the largest is 100, for a range of 100 − 51 = 59. Therefore the range of Class A could be larger, so this choice is wrong.

B) The average test score for Class A is larger than the average test score for Class B.

Similar to what we did to evaluate choice A, we need to look at the smallest the average could be for Class A and the largest it could be for Class B. This means that for Class A we will look at what would happen if each student got the lowest possible score in their range and for class B if each student got the highest score in their range.

Class A min avg = $\dfrac{2(51) + 3(61) + 7(71) + 8(81) + 5(91)}{25} = 75.4$

Class B max avg = $\dfrac{1(50) + 4(60) + 5(70) + 7(80) + 4(90) + 4(100)}{25} = 78.4$

So it is possible for Class B to have the higher average, making choice B incorrect.

C) The median test score for Class A is larger than the median test score for Class B.

For Class A, the median is in the 81–90 range. For Class B, the median is in the 71–80 range. Therefore, the median for Class A <u>must</u> be larger than the median for class B. This answer choice works!

D) The highest test score in Class A is larger than the highest test score for Class B.

Both classes have their highest score in the 91–100 range, but we have no way to know what the scores are within that range, so this statement could be true, but it could also be false, and so this choice is incorrect.

Challenge Problem Set 3

These problems represent the toughest SAT math problems you'll see on test day.

11

Marble Color	Frequency
red	12
yellow	18
green or blue	36

A bag contains 66 solid colored marbles. The table provides information about the color of the marbles. If a marble is drawn from the bag randomly, the probability that it is green, given that it is not red, is $\frac{1}{6}$. How many blue marbles are in the bag?

12

The height of a rock thrown from a bridge can be modeled with a quadratic equation. The initial height of the rock was 12 meters. After 2 seconds, it reaches a maximum height of 52 meters. What was the height of the rock after 3 seconds?

13

Triangle *ABC* is located in the *xy*-plane such that vertex *A* is at $(1,\sqrt{3})$, vertex *B* is at the origin, and vertex *C* is at (1, 0). Which of the following gives the measure, in radians, of an angle that is coterminal with angle *ABC* ?

A) $\dfrac{31\pi}{3}$

B) $\dfrac{28\pi}{3}$

C) $\dfrac{31\pi}{6}$

D) $\dfrac{28\pi}{6}$

14

A 3-foot by 8-foot rectangular tank is filled 45 inches deep with salt water. 196 pounds of salt were used to make the salt water. What is the concentration, in pounds of salt per cubic yard, of the salt water?

15

The function *f* is defined as $f(x) = (x - 2)(x + 3)(x + 7)$. The function *g* is obtained by shifting the graph of *f* right 5 units. Which of the following functions defines *g*?

A) $g(x) = (x - 7)(x - 2)(x + 2)$
B) $g(x) = (x - 7)(x + 3)(x + 7)$
C) $g(x) = (x + 3)(x + 8)(x + 12)$
D) $g(x) = (x + 3)^2(x + 7)$

Explanations

Answers & explanations for Challenge Problem Set 3

....

11.

Marble Color	Frequency
red	12
yellow	18
green or blue	36

A bag contains 66 solid colored marbles. The table provides information about the color of the marbles. If a marble is drawn from the bag randomly, the probability that it is green, given that it is not red, is $\frac{1}{6}$. How many blue marbles are in the bag?

SOLUTION

Since we are told the marble is NOT red, there are 18 + 36 = 54 marbles that we care about.

Since the probability of drawing a green marble from this set is $\frac{1}{6}$, there must be $54 \times \frac{1}{6} = 9$ green marbles.

Since 36 marbles are green **or** blue, there must be 36 − 9 = ⬭27 blue marbles.

12. The height of a rock thrown from a bridge can be modeled with a quadratic equation. The initial height of the rock was 12 meters. After 2 seconds, it reaches a maximum height of 52 meters. What was the height of the rock after 3 seconds?

SOLUTION

We are given the vertex of the parabola, (2, 52), so the equation looks like $y = a(x − 2)^2 + 52$. We can use the initial value (0, 12) to determine a. Plugging in we get $12 = a(0 − 2)^2 + 52$ and solving gives $a = −10$.

Now we have the model $y = −10(x − 2)^2 + 52$ and can plug in $x = 3$ to get a final answer of ⬭42.

TIP

The easiest solution to this problem is to graph it with k as a slider. The only tricky bit then is getting a useful range on the slider.

13. Triangle ABC is located in the xy-plane such that vertex A is at $(1, \sqrt{3})$, vertex B is at the origin, and vertex C is at $(1, 0)$. Which of the following gives the measure, in radians, of an angle that is coterminal with angle ABC?

A) $\frac{31\pi}{3}$

B) $\frac{28\pi}{3}$

C) $\frac{31\pi}{6}$

D) $\frac{28\pi}{6}$

NOTE

It is unclear whether the SAT will actually use the term coterminal, though we have seen them test the concept. They might instead phrase the question something like:

Which of these radian measures could be used to describe angle ABC?

SOLUTION

Step 1 is to recognize that this is one of the special right triangles the SAT gives in the math reference box.

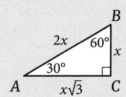

Specifically, it is a 30°-60°-90° triangle and angle ABC is a 60° angle. Converting this to radians, we get $60° \times \frac{\pi}{180} = \frac{\pi}{3}$ radians

This is not directly an answer choice. However, every angle can actually be described in *infinitely* many ways since you could, for example, start at the x-axis and go fully around counter clockwise before continuing up to segment AB.

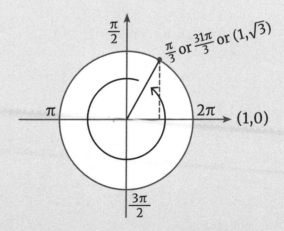

This would give an angle of $2\pi + \frac{\pi}{3} = \frac{7\pi}{3}$ radians.

We could keep looping around adding 2π getting $\frac{13\pi}{3}, \frac{19\pi}{3}, \frac{25\pi}{3},$ and finally $\frac{31\pi}{3}$, which is choice A!

A

14. A 3-foot by 8-foot rectangular tank is filled 45 inches deep with salt water. 196 pounds of salt were used to make the salt water. What is the concentration, in pounds of salt per cubic yard of the salt water?

SOLUTION

To find the concentration we first need to find the volume of the water, in cubic yards. There are 12 inches in a foot and 3 feet in one yard, so the dimensions of the tank are 1 yard by $\frac{8}{3}$ yards and the water is 1.25 yards deep.

This gives us a volume of $(1)(\frac{8}{3})(1.25) = \frac{10}{3}$ cubic yards.

To find the concentration, we take the 196 lbs of salt and divide by $\frac{10}{3}$ cubic yards to get (58.8) pounds of salt per cubic yard. (Fun fact: this is approximately the concentration of sea water.)

15. The function f is defined as $f(x) = (x - 2)(x + 3)(x + 7)$. The function g is obtained by shifting the graph of f right 5 units. Which of the following functions defines g?

A) $g(x) = (x - 7)(x - 2)(x + 2)$
B) $g(x) = (x - 7)(x + 3)(x + 7)$
C) $g(x) = (x + 3)(x + 8)(x + 12)$
D) $g(x) = (x + 3)^2(x + 7)$

TIP

If you aren't comfortable with transforming functions, this question can be solved fairly easily by plugging all 5 functions into Desmos and comparing them.

SOLUTION

To shift a graph 5 units to the right you substitute $x - 5$ for x in the original function. Here that gives:

$$g(x) = f(x - 5) = ((x - 5) - 2)((x - 5) + 3)((x - 5) + 7)$$

Simplifying that gives us $(x - 7)(x - 2)(x + 2)$ which is **choice A**!

Note that choice B comes from only shifting the *first factor* to the right, choice C shifts 5 to the *left*, and choice D makes both mistakes, shifting only the first factor 5 to the left.

BEYOND THE CONTENT

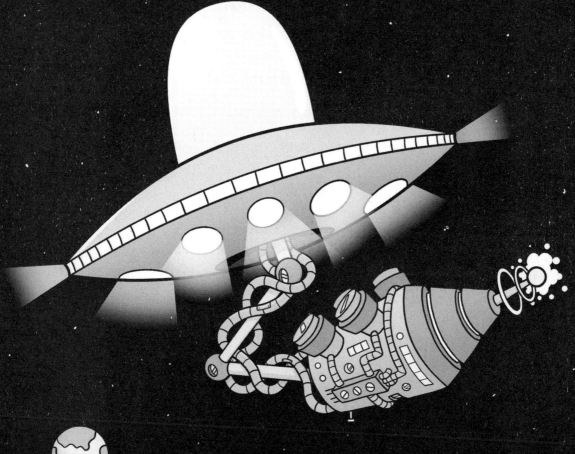

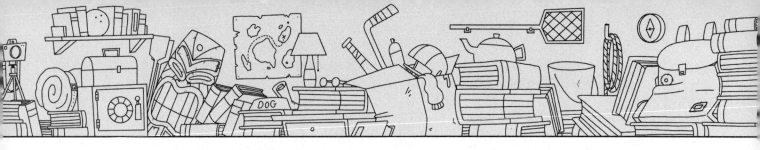

Believe in Yourself

Studies show that your level of self-confidence can affect your score.

Taking a test is its own skill

To fully prepare for the SAT, you need to accomplish 3 goals:

(1) *Understand the **structure and format** of the SAT*

(2) *Master the **content** assessed on all sections of the test*

(3) *Master **test-taking skills** to thrive in a timed, pressured environment*

The final component, test-taking skills, is the most neglected aspect of test preparation. However, for many students, improving this skill is what will give you the most points. So what are test-taking skills? The first, most important aspect deals with **confidence and beliefs**.

Beliefs about yourself affect your score

Whether you believe that you are a good test-taker or a bad test-taker, that **belief** will impact your score on the SAT. In fact, self-appraisal of your ability is a better predictor of how you will do on the SAT than your *actual* level of ability! If you repeatedly tell yourself that you are not going to do well on this test, you can override your actual abilities and sabotage your performance. And conversely, if you believe you will succeed on the SAT, this belief will improve your performance. Thoughts are powerful!

You've got this!

Natural Test-Takers vs. Everybody Else

Some of you may fall under the category of **natural test-takers**. You might even enjoy standardized tests, treating them like a game where you set challenges and work to overcome them. You've likely developed some conscious or subconscious behaviors that help you succeed.

Most people are *not* natural test-takers. Some students get nervous or a little stressed when sit for an SAT. Other students feel **eternally cursed** when it comes to tests. They believe that no matter how much they prepare, they will never do well. If that sounds like you, read on.

Negative Beliefs about Testing

If you feel karmically challenged by the SAT, it's important that you examine the *origins* of your negative beliefs. Ask yourself:

1. When did you start to believe that you were "bad at testing?"
2. Are you focusing on a few isolated instances of poor performance?
3. Are you **ignoring instances of strong performance?**
4. Are you really **always** bad at testing in every possible context?

The truth is doing well or freezing up on a test is all about behavior—and behavior can be changed. The very first behavior to change is how you speak about yourself.

Watch your words: your mind is listening!

When it comes to making global statements about your testing abilities, be careful not to sell yourself short. Rather than saying, "I am miserable at testing," shift and rephrase the statement.

> "I used to struggle with testing, but now I'm open to the **possibility** of doing better."

Your mind likes to be consistent, and it tends to back up your words with actions. Optimists score higher; don't close the door on what's possible!

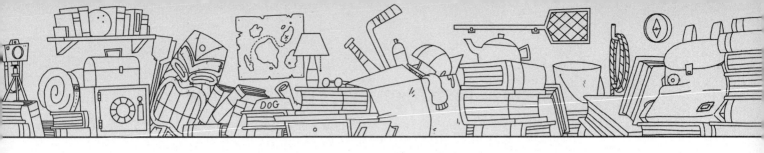

Overcome Anxiety

Test anxiety stems from a potentially useful thought: "Hey, this test counts. I need to do well." When this thought becomes invested with too much energy, however, it starts to hurt your score.

The fight-or-flight reflex can kick in on test day

When you are stressed about an upcoming test, your body reacts in the same way it would to an actual physical threat. These two thoughts cause the *same exact chemicals* to surge through your body:

"Ahh! A test!" and *"Ahh! A lion!"*

When those stress hormones hit your bloodstream, your muscles begin to tense, your heart rate and respiratory rate change, and your breathing may become increasingly shallow. With less oxygen going to your brain, **you start to lose focus.** Distracted, you no longer think or process information as clearly, and your working memory becomes impaired. This increases your chances of escaping a lion... but significantly lowers your chances of acing the SAT!

Some anxiety helps. Too much anxiety hurts.

A **low** level of anxiety is actually **useful** because it drives you to prepare and stay focused during the SAT. There is a tipping point where things shift from good to bad.

The simple graph below illustrates the continuum of anxiety and its impact on performance. What it tells us is that **some** anxiety is good; too much is harmful. We want to reach the optimal point, so we have just the right amount of anxiety.

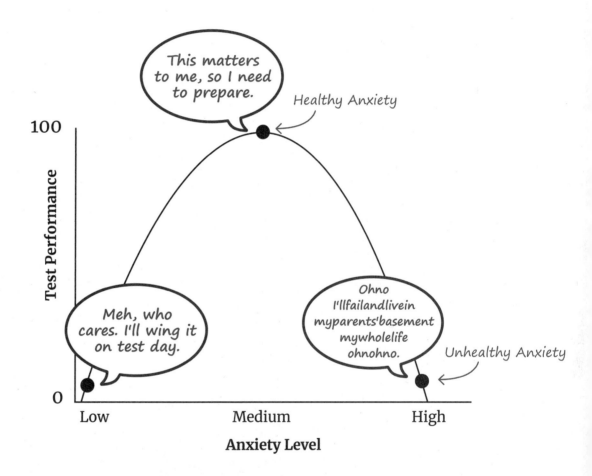

So what can you do about anxiety?

There are several strategies to address heightened anxiety. We each have a number of voices inside our heads (some of us have more voices than others) that provide a running commentary on life. Some of these voices are negative, but others are positive and encouraging. Learning to manage your own inner-dialogue and focus on the positive voices is one of the keys to succeeding on the SAT.

TIP

For most students, their inner coach is actually a composite figure, created from pieces of their favorite coaches, teachers, or mentors from life experience, books, or movies.

Listen to your inner coach

When it comes to inner dialogue, most good test-takers have a major resource on their side: their inner coach. For most students, their inner coach is actually a composite figure, created from pieces of their favorite coaches, teachers, or mentors rooting for them to succeed.

Your inner coach can help you relax or get focused before and during the test by sending you supportive messages.

Pre-game: "You're ready. Go in relaxed. You can knock this out."

Game Time: "You're doing great. It's only one question, don't worry about it. Let it go. Relax... you can do this."

It's not difficult to imagine how receiving these kinds of positive messages could help you remain focused and centered during the SAT. Having a supportive inner dialogue helps you keep yourself paced, calm, and focused. What an advantage!

If your inner voice isn't this positive yet, that's okay! It's something we can change with some practice. The first step is to recognize your anxiety. The next step is to conquer it! On the next page, we'll look at how a negative voice can impact your performance.

TIP

Your inner dialogue will have a big impact on your test-taking performance, so make sure it's working to support you. It can offer a huge boost!

Do not listen to your inner anxiety monster

For other students who have not yet tapped into their inner coach, another creature may appear instead: **the anxiety monster.** The monster feeds on fear and is continually scanning the environment for potential catastrophes. He causes negative statements that cause more negative statements, raising anxiety and dropping performance.

How to conquer the anxiety monster

If you don't deal with the monster directly and **confront** these negative statements, you run the risk of being influenced by them. If you allow yourself to focus your energy on thoughts of failure, your mind may subconsciously begin to turn these thoughts into reality.

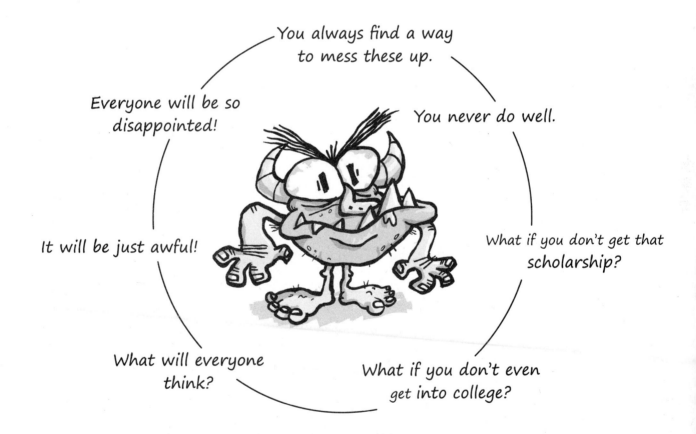

You always find a way to mess these up.

Everyone will be so disappointed!

You never do well.

It will be just awful!

What if you don't get that scholarship?

What will everyone think?

What if you don't even get into college?

Naming the Monster

If you can give your monster a name, you can deal with him more easily and address him directly. Though you will know the right name for your monster, for now, we'll call him Rupert.

It's important to remember that Rupert actually works *for* you (though he's not the world's best employee), and he is taking up space in your head. If you stop feeding Rupert energy and attention, he will disappear.

Taming the Monster

If you are about to take the SAT and Rupert is stoking the fire of anxiety, bringing up those negative thoughts, address him directly. At this point you may banish Rupert to a deserted island, and let him entertain himself while you go in there and rock the SAT.

> "Listen, buddy. I've had enough. I'm ready for this test. I'm **done** listening to your negative statements."

Reinforcing Positive Messages

A positive message might not banish Rupert on the first pass. You need to hear it about 20 times before you'll start to believe it. So reinforce! Leave yourself an encouraging note on your refrigerator. Put up a sticky note on your bathroom mirror. Some students have even been helped by recording a short 5 minute audio track on their voicemail or smart phone reminding themselves to stay positive.

> "You're ready for this. You've worked hard. You can rock this test."

Mix this message in with your favorite songs and positively rock out on the way to the test. In the right frame of mind, you'll get your best score.

Focus on your breath

Just as you can address anxiety by shifting your thoughts and your inner dialogue, you can also address anxiety by making subtle physical adjustments.

The quickest way to shift from anxiety to relaxation is through **breathing**. It is physically impossible to breathe in a deep and relaxed manner and simultaneously feel intense anxiety.

1 Take deep breaths

Deep breaths should come from your diaphragm, not your chest. When you breathe deeply, your stomach should go out (think of the Buddha). If your shoulders rise while you are inhaling, you are breathing from your chest rather than your diaphragm. **Think Buddha.**

2 Slow things down

Count to 3 during the inhalation, pause at the peak of the breath and then count to 3 during the exhalation: this will begin to automatically relax your entire body.

3 Practice breathing while counting backwards

Count backwards from 10 to 1, silently in your head, breathing slowly and deeply from your diaphragm with every count. 10....9....8....7.... With each breath, imagine yourself becoming more and more relaxed.

4 Sigh deeply or make yourself yawn

Yawning is like pressing a reset button in your brain. Yawning has many beneficial effects and can actually help you increase your level of focus and energy.

Use a physical trigger to relax

You can use a physical cue or trigger to bring yourself to a more relaxed state. Create a link between a simple movement and a state of relaxation. Make the movement— start to relax!

1 Choose a cue

You can associate a specific cue with starting to relax. Pick one that works for you, or simply make up your own. Here are a few examples:

- squeezing three fingers together three times
- tapping your knee slowly three times
- putting one hand on top of the other

2 Get relaxed

Once you've officially started to relax with your cue, it's time for calm:

- Close your eyes
- Take 3 deep breaths
- Feel your body become more relaxed
- Tense your muscles, hold for a full breath, and then release
- Take 3 more deep breaths using the 3 count:

> Breathe in. Hold. Breathe Out.
> 1   2   3

3 Link 'em up

Perform your chosen trigger in this relaxed state, and create a mental association between the physical motion and a state of deep relaxation. You will need to do this a few times to create a stronger association.

4 Cue the relaxation during the test

During the test, whenever you feel anxiety coming on, perform your cue to activate your relaxed state. Take deep breaths, and begin to relax.

Test Day Anxiety

Sitting down and taking the test can trigger anxiety in a lot of students. Let's think about good practices at specific moments during the test.

When the Test Begins

Some students become nervous the moment the test begins. They hear the proctor say, "you may now start Module 1." They hear the sound of clicking keyboards fill the room, and they start to sweat. When the proctor says "begin," **pause** and **take a moment for yourself.** Once you're centered and calm, turn the page and begin.

At the Five-Minute Warning

Some students lose their cool at the 5-minute warning. They panic and start to rush, even when they are on track to finish in time. In their rush, they are frequently more careless.

When you see the 5-minute warning on the screen, **pause** and **take a moment for yourself.** Once you're centered and calm, make any necessary adjustments, prioritize the remaining questions, and get back to the test.

A missed problem can feel like a disaster...

Some students start to feel stressed when they just **know** they missed that last problem. They worry so much about that missed point that they have trouble concentrating on the next several questions. They get hung up on one little point and make that missed question feel like a disaster. That anxiety monster starts to drown out the inner coach, kicking that fight-or-flight response into high gear. This just makes it all the more likely they'll miss the **next problem**, starting a negative cycle.

...but it's just a speedbump on the way to success

Here's the thing: you don't need to get every single question right. Not even close! Think of a missed problem as just a **speedbump** on the way to your best score yet. Remember this if you start to feel worried after a tough problem.

Keep cool, keep perspective, and **keep your eyes on the finish line!**

Picture Success

Using your imagination, you can rewire your brain to feel more confident.

Rewiring your brain

To learn the power of imagination, talk to any professional athlete. These folks walk into something very much like a testing environment each time they calmly walk out onto the court or field (in front of millions of people, no less). To get centered, they tap into the power of **creative visualization**. At home, in the locker room, before taking a shot, they picture themselves performing and succeeding.

They do this because it works. The brain has a hard time distinguishing between **imagined** reality and **actual** reality. When you *imagine* lifting your hand, the same parts of the brain are triggered as when you *actually* lift your hand. Similarly, when you vividly imagine yourself calmly taking a test, your brain will *remember* the experience and start to associate confidence with testing.

Later, when you walk into a testing room, your brain will scan the environment to relate the current situation to past experiences and determine how to respond. If you can only remember bad experiences full of anxiety and disappointment, walking into that room will cause anxiety. But by using creative visualization, you can **break that cycle.** You actually have the power to create a new "script" for your brain to follow when you confront new testing situations.

TIP

If you can vividly imagine an event, engage your senses and emotions, and reinforce it through repetition, your brain will begin to treat the event like it is real rather than imagined.

Create a new script with creative visualization

Let's walk through an example of how simply imagining the many details of success on the SAT can increase your confidence and reduce anxiety. To establish a new, positive "memory," we'll need to be detailed so your brain will buy it. Let's walk through a script.

You wake up confident & refreshed

Imagine yourself waking up the morning of the SAT. You turn off your alarm and get out of bed. You do your morning routine and have a **healthy breakfast**. You begin to feel awake and alert, ready for the task ahead of you. You grab your backpack with your fully charged testing device and its charger, admission ticket, ID, pencils, calculator, water, and snacks and head to the test center.

Before you enter, you take a deep breath. "I've worked hard. I'm ready for this test; I'm going to go in there and knock this out," you tell yourself. You walk to the registration line. You show your ID and ticket, and make your way to your testing room where other students are getting situated. Some are fidgety; others are barely awake. You spot an empty seat.

You take a seat and get ready

You find your seat, put away your things and settle in. Visualize yourself **feeling ready and relaxed**. You'll log into the center's Wi-Fi and open the Bluebook application, which will guide you through pretest instructions. The proctor will give you a start code. Once you enter the start code, testing will begin.

Continued on next page →

Writing
10) D
11) A
12) D
13) B
14) A
15) C

Tense Switch

1) D
2) C
3) B
4) C
5) C
6) C
7) B
8) A
9) D
10) A
11) B
12) A

Subject-Verb Agreement

1) B
2) A
3) D
4) D
5) C
6) B
7) B
8) A
9) B
10) B
11) B
12) C

Pronouns

1) B
2) C
3) B
4) A
5) B
6) D
7) C
8) B
9) A
10) B
11) B
12) B

Possessive

1) B
2) C
3) B
4) A
5) C
6) A
7) B
8) D
9) A
10) B
11) D
12) A

Misplaced Modifier

1) C
2) C
3) A
4) A
5) B
6) C
7) C
8) D
9) C
10) B

11) A
12) B

Transitions

1) B
2) D
3) D
4) D
5) D
6) B
7) A
8) C
9) C
10) A
11) B
12) C

Rhetorical Synthesis

1) A
2) B
3) B
4) C
5) C
6) A
7) A
8) D
9) B
10) D

Math

Mixed Practice

1) D, WB
2) A, PN
3) C, WB
4) B, WB
5) D, PN
6) D, WB
7) C, WB
8) D, PN
9) C, WB
10) C, PN
11) A, PN

Basic Algebra

1) C
2) A
3) B
4) C
5) B
6) 8
7) C
8) D
9) C
10) C
11) C
12) A
13) A
14) D
15) B

Exponents

1) A
2) D
3) C
4) D
5) C
6) D
7) 9
8) D

9) B
10) –4
11) A
12) A
13) A
14) B
15) D

Fractions

1) B
2) D
3) D
4) C
5) B
6) A
7) D
8) B
9) D
10) C
11) C
12) B
13) B
14) 1/7
15) 5
16) 12
17) B
18) B

Linear Equations

1) D
2) C
3) B
4) 2/3
5) B
6) C
7) D
8) –6/5 or –1.2
9) A
10) B
11) A
12) B
13) D
14) D

Function Machines

1) 13
2) B
3) A
4) C
5) 24
6) A
7) C
8) C
9) B
10) C
11) B
12) C
13) D
14) D
15) B
16) B

Factoring Basics

1) D
2) C
3) D
4) A
5) A
6) D
7) D
8) A
9) C
10) A
11) D
12) B
13) 4
14) C
15) C

Math

Zeros, Solutions, and Roots

1) C
2) C
3) B
4) 6
5) A
6) B
7) B
8) C
9) B
10) D
11) C
12) B
13) A
14) A

Pattern Matching

1) D
2) B
3) B
4) C
5) B
6) A
7) B
8) A
9) A

Advanced Algebra

1) 6
2) D
3) B
4) 8
5) 3
6) 4
7) A
8) B
9) C
10) C
11) A

12) B
13) D
14) –7
15) –10, 6

All About Graphs

1) 2
2) D
3) –20/7 or –2.857
4) C
5) B
6) C
7) B
8) –1.6 OR –8/5
9) D
10) A
11) A
12) –15
13) B
14) B

Inequalities

1) A
2) D
3) B
4) –1/5
5) D
6) C
7) B
8) –7
9) C
10) D

Linear Systems

1) C
2) B
3) C
4) D
5) A
6) B
7) –5/8 or –0.625
8) 7

9) B
10) C
11) C
12) D
13) 4/3 or 1.333
14) B

Non-Linear Systems

1) D
2) 4
3) D
4) B
5) A
6) C
7) C
8) A
9) C
10) C
11) D
12) C
13) B
14) B
15) –196

Linear Modeling

1) D
2) A
3) C
4) D
5) C
6) C
7) D
8) A
9) A
10) C

Math

Modeling Systems

1) C
2) B
3) 44
4) D
5) 4
6) B
7) 57
8) A
9) D
10) B

Quadratic Modeling

1) D
2) C
3) A
4) 1500
5) A
6) A
7) B
8) 5
9) B
10) 6
11) 1125
12) B

Exponential Modeling

1) D
2) C
3) A
4) B
5) A
6) 320
7) A
8) B
9) C
10) B

Applied Algebra

1) A
2) B
3) D
4) A
5) C
6) D
7) A
8) C
9) C

Percentages

1) C
2) A
3) 378
4) C
5) B
6) C
7) C
8) C
9) D
10) C
11) B
12) 20

Ratios and Proportions

1) 2100
2) C
3) D
4) B
5) 2.3
6) C
7) A
8) C
9) B
10) D
11) C

Probability

1) 8/40 or 1/5 or 0.2
2) B
3) A
4) A
5) 12
6) D
7) D
8) B
9) 11
10) 14/41 or 0.341

Basic Statistics

1) 22
2) A
3) B
4) C
5) C
6) B
7) C
8) C
9) 0.8
10) A
11) D
12) 660
13) A
14) C

Two Variable Statistics

1) D
2) B
3) A
4) B
5) C
6) C
7) B
8) B
9) A
10) A
11) C
12) A
13) D

Math

Study Design

1) D
2) B
3) B
4) C
5) D
6) C
7) B
8) D
9) C

Angles and Triangles

1) A
2) C
3) D
4) D
5) 50
6) 47
7) A
8) 43.75
9) C
10) B
11) B
12) 16
13) C
14) D
15) B
16) 52.5
17) B

Measuring Shapes

1) B
2) 13
3) 3120
4) D
5) B
6) 6
7) C
8) B

9) 38
10) C
11) 64
12) D
13) 26
14) 2288
15) B

Trig

1) 3/5
2) A
3) 3
4) C
5) 3
6) C
7) A
8) B
9) 6
10) C
11) D
12) 28
13) B

Circles

1) C
2) 87
3) A
4) C
5) 18
6) C
7) A
8) B
9) B
10) D

Challenge Problems

1) −29
2) 77/36
3) C
4) D
5) 49
6) C
7) −15
8) B
9) 24
10) C
11) 27
12) 42
13) A
14) 58.8
15) A

739

SAT Question Tag Index

For easy cross-reference, we've listed the pages for each SAT question type tag below. You'll also find these tags listed beneath chapter headers. When multiple chapters apply, starting pages are listed.